DATE DUE

			PRINTED IN U.S.A.

Authors
& Artists
for Young
Adults

ISSN 1040-5682

Authors & Artists for Young Adults

VOLUME 7

**Laurie Collier,
Editor**

 **Gale Research Inc.** • *DETROIT* • *LONDON*

The paper used in this publication meets the minimum requirements of American National Standard for Information Sciences—Permanence Paper for Printed Library Materials, ANSI Z39.48-1984.

Library of Congress Catalog Card Number 89-641100
ISBN 0-8103-5056-4
ISSN 1040-5682

Printed in the United States of America

Published simultaneously in the United Kingdom
by Gale Research International Limited
(An affiliated company of Gale Research Inc.)

Contents

Introduction

Authors and Artists for Young Adults is a reference series designed to bridge the gap between Gale's *Something about the Author*, created for children, and *Contemporary Authors*, intended for older students and adults.

Authors and Artists for Young Adults is aimed entirely at the needs and interests of the often overlooked young adults. We share the concerns of librarians who must send young readers to the adult reference shelves for which they may not be ready. *Authors and Artists for Young Adults* will give high school and junior high school students information about the lives and works of their favorite creative artists—the people behind the books, movies, television programs, plays, lyrics, cartoon and animated features that they most enjoy.

Although most of the entries in *Authors and Artists for Young Adults* will cover contemporary artists, the series will include artists of all time periods and all countries whose work has a special appeal to young adults today. Some of these artists may also be profiled in *Something about the Author* or *Contemporary Authors*, but their entries in *Authors and Artists for Young Adults* are tailored specifically to the information needs of the young adult user.

Entry Format

Each volume of *Authors and Artists for Young Adults* will furnish in-depth coverage of about twenty authors and artists. The typical entry consists of:

— A detailed biographical section that includes date of birth, marriage, children, education, and addresses.

— A comprehensive bibliography or filmography including publishers, producers, and years.

— Adaptations into other media forms.

— Works in progress.

— A distinctive essay featuring comments on an artist's life, career, artistic intentions, world views, and controversies.

— References for further reading.

— Extensive illustrations, photographs, movie stills, manuscript samples, book covers, and other relevant visual material.

A cumulative index to featured authors and artists appears in each volume.

Compilation Methods

The editors of *Authors and Artists for Young Adults* make every effort to secure information directly from the authors and artists through personal correspondence and interviews. Sketches on living authors and artists are sent to the biographee for review prior to publication. Any sketches not personally reviewed by the biographee are marked with an asterisk (°).

Highlights of Forthcoming Volumes

Among the authors and artists planned for future volumes are:

Vivien Alcock	Leon Garfield	Jayne A. Phillips
Isaac Asimov	Jean Craighead George	Ouida Sebestyen
Margaret Atwood	Matt Groening	Scott Spencer
Avi	Deborah Hautzig	Steven Spielberg
James Blish	Robert Heinlein	Mary Stolz
Robin F. Brancato	Ron Howard	Mildred D. Taylor
Sue Ellen Bridgers	Janni Howker	John Rowe Townsend
Bruce Brooks	John Irving	Jill Paton Walsh
Alice Childress	Maxine Hong Kingston	Bill Watterson
Agatha Christie	Linda Lewis	Simon Wiesenthal
Pat Conroy	Lael Littke	Jack Williamson
Chris Crutcher	Margaret Mahy	Maia Wojciechowska
Jim Davis	Milton Meltzer	Patricia C. Wrede
Peter Dickinson	Nicholasa Mohr	Tom Wolfe

The editors of *Authors and Artists for Young Adults* welcome any suggestions for additional biographees to be included in this series. Please write and give us your opinions and suggestions for making our series more helpful to you. Direct your comments to: Editors, *Authors and Artists for Young Adults*, Gale Research Inc., 835 Penobscot Building, Detroit, Michigan 48226-4094.

Authors & Artists for Young Adults

Maya Angelou

■ Personal

Surname is pronounced "*Ahn*-ge-low"; given name, Marguerite Annie Johnson; born April 4, 1928, in St. Louis, MO; daughter of Bailey (a naval dietician) and Vivian (Baxter) Johnson; married Tosh Angelos, 1950 (divorced); married Paul Du Feu, December, 1973 (divorced, 1981); children: Guy. *Education:* Attended public schools in Arkansas and California; studied music privately, dance with Martha Graham, Pearl Primus, and Ann Halprin, and drama with Frank Silvera and Gene Frankel.

■ Addresses

Home—Sonoma, CA. *Office*—Department of Humanities, Wake Forest University, Reynolds Station, Winston Salem, NC 27109.

■ Career

Author, poet, playwright, educator, professional stage and screen performer, singer, and dancer. Appeared in *Porgy and Bess* on twenty-two nation tour sponsored by the U.S. Department of State, 1954-55; appeared in Off-Broadway plays, *Calypso*

Heatwave, 1957, and Jean Genet's *The Blacks*, 1960; with Godfrey Cambridge wrote, produced, and performed in *Cabaret for Freedom*, Off-Broadway, 1960; appeared in *Mother Courage* at University of Ghana, 1964, and in *Medea* in Hollywood, 1966; made Broadway debut in *Look Away*, 1973. *Arab Observer* (English-language newsweekly), Cairo, Egypt, associate editor, 1961-62; University of Ghana, Institute of African Studies, Legon-Accra, Ghana, assistant administrator of School of Music and Drama, 1963-66; free-lance writer for *Ghanaian Times* and Ghanaian Broadcasting Corp., 1963-65; *African Review*, Accra, feature editor, 1964-66. Lecturer at University of California, Los Angeles, 1966; writer-in-residence at University of Kansas, 1970; distinguished visiting professor at Wake Forest University, Wichita State University, and California State University, Sacramento, 1974. Reynolds Professor of American Studies at Wake Forest University, 1981—. Northern coordinator, Southern Christian Leadership Conference, 1959-60; appointed member of American Revolution Bicentennial Council by President Gerald R. Ford, 1975-76; television narrator, interviewer, and host for Afro-American specials and theater series, 1972—. *Member:* American Film Institute (member of board of trustees, 1975—), Directors Guild of America, Equity, American Federation of Television and Radio Artists, Women's Prison Association (member of advisory board).

■ Awards, Honors

National Book Award nomination, 1970, for *I Know Why the Caged Bird Sings*; Pulitzer Prize nomination, 1972, for *Just Give Me a Cool Drink of Water 'fore I Diiie;* Tony Award nomination, 1973, for performance in *Look Away;* named Woman of the Year in Communications, *Ladies' Home Journal,* 1976; appointed first Reynolds Professor of American Studies at Wake Forest University, 1981; Matrix Award in the field of books, Women in Communication, Inc., 1983. Yale University fellow, 1970; Rockefeller Foundation scholar in Italy, 1975; honorary degrees, Smith College, 1975, Mills College, 1975, and Lawrence University, 1976.

■ Writings

AUTOBIOGRAPHY

I Know Why the Caged Bird Sings (Book-of-the-Month Club selection; also see below), Random House, 1970.

Gather Together in My Name (Book-of-the-Month Club selection), Random House, 1974.

Singin' and Swingin' and Gettin' Merry Like Christmas (Book-of-the-Month Club selection), Random House, 1976.

The Heart of a Woman (also see below), Random House, 1981.

All God's Children Need Traveling Shoes, Random House, 1986.

Mrs. Flowers: A Moment of Friendship (selection from *I Know Why the Caged Bird Sings*), illustrations by Etienne Delessert, Redpath Press, 1986.

I Know Why the Caged Bird Sings [and] *The Heart of a Woman* (selections), Literacy Volunteers of New York City, 1989.

POETRY

Just Give Me a Cool Drink of Water 'fore I Diiie, Random House, 1971.

Oh Pray My Wings Are Gonna Fit Me Well, Random House, 1975.

And Still I Rise (also see below), Random House, 1978.

Shaker, Why Don't You Sing?, Random House, 1983.

Poems: Maya Angelou, four volumes, Bantam, 1986.

Now Sheba Sings the Song, illustrations by Tom Feelings, Dutton, 1987.

I Shall Not Be Moved, Random House, 1990.

PLAYS

(With Godfrey Cambridge) *Cabaret for Freedom* (musical revue), first produced in New York City at Village Gate Theatre, 1960.

The Least of These (two-act drama), first produced in Los Angeles, 1966.

(Adapter) Sophocles, *Ajax* (two-act drama), first produced in Los Angeles at Mark Taper Forum, 1974.

(And director) *And Still I Rise* (one-act musical), first produced in Oakland, CA, at Ensemble Theatre, 1976.

Also author of drama, *The Best of These,* of two-act drama, *The Clawing Within,* 1966, of two-act musical, *Adjoa Amissah,* 1967, and of one-act play, *Theatrical Vignette,* 1983.

FILM AND TELEVISION

Georgia, Georgia (screenplay), Independent-Cinerama, 1972.

(And director) *All Day Long* (screenplay), American Film Institute, 1974.

Sister, Sister (television drama), National Broadcasting Co., Inc. (NBC-TV), 1982.

Author of "Black, Blues, Black," a series of ten one-hour programs, broadcast by National Educational Television (NET-TV), 1968. Also author of "Assignment America," a series of six one-half-hour programs, 1975, and of "The Legacy" and "The Inheritors," two Afro-American specials, 1976.

OTHER

Miss Calypso (audio recording of songs), Liberty Records, 1957.

The Poetry of Maya Angelou (audio recording), GWP Records, 1969.

An Evening with Maya Angelou (audio cassette), Pacific Tape Library, 1975.

I Know Why the Caged Bird Sings (audio cassette with filmstrip and teacher's guide), Center for Literary Review, 1978, abridged version read by Angelou, Random House, 1986.

Women in Business (audio cassette), University of Wisconsin, 1981.

Making Magic in the World (audio cassette), New Dimensions, 1988.

Composer of songs, including two songs for movie, *For Love of Ivy,* and composer of musical scores for both her screenplays. Short stories are included in anthologies such as *Harlem* and *Ten Times Black.* Contributor of articles, short stories, and poems to national periodicals, including *Harper's, Ebony, Mademoiselle, Redbook, Ladies' Home Journal,* and *Black Scholar.*

■ Adaptations

I Know Why the Caged Bird Sings was adapted as a television movie by Columbia Broadcasting System, Inc. (CBS-TV), 1979.

And Still I Rise was adapted as a television special by Public Broadcasting Service (PBS-TV), 1985.

■ Sidelights

Creative and charismatic, Maya Angelou is hailed as one of the great voices of contemporary Black literature. Having earned respect as a poet, dramatist, educator, composer, actress, singer, and dancer, she is most highly regarded as the author of five autobiographies: *I Know Why the Caged Bird Sings, Gather Together in My Name, Singin' and Swingin' and Gettin' Merry Like Christmas, The Heart of a Woman,* and *All God's Children Need Traveling Shoes.* According to Lynn Z. Bloom in an essay in *Dictionary of Literary Biography,* "Angelou's literary significance rests upon her exceptional ability to tell her life story as both a human being and a black American woman in the twentieth century." In the opinion of Sidonie Ann Smith in *Southern Humanities Review,* "Her genius as a writer is her ability to recapture the texture of the way of life in the texture of its idioms, its idiosyncratic vocabulary and especially in its process of image-making."

Although Angelou began her diverse artistic career as a nightclub entertainer and stage actress, she is a gifted storyteller and began producing books after some notable friends, including James Baldwin—a celebrated author whose work often explores the psychological implications of racism—heard her relate stories about her youth. Angelou's first autobiography, *I Know Why the Caged Bird Sings,* tells the story of her childhood growing up in Arkansas, Missouri, and California, until her debut as a dancer at the Purple Onion cabaret in her late twenties. Widely considered to be the best of her autobiographies, it enjoyed a commercial as well as critical success and was nominated for a National Book Award in 1970. Admitting that she "really got roped into writing *The Caged Bird,*" Angelou explains in *Black Women Writers at Work:* "James Baldwin took me to a party at [cartoonist and playwright] Jules Feiffer's house.... We sat up until three or four o'clock in the morning, drinking scotch and telling tales. The next morning Judy Feiffer [Jules' wife] called a friend of hers at Random House and said, 'You know the poet, Maya Angelou? If you can get her to write a book....' Then Robert Loomis at Random House phoned, and I said, 'No, I'm not interested.' I went out to

California and produced my series for WNET. Loomis called two or three times, and I said 'No, I'm not interested. Thank you so much.' Then, I'm sure he talked to Baldwin because he used a ploy which I'm not proud to say I haven't gained control of yet. He called and said, 'Miss Angelou, it's been nice talking to you. I'm rather glad you decided not to write an autobiography because to write an autobiography as literature is the most difficult thing anyone could do.' I said, 'I'll do it.' Now that's an area I don't have control of yet at this age. The minute someone says I can't, all my energy goes up and I say, what? What? I'm still unable to say that you may be wrong and walk away."

In *I Know Why the Caged Bird Sings,* Angelou describes being shuttled between rural, segregated Stamps, Arkansas, where her devout grandmother ran a general store, and St. Louis, Missouri, where her worldly, glamorous mother lived. "Marguerite and [her older brother] Bailey—who gave his sister the nickname Maya ('mine')—spent their formative years in Stamps," remarks Paul Bailey in the *Observer.* In a discussion of the book in *Harvard Educational Review,* Ernece B. Kelly observes that "Angelou confidently reaches back in memory to pull out the painful childhood times: when children fail to break the adult code, disastrously breaching faith and laws they know nothing of; when the very young swing easy from hysterical laughter to awful loneliness; from a hunger for heroes to the voluntary Pleasure-Pain game of wondering who their *real* parents are and how long before they take them to their authentic home."

"If you want to know what it was like to live at the bottom of the heap before, during and after the American Depression, this exceptional book will tell you," observes Bailey about *I Know Why the Caged Bird Sings,* remarking that Stamps was "a small town regularly visited by the Ku Klux Klan." According to Angelou, "Stamps, Arkansas, was Chitlin' Switch, Georgia; Hang 'em High, Alabama; Don't Let the Sun Set on You Here, Nigger, Mississippi; or any other name just as descriptive. People in Stamps used to say that the whites in our town were so prejudiced that a Negro couldn't buy vanilla ice cream. Except on July Fourth. Other days he had to be satisfied with chocolate." Growing up in the racially biased South was to witness or experience intolerance and overt cruelty; but its effects could also be more subtle and pervasive. Angelou recalls that it was during this period when she first encountered the works of William Shakespeare: "He was my first white love. Although I enjoyed and respected Kipling, Poe,

Maya Angelou
I Know Why the Caged Bird Sings

Angelou's 1970 book about her turbulent childhood is widely considered the best of her five autobiographies.

Butler, Thackeray and Henley, I saved my young and loyal passion for Paul Lawrence Dunbar, Langston Hughes, James Weldon Johnson and W. E. B. DuBois' 'Litany at Atlanta.' But it was Shakespeare who said, 'When in disgrace with fortune and men's eyes.' It was a state with which I felt myself most familiar. I pacified myself about his whiteness by saying that after all he had been dead so long it couldn't matter to anyone any more.''

Sent to live with their grandmother upon the divorce of their parents "when I was three and Bailey four," Angelou says, "we had arrived in the musty little town wearing tags on our wrists which instructed—'To Whom It May Concern'—that we were Marguerite and Bailey Johnson Jr., from Long Beach, California, en route to Stamps, Arkansas, c/o Mrs. Annie Henderson. Our parents had decided to put an end to their calamitous marriage, and Father shipped us home to his mother. A porter had been charged with our welfare—he got off the train the next day in Arizona—and our tickets were pinned to my brother's inside coat pocket. I

don't remember much of the trip, but after we reached the segregated southern part of the journey, things must have looked up. Negro passengers, who always traveled with loaded lunch boxes, felt sorry for 'the poor little motherless darlings' and plied us with cold fried chicken and potato salad. . . . The town reacted to us as its inhabitants had reacted to all things new before our coming. It regarded us a while without curiosity but with caution, and after we were seen to be harmless (and children) it closed in around us, as a real mother embraces a stranger's child. Warmly, but not too familiarly.''

Angelou reminisces about living with her grandmother and uncle behind the store that her grandmother had owned for twenty-five years: "Early in the century, Momma (we soon stopped calling her Grandmother) sold lunches to the sawmen in the lumberyard (east Stamps) and the seedmen at the cotton gin (west Stamps). Her crisp meat pies and cool lemonade, when joined to her miraculous ability to be in two places at the same time, assured her business success. From being a mobile lunch counter, she set up a stand between the two points of fiscal interest and supplied the workers' needs for a few years. Then she had the Store built in the heart of the Negro area. Over the years it became the lay center of activities in town.''

Among the significant lessons about life that Angelou learned from her grandmother was that through diligence and determination, one might direct one's own destiny. However, she recalls that her grandmother also waged a personal and ferocious war against soil and sass: " 'Thou shall not be dirty' and 'Thou shall not be impudent' were the two commandments of Grandmother Henderson upon which hung our total salvation," remembers Angelou. "Each night in the bitterest winter we were forced to wash faces, arms, necks, legs and feet before going to bed. She used to add, with a smirk that unprofane people can't control when venturing into profanity, 'and wash as far as possible, then wash possible.' We would go to the well and wash in the ice-cold clear water, grease our legs with the equally cold stiff Vaseline, then tiptoe into the house. We wiped the dust from our toes and settled down for schoolwork, cornbread, clabbered milk, prayers and bed, always in that order. Momma was famous for pulling the quilts off after we had fallen asleep to examine our feet. If they weren't clean enough for her, she took the switch (she kept one behind the bedroom door for emergencies) and woke up the offender with a few aptly placed burning reminders.''

Diahann Carroll portrayed Angelou's glamorous mother in the television adaptation of *I Know Why the Caged Bird Sings.*

Although Angelou learned great pride in herself and confidence in her surroundings from her grandmother, this tumbled when she was eight years old and was sent for a brief visit with her mother, then living in St. Louis. "To describe my mother would be to write about a hurricane in its perfect power," writes Angelou in *Singin' and Swingin' and Gettin' Merry Like Christmas*. "Or the climbing, falling colors of a rainbow.... It is remarkable how much truth there is in the two expressions: 'struck dumb' and 'love at first sight.' My mother's beauty literally assailed me. Her red lips (Momma said it was a sin to wear lipstick) split to show even white teeth and her fresh-butter color looked see-through clean. Her smile widened her mouth beyond her cheeks beyond her ears and seemingly through the walls to the street outside. I was struck dumb. I knew immediately why she had sent me away. She was too beautiful to have children. I had never seen a woman as pretty as she who was called 'Mother.' Bailey on his part fell instantly and forever in love. I saw his eyes shining like hers; he had forgotten the loneliness and the nights when we had cried together because we were 'unwanted children.' He had never left her warm side or shared the icy wind of solitude with me. She was his Mother Dear and I resigned myself to his condition. They were more alike than she and I, or even he and I. They both had physical beauty and personality, so I figured it figured."

"I decided that St. Louis was a foreign country," states Angelou in *Singin' and Swingin' and Gettin' Merry Like Christmas*. About the title, Angelou explains in *Black Women Writers at Work* that it "comes from a time in the twenties and thirties when black people used to have rent parties. On Saturday night from around nine when they'd give these parties, through the next morning when they would go to church and have the Sunday meal, until early Sunday evening was the time when everyone was encouraged to sing and swing and get merry like Christmas so one would have some fuel with which to live the rest of the week." In her autobiography, she says, "I would never get used to the scurrying sounds of flushing toilets, or the packaged foods, or doorbells or the noise of cars and trains and buses that crashed through the walls or slipped under the doors. In my mind I only stayed in St. Louis for a few weeks. As quickly as I understood that I had not reached my home, I sneaked away to Robin Hood's forest and the caves of Alley Oop where all reality was unreal and even that changed every day. I carried the same shield that I had used in Stamps: 'I didn't come to stay.'"

At the age of eight, Angelou was raped by her mother's boyfriend, who was later found "dropped ... [or] kicked to death" by her uncles, she says in *I Know Why the Caged Bird Sings*; feeling somehow responsible for his murder, Angelou decided "to stop talking." Shortly after this traumatic incident, she and her brother were returned to their grandmother in Arkansas. "The barrenness of Stamps was exactly what I wanted, without will or consciousness," continues Angelou. "After St. Louis, with its noise and activity, its trucks and buses, and loud family gatherings, I welcomed the obscure lanes and lonely bungalows set back deep in dirt yards. The resignation of its inhabitants encouraged me to relax. They showed me a contentment based on the belief that nothing more was coming to them, although a great deal more was due. Their decision to be satisfied with life's inequities was a lesson for me. Entering Stamps, I had the feeling that I was stepping over the border lines of the map and would fall, without fear, right off the end of the world. Nothing more could happen, for in Stamps nothing happened. Into this cocoon I crept.

Angelou's second autobiographical volume appeared in 1974.

For an indeterminate time, nothing was demanded of me or of Bailey." Asked by several people why she chose to write about rape in the Black community, Angelou indicates in *Black Women Writers at Work,* "I wanted people to see that the man was not totally an ogre. The hard thing about writing or directing or producing is to make sure one doesn't make the negative person totally negative. I try to tell the truth and preserve it in all artistic forms."

Befriended by an educated Black woman, Angelou acknowledges Mrs. Flowers, who "made me proud to be a Negro, just by being herself," in *I Know Why the Caged Bird Sings.* In 1986, Angelou published *Mrs. Flowers: A Moment of Friendship,* excerpts from her autobiography in which she explains her profound debt to this woman. Calling her "the aristocrat of Black Stamps," Angelou describes Mrs. Flowers: "Her skin was a rich black that would have peeled like a plum if snagged, but then no one would have thought of getting close enough to Mrs. Flowers to ruffle her dress, let along snag her skin. She didn't encourage familiarity. . . . She acted just as refined as whitefolks in the movies and books and she was more beautiful, for none of them could have come near that warm color without looking gray by comparison." Mrs. Flowers recognized in Angelou a gift for the written word and requested the young Marguerite to stop by her home for lemonade, cookies, and a chat. Angelou recalls that Mrs. Flowers mentioned her excellent written work at school but emphasized how important the spoken word was as well: "Words mean more than what is set down on paper," she told the young girl. "It takes the human voice to infuse them with the shades of deeper meaning." She then instructed Angelou to return another day prepared to recite a poem from memory. Angelou writes that Mrs. Flowers also provided her with many lessons about living: "She said that I must always be intolerant of ignorance but understanding of illiteracy. That some people, unable to go to school, were more educated and even more intelligent than college professors. She encouraged me to listen carefully to what country people called mother wit. That in those homely sayings was couched the collective wisdom of generations."

Slowly, Angelou regained her self-confidence, pride, and speech. After graduating at the top of her eighth grade class, though, her fun-loving mother, now a professional gambler, moved the children from Stamps to San Francisco. "Knowing Momma, I knew that I never knew Momma," recalled Angelou in *I Know Why the Caged Bird*

Angelou explores her life through poetry in this 1975 volume.

Sings. "Her African-bush secretiveness and suspiciousness had been compounded by slavery and confirmed by centuries of promises made and promises broken. . . . Momma told us one day she was taking us to California. She explained that we were growing up, that we needed to be with our parents, that Uncle Willie was, after all, crippled, that she was getting old. All true, and yet none of those truths satisfied our need for The Truth. . . . I was as unprepared to meet my mother as a sinner is reluctant to meet his Maker. And all too soon she stood before me, smaller than memory would have her but more glorious than any recall. . . . My picture of Mother and Momma embracing on the train platform has been darkly retained through the coating of the then embarrassment and the now maturity. Mother was a blithe chick nuzzling around the large, solid dark hen. The sounds they made had a rich inner harmony. Momma's deep, slow voice lay under my mother's rapid peeps and chirps like stones under rushing water."

Angelou's formal education consisted of attending George Washington High School in San Francisco during World War II, while concurrently taking dance and drama lessons at the California Labor School, where she was given a scholarship. "In San Francisco, for the first time, I perceived myself as part of something," says Angelou in *I Know Why the Caged Bird Sings*. "Not that I identified with the newcomers, nor with the rare Black descendants of native San Franciscans, nor with the whites or even the Asians, but rather with the times and the city.... The undertone of fear that San Francisco would be bombed which was abetted by weekly air raid warnings, and civil defense drills in school, heightened my sense of belonging. Hadn't I, always, but ever and ever, thought that life was just one great risk for the living?"

Her informal schooling, in the rooming house her mother ran in the Fillmore District, was much more extensive. From her mother she learned posture and table manners; from her stepfather, how to play poker and blackjack; from the household, the ways of shipyard workers and prostitutes. On her own as a teenager, by the age of twenty, Angelou had been a Creole cook, San Francisco's first Black woman streetcar conductor, a cocktail waitress, a dancer, a madam, and an unwed mother. "My son was born when I was sixteen, and determined to raise him, I had worked as a shake dancer in night clubs, fry cook in hamburger joints, dinner cook in a Creole restaurant and once had a job in a mechanic's shop, taking the paint off cars with my hands," recalls Angelou in *Singin' and Swingin' and Gettin' Merry Like Christmas*. Bloom reports that according to Angelou, by the time she was eighteen, she had "managed in a few tense years to become a snob at all levels, racial, cultural and intellectual. I was a madam and thought myself morally superior to the whores. I was a waitress and believed myself cleverer than the customers I served. I was a lonely unmarried mother and held myself to be freer than the married women I met."

Angelou's *Gather Together in My Name* and *Singin' and Swingin' and Gettin' Merry Like Christmas* take her life's story from late adolescence, when she trifled briefly with prostitution and drug addiction, to early adulthood as she established a reputation as a performer among the avant-garde of the early 1950s. Not as commercially successful as their predecessor, the two books were nevertheless praised by some critics. Lynn Sukenick, for example, remarked in *Village Voice* that *Gather Together in My Name* was "sculpted, concise, rich with flavor and surprises, exuding a natural confidence

and command." Ann Gottlieb added in a *New York Times Book Review* article that "Angelou writes like a song, and like the truth. The wisdom, rue and humor of her storytelling are borne on a lilting rhythm completely her own, the product of a born writer's sense nourished on black church singing and preaching, soft mother talk and salty street talk, and on literature."

Angelou married Tosh Angelos in 1950. An ex-sailor and white, "Tosh grew up in a Greek community, where even Italians were considered foreign," relates Angelou in *Singin' and Swingin' and Gettin' Merry Like Christmas*. "His contact with Blacks had been restricted to the Negro sailors on his base and the music of the bebop originators. I would never forget the slavery tales, or my Southern past, where all whites, including the poor and ignorant, had the right to speak rudely to and even physically abuse any Negro they met. I knew the ugliness of white prejudice. Obviously there was no common ground on which Tosh and I might meet.... During the first year of marriage I was so enchanted with security and living with a person whose color or lack of it could startle me on an early-morning waking, and I was so busy keeping a spotless house, teaching myself to cook and serve gourmet meals and managing a happy, rambunctious growing boy that I had little time to notice public reactions to us. Awareness gradually grew in my mind that people stared, nudged each other and frowned when we three walked in the parks or went to the movies. The distaste on their faces called me back to a history of discrimination and murders of every type.... I stared back hard at whites in the street trying to scrape the look of effrontery off their cruel faces. But I dropped my eyes when we met Negroes. I couldn't explain to all of them that my husband had not been a part of our degradation. I fought against the guilt which was slipping into my closed life as insidiously as gas escaping into a sealed room."

After the brief but ill-fated marriage ended, Angelou studied dance in New York City, and appeared as a singer in San Francisco's "Purple Onion" cabaret. In 1954 and 1955, she toured twenty-two countries as a member of the cast of *Porgy and Bess;* and in Rome and Tel Aviv, she managed to exchange lessons in modern dance and African movement for those in Middle Eastern dance. Headed for Morocco and then Spain, Angelou hated to leave Tel Aviv. "I had felt an emotional attachment to Egypt and made an intellectual identification with Israel," explains Angelou in *Singin' and Swingin' and Gettin' Merry Like Christ-*

mas. "The Jews were reclaiming a land which had surrendered its substance to the relentless sun centuries before. They brought to my mind grammar school stories of pioneer families and wagon trains. The dislodged Palestinians in the desert were as remote in my thoughts as the native Americans whose lives had been stifled by the whites' trek across the plains of America." After Switzerland and Italy, Angelou left the tour and returned to her son, Guy, in the United States.

Angelou continued to work as a singer in nightclubs on the West Coast and in Hawaii during the late 1950s. She also moved into a houseboat commune in Sausalito with her son. "Strangely, the houseboat offered me respite from racial tensions, and gave my son an opportunity to be around whites who did not think of him as too exotic to need correction, nor so common as to be ignored," writes Angelou in *The Heart of a Woman.* "In less than a year, I began to yearn for privacy, wall-to-wall carpets and manicures. Guy was becoming rambunctious and young-animal wild. He was taking fewer baths than I thought healthy, and because my friends treated him like a young adult, he was forgetting his place in the scheme of our mother-son relationship. I had to move on. I could go back to singing and make enough money to support myself and my son. I had to trust life, since I was young enough to believe that life loved the person who dared to live it. I packed our bags, said goodbye and got on the road." Inspired by author and social activist John Killens, who praised her work and encouraged her to go to New York and join the Harlem Writers Guild, Angelou moved to Brooklyn to master the craft of writing.

She also turned to the New York stage, appearing in such Off-Broadway plays as *Calypso Heatwave* in 1957 and in Jean Genet's *The Blacks* in 1960. That same year, Angelou collaborated with Godfrey Cambridge in writing, producing, directing, and starring in *Cabaret for Freedom,* a musical revue at New York's Village Gate. She describes this period of accomplishment and hope for the future in *The Heart of a Woman:* "Time, opportunity and devotion were in joint. Black actors, bent under the burden of unemployment and a dreary image of cinematic and stage Uncle Tom characterizations, had the chance to refute the reflection and at the same time, work toward the end of discrimination. After 'Cabaret for Freedom,' they would all be employed by suddenly aware and respectful producers. After Martin Luther King won freedom for us all, they would be paid honorable salaries and would gain the media coverage that their talents

This 1990 poetry collection was praised for Angelou's lyrical use of language.

deserved. It was an awakening summer of 1960 and the entire country was in labor. Something wonderful was about to be born, and we were all going to be good parents to the welcome child. Its name was Freedom. Then, too soon, summer and the revue closed. The performers went back to the elevator-operating or waiting-on-tables jobs they had interrupted. A few returned to unemployment or welfare lines. No one was hired as a leading actor in a major dramatic company nor as a supporting actor in a small ensemble, or even as a chorus member in an Off-Off-Broadway show. Godfrey was still driving his beat-up cab, . . . and I was broke again. I had learned how to work office machines, and how to hold a group of fractious talented people together, but a whole summer was gone; I was out of work and Guy needed school clothes."

Angelou left New York with South African freedom fighter Vusumzi Make. In Cairo, Egypt, she worked as an associate editor for an English language weekly newspaper. "I stayed at the *Arab Observer* for over a year and gradually my ignorance receded," relates Angelou in *The Heart of a Woman*. "I learned from Abdul Hassan how to write an opinionated article with such subtlety that the reader would think the opinion his own. Eric Nemes, the layout artist, showed me that where an article was placed on a page, its typeface, even the color of ink, were as important as the best-written copy. David DuBois demonstrated how to select a story and persevere until the last shred of data was in my hands. Vus supplied me with particulars on the politically fluid, newly independent African states. I received a raise from Dr. Nagati, the respect of my fellow workers and a few compliments from strangers."

Angelou left Egypt in 1962 for West Africa, and describes the atmosphere of this land in *All God's Children Need Traveling Shoes:* "The breezes of the West African night were intimate and shy, licking the hair, sweeping through cotton dresses with unseemly intimacy, then disappearing into the utter blackness. Daylight was equally insistent, but much more bold and thoughtless. It dazzled, muddling the sight. It forced through my closed eyelids, bringing me up and out of a borrowed bed and into brand new streets.... I planned staying for two weeks with a friend of a colleague, settling Guy into his dormitory, then continuing to Liberia to a job with the Department of Information. Guy was seventeen and quick. I was thirty-three and determined. We were Black Americans in West Africa, where for the first time in our lives the color of our skin was accepted as correct and normal." Although a serious automobile accident delayed her son's entrance to the University of Ghana, Angelou found a job there as an assistant administrator of the School of Music and Drama, in addition to free-lancing as a writer and serving as feature editor for *African Review.*

"I worked wherever I was needed...," says Angelou in *All God's Children Need Traveling Shoes.* "Sometimes I handled theatre reservations or sold tickets at the box office in town. When Ireland's Abbey Theatre director, Byrd Lynch, came to teach at Legon, she chose to present Bertolt Brecht's *Mother Courage* in full production, and I was chosen to play the title role. I received no housing, tuition, or dislocation allowances. On the first day of every month, when the small manilla envelopes of cash were delivered to the offices, I would open mine with a confusion of sensations. Seventy-five pounds. Around two hundred dollars. In San Francisco, my mother spent that amount on

two pairs of shoes. Then I would think, seventy-five pounds, what luck! Many Ghanians at the university would take home half that much with gratitude. My feelings slid like mercury. Seventy-five pounds. Sheer discrimination. The old British philosopher's packet was crammed with four times that, and all I ever saw him do was sit in the Lecturers' Lounge ordering Guinness stout and dribbling on about Locke and Lord Acton and the British Commonwealth. I would count out the paper money, loving the Black president's picture. Thirty pounds for rent; thirty for my son's tuition, being paid on the installment play; ten for beer, cigarettes, food. Another five for the houseman who my friends and I paid fifteen pounds per month to clean the bungalow."

When Angelou returned to the United States in the mid-1960s, she became an educator, lecturing at the University of California in Los Angeles, serving as writer-in-residence at the University of Kansas, and as distinguished visiting professor at several universities. In 1981, she was honored by being named the first Reynolds Professor of American Studies at Wake Forest University—a post she continues to hold. However emotionally wrenching leaving Africa was for Angelou, she indicates in *All God's Children Need Traveling Shoes* that she was able to feel the essence of that land of her ancestors in the culture of its uprooted and transplanted descendants: "Many years earlier I, or rather someone very like me and certainly related to me, had been taken from Africa by force. This second leave-taking would not be so onerous, for now I knew my people had never completely left Africa. We had sung it in our blues, shouted it in our gospel and danced the continent in our break-downs. As we carried it to Philadelphia, Boston and Birmingham we had changed its color, modified its rhythms, yet it was Africa which rode in the bulges of our high calves, shook in our protruding behinds and crackled in our wide open laughter. I could nearly hear the old ones chuckling."

Acclaimed for her profuse and varied artistic accomplishments, Angelou has also gained recognition for several volumes of poetry that explore experiences common to American Blacks—discrimination, exploitation, and poverty. In *School Library Journal*, Candelaria Silva praises Angelou's poetry as "easily accessible" and rhythmic, adding that Angelou "writes about love, beauty, the South, the human struggle for freedom and the incredible dignity black people have maintained against all odds." According to an assessment of a *Publishers Weekly* reviewer, "Hers is not a major poetical voice; she seldom dazzles—or tries to. . . . But her human warmth, honesty, strength and deep-rooted sense of personal pride—call it defiance—come through in almost every word she sets down." However, in the genre of autobiography, claims David Levering Lewis in the *Washington Post Book World*, Angelou "has achieved a kind of literary breakthrough which few writers of any time, place, or race achieve. Moreover, since writing *The Caged Bird Sings,* she has done so with stunning regularity."

Discussing the importance of her craft to her, Angelou states in *Black Women Writers at Work:* "Writing is a part of my life; cooking is a part of my life. Making love is a part of my life; walking down the street is a part of it. Writing demands more time, but it takes from all of these other activities. They all feed into the writing. I think it's dangerous to concern yourself with it, just get it done. The pondering pose—the back of the hand glued against the forehead—is baloney. People spend more time posing than getting the work done. The work is all there is, and when it's done, then you can laugh, have a pot of beans, stroke some child's head, or skip down the street. My responsibility as a writer is to be as good as I can be at my craft. So I study my craft. I don't simply write what I feel, let it all hang out. That's baloney. That's no craft at all. Learning the craft, understanding what language can do, gaining control of the language, enables one to make people weep, make them laugh, even make them go to war. You can do this by learning how to harness the power of the word. So studying my craft is one of my responsibilities.

"The other is to be as good a human being as I possibly can be so that once I have achieved control of the language, I don't force my weaknesses on a public who might then pick them up and abuse themselves. So first, I am always trying to be a better human being, and second, I continue to learn my craft. Then, when I have something positive to say, I can say it beautifully. That's my responsibility. I try to live what I consider a 'poetic existence.' That means I take responsibility for the air I breathe and the space I take up. I try to be immediate, to be totally present for all my work. *I try. . . .* That to me is poetic. I try for concentrated consciousness which I miss by more than half, but I'm trying."

Maya Angelou during one of her many interviews.

■ **For More Information See**

BOOKS

Angelou, Maya, *I Know Why The Caged Bird Sings,*
Random House, 1970.

Angelou, *Gather Together in My Name,* Random
House, 1974.

Angelou, *Singin' and Swingin' and Gettin' Merry
Like Christmas,* Random House, 1976.

Angelou, *The Heart of a Woman,* Random House,
1981.

Angelou, *All God's Children Need Traveling Shoes,*
Random House, 1986.

Angelou, *Mrs. Flowers: A Moment of Friendship,*
illustrations by Etienne Delessert, Redpath
Press, 1986.

Contemporary Literary Criticism, Gale, Volume 12,
1980, Volume 35, 1985.

Dictionary of Literary Biography, Volume 38: *Afro-
American Writers after 1955: Dramatists and
Prose Writers,* Gale, 1985.

Jelinek, Estelle C., editor, *Women's Autobiography: Essays in Criticism,* Indiana University
Press, 1980.

Tate, Claudia, editor, *Black Women Writers at
Work,* Continuum, 1983.

PERIODICALS

Black Scholar, January-February, 1977; summer,
1982.

Black World, July, 1975.

Bulletin of Bibliography, January-March, 1979.

Chicago Tribune, November 1, 1981.

Chicago Tribune Book World, March 23, 1986.

Detroit Free Press, May 9, 1986.

Ebony, April, 1970.

Essence, May, 1983.

Harper's Bazaar, November, 1972.

Harvard Educational Review, November, 1970.

Intellectual Digest, June, 1973.

Kansas Quarterly, summer, 1975.

Ladies' Home Journal, May, 1976.

Los Angeles Times, May 29, 1983.

Los Angeles Times Book Review, April 13, 1986.

Momentum, December, 1985.

Ms., January, 1977.

New Republic, July 6, 1974.

Newsweek, March 2, 1970.

New York Post, November 5, 1971.

New York Times, February 25, 1970; March 24,
1972.

New York Times Book Review, June 16, 1974.

Observer, April 1, 1984.

Parnassus: Poetry in Review, fall-winter, 1979.

Poetry, August, 1976.

Publishers Weekly, July 31, 1978.

School Library Journal, September, 1983.

South Atlantic Bulletin, May, 1976.

Southern Humanities Review, fall, 1973.

Time, March 31, 1986.

Times Literary Supplement, February 17, 1974;
June 14, 1985; January 24, 1986.

Village Voice, July 11, 1974; October 28, 1981.

Viva, March, 1974.

Washington Post, October 13, 1981.

Washington Post Book World, October 4, 1981;
June 26, 1983; May 11, 1986.

Wilson Library Bulletin, June, 1986.

Writers Digest, January, 1975.°

Jean M. Auel

■ Personal

Surname is pronounced "owl"; full name, Jean Marie Auel; born February 18, 1936, in Chicago, IL; daughter of Neil S. (a painter and decorator) and Martha (Wirtanen) Untinen; married Ray B. Auel (wife's business manager), March 19, 1954; children: RaeAnn, Karen, Lenore, Kendall, Marshall. *Education:* Attended Portland State University during the 1960s; University of Portland, M.B.A., 1976. *Politics:* Independent. *Hobbies and other interests:* Writing poetry, cooking, math, wine-tasting, art collecting, archaeology, anthropology, science in general, traveling, giving lectures, and studying French.

■ Addresses

Agent—Jean V. Naggar Literary Agency, Inc., 216 East Seventy-fifth St., New York, NY 10021.

■ Career

Worked in the office of the mayor of Chicago, IL, 1954; keypunch operator for J. C. Penney and numerous other companies; Tektronix, Inc., Beaverton, OR, clerical/office work, 1964-66, circuit board designer, 1966-73, technical writer, 1973-74, credit manager, 1974-76; writer. Lecturer at various universities and museums, including the Smithsonian Institution, Washington, DC, American Museum of Natural History, New York, Academy of Science, San Francisco, CA, and Royal Ontario Museum, Toronto, Canada. Speaker at numerous conferences, including Circum-Pacific Conference on Evolution, Seattle, WA, and annual meeting of Society for American Archaeologists, and for many writing organizations, anthropologists' groups, community organizations, and fundraisers. Member of board of International Women's Forum. *Member:* Authors League of America, Authors Guild, PEN, Mensa, Oregon Writers Colony, Willamette Writers Club.

■ Awards, Honors

Award for excellence in writing from Pacific Northwest Booksellers Association, 1980, Vicki Penziner Matson Memorial Award from Friends of Literature, 1981, American Book Award nomination for best first novel, 1981, and New York Public Library's Books for the Teen Age, 1981 and 1982, all for *The Clan of the Cave Bear;* D.L., University of Portland, 1983; D.H., University of Maine, 1985; D.H.L., Mt. Vernon College, 1985; Golden Plate award from American Academy of Achievement, 1986; Cultural Resource Management Award from Department of the Interior, and Publieksprijs voor het Nederlandse Boek (Holland), both 1990; keynote speaker for First World Summit on the Peopling of the Americas, Center for the Study of Early Man (now Center for the

Study of First Americans); award from National Zoo, Washington, DC; several other awards.

■ Writings

"EARTH'S CHILDREN" SERIES

The Clan of the Cave Bear, Crown, 1980.
The Valley of Horses, Crown, 1982.
The Mammoth Hunters, Crown, 1985.
The Plains of Passage, Crown, 1990.

OTHER

Poetry represented in *From Oregon with Love,* edited by Anne Hinds, Heron's Quill.

Auel's works have been issued in twenty-two nations, including Great Britain, the Netherlands, Japan, Israel, Yugoslavia, Portugal, Greece, and Argentina, and translated into eighteen languages, including Serbo-Croatian, Portuguese, Japanese, Italian, Dutch, Hebrew, Finnish, and Spanish. Her works are required reading in many anthropology classes in the United States and Europe.

■ Adaptations

The Clan of the Cave Bear was adapted into a film of the same name, starring Daryl Hannah and released by Warner Bros., 1986; *The Clan of the Cave Bear, The Mammoth Hunters, The Valley of Horses,* and *The Plains of Passage* are all available on audiocassette, distributed by Brilliance Corporation, Recorded Books, Books on Tape, and other companies.

■ Work in Progress

Completion of the six-volume "Earth's Children" series.

■ Sidelights

Self-assured and engaging, Jean M. Auel is the author of the phenomenally successful "Earth's Children" series. From 1980's *The Clan of the Cave Bear* to 1990's *The Plains of Passage,* Auel's prehistoric saga has propelled this working mother of five into a best-selling author whose novels are published worldwide. Auel began writing at age forty, after earning her master's degree in business administration (M.B.A.) and working her way up to credit manager at a manufacturing company. Her ensuing prehistorical novels shattered publishing records and earned her a multitude of readers as well as the respect of numerous anthropologists, archaeologists, and other scientists. "I'm doing

what I want to do more than anything else," Auel proudly declared in *Contemporary Authors.* "With all the frustration, I love writing fiction and telling stories."

Auel was born in 1936 in Chicago, Illinois, the second of five children of a housepainter and his wife. Auel recalls an early love for reading; as a kindergartner she was told she would have to wait until she reached first grade to learn to read. "I cried after my first day in first grade because I hadn't learned to read yet," Auel told *Authors and Artists for Young Adults (AAYA).* "I had expected it to happen instantly!" A vivid imagination accompanied this love of words, and the author remembers creating make-believe playmates, who often helped her with household chores. When she finally did learn to read, she found the characters in fairy tales and young people's literature fascinating. The author became "hooked" on science fiction, she recalled, "but continued to read everything else as well." The radio of the 1940s also captivated the adolescent Auel. "On Saturday mornings there was a program called 'Let's Pretend,' based on fairy tales and other stories," she recalled in the *Washington Post.* "I learned a lot from radio about telling stories. It placed a heavy premium on character development and narrative. Writing is not so different in some ways."

In 1954 Auel married Ray B. Auel, whom she had known since grade school. "I was married at age 18," the author explained to Marian Christy in the *Boston Globe.* "My mother wanted me to get married. It was expected of my generation." Auel was consequently fired from her job in the mayor's office: "In those days you could get fired for getting married," Auel pointed out to Norma Libman in the *Chicago Tribune.* By the time Auel was twenty-five, she found herself with five children under the age of six. During this period the author also worked for various companies as a free-lance keypunch operator. "I picked my own hours—evenings, weekends, times when my husband was not working," Auel noted to *AAYA.* "At the time, that skill, now called data-entry, was the highest paid office work you could find, and we needed the money. Five children are expensive to raise."

In between working and managing the household, something was brewing inside Auel—a desire and a need for something more, something other than the laundry, cleaning, car pooling, and other work she encountered in daily life. She was assisting her husband through college, and Ray would often bring home his history or philosophy books, as well as work from his other classes, including architecture and engineering. To help, Auel would study with him, and her love of literature and learning resurfaced. She discovered philosophers such as Aristotle, Plato, Friedrich Nietzsche, Jean-Paul Sartre, and Simone de Bouvior. "And then along came Betty Friedan's book," Auel recalled in the *Los Angeles Times.*

Feminist author Friedan's 1963 *The Feminine Mystique* sparked a turning point in Auel's life. Friedan proposed that American women embrace educational opportunities and pursue interests outside the home. "I identified with Friedan's premise not because I was a fatigued, incomplete housewife, but because I wanted more," Auel explained to *AAYA*. "I was working and taking care of the family, but even then, my husband did a lot in terms of helping with the children." "I'm a product of the Betty Friedan generation," Auel told Julia Braun Kessler in the *Los Angeles Times.* "I'm the very person she was talking to. When my last child was born I stayed home a few years to do the things that women in the '50s were taught to do." After reading Friedan, Auel felt a certain amount of liberation; the young mother felt free to do what *she* wanted to do. "Friedan seemed to say to me: 'You don't have to be fulfilled by motherhood alone,'" Auel recalled in the *Boston Globe.* "'Don't feel guilty about fulfilling your desires.'" Auel also felt assured that as a woman she too had the right to broaden herself. "I wanted to go to college, I wanted to learn, I wanted to grow," Auel recalled, "and Betty Friedan gave me 'permission,' which the general culture did not."

So in 1964, in her late twenties, Auel decided to become a physicist, a decision hardly welcomed by her husband. The couple battled, yet Auel held firmly to her own determination to learn. In the end she went to school, although quite against Ray's wishes, and began night classes at Oregon's Portland State University to study mathematics, physics, electronics, and Russian. During the same year she also began work at Tektronix, a large manufacturer of electronic test equipment, first as a keypunch operator, then as a typist, and later as a circuit board designer in the company's engineering department. These positions were then followed by about a year as a technical writer. "That's professional writing in a sense, although 'Engage the power supply, check the time base, and adjust the altitude' is nothing very exciting," Auel noted in Lee Michael Katz's *USA Today* article. "Nothing you learn though is not worthwhile, because even from that you learn how to be clear and concise."

While a technical writer Auel began exploring the M.B.A. program at the University of Portland. "Though Ray and I didn't have bachelor degrees, we had to take the same 'Admission Test for Graduate Study in Business' that anyone with a bachelor's degree had to take," the author recalled to *AAYA*, "only we had to score substantially higher than those who held a degree. That was to show that the University of Portland was not a graduate school admitting people without a bachelor's, but one that would give an opportunity to people who had earned it." The couple began night classes in the program in 1972 and completed their degrees four years later, in 1976.

At age forty then, Auel had earned her M.B.A. and completed management training programs at Tektronix, where she had risen to the level of credit manager and was one of five employees responsible for nearly a billion dollars in annual accounts receivable. Dissatisfied, however, with her male boss who felt intimidated by a female employee fourteen years his senior, and desiring a position with more potential for growth, Auel resigned later that year, drastically cutting the family income. With three children in college, Auel knew she needed another job; the problem, though, was deciding what to do. She began looking for a more fulfilling position, yet she later admitted to putting forth merely a half-hearted effort. "I had been spending a great deal of time and energy working, going to school, raising a family, and suddenly, after I quit my job, there were no demands on me," the author said to *AAYA*. "My children were nearly grown, I was no longer going to school or doing homework, and suddenly, I wasn't working. It was a very free-floating state that was open, perhaps, to new ideas."

Then one cold winter night in 1977, "it was eleven o'clock," Auel recounted in *At the Field's End: Interviews with Twenty Pacific Northwest Writers,* "my husband said, 'C'mon, let's go to bed.' I said, 'Wait a minute. I want to see if I can do something.' An idea had been buzzing through my head of a girl or young woman who was living with people who were different. I was thinking prehistory, but I don't know why. I was thinking, 'These people were different, but they think she's different.' They were viewing her with suspicion, but she was taking care of an old man with a crippled arm, so they let her stay. This was the beginning. That night I started to write the story. I had never written fiction before. It got to be the wee hours of the morning, I was about ten or twelve pages into it and I decided, 'This is kind of fun.' Characters, theme and story were starting.''

Auel, who had previously written only a handful of poems for publication, became exhilarated by her work. ''All the determination and purpose that I had been devoting to work, school, and children focused into writing,'' she exclaimed. The author wanted to know *all* about her characters: their appearance, their dress, their lifestyle, their eating habits. At the same time she realized she didn't know what she was writing about. ''I'd want to describe something and I wouldn't know how or where they lived or what they looked like, what they wore, or what they ate, or if they had fire,'' the author acknowledged in *At the Field's End.* ''I didn't have any sense of the place or the setting. So I thought, 'I'll do a little research.'''

Her ''little'' research took her first to the encyclopedia and then to the library, where she gathered almost fifty books (the author has since acquired her own research library filled with more than two thousand books as well as files of papers and

Published in 1980, this prehistoric saga propelled Auel into the front ranks of best-selling authors.

articles). Through her reading Auel learned that Neanderthal man lived somewhere between two or three hundred thousand years ago until approximately thirty thousand years ago, during the Middle Paleolithic age. These people used fire and stone tools and were the first to observe religious rites and burials. The advanced culture of the Cro-Magnon man, the same species as modern man, appeared in Europe approximately thirty-five to forty thousand years ago, during the Upper Paleolithic period. These more developed people stood taller than six feet, were skilled toolsmen, hunted as a community, fished, and composed cave drawings. Auel found evidence that the Cro-Magnons and Neanderthals could have overlapped and perhaps even interbred for at least ten thousand years. It was this interaction of peoples and cultures that caught the author's imagination. ''The stereotype of Neanderthal is of a knuckle-dragging ape,'' she noted in *At the Field's End,* ''but they were Homo sapiens also, quite advanced human beings. I felt as though I'd made a discovery. 'Why don't we know this? Why aren't people writing about our ancestors the way these books are depicting them?' That became the story I wanted to tell: the scientifically valid, updated version.''

''The more I read, the more the story kept growing,'' Auel reflected, as quoted by Libman in the *Chicago Tribune,* ''and I'd read about something and think of something new to add to the story. And I got so fired up about it. I thought: 'Here's this whole world and it's fresh, it's green; you can write fiction that's never been written before. And it's not cave man, Hollywood-style. We're talking about people who were modern humans.'' Her research only furthered this belief: Auel read about the discovery of the physically damaged skeleton of a prehistoric elderly man. Because this disabled man had lived to such an old age—he had suffered from both paralysis and blindness—she surmised that the prehistoric frail were sheltered by their clansmen. ''Suddenly I was seeing a real humanity in these people,'' Auel divulged to Roy Bongartz in *Publishers Weekly,* ''and that became my obsession—what I really wanted to tell.''

Auel's extensive research took her to the Oregon Museum of Science and Industry, which offered a wilderness survival course that Auel and her husband attended. ''I had characters who were living in ice-age conditions,'' Auel told Jean M. Ross in a *Contemporary Authors New Revision Series (CANR)* interview. ''I had to know how people could survive in that kind of situation.'' Guided by an

Darryl Hannah, as Ayla, experiences a moment of fear in the film version of *The Clan of the Cave Bear.*

Arctic survival expert, the Auels not only built a snow cave on Oregon's Mt. Hood, they spent the night in it. Additionally, Auel attended courses where she learned about animal traps and making stone tools and how to identify edible wild plants and use deer brains to tan animal skins—skills she would later incorporate in her books. She does admit, however, that in some areas of her "Earth's Children" books—where the information is sparse or lacking—she uses logical extrapolation and imagination based on factual, scientific material. As Auel asserted in *At the Field's End,* "I want the background to be as accurate as I can make it."

Throughout Auel's research her story idea continued to develop. She put together a one-page outline of the notes she jotted down and "sat down at the typewriter and started to type, telling the story to myself. Some four to six months later," Auel told Ross in *CANR,* "I had a huge manuscript, something like 450,000 words, and I was obsessed . . . I didn't want to do anything else. It was almost an interference to take a shower before I sat down

to work. I would work from the time I got up until I was so tired I couldn't hold my eyes open. Then I'd fall into bed, and as soon as I got up, I'd be right back at it. It was twelve, fourteen, sixteen hours, however many hours I could squeeze into a day, at that machine."

"I was well into the story before I took any of the classes or research trips," Auel said to *AAYA,* "and every time I needed a new piece of information for the story, I was back at the books. It was a very unstructured, almost organic process, growing like a warm yeast dough, doing what I needed to do when I needed to." By the time Auel finished composing, she had amassed a gigantic rough draft. However, "when I re-read it," Auel admitted to Teresa Byrne-Dodge in the *Houston Post,* "it was awful. The worst thing I'd ever read."

Auel recognized that she "had to learn something about writing," she told Ross, because "all of the wonderful passion that I felt was not on the page." Auel pondered whether she should take a creative writing course, but decided against it when she

Like her previous books, this third volume in the "Earth's Children" saga reflects Auel's keen interest in researching the historical details of the era.

realized the amount of time it would require. "I knew from years of going to school that a course would be two to three hours a day, two to three days a week—writing what some teacher wanted me to write," Auel explained to *AAYA*. "I wanted to keep working at the pace I was going—fourteen hours a day, every day, and no teacher was going to put in those kind of hours." So she armed herself with Leon Surmelian's *Techniques of Fiction Writing: Measure and Madness* and Lajos Egri's *The Art of Dramatic Writing* and absorbed everything she could of pacing, characterization, point of view, and setting. She also attended her first writer's conference, where she met Jean V. Naggar, who would later become her literary agent. Equipped with her new knowledge of writing, Auel was then *certain* her 450,000-page draft possessed the makings of a good story. It just needed some work.

The work turned out to be a tremendous rewrite, with the intent being condensation; ironically,

before Auel completed the first half of her first section, she had compiled one-hundred thousand words *extra*. By adding details, dialogue, and description, she had accumulated much more than she had cut. "I thought, 'I'm doing something wrong,'" Auel recalled in *At the Field's End*. "'At this rate I'm going to end up with a million-and-a-half words.'" Taking a closer look at her draft, it became clear to Auel that she had *too much* material for merely one novel. "What I had was six different books," Auel continued. "I can still remember telling my husband, 'I've got six books.' He said, 'You've never written a short story, and now you're going to write six books?'"

The first "Earth's Children" novel, after four rewrites, became *The Clan of the Cave Bear*. Exploring the interaction of Neanderthal and Cro-Magnon peoples about thirty thousand years ago in Eurasia, *The Clan of the Cave Bear* features Ayla, a five-year-old Cro-Magnon girl adopted by the lower-order Neanderthals after her family has perished. As a Cro-Magnon, Ayla is fair, tall, slender, and graced with a quick intellect, well-developed linguistic skills, and a capacity for creative thought. She strives to be accepted by the dark, stocky Neanderthal clan, whose people are instinctive, telepathic, and ritualistic. Still, unable to reconcile cultural differences between themselves and the one they refer to as an "Other," the Clan casts out the, by then, fourteen-year-old, who consequently embarks on a search to locate her own people.

Each "Earth's Children" book centers on Ayla—following the strong female character as she searches for an identity and a community where she and her skills will finally find acceptance. According to the author, Ayla's life is the cord that ties the entire series together; as Ayla encounters various civilizations throughout her late Ice Age trek, Auel reveals both man's ageless struggle for coexistence and her heroine's extraordinary ability to endure. "What lifts Ayla beyond caricature," *Washington Post* staff writer Ken Ringle pointed out, "is the compelling logic of her development, driven as she is to discover self-reliance in the face of alienating differences of race and culture." "I see [Ayla] as the kind of woman every woman can be," Auel told Bill Feret in a *Starlog* interview. "There's some of her in every woman. I suppose she's the sort of heroine I never had as a child. When I was reading stories, the hero was always a man, and the women always tended to be non-entities. Sometimes, I identified more with the male's heroism than the woman's. Later, books were written with strong women, but often they were just carbon copies of men."

Two years after the publication of *The Clan of the Cave Bear*, Auel published her second book in the series, *The Valley of Horses*. While the focus of Auel's first "Earth's Children" book is on Neanderthal culture, the focus of this second book is on the advanced Cro-Magnon people. Ayla, exiled by the Clan and seeking shelter from the forthcoming winter, makes her home in a lush valley near the Black Sea. Out of necessity she perfects her hunting skills—violating the Neanderthal taboo against hunting by women—invents horseback riding, creates tools, raises a lion cub, and displays her Cro-Magnon ingenuity in various ways. She saves a fellow "Other," Jondalar, from a vicious animal attack and, with her mastery of medicinal healing, nurses him to health. From this handsome Cro-Magnon, Ayla experiences a reversal of her Clan upbringing, for, with him, she learns to converse verbally rather than in signs, she is allowed to communicate her opinions and ideas on vital matters, she can accompany him on hunts, and she shares sexual pleasures with him, something she has never before experienced. For the first time, Ayla finds true companionship and love; in the end the two begin their journey to western Europe, where they hope to join the Zelandonii, Jondalar's kin.

The same year that *The Valley of Horses* was published, Auel fulfilled a long-standing desire to visit the European caves that had housed Stone Age man. Auel toured the Dordogne region of southwest France, researching ancient sculptures, fossilized footsteps, stone and ivory carvings, musicals instruments, and various tools and inventions. She was fascinated by the intricate and elaborate cave paintings at such sites as Font-de-Gaume, Les Combarelles, and Rouffignac. However, the most inspiring excursion was to Lascaux—a well-protected cave that holds perhaps the greatest example of Paleolithic art. In an article she wrote for the *New York Times,* Auel described her exhilarating experience at the cave. "Nothing prepared me for the impact of that sanctuary. Tears sprang forth, unnoticed until I tried to stifle a sob in the awful silence; they still do at the memory.... The paintings are rich and vivid, and unbelievably fresh. Clear calcite has formed on top of the paintings, preserving their color and authenticating their great age.... The paintings glow. The artists, in complete control of the medium, deftly used the bumps and ridges of the cave wall to add dimension

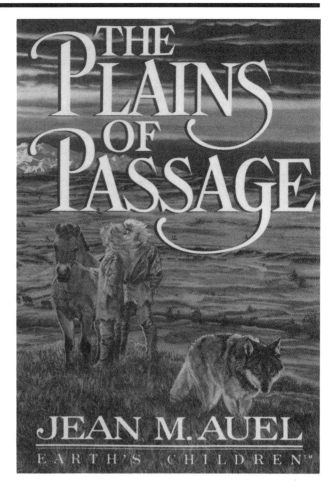

Auel's 1990 best-seller traces the steps of Ayla and Jondolar as they trek across Europe's Ice Age plains.

to the perspective already gained by molding and shading with color."

Utilizing the prehistoric knowledge gleaned from her European tour, Auel completed *The Mammoth Hunters* in 1985. This third part of Ayla's saga examines the role of the individual in a society, tracing Ayla and Jondalar's involvement with the Mamutoi, or mammoth hunters. The first Cro-Magnon tribe Ayla encounters, the Mamutoi are fascinated with Ayla's extraordinary hunting, healing, and language abilities, although also wary of the mysterious and graceful woman, for she was reared by the Clan of the Cave Bear, whom they regard as animalistic. Further inciting mistrust is Ayla's defense of the Clan's capacity for communication and human compassion. She even suggests an evolutionary connection between the two Ice Age groups. At the same time Jondalar becomes ashamed of his attachment to the Clan-raised Ayla and fears taking her to his people, who he thinks may reject her. So, when an ivory carver vies for Ayla's affections, the heroine finds herself torn. Ultimately Jondalar reasserts his love for Ayla, and the two are again united. Ayla, too, accepted by the Mamutoi, grows in her individuality, having softened the Mamutoi's bias toward the Clan.

Research for Auel's fourth book, the highly anticipated 1990 *The Plains of Passage,* took her to Czechoslovakia, Hungary, Austria, and Germany. In this "travel book," as Auel refers to it in the book's acknowledgements, Ayla and Jondalar continue their trek across Europe's Ice Age plains, enroute to the Zelandonii. Because of their awe-inspiring talents—the lovers ride domesticated horses and travel alongside a wolf—they invoke suspicion in those they meet, although their healing and fire-building abilities do gain the favor of many. Throughout brushes with hostile, territorial peoples, sudden floods, and ice-caked rivers, Ayla and Jondalar preserve and strengthen their spiritual and physical devotion to each other during their lengthy journey.

Although Auel's entire "Earth's Children" series—which she continues to write and research—has won her widespread acclaim among popular audiences, critical reaction to the cave-dweller saga is mixed. Many critics fault the juxtaposition of what they consider to be modernized dialogue with technical jargon. A point of contention too is the saga's sexual scenes—at least one high school library has pulled *The Valley of Horses* from its shelves—which some reviewers feel are included merely for popular appeal. "I did not have to put [sex] in there to sell books—nor did I," responded Auel in a *Writer* article. "It was a carefully considered decision based on research, storyline, and personal philosophy.... The sexuality was used partly to define a culture that certainly had to be different from our own. Looking at both archeological and anthropological evidence, I believe my interpretation is close to the reality of the era."

Sex and language aside, Auel's saga impressed other reviewers, who applauded her detailed and imaginative narrations. A "master storyteller" many deemed her. "Auel's books are fascinating and sometimes moving depictions of a time and a people shrouded in mystery and speculation," judged Jane Stewart Spitzer in the *Christian Science Monitor.* Auel "has gone beyond the cliche of leopard-skin-covered, club-wielding grunters and presented a panorama of human culture in its infancy," declared Susan Isaacs in the *New York Times Book Review.* Willard Simms, in his *Los Angeles Times Book Review* appraisal of *The Clan of the Cave Bear,* complimented Auel's realistic portrayal of Stone Age life. "There's an authenticity about the life styles and survival techniques of

these cavemen that's deeply moving. When it's man against the elements, struggling to survive in a forbidding and hostile world he doesn't understand, the writing rings clear and true."

Auel's painstaking research into her prehistoric setting also earned the admiration of many archaeologists, anthropologists, and other scholars. Donald Johanson, director of the Institute of Human Origins at the University of California at Berkeley, claimed in the *Washington Post* that Auel "has done a great deal to bring alive all of these bones that have hung around in museums all these years." "We learn about the plants that an Ice Age medicine woman might use to cure different ills," asserted Lindsy Van Gelder in *Ms.,* "how to build an earthlodge out of mammoth bones and skins, how to knap flint, how to use mashed animal brains and stale human urine to process soft, white leather, and much, much more." Jack Fincher in his *People* article likewise commended Auel. "Not since [*Roots* author] Alex Haley crossed the Atlantic in the cargo hold of a ship to relive the slave experience has an author so ardently sought historical verisimilitude." And Brian M. Fagan noted in a *Scientific American* article that "because of these books, everyone should ultimately learn a great deal more about what may well have been a Golden Age after all."

Intermixed with her crowd of critical and scientific enthusiasts are Auel's scores of fans, among the author's most ardent advocates, who are responsible for the tremendous success of her "Earth's Children" books. These Auel supporters, many of whom have children named Ayla, have helped her books become gigantic best-sellers, garnering millions in revenues for the author. Each individual book has sold more than five million copies both in hardcover and in paperback, and, according to her publisher, Crown, each new novel has sparked the additional sales of the previous ones in the series. Moreover, Auel's books consistently appear on best-seller lists—*The Clan of the Cave Bear* and *The Mammoth Hunters* both remained on fiction best-seller lists for almost two years—and regularly topple publishing records.

Success has not changed Auel's basic intent; she is still doing what she loves to do: fulfilling the desire she felt when she first sat down to write. The purchase of an ocean-front house in Oregon along with plane tickets for her children have been the only major changes in Auel's life, aside from her husband becoming her full-time business manager. Foremost in the author's thoughts is her original premise, to write the story she feels she needs to

Jean M. Auel in 1985.

tell. "I write these books for myself," Auel told Margaret Carlin in the *Chicago Tribune*. "The story of Ayla and Jondalar—our beginnings 35,000 years ago—is profoundly interesting. I love the travel and research."

Auel continues to write, working from evening until dawn—her favorite composing time—believing that nothing could satisfy her more than to spend her life learning new things and writing the story she has always wanted to read. "One publisher told me my story was too long, that no one would pay the money to buy such a long book by an unknown author," Auel remarked to Libman in the *Chicago Tribune*. "But if you believe in what you're doing, you just don't give up." Simply put, as Auel is quoted in *Maclean's:* "I'm living every writer's fantasy."

■ Works Cited

Auel, Jean M., in comments provided to Denise E. Kasinec for *Authors and Artists for Young Adults*.

Auel, Jean M., in an interview with Norma Libman, *Chicago Tribune*, December 16, 1990.

Auel, "'Commercial' vs. 'Literary'—The Artificial Debate," *Writer*, October, 1987, pp. 9-12, 46.

Auel, "A Pilgrimage into Prehistory: The Traces of Early Man and His Art," *New York Times*, November 21, 1982.

Auel, *The Plains of Passage*, Crown, 1990.

Bongartz, Roy, "PW Interviews: Jean Auel," *Publishers Weekly*, November 29, 1985, pp. 50-51.

Byrne-Dodge, Teresa, "Breathing Life into Prehistoric Man (and a New Career)," *Houston Post*, October 10, 1982.

Carlin, Margaret, "Love in the Ice Age: Author Jean Auel's Characters Come to Meet Her," *Chicago Tribune*, December 24, 1990.

Christy, Marian, "From Boredom to Best Sellers," *Boston Globe*, January 15, 1986, pp. 59, 62.

Contemporary Authors, Volume 103, Gale, 1981.

Contemporary Authors New Revisions Series, Volume 21, Gale, 1987.

Fagan, Brian M., "Life with Ayla and Her Friends: Jean Auel and the New Phenomenon of Ice Age Fiction," *Scientific American*, June, 1987, pp. 132-135.

Feret, Bill, "Starlog Interview: Jean M. Auel; The Mother of 'Earth's Children,'" *Starlog*, June, 1986, pp. 50-51, 63.

Fincher, Jack, "Author Jean Auel Makes Literary Hay by Thinking Like a Neanderthal," *People*, November 10, 1980, pp. 96, 98.

Hopkins, Thomas, "Perils of a Pre-Historic Pauline," *Maclean's*, October 6, 1980.

Isaacs, Susan, "Ayla Loves Jondalar," *New York Times Book Review*, September 26, 1982, p. 14.

Katz, Lee Michael, "Neanderthals Had Caring, Human Side," *USA Today*, June 4, 1986, p. 9A.

Kessler, Julia Braun, "Writing Phenomenon Auel Makes Prehistory," *Los Angeles Times*, February 9, 1986.

O'Connell, Nicholas, editor, *At the Field's End: Interviews with Twenty Pacific Northwest Writers*, Madronas Publishers, 1987, pp. 208-219.

Ringle, Ken, "Jean M. Auel: The Smashing Saga of the 'Cave' Woman; Ice Age Melodramas and Mammoth Success," *Washington Post*, February 21, 1986, pp. D1ff.

Simms, Willard, "Neanderthal as a Dummy," *Los Angeles Times Book Review*, November 2, 1980, p. 4.

Spitzer, Jane Stewart, "Turning Prehistoric Sagas into Best-Selling Novels," *Christian Science Monitor*, December 30, 1985, pp. 19-20.

Van Gelder, Lindsy, "Lindsy Van Gelder on Jean Auel," *Ms.*, March, 1986, pp. 64, 70.

■ For More Information See

BOOKS

Contemporary Literary Criticism, Volume 31, Gale, 1985.

PERIODICALS

Chicago Tribune, September 14, 1980; November 11, 1985; February 16, 1986.

Cosmopolitan, April, 1986.

Detroit News, December 8, 1985.

Houston Post, November 2, 1980; February 9, 1986; November 27, 1986.

Los Angeles Times, November 3, 1982.

Los Angeles Times Book Review, September 12, 1982; November 24, 1985; October 14, 1990.

Newsday, November 25, 1986.

Newsweek, November 18, 1985.

New York Times, November 28, 1985.

New York Times Book Review, July 27, 1980; October 26, 1980.

People, December 16, 1985.

Publishers Weekly, October 8, 1979; December 22, 1989; August 31, 1990.

San Francisco Examiner, September 26, 1982.

School Library Journal, February, 1983; May 1986.

Tribune Books (Chicago), October 7, 1990.

USA Today, November 15, 1985.

Vogue, December, 1985.

Washington Post Book World, September 28, 1980; December 15, 1985.

—Sketch by Denise E. Kasinec

Claude Brown

■ Personal

Born February 23, 1937, in New York City; son of Henry Lee (a railroad worker) and Ossie (a domestic worker; maiden name, Brock) Brown; married Helen Jones, September 9, 1961 (divorced); children: two. *Education:* Howard University, B.A., 1965; further study at Stanford University and Rutgers University.

■ Career

Writer and lecturer. Member of Harlem Buccaneers Gang's "Forty Thieves" division during the 1940s; worked confidence games and dealt drugs in Harlem, 1953-54; worked variously as a busboy, watch crystal fitter, shipping clerk, and jazz pianist in Greenwich Village, 1954-57. Member of Harlem Improvement Group.

■ Awards, Honors

Grant from Metropolitan Community Methodist Church, 1959; Ansfield-Wolf Award, 1966, for furthering race relations.

■ Writings

Manchild in the Promised Land, Macmillan, 1965.
The Children of Ham, Stein & Day, 1976.

■ Sidelights

In a 1984 article for the *New York Times* Sunday magazine, Claude Brown wrote that "nobody is more ruthless in his relationships with his peers than the poor child." Brown understood this ruthlessness very well. As a child growing up in Harlem, Brown learned how to steal, hustle, skip school, and evade the police. Most of his teenage years were spent in New York state reformatories, whose programs punished his behavior but did nothing to alter it. It was not until Brown met Wiltwyck Reformatory director Ernest Popanek that he first realized he could change his life for the better. Armed with the insights he gained from people like Popanek, Brown was eventually able to move out of Harlem and find work. No matter how far from Harlem he travelled, however, Brown was unable to forget the people he had left behind, many of whom fell prey to drugs and crime. In his landmark autobiography, *Manchild in the Promised Land*, Brown presented an unflinching look at the Harlem of his youth, including his own troubled childhood and how he escaped it. By both drawing attention to the plight of urban blacks and showing that there was a way out of the ghetto, Brown offered hope to other young people facing similiar obstacles.

Brown, called Sonny by family and friends, was the second of four children. He had two sisters, Margie and Carol, and a younger brother named Pimp (named by his godmother, a prostitute who paid the cab fare so Pimp could be born in a hospital). Brown's parents had moved from South Carolina to the "Promised Land" of New York City in 1935. From the beginning, Brown's parents (especially his mother) attempted to maintain a sense of their southern roots. This proved an embarrassment to their children, who pictured the South as an "uncool" backwater. Brown recalled: "It seemed as though the folks, Mom and Dad, had never heard anything about Lincoln or the Emancipation Proclamation. . . . [My parents] were in New York, but their minds were in the South Carolina cotton fields. Pimp, Carol, and Margie had to suffer for it. I had to suffer for it, too, but because I wasn't home as much as the others, I suffered less than anybody else."

Brown was especially angered by his grandfather's somewhat sentimental stories about life on a chain gang. The elder Brown once referred to a chain gang boss as being "nice" for allowing him back on the work detail after he'd tried to run away and see his family. Young Brown found his grandfather's benevolent attitude puzzling, to say the least. "I couldn't imagine them treating [my grandfather] nice, because I didn't know anybody in the South who was treated nice, let alone on a chain gang. . . . I wanted to smack him. If he weren't my grandfather, I would have," Brown wrote in *Manchild*.

Brown's relationships with other family members were also strained. A large part of this strain was caused by the mixed messages Brown's parents sent to their children. Brown's father was a heavy drinker, but only on the weekend. Every Saturday night, he would get drunk, sing spirituals, and sometimes become violent towards his family. Many Saturday nights, Brown would get drunk and keep his father company. Mrs. Brown was disturbed by her son's drinking, but chastising him did no good—largely because her husband didn't think drinking would hurt the boy. As he got older, Brown began to accompany his father to the neighborhood "King Kong" joints, or gin mills. The joints were usually located in a basement apartment and operated by a friend or relative. Brown's father knew where all the joints were, and he would often take his son to a number of them in a single night.

Brown rarely got along with his father. As a result, their discussions usually wound up as fierce fights. Part of the problem was that Brown had a difficult time taking his father seriously. "Sometimes I would bullshit him by looking real serious and saying something to make him think he was saying something real smart," Brown admitted. "But most of the time he would be too mad to be bullshitted, and he would end up pounding me anyway. I really didn't care, because I was just waiting and wondering—waiting till I got big enough to kick his ass and wondering if he would want to talk then."

Despite the often turbulent nature of his home life, Brown found some solace in the seldom-changing routine of his neighborhood. According to Michael Stone of *New York* magazine, Brown "knew the people who lived in his building, on his block, and up and down Eighth Avenue. He knew the cops on the beat, the store owners along Seventh Avenue, the pastors of a dozen churches—and, of course, they knew him." In *Manchild*, Brown describes the tenement in which he grew up as both a dilapidated, graffitti-scarred wreck and a playground for pranks and mischief for area kids. Many of the boys in the neighborhood got mixed up in petty scams at an early age. Brown recalled many days spent on the tenement stoop with his friend Danny, who taught him how to play hookey and chase girls. Brown's father beat him severely for skipping school and carousing, but the beatings had little long-term effect. Over time, Brown became an expert at evading teachers, traunt officers, and his father. He even learned to judge when truancy slips were being mailed in the hope of getting them out of the mailbox before his father saw them.

Eventually, Brown's truancy record led to his expulsion from school. His mother responded by sending him to live with his grandparents in another school district. Instead of improving the situation, however, the move only made Brown more rebellious. One day, Brown's mother received a note from Bellevue Psychiatric Hospital informing her that her son Claude was being held for observation. According to Brown, the incarceration stemmed from a misunderstanding at school. "My teacher had told [my mother] that I had persuaded a boy to look out of the window at an accident that hadn't taken place. Because of the window's edge, I was holding the boy's legs while he leaned out of the window. The boy started screaming and calling for help. When he got down out of the window, the boy said I had been trying to push him out of the window. Just because we had fought the day before and I was the only one who saw the accident, I ended up in the nuthouse."

The court ordered Brown out of New York state, and he was sent to live with his grandparents in South Carolina for a year. While there, he was expected to help out on the family farm by doing chores such as killing hogs and weeding vegetable patches. Despite the incongruity of being a city boy in a country setting, Brown actually enjoyed much of his time on the farm. He got to know his grandparents better and came to appreciate the slower pace (and relative safety) of country living.

Once back in the city, Brown fell in with his old crowd. He got into many scrapes and stayed away from home for long periods. By the time he was twelve, Brown was a hardened thief and gang member. He participated in a number of petty crimes, but always managed to stay one step ahead of the law. Eventually, however, Brown ran out of luck. He was caught breaking into a store and stealing merchandise. Because of his past record, Brown was sent to the Wiltwyck Reformatory. At Wiltwyck, Brown continued to scam, stealing from the other boys and staff members. The only person Brown could not con was Wiltwyck's new director, Ernest Popanek. Popanek was a patient man who treated his boys with more respect than many of them had ever experienced. Brown found Popanek "hard to fight" because of his honesty and integrity. He tried all kinds of tricks to get Popanek angry, but none worked. In the end, Brown found himself liking the director, even taking some of his advice to heart.

Brown also befriended Mrs. Meitner, his housemother. A refugee from a Nazi concentration camp, Mrs. Meitner saw Brown as more of a hurt child than petty criminal. During the long months of his incarceration, Mrs. Meitner gave the youth equal doses of love and encouragement. She was also instrumental in introducing Brown to Eleanor Roosevelt, one of Wiltwyck's sponsors. Every year, Mrs. Roosevelt would invite all the boys from the reformatory to her home in Hyde Park for lunch. Brown was amazed by both the size of the Roosevelt home and the fact it had no roaches. "I thought they just might have been hiding the whole time I was there," Brown recalled. "But it wasn't like roaches to hide when there were a lot of people around eating food and stuff. That's why Mama didn't like roaches—they were always coming out and showing off when company came."

Upon his release from Wiltwyck, Brown suffered from culture shock. His friends were still getting into trouble, and many of them were taking the current drug of choice—heroin. After a little hesitation, Brown tried it and became violently ill. He was sick for three days, and the experience turned him off heroin for good. Brown began to look at his friends and wonder how they could

Brown's autobiography created a sensation at the time of its publication in 1965.

continue to abuse the drug and themselves. He also questioned the value of gang membership and the lure of criminal activity. "I don't think anybody was too happy. It was a bad time. It was a bad time for me because I was sick. I was sick of being at home. I was sick of the new Harlem, the Harlem I didn't know, the Harlem I couldn't find my place in."

Brown started going to the Wiltwyck office on 125th Street to talk with Mr. Popanek about his growing feelings of alienation. Popanek listened patiently, offering advice when it seemed appropriate. Unfortunately, Brown had little time to use the advice. In a gang-related incident, he was shot in the stomach for stealing bedsheets off a clothesline. Brown recovered and was sent to the Warwick Reformatory, a tough state institution for "hard to handle" older boys. Warwick was run

This 1976 book examines the lives of a group of abandoned ghetto children who band together to form a "family."

more like a prison than a reform school. There were work gangs, trustees, and "real criminals"— car thieves, pick pockets, and drug dealers. Brown served a nine-month term and was released with the stipulation that he attend the High School of Commerce. Brown tried school for a while, but soon found himself longing for more freedom and money. He began to cut school and sell marijuana. His father found out and kicked him out of the house. With no place else to go, Brown returned to Warwick.

Just as Ernest Popanek had counseled Brown at Wiltwyck, the Cohens, a married couple on staff at the institution, helped him at Warwick. Mrs. Cohen encouraged Brown to aim for bigger and better things—including college. She loaned him books on a variety of subjects. Brown read about Einstein, Albert Schweitzer, Jackie Robinson, and Sugar Ray Robinson. At first reluctant to open up to new ideas, Brown began to enjoy the learning process. "After reading about a lot of these people, I started getting ideas about life.... I wanted to

know things and I wanted to do things. It made me start thinking about what might happen if I got out of Warwick and didn't go back to Harlem." The books also afforded Brown some privacy. "I didn't bother with people and nobody bothered with me. This was a way to be in Warwick and not be there at the same time. I could get lost in a book. Cats would come up to me and say 'Brown, what you readin'' and I'd just say 'Man, get the f—— on away from me, and don't bother me.'"

Brown was released from Warwick in 1953. After some careful thought, he moved downtown, out of Harlem, and got a low-paying job in the garment district. Brown also began attending Washington Irving High School in the evenings. On his way to class, some of his old friends would stand on the street corner and tease him. They were still making big money selling drugs and didn't see the point of going to school and working for low wages. Brown ignored their taunts, having made up his mind that the street life was far behind him. Still, there were discouraging moments. Because of his spotty academic record, Brown had to start school all over again. Classes like math were especially difficult, but Brown didn't drop out. Eventually, he passed most of his classes with very high marks.

To support himself, Brown held a variety of jobs. He was a cook, watch repairman, postal clerk, and cosmetics salesman. No matter how tough things got, however, Brown felt his life outside Harlem was worth the price. "I gave my gun away when I moved out of Harlem," he wrote in *Manchild.* "I felt free.... I didn't need any kind of protection because I wasn't afraid anymore. I had been afraid in Harlem all my life." Though only seventeen when he made the move downtown, Brown realized the fact that he was, for all intents and purposes, an adult on his own. "I felt I was a grown man, and I had to go out and make my own life. This was what the moving was all about, growing up and moving out on my own."

In his rare free time, Brown began playing the piano and hanging out with a group of jazz musicians who played clubs in Greenwich Village. Although learning new pieces was very hard for him at first, Brown kept practicing and progressed farther than he'd ever dreamed. While playing with the band, Brown also managed to finish high school and get his diploma. He was twenty-one years old.

Brown wanted to go to college, but he had no money and few prospects. He didn't think that he was smart enough to get a scholarship. His problem was solved by a friend, Reverend James of the Metropolitan Community Methodist Church. At James's suggestion, the church awarded Brown a scholarship to Howard University. While at Howard, Brown became involved in the civil rights movement. He began to write letters to magazines and newspapers about minority issues. One of these letters reached *Dissent* magazine. Impressed with Brown's literate arguments, *Dissent* requested he write an essay about growing up in Harlem. The result was an article that later became part of *Manchild in the Promised Land.*

While Brown was finding success in college, other members of his family were not so fortunate. Pimp had unsuccessfuly tried to kick his heroin habit. The night before he was to leave for a rehabilita-

tion center he was arrested for attempted robbery and sent to jail. Brown's mother was robbed and stabbed not far from her house. Although angered by these events, Brown resisted the urge to violently retaliate as he might have in the past.

In 1961, the same year that Brown married Helen Jones, Macmillan offered him a contract for his autobiography based on the *Dissent* piece. Completed in 1963, *Manchild in the Promised Land* created quite a stir at the time of its publication. Romulus Linney, writing in the *New York Times Book Review,* praised the book for its "brutal and unvarnished honesty in the plain talk of the people, in language that is fierce, uproarious, obscene and tender, but always sensible and direct. And to its enormous credit, this youthful autobiography gives

Brown in his Harlem neighborhood.

us its devastating portrait of life without one cry of self-pity, outrage, or malice, with no caustic sermons or searing rhetoric." While acknowledging the technical brilliance of the book, Martin Tucker of *Commonweal* felt that the "miraculous autobiography suffers from a canker: the miracle of his salvation is presented brilliantly, but the causes for it remain vague. Brown himself seems evasive when he discusses the spiritual and psychological changes that separated him from his gang and made possible his new life. . . . The disappointment is certainly minor compared to the success Brown has accomplished in his vignettes of Harlem life, but it is a flaw that stands out in his achievements."

While the success of *Manchild* gave him both critical recognition and, to a certain extent, financial freedom, Brown did not produce another book until *The Children of Ham* in 1976. *Children* is a collection of portraits of orphaned and abandoned children in Harlem who get together to form a loose support network or "family." The Harlem these young people live in is much more violent than the one Brown fled years earlier. Unemployment is rampant, junkies roam the streets, and the family unit is largely a thing of the past. Entire blocks of Harlem are vacant, and the buildings that remained are rat infested, empty shells. By taking over one of these abandoned buildings, the children give themselves a home of sorts, complete with furniture salvaged from nearby junkyards and the streets.

Children received a harsher critical reception than *Manchild*. Many critics felt that Brown spent too much time detailing the prurient aspects of the children's lives and not enough time examining the sociological reasons for their plight. "*The Children of Ham* suffers from a monotony of negatives and oversimplifications, and these do not sound any better when they are ungrammatically phrased," wrote Anatole Broyard in the *New York Times*. Arnold Rampersad of the *New Republic* praised Brown's ability to capture the ugly realities of ghetto life, but found that Brown "exemplifies the predicament not of the author but of the reader, the person of means and education from whom the accusations of neglect and abuse demand response."

Although he had moved to Newark, New Jersey, to raise his two sons after his divorce, Brown returned to Harlem many times after writing *The Children of Ham*. With every trip, he was amazed by how much his old neighborhood continued to deteriorate. In 1984, Brown wrote an article for the *New York Times* in which he attempted to describe the changes he'd seen. He was most struck by the increase in violent crimes committed by young teens. In Brown's youth, gang members carried knives and pop guns, but rarely used them to kill or maim. By 1984, shootings (and killings) were commonplace in Harlem. When Brown asked a boy why he would use a gun to get a pair of shoes or a coat, the boy replied "That's what they do now. . . . Yeah, it's wrong to kill somebody. But you've gotta have dollars, right?"

In his article, Brown noted that Harlem is not just a geographical place in New York City. It is a symbol of all urban areas where opportunity is virtually nonexistent. He wrote: "Harlem U.S.A is defined by a common culture. . . . All street kids are at least semi-abandoned, out on those mean streets for the major portion of day and night. They are at the mercy of a cold-blooded and ruthless environment; survival is a matter of fortuity, instinct, ingenuity, and unavoidable conditioning." Obviously dismayed by the "doom and gloom" prevalent in present-day ghetto areas, Brown proposed that government take a serious look at the future of inner-city children. "The manchild of 1984 must be convinced there is reason for hope," Brown pointed out. "He must be convinced that the quality of life actually does improve as he gets older, . . . that most of the major mysteries are solved by life's greatest two detectives, time and experience." When asked how he would fare in today's Harlem, Brown replied: "I'd be dead."

■ Works Cited

Brown, Claude, *Manchild in the Promised Land*, Macmillan, 1965.

Brown, Claude, "Manchild in Harlem," *New York Times Magazine*, September 16, 1984, pp. 36-40, 54, 76-77.

Linney, Romulus, "Growing Up the Hard Way," *New York Times Book Review*, August 22, 1965, pp. 1, 14.

Stone, Michael, "Three Lives," *New York*, January 30, 1989, pp. 35-42.

Tucker, Martin, "The Miracle of a Redeemed Harlem Childhood," *Commonweal*, September 24, 1965, pp. 700-702.

■ For More Information See

BOOKS

Black Writers, Gale, 1989.

PERIODICALS

New Republic, May 8, 1976.

Newsweek, August 16, 1965.
New York Times Book Review, August 15, 1976.
Times Literary Supplement, August 11, 1966.

Washington Post Book World, April 11, 1976.°

—*Sketch by Elizabeth A. Des Chenes*

Daniel Cohen

Scientific Investigation of Claims of the Paranormal, fellow. *Member:* International Cryptological Society, Authors Guild, Authors League of America, Audubon Society, Appalachian Mountain Club, Watson's Erroneous Productions, Wodehouse Society.

■ Writings

Myths of the Space Age, Dodd, 1967.
Mysterious Places, Dodd, 1969.
A Modern Look at Monsters, Dodd, 1970.
Masters of the Occult, Dodd, 1971.
Voodoo, Devils, and the New Invisible World, Dodd, 1972.
The Far Side of Consciousness, Dodd, 1974.
Biorhythms in Your Life, Fawcett, 1976.
Close Encounters with God, Pocket Books, 1979.
The Great Airship Mystery: A UFO of the 1890s, Dodd, 1981.
Re-Thinking: How to Succeed by Learning How to Think, M. Evans, 1982.
The Encyclopedia of Monsters, Dodd, 1983.
Movie Musicals, Bison, 1983.
The Encyclopedia of Ghosts, Dodd, 1984.
Horror Movies, Bison, 1984.
(With wife, Susan Cohen) *Screen Goddesses,* Bison, 1984.
The Encyclopedia of the Strange, Dodd, 1985.
(With S. Cohen) *Hollywood Hunks and Heroes,* Bison, 1985.
(With S. Cohen) *The Encyclopedia of Movie Stars,* Bison, 1986.
(With S. Cohen) *A History of the Oscars,* Bison, 1986.

■ Personal

Born March 12, 1936, in Chicago, IL; son of M. Milton and Sue (Greenberg) Cohen; married Susan Handler (a writer), February 2, 1958; children: Theodora (deceased). *Education:* University of Illinois, journalism degree, 1959. *Hobbies and other interests:* Hiking, animals.

■ Addresses

Home and office—24 Elizabeth St., Port Jervis, NY 12771. *Agent*—Henry Morrison, Inc., P.O. Box 235, Bedford Hills, NY 10507.

■ Career

Time, Inc., Chicago, IL, member of staff during the 1950s; *Science Digest* (magazine), New York City, assistant editor, 1960-65, managing editor, 1965-68; writer, 1969—. Has given talks at colleges, universities, secondary schools, and elementary schools in the United States and Canada; has appeared on radio and television programs, including the television special "Everything You Wanted to Know about Monsters But Were Afraid," Columbia Broadcasting System. Committee for the

500 Great Films, Bison, 1987.
The Encyclopedia of Unsolved Crimes, Dodd, 1987.

YOUNG ADULT NONFICTION

Secrets from Ancient Graves, Dodd, 1968.
Vaccination and You, Messner, 1968.
The Age of Giant Mammals, Dodd, 1969.
Animals of the City, McGraw, 1969.
Night Animals, Messner, 1970.
Conquerors on Horseback, Doubleday, 1970.
Talking with the Animals, Dodd, 1971.
Superstition, Creative Education Press, 1971.
A Natural History of Unnatural Things, Dutton, 1971.
Ancient Monuments and How They Were Built, McGraw, 1971.
Watchers in the Wild: The New Science of Ethology, Little, Brown, 1972.
In Search of Ghosts, Dodd, 1972.
The Magic Art of Foreseeing the Future, Dodd, 1973.
How Did Life Get There?, Messner, 1973.
Magicians, Wizards, and Sorcerers, Lippincott, 1973.
How the World Will End, McGraw, 1973, published as *Waiting for the Apocalypse: Doomsday Deferred*, Prometheus Books, 1983.
Shaka: King of the Zulus, Doubleday, 1973.
ESP: The Search beyond the Senses, Harcourt, 1973.
The Black Death, 1347-1351, F. Watts, 1974.
The Magic of the Little People, Messner, 1974.
Curses, Hexes, and Spells, Lippincott, 1974.
Intelligence: What Is It?, M. Evans, 1974.
Not of the World: A History of the Commune in America, Follett, 1974.
Human Nature—Animal Nature: The Biology of Human Behavior, McGraw, 1974.
The Mysteries of Reincarnation, Dodd, 1975.
The Greatest Monsters in the World, Dodd, 1975.
The Body Snatchers, Lippincott, 1975.
The Human Side of Computers, McGraw, 1975.
Monsters, Giants, and Little Men from Mars, Doubleday, 1975.
The New Believers: Young Religion in America, M. Evans, 1975.
The Spirit of the Lord: Revivalism in America, Four Winds, 1975.
Animal Territories, Hastings House, 1975.
Mysterious Disappearances, Dodd, 1976.
The Ancient Visitors, Doubleday, 1976.
Dreams, Visions, and Drugs, F. Watts, 1976.
Gold: The Fascinating Study of the Noble Metal through the Ages, M. Evans, 1976.
Supermonsters, Dodd, 1977.
Ghostly Animals, Doubleday, 1977.

The Science of Spying, McGraw, 1977.
Real Ghosts, Dodd, 1977.
Meditation: What It Can Do for You, Dodd, 1977.
What Really Happened to the Dinosaurs?, Dutton, 1977.
Creativity, What Is It?, M. Evans, 1977.
Ceremonial Magic, Four Winds, 1978.
The World of UFOs, Lippincott, 1978.
Creatures from UFOs, Dodd, 1978.
The World's Most Famous Ghosts, Dodd, 1978.
Young Ghosts, Dutton, 1978.
Frauds, Hoaxes, and Swindles, F. Watts, 1979.
Missing! Stories of Strange Disappearances, Dodd, 1979.
Mysteries of the World, Doubleday, 1979.
What's Happening to Our Weather, M. Evans, 1979.
Dealing with the Devil, Dodd, 1979.
Famous Curses, Dodd, 1979.
Great Mistakes, M. Evans, 1979.
The Monsters of "Star Trek," Pocket Books, 1980.
Monsters You Never Heard Of, Dodd, 1980.
The Tomb Robbers, McGraw, 1980.
Bigfoot: America's Number One Monster, Pocket Books, 1980.
Everything You Need to Know about Monsters and Still Be Able to Sleep, Doubleday, 1981.
A Close Look at Close Encounters, Putnam, 1981.
Ghostly Terrors, Putnam, 1981.
The Headless Roommate and Other Tales of Terror, M. Evans, 1981.
The Last Hundred Years: Medicine, M. Evans, 1981.
How to Buy a Car, F. Watts, 1982.
Video Games, Pocket Books, 1982.
Horror in the Movies, Clarion Books, 1982.
How to Test Your ESP, Dutton, 1982.
Real Magic, Dodd, 1982.
The Last Hundred Years: Household Technology, M. Evans, 1982.
Monster Hunting Today, Dodd, 1983.
The Simon and Schuster Question and Answer Book: Computers, Simon & Schuster, 1983 (published in England as *The Hamlyn Book of Computer Questions and Answers*, Hamlyn, 1984).
Southern Fried Rat and Other Gruesome Tales, M. Evans, 1983.
Monster Dinosaur, Lippincott, 1983.
The Restless Dead: Ghostly Tales from around the World, Dodd, 1983.
(With S. Cohen) *The Kid's Guide to Home Computers*, Pocket Books, 1983.
Hiram Bingham and the Dream of Gold, M. Evans, 1984.
Masters of Horror, Clarion Books, 1984.

(With S. Cohen) *Teenage Stress: Understanding the Tensions You Feel at Home, at School and among Your Friends*, M. Evans, 1984.

(With S. Cohen) *The Kids' Guide to Home Video*, Pocket Books, 1984.

Henry Stanley and the Quest for the Source of the Nile, M. Evans, 1985.

(With S. Cohen) *Rock Video Superstars*, Pocket Books, 1985.

(With S. Cohen) *Wrestling Superstars*, Pocket Books, 1985.

(With S. Cohen) *Wrestling Superstars II*, Pocket Books, 1986.

(With S. Cohen) *Heroes of the Challenger*, Pocket Books, 1986.

(With S. Cohen) *A Six-Pack and a Fake I.D.: Teens Look at the Drinking Question*, M. Evans, 1986.

(With S. Cohen) *How to Get Started in Video*, F. Watts, 1986.

Strange and Amazing Facts about "Star Trek," Archway, 1986.

ESP: The New Technology, Messner, 1986.

(With S. Cohen) *Teenage Competition: A Survival Guide*, M. Evans, 1987.

Hollywood Dinosaur, Archway, 1987.

Carl Sagan, Superstar Scientist, Putnam, 1987.

(With S. Cohen) *Young and Famous: Hollywood's Newest Superstars*, Archway, 1987.

The UFOs' Third Wave, M. Evans, 1988.

(With S. Cohen) *Going for the Gold*, Archway, 1988.

(With S. Cohen) *What You Can Believe about Drugs: An Honest and Unhysterical Guide for Teens*, Holt, 1988.

Phone Call from a Ghost: Strange Tales from Modern America, Putnam, 1988.

(With S. Cohen) *What Kind of Dog Is That?: Rare and Unusual Breeds of Dogs*, Cobblehill Books, 1989.

(With S. Cohen) *When Someone You Know Is Gay*, M. Evans, 1989.

(With S. Cohen) *Zoo Superstars*, Pocket Books, 1989.

The Ghosts of War, Putnam, 1990.

Phantom Animals, Putnam, 1991.

Railway Ghosts and Other Highway Horrors, Cobblehill Books, 1991.

(With S. Cohen) *Where to Find Dinosaurs*, Cobblehill Books, 1991.

JUVENILE NONFICTION

America's Very Own Monsters, Dodd, 1982.
America's Very Own Ghosts, Dodd, 1985.
Dinosaurs, Doubleday, 1987.
Prehistoric Animals, Doubleday, 1988.

Ancient Egypt, Doubleday, 1989.
Ancient Greece, Doubleday, 1990.
Great Ghosts, Dutton, 1990.
Ancient Rome, Doubleday, 1991.
(With S. Cohen) *Zoos*, Doubleday, 1991.

OTHER

Contributor to *People's Almanac, New York Kids' Book, Doubleday Encyclopedia of UFOs, World Book Encyclopedia,* and *Science and the Paranormal;* contributor to periodicals, including *Omni, Popular Mechanics, Nation,* and *Parapsychology Review.* Contributing editor, *Science Digest.*

■ **Sidelights**

Daniel Cohen is the author of more than one hundred books on subjects ranging from monsters, UFOs, and the paranormal to video games, rock stars, and social issues like drug abuse and homosexuality. Although the majority of his books deal with the fantastic, mysterious, and unexplained, Cohen is willing to tackle almost any subject. His books are classified as high interest-low reading level titles designed to attract readers who usually do not visit libraries and book stores. Cohen and his wife Susan, who has co-written a number of books with her husband, "are quite proud to point out that many of their readers are kids who don't normally read," reports Cheryl Abdullah in *Book Report.* By tantalizing young readers with subjects that truly interest them, Cohen hopes to reach an audience he feels is neglected by librarians and other authors. "I write for the fat, spotty kid in the third row who is picking his nose," the writer relates in his *Something about the Author Autobiography Series* entry, "or for the scruffy kid wearing the Twisted Sister tee shirt, who is looking out the window waiting for class to end."

As a schoolboy, Cohen was himself a somewhat odd-looking student who thought class was very boring. Coming from a poor family, Cohen describes himself as a child as "a fat kid in ill-fitting clothes" that were mostly hand-me-downs. The Dick and Jane books he read in school that portrayed the idealized middle-class American family seemed preposterous to him. Early in his autobiographical essay, Cohen says, "I remember thinking that I'm not like that. I live in an apartment with roaches, my mother works, my father is in the hospital. I don't even know anybody who lives in a house." An average student, the author remembered: "I spent most of my time looking at the clock waiting for class to end."

A change came in Cohen's life during his senior year in high school. He began to spend more and more of his time on campus at the University of Chicago, which is located in his old Hyde Park neighborhood. But the young Cohen was not attracted to the highly academic atmosphere of the prestigious university. Rather, he was drawn to the rag-tag collection of "artists or would-be artists, and others who lived on the fringes of respectable academic society. It was into this world that I began to drift. In addition to the artists there were a variety of political, sexual, and religious radicals, a few alcoholics and potheads, as well as the occasional thief and con man. These were my kind of people, a wonderful antidote to the blandness and utter boredom of high school.

"Now here is where the contradiction in my life comes in. I was not at all wild. I went to school and worked afterwards, usually in movie theatres. Indeed I was often the only one in my crowd who was working, and I kept a couple of friends from starvation by supplying them with enormous quantities of buttered popcorn. I was an observer, a hanger on, tolerated and perhaps liked because I was a pretty good listener, and there was always the popcorn."

Feeling that he did not belong with his more artistic and bohemian friends, Cohen was practical and attended a two-year branch of the University of Illinois in Chicago. He loved animals and so decided to major in biology, but he discovered that

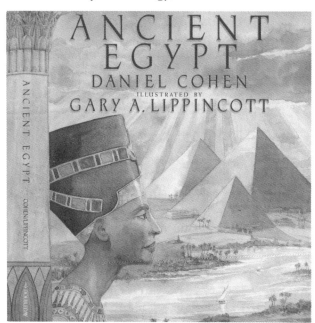

Cohen first explored the mysteries of the past in 1989's *Ancient Egypt*.

studying cells under a microscope was not nearly as enjoyable as being with living animals. Not knowing what to do next, he started working for the student newspaper because his friend was the editor and it was something he could do to occupy his time. At the time he was working on the newspaper, Cohen had not thought about becoming a professional writer, although he enjoyed reading science fiction and horror stories and had submitted science-fiction stories to the magazine, *Thrilling Wonder Stories.* However, he did have fun being a student journalist and eventually became the editor-in-chief.

When Cohen finished his classes in Chicago, he continued his studies at the University of Illinois's main campus at Urbana-Champaign. The classes he took there were like a flashback to his high school days because they were just as useless and uninteresting to him. He studied journalism, but the courses in typesetting by hand and running a small newspaper seemed outdated and impractical. He joined the staff of the college newspaper, but because most of the positions there were already filled by other students, he was not able to participate as much as he wished. "It was quite a comedown from being editor-in-chief," Cohen relates in his essay, "and my passion for journalism was rapidly cooling."

Cohen graduated with a degree in journalism and soon married Susan Handler, who was a sociology student at the time. Uncertain of what type of job he could find in journalism, he eventually took a position as a proofreader at the Chicago office of Time, Inc. Again, Cohen was terribly bored by the menial work he was required to do. It seemed as if he would never find his niche in life, until, in frustration, the young journalist left Time, Inc., and joined the staff of *Science Digest* magazine. Here he was allowed to do a little bit of everything—including some writing—to put the small magazine together. The work was as enjoyable as his early years at his college newspaper. He loved his job so much that when the magazine moved to New York City Cohen agreed to leave his hometown and move, too.

Life in New York City was not easy for Cohen at first. Working conditions at *Science Digest* were chaotic while the staff adjusted to its new location. The original editor died suddenly, and Cohen's next boss was incompetent and was later fired by the management. During this time the magazine was actually put together with the efforts of only Cohen and one co-worker. After a more experienced editor was found and the staff of two was

Egyptian royalty was buried with lavish displays of wealth and ritual.

increased to four, time became available for Cohen to contribute his own articles to the magazine. "I learned to write quickly and clearly if not elegantly," he remembers in his essay.

After publishing several popular science articles for *Science Digest*, Cohen began to write about the out-of-the-ordinary topics that would later become the subjects of most of his books. His first such article, published in 1966, was a review of John Fuller's UFO book, *Incident at Exeter*. It was the first article that Cohen had written for *Science Digest* that drew very much attention to the journalist. He received several dozen letters from readers, and although some of them were positive responses, most of them were from angry readers who objected to Cohen's skeptical attitude about

whether UFOs actually existed. But Cohen relished the attention—both bad and good—because it proved that people were at least reading his work.

Even more surprising to the author was that he was invited to appear on television and radio programs to discuss the UFO phenomenon. "My television debut was an appearance on educational television with John Fuller who wrote *Incident at Exeter*. The show was supposed to be a dignified low-key discussion, but it immediately turned into an angry shouting match—quite lively for educational television at that time. Years later I met Fuller at a publishing party. He didn't remember me or the show. Apparently it had been a good deal more important to me than it was to him."

Realizing that there was a large audience for articles about strange phenomena, Cohen next wrote a lengthy piece on extra-sensory perception (ESP). The *Science Digest* issue in which it appeared sold a record number of copies for that magazine. This success encouraged the author to write more such articles and submit them to other magazines. Eventually, he had collected enough material for his first book, *Myths of the Space Age*. He was asked to be on more television and radio shows and, later, he began to give talks at colleges and universities. Cohen credits his popularity with talk show hosts to his tendency to talk about a topic for long periods of time: "Hosts of late-night talk shows could leave the studio to go to the bathroom, or possibly to take a nap and feel perfectly confident that I would keep right on talking; there would be no dead airtime so long as I was around. Later, when I did some lecturing, I displayed the same tendencies—at one college they actually had to turn the lights out in the auditorium to shut me up. I thoroughly enjoyed being a minor celebrity."

Although Cohen still liked his position at *Science Digest* and had become managing editor of the magazine, he believed it to be a dead-end career. His newfound success as an author inspired him to become a freelance writer. Since his wife Susan was also dissatisfied with her job as a social worker and they were both tired of life in New York City, the Cohens quit their jobs and moved to the countryside. At first, the author tried to publish the kind of popular science writing he had done for *Science Digest*, but he soon discovered that the demand for such books was not very great. "However my writings about ghosts and monsters and psychic phenomena found a ready market, and more and more of my time was spent on those subjects."

For the author, writing about the supernatural was not the same as believing in it. As with the artistic groupies he was friends with in high school—as well as the bohemian friends he had in Chicago and New York City—Cohen was just as fascinated by the people who talked about witches, aliens, ghosts, and Bigfoot as he was about the subjects themselves. He was once again the objective outsider, trying to mix in with people whose beliefs he did not really share. "Even when I find such people obviously wrong, foolish, crazy, or know that they are lying and trying to con me, I still find them interesting," he remarks in his essay.

Despite his skepticism, Cohen has said that he would be delighted if in fact he did encounter one of the creatures he describes in his books. His readers often ask him whether he has seen a ghost. "Sadly, the answer is no," the author responds in *Cricket Magazine*. "But it's not for want of trying. I've crept around haunted houses, I've attended seances, and I even spent a damp and chilly night in an English churchyard that was supposed to be haunted." Cohen cautions, however, that lack of evidence does not prove or disprove anything. He points out that scientific "facts" should not be accepted without question. In *Book Report* he says: "It's not wise and not correct to leave any reader, young or old, with the feeling that all of the questions have been answered, particularly in writing about science. Sometimes writers present science as 'revealed truth,' with all of the questions answered. But science is a process, and there are always unanswered questions. It's important to get kids to understand that gray-area truths are merely conditional, at least until new evidence comes in."

Cohen's books about monsters and the supernatural characteristically end on a "what if" note. For example, in *Creatures from UFO's*, which tells several stories about people who claim to have seen alien beings and spaceships, Cohen concludes: "This is only a sample, a very small sample, of hundreds and hundreds of reports that have been received from around the world. I'm sure you will agree they are sensational. But are they true? Do they describe things that really happened? Or did people dream these encounters, or make them up altogether? We cannot say for sure. None of these cases has been thoroughly investigated. As we have seen, investigations often show things did not happen as they are reported to have happened. Investigations have often shown a story to be a hoax. So we must treat these stories with care. But that should not keep us from enjoying them. It is quite thrilling to think that one day we may look out our window and see a UFO. Then slowly a door in the UFO opens, and three little men float out...."

Reviews of Cohen's numerous books have been mixed. Some critics have praised the author's research and easy-to-understand writing, while others have complained that in some cases his coverage of a topic is superficial and too generalized. In a review of *In Search of Ghosts*, for example, *School Library Journal* contributor Michael Cart argues that the text is "marred by undocumented, sweeping generalizations." A *Science Books and Films* evaluation of *The Ancient Visitors* also skeptically notes that "Cohen fails to do original research, relying instead on secondary sources and his own logic." On the other hand, another *School Library Journal* reviewer regards Cohen's *ESP: The New Technology* to be a "balanced, noncondescending, factual, and credible book." A number of other critics have also praised the author's ability to objectively and entertainingly introduce young readers to subjects that appeal to them. Calling *The World of UFO's* "an extraordinary and delightful book," an *Appraisal* writer approves of Cohen's ability to be enthusiastic about a subject that he does not really believe in: "Throughout the work Cohen's own involvement in and enjoyment of the subject is evident and contagious. I cannot recommend this book highly enough."

Although many of Cohen's books deal with the supernatural and unexplainable, his interest in animals and popular science has lead him to write about subjects for which there is more scientific evidence. These books still address areas of interest to young readers, however. Some, such as the author's books on dinosaurs, cover topics that have always fascinated many people. Nevertheless, Cohen still has a fondness for the bizarre. Many of his books demonstrate that fact can be just as strange as fiction. *The Body Snatchers,* for example, is an informal history about grave robbing. In his typically straightforward and noncondescending manner, Cohen tells of Egyptian tomb robbings and nineteenth-century anatomical experiments. Along the way he adds such tidbits as how to properly hang someone and where the expression "kick the bucket" comes from (executioners used to hang prisoners by putting a noose around the convicts' necks, standing them on a bucket, and kicking it out from under their feet). In a *New York Times Book Review* article on *The Body Snatchers,* Peter Andrews observes that what "could have been a distasteful story in lesser hands becomes spritely and fascinating reading. Mr. Cohen has crafted a model of good juvenile literature."

Cohen, an animal lover since his youth, recognizes that animals are also a favorite topic among his readers. After he graduated from high school, the author toyed with the idea of working for Lincoln Park Zoo in Chicago. But he decided against the idea. "Being a zookeeper was an unskilled job and therefore not quite respectable. [My family] ... expected that I would go to college," Cohen writes in his autobiography. Earlier he reflects, "Even today I often wonder if my failure of nerve at that moment was not one of the biggest mistakes of my life." Cohen instead has used his writing talents to share his interest in animals with his readers. Some of the author's animal books include *The Age of*

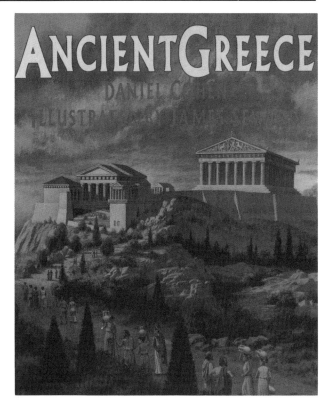

The history and mythology of ancient Greece was the topic of this 1990 book.

Giant Mammals, Night Animals, Human Nature—Animal Nature: The Biology of Human Behavior, Talking with the Animals, and *Animal Territories.* A number of critics have praised Cohen's studies of animals and their relationships with human beings as valuable introductions to zoology and its related fields. A *Science Books* contributor, for instance, calls *Talking with the Animals* an "attractively written, clear, but not simplistic overview of animal communication."

In the early 1980s, after writing dozens of books, Cohen suddenly found himself getting far behind in his writing. He had several deadlines approaching for books that his editors were demanding he finish, but it was a lot more work than he could do on his own. Soliciting help from his wife Susan, who had just begun to write her own books, the couple managed to complete the assignments on time. They were pleasantly surprised at how well the collaboration worked, and so they decided to write more books together. Susan's background in sociology led the Cohens to write such books as *Teenage Stress: Understanding the Tensions You Feel at Home, at School and among Your Friends; A Six Pack and a Fake I.D.: Teens Look at the Drinking Questions; Teenage Competition: A Survival Guide; What You Can Believe about Drugs: An Honest and*

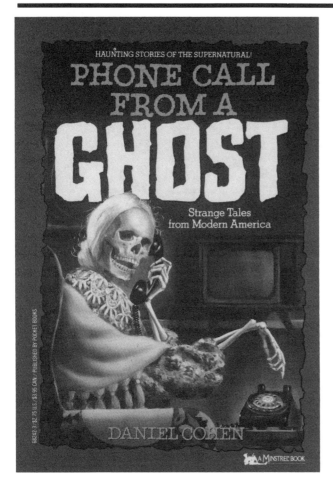

Cohen provides plenty of spooky stories about "real" ghosts in his 1988 collection.

Unhysterical Guide for Teens; and *When Someone You Know Is Gay.*

The Cohens' daughter, Theodora, also inspired several books. Having "a teenage daughter in the house made us realize that rock video had become a major cultural force among today's kids," Cohen recalls in his autobiographical essay. He and Susan decided they wanted to do a rock video book together. "It took us quite a while to convince an editor of this. It seems to me that many children's-book editors are strangely isolated from the interests of the audience they are supposed to be trying to reach. They generally discover a hot topic only after someone else has been successful, and then they all rush to imitate the success, resulting in a glut of books. Timing is everything." The book, *Rock Video Superstars,* sold well, proving Cohen right about the importance of timing. Researching the book (which mostly involved watching hours of MTV) was also a rewarding experience, according to Cohen. "I learned a lot about the interplay of music and electronics and about video technology. And I also think I learned something about today's

kids, a useful lesson if your business is writing for them."

A sympathetic father as well as writer, Cohen had no objection when his own daughter announced that she wished to become an actress, even though many parents would want their children to pursue less risky careers. "Who are we to tell her it is a crazy and unstable way to try to make a living," the author says in his essay, which was written just after Theodora graduated from high school. "She thinks a writer's life is dull, and she's probably right." Tragically, three years later the Cohens lost their daughter. The author told *Authors and Artists for Young Adults (AAYA):* "Since that autobiography was written, one quite terrible thing has happened. My daughter, Theo, was one of the Syracuse University students killed in the bombing of Pan Am 103 [which crashed in Scotland] in December, 1988. As you can imagine, this has left Susan and I quite shattered. I think it was Mark Twain who said, 'I don't know how anyone survives the loss of a child.' I don't know either, I'm just trying to get along. You don't get over something like this; you simply live with it.... Susan and I have both been very public about what has happened. We feel that it is only through maximum publicity that there will be any form of justice for this crime. And only keeping people aware of what has happened will keep it from happening again to others. However, at this time I have no desire to write about what has happened. That may come someday, but not yet."

Cohen has managed to keep on writing and has also returned to lecturing on a regular basis. As before, he continues to write about animals, popular science, subjects that are of special interest to teenagers, and the paranormal, as well as books that are meant for children instead of teenagers. His more recent books about the supernatural have mostly dealt with ghosts, including *The Ghosts of War, Great Ghosts, Phone Call from a Ghost: Strange Tales from Modern America,* and *Phantom Animals.* The writer prides himself on the wide variety of topics he has written about. At one point in his autobiography, he states, "There are certain things that I can't write, and certain things that I won't write. For example, I could never do a book on mathematics, because I don't understand mathematics, and I wouldn't do one of the currently fashionable books on the glories of disciplining your children so that they turn out to be perfect little twerps. But between those extremes I've turned out books on an alarming number of subjects."

Because of his peculiar choice of subjects, Cohen has had to deal with some resistance to his books. His writings on monsters, aliens, and the supernatural, for instance, have provoked protests from religious fundamentalists. He relates in his essay: "On a few occasions I've run into problems with religious groups. Without ever having read anything I had written, they decided that I was going to lead their children down the path of Satan worship and spiritualism. When I point out to them that I am neither a Satan worshiper nor a spiritualist, indeed that I strongly debunk both beliefs, they are not appeased, because my type of belief is not what they are looking for. Such folks do not want the subject discussed at all, from any point of view except their own, narrow, ignorant, and unhistoric view. It isn't enough to say that spiritualism is silly. They only want to hear someone who says it is Satanic. To say, as I do, that the company of Satan worshippers is small, crazed, stupid, or simply not serious, is offensive. They want someone who says that the legion of the Devil is enormous and powerful, and that it includes everyone who disagrees with them." Pressure from such special interest groups has caused some school libraries to keep Cohen's books off their shelves, especially *Curses, Hexes and Spells*, which suffered this fate in libraries throughout the United States. Cohen also told *AAYA* that the *New York Times* listed *Curses, Hexes and Spells* "as one of the ten books most frequently stolen from libraries.... [It ranks] just below *The Joy of Sex*. I don't know what this means."

Other books by Cohen and his wife have also been met with protests. *When Someone You Know Is Gay*, Susan Cohen recalls in *Book Report*, posed a particular problem: "We did have trouble selling it. Through our agent, we submitted to at least 15 children's publishers and got either 'The librarians will never accept it' or 'This has been done before.' Well, it *hadn't* been done before, not from the approach we took. Only a couple said right out that they didn't want the grief that might result from printing this type of book." The Cohens did finally publish *When Someone You Know Is Gay* and were rewarded by a favorable response from both audiences and critics alike.

While Cohen is concerned with publishing enough books to earn a living as a freelance writer, he does not try to cater to public tastes in order to make money. If a certain subject interests him—even if he knows it has no great selling potential—the author will sometimes try to convince his editor to invest in his book idea anyway. This has been

especially true with the biographies that Cohen has written about such people as Henry Stanley and Hiram Bingham. The books have received positive reviews from critics, but only a relatively small audience has read them.

Because some of Cohen's books earn less money than others, the author writes as many books as he can to have a steady income. But even if he had all the money he needed, he says in his essay, "I think I would still write—though at a somewhat more relaxed pace. I am not in any way driven to express myself; it's just that writing has been the central part of my life for so many years, I'm not at all sure how I would get along without it. For me, writing is a habit." It is not a dull habit to him, however. Today, Cohen writes the same type of books that have fascinated him since childhood, what he calls "gee-whiz" books in his *Book Report* interview. Whether he writes about rock and roll superstars or beings from another planet, the author believes

From haunted battlefields to soldiers' premonitions of death, Cohen's 1990 story collection includes some chilling tales.

that "if you open yourself up to it, you can learn a great deal about the world no matter what subject you approach." "When children make interest and fascination part of life," he concludes at one point, "they may in fact enjoy life just a little bit more. That deep fascination is what I try to stimulate in my writing."

■ Works Cited

Abdullah, Cheryl, "Daniel & Susan Cohen," *Book Report*, May-June, 1990, pp. 34-39.

Andrews, Peter, *New York Times Book Review*, July 6, 1975, p. 8.

Appraisal, fall, 1979.

Cart, Michael, *School Library Journal*, November, 1972, p. 66.

Cohen, Daniel, in comments provided to Kevin S. Hile for *Authors and Artists for Young Adults*.

Cohen, Daniel, *Creatures from UFO's*, Dodd, 1978, p. 109.

"Meet Your Author, Daniel Cohen," *Cricket Magazine*, October, 1980, p. 27.

School Library Journal, October, 1986.

Science Books, December, 1972, p. 245.

Science Books and Films, December, 1976, pp. 125-126.

Something about the Author Autobiography Series, Volume 4, Gale, 1987, pp. 147-165.

■ For More Information See

BOOKS

Children's Literature Review, Volume 3, Gale, 1978.

PERIODICALS

Books and Bookmen, December, 1977.

Childhood Education, April, 1977.

Christian Science Monitor, April 1, 1971.

Commonweal, November 10, 1978.

New York Times Book Review, April 16, 1972; July 6, 1975.

School Library Journal, October and November, 1972.

Science Books and Films, December, 1976.

Scientific America, December, 1976.

Teacher, December, 1974.

Times Educational Supplement, February 3, 1978.

—*Sketch by Kevin S. Hile*

Evan S. Connell

■ Personal

Born August 17, 1924, in Kansas City, MO; son of Evan Shelby (a surgeon) and Elton (Williamson) Connell. *Education:* Attended Dartmouth College, 1941-43; University of Kansas, A.B., 1947; graduate study at Stanford University 1947-48, Columbia University, 1948-49, and San Francisco State College (now University).

■ Addresses

Home—Fort Marcy, Apt. 13, Santa Fe, NM 87501.
Agent—Harold Matson Co., 276 Fifth Ave., New York, NY 10001.

■ Career

Writer. *Military service:* U.S. Navy, pilot, 1943-45; served as flight instructor.

■ Awards, Honors

Eugene F. Saxon fellow, 1953; nomination for National Book Award, 1960, for *Mrs. Bridge,* and 1974, for *Points for a Compass Rose;* Guggenheim fellow, 1963; Rockefeller Foundation grant, 1967;

nomination for award for general nonfiction from National Book Critics Circle, 1984, and Literary Award of Little Bighorn Associates, 1985, both for *Son of the Morning Star;* award from American Academy and Institute of Arts and Letters, 1987; induction to Institute of American Academy and Institute of Arts and Letters, 1988.

■ Writings

The Anatomy Lesson and Other Stories, Viking, 1957.
Mrs. Bridge (novel), Viking, 1959.
The Patriot (novel), Viking, 1960.
(Editor) Jerry Stoll, *I Am a Lover,* Angel Island Publications, 1961.
Notes from a Bottle Found on the Beach at Carmel, Viking, 1963.
At the Crossroads: Stories, Simon & Schuster, 1966.
The Diary of a Rapist (novel), Simon & Schuster, 1966.
Mr. Bridge (novel), Knopf, 1969.
(Editor) *Woman by Three,* Pacific Coast Publishers, 1969.
Points for a Compass Rose, Knopf, 1973.
The Connoisseur (novel), Knopf, 1974.
Double Honeymoon (novel), Putnam, 1976.
A Long Desire (nonfiction), Holt, 1979.
The White Lantern (nonfiction), Holt, 1980.
St. Augustine's Pigeon: The Selected Stories, North Point Press, 1980.
Son of the Morning Star: Custer and the Little Bighorn (nonfiction), North Point Press, 1984.
The Alchymist's Journal (novel), North Point Press, 1991.

Author of preface to *The Sea and the Jungle*, by H. M. Tomlinson, Marlboro Press, 1989; author of introduction to the reissue of *The Rise of Silas Lapham*, by William Dean Howells, Vintage Books, 1991. Contributor of short stories to periodicals, including *Carolina Quarterly, Paris Review*, and *Esquire.* Editor of *Contact* (literary magazine), 1959-65.

■ Adaptations

Mrs. Bridge and *Mr. Bridge* have been adapted for a Merchant Ivory film titled *Mr. and Mrs. Bridge*, starring Joanne Woodward and Paul Newman, 1990.

Son of the Morning Star has been adapted for a television miniseries, starring Gary Cole, which aired on ABC, February, 1991.

■ Sidelights

Evan S. Connell is a distinguished author best known for his novels probing the complexities of human behavior. His most popular works, *Mrs. Bridge* and its companion novel *Mr. Bridge*, showcase the lives of an affluent midwestern family whose unfulfilled lives are ruled by social pretense. In addition to his fiction, Connell has written celebrated books of nonfiction, the most popular of which is the 1984 *Son of the Morning Star.* A study of the people and events connected with the defeat of General George A. Custer at Little Bighorn, the immensely popular work has been adapted as a television miniseries.

Connell was born on August 17, 1924, in Kansas City, Missouri. "We lived in a square, white midwestern house with green shutters, a clammy basement full of spiders, and a musty attic reached by a sliding ladder," Connell declared in *Contemporary Authors Autobiography Series (CAAS).* "Our house could be distinguished from others on the block by a steep driveway leading to the garage, and every winter for several years, my father—sometimes my mother, at times myself and my (years younger) sister—could be seen scattering rock salt or ashes from the fireplace on this short, steep grade. Scattering salt or ashes was not of itself disagreeable, but I would be called to do this on icy winter evenings just before my father returned from the office. If he could not get up the hill to park the Reo in the garage, he would not be able to get it started the next morning. So we attended to this on wretched winter nights, year after year, until at last my father employed somebody with a road grader to eliminate the hump

where the car always got stuck. Thereafter he was able to drive up the slope. I have wondered many times why he did not do this after the experience of his first winter in that house, but it was not the sort of question he liked. He did not accept critical questions with much grace. I never saw him so enraged that he expressed himself physically, but he could be irritable, and there never was the least doubt who commanded the affairs of our house."

Connell's stern and autocratic father—later the prototype for Walter Bridge in Connell's novels *Mrs. Bridge* and *Mr. Bridge*—was a highly skilled and successful ophthalmic surgeon, performing somewhere between thirty and fifty thousand cataract operations in fifty years. "Extraordinarily delicate surgery," Connell revealed in an interview for *Authors and Artists for Young Adults (AAYA).* "The way he could handle a scalpel impressed me enormously. He was intimidating; he ran a tight ship, and was a quite humorless man. I don't think he ever made a joke; he must have, but I can't remember it. My father's father was also a doctor. I think my father was disappointed that I didn't

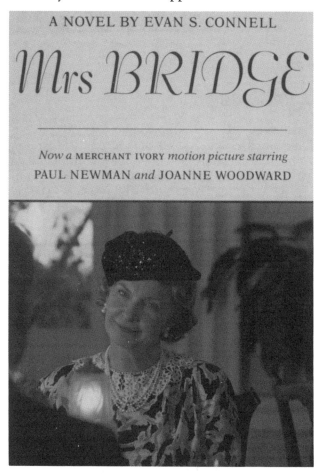

A NOVEL BY EVAN S. CONNELL

Mrs BRIDGE

Now a MERCHANT IVORY *motion picture starring*
PAUL NEWMAN *and* JOANNE WOODWARD

Connell's story about a "perfect" wife and mother was a best-seller in 1959.

become one as well, although he did say 'I don't care what you do. Just do it well.' If he read my stuff, he never said anything to me about it."

In addition to a "clean and surgical" approach to his own work as a writer, Connell inherited from his father a scrupulous sense of honesty. "My father believed you always told the truth and always paid your debts," the author told *AAYA*. "When Harry Truman lived in Missouri, before he was vice-president, and then president, he borrowed some money from one of my father's friends and never paid it back. At least once, when Truman's name came up, my father said angrily: 'That fellow doesn't pay his debts.' When *Mrs. Bridge* came out, all he said was 'as long as he portrays Kansas City honestly.' I share his belief in the importance of honesty; I have since I was a kid. Very late one Christmas Eve, my grandfather Williamson carried our Christmas tree into the house. I saw it. And at that instant, peeping out the window when I was supposed to be asleep, I understood that Santa Claus did not exist. The whole thing was a lie. Parents know this must happen sooner or later but assume the pleasure in believing in Santa Claus more than compensates for the ultimate disenchantment. As for myself, I think not. I have never forgiven anybody who lied to me."

The home in which Connell grew up was, if not anticultural, certainly acultural: "My father read mystery stories to put himself to sleep," Connell told *AAYA*, "but he didn't admit he enjoyed it; he thought it was frivolous. He worked fiercely and expected other people to do the same. There wasn't a real 'library' in our home. There were medical books and a miscellaneous collection of Christmas gift books and cook books, but nobody really went out and bought books to read.

"My first reading interest was the West, when I was about ten. The X-bar-X Boys, a series about a ranch, Will James' books, and Albert Payson Terhune were all in the school library. I thought *The Aztec Treasure House* was the greatest novel ever written. I can't remember who wrote it; the hero was an archaeologist. There's a dying priest in the desert who gives him a map and off goes the hero to find the fabulous walled city of Culhuacan. Years later, I started collecting pre-Columbian art and based a book (*The Connoisseur*) on that interest. In the same way my interest in alchemy (*The Alchymist's Journal*) started when I picked up a book on [Sixeenth-century German alchemist] Paracelsus forty years ago.

"I had always enjoyed graphic arts, as well, because there was an immediate satisfaction in painting and drawing. When I got into college I took quite a few art courses, and I think, had I had my druthers, I'd like most of all to have been a sculptor. At Columbia graduate school I took a clay modeling class and knew immediately that I was good at it; I was the only first-year student who got an 'A.' But I had a feeling that I might just have wound up teaching if I'd gone into the graphic arts. I think that painters, sculptors, and poets have a much tougher time supporting themselves through their work. Those things didn't concern me as the primary motivating factor, but probably because of my midwestern background they did concern me. You're supposed to make a living. I think my father thought that even the writing was rather impractical.

"I wrote my first stories at around eighteen or nineteen. I wasn't good at assigned writing. When I was a freshman at Dartmouth, I was put in a class with twenty-four others who'd scored highest on the English exam, but after a semester I was demoted. In my 'ordinary' English class every other theme was optional, and I got an 'A' on each optional theme and a 'C' or 'D' on each assigned theme. The instructor said, 'I've had brilliant students and stupid students, but I've never had one quite like you.' The explanation, of course, was simple; I like to think up my own subject matter."

World War II interrupted Connell's university studies, and he entered the U.S. Navy as an aviation cadet. Receiving his wings on V.E. Day, he served thereafter as a flight instructor until his discharge. "By 1941 it had become apparent, even to someone my age, that the Nazi maelstrom was gathering strength," Connell related in *CAAS*. "Accordingly, I thought I should join the Marines. My father thought not. I was sixteen and he decreed that I should attend college until the government sought my services.... My father might have been relieved when [two years later] the government looked at me with basilisk eyes, because he had spent quite a lot of money on my Dartmouth education and the results were unimpressive. All I could show for two years at this excellent school were my green athletic sweaters, an inexplicable demotion in English, and a failing grade in chemistry—a course I detested.... Military service was inevitable, so one might as well get on with it. I had applied for admission to Naval Aviation training, which sounded better than marching around with a rifle, eating from a mess kit, and throwing hand grenades. And some years earlier I had seen a wonderful movie called *The Dawn Patrol* starring Errol Flynn, which may have had something to do with it."

Connell served two years as a navy pilot without seeing overseas action. He then returned to his writing studies at the University of Kansas. "The importance of university study for writers depends, I think, on the individual," Connell disclosed to *AAYA*. "My father wanted me to get a degree, just in case I couldn't make a living as a writer, but there wasn't undue pressure. I enrolled later at San Francisco State because Walter Van Tilburg Clark was teaching there and I wanted to study with him. I'd read a number of his Western stories and thought they were really fine. I was studying with Clark while working on *The Patriot*, based on my navy experiences. I was turning in sections of it to Clark and getting conflicting advice from him and from my editor at Viking. The Viking editor wanted me to put everything in there and make it a big, robust Ken Kesey-type of book. Walter Clark thought that I should eliminate everything but what was essential to the narrative—pare it down—keep it lean. So I tried listening to both of them and struggled with it."

Although Connell was building a respected reputation among writers and critics in the fifties, his first major commercial success came in 1959 with the publication of *Mrs. Bridge*. "Her first name was India—she was never able to get used to it," Connell writes in the novel. "It seemed to her that her parents must have been thinking of someone else when they named her. Or were they hoping for another sort of daughter? As a child she was often on the point of inquiring, but time passed, and she never did." *Mrs. Bridge* was on the *New York Times* best-seller list for three months. *Mr. Bridge* was published ten years later and received similar high critical praise without achieving the same degree of popular success as the earlier book. Nonetheless, Connell feels that *Mr. Bridge*, which deals with the same upper-class Kansas City family, is the better work. "It's better craftsmanship," Connell declared to *AAYA*. "When North Point was going to reissue them, I read both of them over and wanted to make changes in *Mrs. Bridge* because I just thought a lot of the sentences were sloppy. It also seems to me that Mr. Bridge is a more complex and interesting character."

In addition to his novels and short stories, Connell has published five books of nonfiction. "Nonfiction is easier to write," Connell told *AAYA*. "You don't have to use as much imagination. Imaginative things are far more difficult than what you derive from just your critical sense and your intelligence. Curt Gentry [author of *Helter, Skelter*] gets incensed at me for saying this; he thinks good essays are just as difficult as fiction, but I disagree. That is not to say that nonfiction can't be good or that it's less important—it's just easier for me to write a long, heavily researched book like *Son of the Morning Star* than a much shorter fiction book like *Diary of a Rapist*. No work is purely fictional, but the farther you get from yourself, the harder it is. Essays are easier because you don't have to invent something and make it plausible. *Notes from a Bottle* and *Points for a Compass Rose* are sometimes filed in the poetry sections of book shops and sometimes in the nonfiction sections. I understand both decisions, but I've not really written poetry, in the purest sense, since I was in school. I call those books of mine mosaics, nonfiction collages— but I've never said they're poetry."

With the publication of *Son of the Morning Star*, Connell found himself in the middle of a popular success eclipsing even that of *Mrs. Bridge*. *Son of the Morning Star* remained on the *New York Times* nonfiction best-seller list for six months. "I worked on that book steadily for about three-and-a-half years—seven days a week," the author told *AAYA*. "I took one vacation after a couple of years and flew to Cancun for a week, where I spent the entire week sitting on the beach thinking about the book, saying things like 'three more days and I'll get outta here.' The 'vacation' was a big waste of time.

"I'd started out to write a book of essays with the Old West as a theme, thinking I'd do the same sort of thing that I'd done with *The White Lantern* and *A Long Desire*. So I made a list of subjects, of which Custer was an obvious choice. I took off on a research trip, including the Custer battlefield, where I took a lot of notes, and Lincoln, New Mexico, the town Billy the Kid shot up. When I went back to San Francisco I did a twenty page Billy the Kid sketch, and then I started doing the Custer sketch and suddenly had about eighty pages. I knew I either had to stop writing about Custer or change the project, but I was having so much fun that I just gave up the original idea and decided to do an entire book about Custer. Then a second decision was required because I was using a discursive method that I think can be utilized in an essay, but I didn't want to do an entire book like that. So, it was either start all over again, or continue, taking a gamble on where it might lead. I chose the latter method. There's been some criticism because of that; when you write a history book, some feel it should be more formal—a 'proper history book.'

"What pleases me most about the Custer thing is that it seems to have incited other people to do things. The southwestern painter Paul Pletka, for example, did an entire Custer show because the book interested him so much. And there's a new book coming out about the Alamo. The author wrote me that he got so excited about the Custer book that it inspired him to write his own book.

"In researching the book, I had the pleasure of getting to know and work with the late John Carroll, who was probably the foremost Custer scholar. He'd studied Custer all his life, and his name turned up constantly in my research. He was an immeasurable help."

"Even now, after a hundred years, his name alone will start an argument...." Connell writes of Custer in *Son of the Morning Star*. "More significant men of his time can be discussed without passion because they are inextricably woven into a tapestry of the past, but his hotspur refuses to die. He stands forever on that dusty Montana slope."

In 1989 *Son of the Morning Star* and *Mrs. Bridge* and *Mr. Bridge* were filmed. *Mrs. Bridge* and *Mr. Bridge* were made into a theatrical feature film (logically titled *Mr. and Mrs. Bridge*) by the Academy Award-winning producer/director team of Ismail Merchant and James Ivory. The film stars Paul Newman and Joanne Woodward. "I'm glad, I think, about my books being adapted for film and TV," Connell told *AAYA*, "but it does make me a little uneasy. The money's changed. I realize I don't have to worry about next month. I'm not quite used to it.

"It was interesting being on the set in Kansas City and seeing what Joanne Woodward brought to the character of India Bridge. Joanne is quite different physically from my mother, on whom the character was based. She's wonderful though, and I think it's a moving performance. In my mind, I had seen George C. Scott as Mr. Bridge. I was surprised by the way in which Paul Newman changed himself to play the role."

"Gale Garnett, who plays Mrs. Bridge's friend Mabel Ong in the film, made a very interesting comment on the set," Connell disclosed in an interview with Graham Fuller in *Interview* magazine. "I had said that my only reservation about Paul Newman playing Mr. Bridge was that he's just so handsome, and after all, your basic attorney does not look like Paul Newman. Gale, after seeing

him at work, said, 'He's thinned himself inside and out,' and I thought that was a remarkable way of expressing what he had done to change himself. He shows the kind of severe expression and manner that was indeed characteristic not only of my father but of many men of his generation in the Midwest."

"The project really happened, I think, because of Joanne Woodward," Connell related to *AAYA*. "I'm told she had been interested in doing the role since the book first came out in 1959, and she had made a couple of offers for it over the years. Then she was doing a film for the producer Robert Halmi a few years ago, and I believe she told him that if he would buy the rights, she would play the role on television. So Halmi made an offer, which I accepted. Some time afterward, Joanne was having dinner with Jim Ivory and Ismail Merchant, and began talking about it. Ivory knew the book very well, and, if I'm not mistaken, he asked her if she'd thought about doing it as a 'big screen' film. Jim and Ismail thought it should be a theatrical film and so they made some sort of deal with Halmi. Paul

A NOVEL BY EVAN S. CONNELL

Mr BRIDGE

Now a MERCHANT IVORY *motion picture starring*
PAUL NEWMAN *and* JOANNE WOODWARD

Marriage as seen from a male point of view is the subject of this 1969 novel.

Newman read it, liked it, and said he would do the role of Walter Bridge. Then Jim and I met in San Francisco when he was there for the opening of his film *Maurice,* and he seemed very enthusiastic. I'd been through the process before, and so I kind of viewed Jim's interest as more of an inquiry than a final 'deal.' But they went forward with it."

Son of the Morning Star has also been filmed, with a script by Melissa Mathison, who worked very closely with Connell and John Carroll. The miniseries, starring Gary Cole as Custer, aired on ABC in February, 1991. "The film company built an entire fort about fifteen miles outside of Billings, Montana, on somebody's ranch," Connell told *AAYA.* "I understand they're going to turn it into a tourist attraction—'The Place Where They Filmed *Son of the Morning Star*'—something like that.

"I was very pleased by the casting of the Indians; the Sioux speak in Sioux, the Cheyenne in Cheyenne—there are no Anglos wearing paint and speaking pidgin English. And the voice-over narration of Kate Bighead, a key Indian figure, is being done by the Canadian Cree singer, songwriter, and actress Buffy Sainte-Marie."

Connell's latest book, *The Alchymist's Journal,* is "mostly fiction and purports to be the journals of seven different alchemists," the author said to *AAYA.* "The first one is Paracelsus, called by his name. The others are anonymous; I cannot explain why. I invented them, the other six, but I read several biographies of Paracelsus. I had him write some things he didn't actually write, but they stick to his known personality and stated beliefs. The others are developed characters, but their attitudes toward alchemy differ. One is a physician, another is a religious novice, another a revolutionary who is trying to assassinate the king. They all live in the fifteenth and sixteenth centuries, but they don't know each other. In the book, each one makes the mistake of mentioning the serpent Ourobouros, who swallows his tail symbolizing the resurrection. Now, as soon as the fatal word 'Ourobouros' is mentioned, lo and behold, in the very next passage, there comes a 'mysterious stranger,' and that's the end of that alchemist.

"Why this book?," Connell continued. "I don't know. I came across a reference to the serpent swallowing his tail and I thought it interesting. The reason this book took so long (three years) was that I'd done about three hundred pages and then started to feel it was too easy, that I was 'playing tennis without a net,' so I started developing the individual characters more. They're all men; I tried to include a woman, but there were very, very few female alchemists.

"I chose the 'Y' spelling of alchemist [for my book] because it removed the word from the present and gave things a kind of anachronistic flavor. It was frequently spelled that way in those times; English words were spelled every which way until Dr. Johnson set down rules for these things."

After thirty-five years of living in the San Francisco Bay area, Connell has recently moved to Santa Fe, New Mexico, where his Santa Fe-style condominium is filled with a collection of pre-Columbian and Native American art. "I moved to Santa Fe because it was getting more and more crowded in San Francisco," Connell revealed to *AAYA.* "There was too much traffic on the freeway, and I got tired of big city life. I'd visited the Southwest many times and always liked it. Seattle is also a pretty place, but there's too much rain. So many people say they can't live without the ocean; I like the ocean, but I really like mountains and the desert, the dryness of New Mexico. It's mostly about mountains; when I was a kid I went to summer camp in Colorado and have loved the mountains ever since."

As with most writers, Connell has developed work habits and preferences over the years. "I write with an Olympia portable, manual typewriter," Connell further told *AAYA.* "It's the same kind I've used for years—I've had this particular one for twenty-five years. The 'P' and 'G' are not working properly—perhaps I use them more than other writers.

"When I'm doing my own work, I get up between seven and seven thirty in the morning and walk down the hill to have breakfast. I never write before breakfast. Mid-morning I start to work until I'm exhausted. With the Custer book, I was so interested that sometimes I'd work until eight o'clock at night. Then I'd have dinner and go back to working until I fell asleep—I'd even dream about certain passages.

"I think living with someone and writing would have been a problem. It's one of the reasons I've not married. I didn't necessarily look at it consciously or deliberately, but I didn't want the responsibility of having to go to work nine to five to support a family. Having other humans around when I was working would also probably have been difficult. Apart from when I was a kid and in college, I've never lived with anyone for any length of time."

"A new American classic." —Time

★ SON OF THE ★
MORNING STAR
Custer and the Little Bighorn

THE NATIONAL BESTSELLER BY
EVAN S. CONNELL

Published in 1984, Connell's history explores the Battle of the Little Bighorn through the testimony of both cavalry and Indian participants.

Even without "other humans around," Connell is often left with limited free time for solitary pleasures. "Many writers don't read, or stop reading when they start writing, due to lack of time," the author told *AAYA*. "I used to read all sorts of things, but now I tend to read primarily when it's a subject that interests me, or research, or books of friends. I read a lot about southwestern pottery because I collect it. I tend to read more nonfiction than fiction now, because nonfiction—if it's reasonably well done—gives you information. Fiction I read here and there to see what writers are up to. If I come across a piece of fiction by a certain writer I admire, I read it automatically—say William Styron or Janet Lewis, who wrote a wonderful book called *The Wife of Martin Guerre*. She turned ninety recently and is still a ball of fire—an exceptional writer. When I read other people's work, I look for a precision and an originality of expression. I don't like approximations; I do like a sense of vitality."

Concerning the difficulties inherent in writing books, Connell told *AAYA* that "some books of mine brew for a long time; others do not. *Diary of a Rapist* came quickly. There were some newspaper articles about a case in which the man came back a second time. That's what intrigued me—that he risked his life by doing that. He seemed to me to have a romantic dream, to believe that if the woman got to know him, she would really love him, and they could live happily ever after. This is unusual pathology for a rapist and seemed to me uniquely American.

"When I write fiction I don't usually do much research, but I wanted to research that book because I felt I was relying too much on my imagination. I'm sure there's more information now, but in 1966 there was almost nothing; I could find out very little and was never really satisfied with the book because I didn't feel that its factual foundation was solid enough. As I worked on it, I did feel that even with the character's romanticism, it had more to do with rage against women, with fury.

"I think it's extremely difficult to write about sexuality because it's so emotionally loaded. It's like writing about religion. In the navy, they have a rule: there are three things you don't discuss at dinner—sex, religion, and politics. I've tried writing detailed sexual scenes, and it's not good—it's dreadful. I can read *Lolita* and think [Vladimir] Nabokov wrote successfully about sexuality; Anais Nin wrote 'pornographic' stories and they were good. You can go back some centuries and find wonderful work in this area. But much of what you come across in contemporary literature is just embarrassing because it seems so badly written. Somebody once said that in certain areas, every writer is as powerless as a dead snake. Different writers, different snakes.

"I read and revise as I write," the author further told *AAYA*. "I write a page, and as I'm writing the next page, I realize there's something I want to fix on the previous page, and I go back and do that. When it's still in the formative stage, I tend to re-read more subjectively and worry about whether I'm getting across what I want to get across. Later on, when it's more finished, I try to stand back a bit and look at it as though I've never seen it before. Some of that is technical—literally looking for too many words that end in 'ly' like 'literally.' I go over it and over it and over it, keeping tabs on things like how times I've used an unusual word; 'egregious' for example. That's a good word, but if you

Son of the Morning Star became a 1991 ABC miniseries starring Gary Cole as Custer.

use it more than once every twenty pages, it sticks out in a bad way."

Connell has traveled extensively, including two "'round the world" journeys—"one each way." He picks up and goes when he feels the need, but he does not write when he travels. "I'll scribble an idea sometimes," Connell said to *AAYA*, "but I don't do any actual work on that idea until I'm back home. I decided to do *Mr. Bridge* while I was in Greece. I took some notes and then got anxious to finish the trip so I could go home and start writing. Traveling is a recreational activity for me, in between periods of writing. Occasionally I want to see what's on the other side of the hill. I tend to notice more of what is different in people, one from another, than what is the same. It's like looking at the Rockies; if all the peaks are snow covered but one, you notice the one that isn't."

To the novice writer, Connell advises: "You learn from working. When I was first writing, I did a story where I mentioned 'the yellow stub' of a cigarette about six times. I wouldn't do that now.

"Showing your work to others can be of value," Connell continued to tell *AAYA*. "Some writers get very nervous and discouraged by criticism while they're working on something; it inhibits them. Others are helped and stimulated by it. My own attitude is that it's a good idea; you ought to grit your teeth and show your work to people whose opinions you respect. I was showing parts of the Custer book to a friend, a chapter at a time, and then I'd listen, think about what was said, and make decisions. The person with whom I was doing this is not a professional writer, but he is thoroughly different from myself, very widely read, and totally honest with me. I think 'widely read' may be a more important criterion than whether or not someone writes."

"I have never encouraged anyone to write with the hope of being published, because the odds against it are formidable," Connell maintained in an article for *The Writer*. "However, . . . assuming that you plan to indulge this quaint mania, . . . it seems to me that when you have a fast, solid start on a story, or a book, you will probably write the whole thing without too much difficulty. That is, the middle and the end will come about naturally. I suspect that there is a psychological reason for this, but it is irrelevant; what matters is finding a beginning."

Except during his travels, Connell is rarely idle as a writer. He has recently written the introduction to a reissue of William Dean Howells's *The Rise of Silas Lapham*. "Vintage Press is reissuing a lot of nineteenth-century work: [Ralph Waldo] Emerson, [Henry David] Thoreau, etc.," Connell told *AAYA*. "And I want to do something on the Anasazi—it's a Navajo word, meaning 'The Ancient Ones.'

"If somebody wanted me to write a screenplay, adapt my own work or do something else that interested me for the screen, I would do it. I don't think it's mysterious, and I'd like to try my hand. And there is one other thing I've always wanted to do; I'd like to be the guy in the cowboy movie who says, 'They went thattaway.'"

■ Works Cited

Connell, Evan S., in an interview with Gale Garnett for *Authors and Artists for Young Adults*.

Connell, *Mrs. Bridge*, Viking, 1959, p. 1.

Connell, "Beginnings," *The Writer*, September, 1970, p. 9.

Connell, *Son of the Morning Star*, North Point Press, 1984.

Contemporary Authors Autobiography Series, Volume 2, Gale, 1985.

Fuller, Graham, in an interview with Connell, *Interview*, November, 1990, p. 130.

■ For More Information See

BOOKS

Contemporary Authors New Revision Series, Volume 2, Gale, 1981.

Contemporary Literary Criticism, Gale, Volume 4, 1975, Volume 6, 1976, Volume 45, 1987.

Dictionary of Literary Biography, Volume 2: *American Novelists since World War II*, Gale, 1978.

Dictionary of Literary Biography Yearbook: 1981, Gale, 1982.

PERIODICALS

Brick-A Journal of Reviews, winter, 1984.

Commonweal, February 13, 1959.

Fame, November, 1990.

Mirabella, November, 1990.

Nation, July 4, 1966.

Observer, July 17, 1983.

Pacific Sun, July 18-24, 1980.

New Republic, October 14, 1957.

Newsday, November, 1990.

New York Herald Tribune, May 26, 1957.

New York Times, January 20, 1985; February 13, 1985.

Saturday Review, September 24, 1960; July 7, 1965.

Time, January, 1985.
Washington Post, June 6, 1976.

Thomas J. Dygard

■ Personal

Born August 10, 1931, in Little Rock, AR; son of Thomas J. (a tailor) and Nannie (a musician; maiden name, Smith) Dygard; married Patricia Redditt, November 23, 1951; children: Thomas J., Nancy Adams Stevens. *Education:* Attended Little Rock Junior College, 1949-50, 1950-51; University of Arkansas, Fayetteville, B.A., 1953. *Politics:* Independent. *Religion:* Episcopal.

■ Addresses

Home—1-13, Kami-Osaki 3-chome, Shinagawa-ku, Tokyo 141, Japan. *Office*—Associated Press, CPO Box 607, Tokyo 100-91, Japan.

■ Career

Arkansas Gazette, Little Rock, sportswriter and reporter, 1949-53; Associated Press, reporter in Little Rock, 1954-56, Detroit, MI, 1956-58, Birmingham, AL, 1958-62, and New Orleans, LA, 1962-64, bureau chief in Little Rock, 1964-66, Indianapolis, IN, 1966-71, Chicago, IL, 1971-85, and Tokyo, Japan, 1985—. *Member:* Chicago Headline Club (president, 1974), Chicago Press Club (president, 1978), Foreign Correspondents' Club of Japan.

■ Awards, Honors

Outside Shooter was selected one of New York Public Library's Books for the Teen Age, 1980, *Point Spread,* 1981, and *Soccer Duel,* 1982; *Halfback Tough* was selected one of Child Study Association of America's Children's Books of the Year, 1987.

■ Writings

NOVELS

Running Scared, Morrow, 1977.
Winning Kicker, Morrow, 1978.
Outside Shooter (Junior Literary Guild selection), Morrow, 1979.
Point Spread (Junior Literary Guild selection), Morrow, 1980.
Soccer Duel (Junior Literary Guild selection), Morrow, 1981.
Quarterback Walk-On, Morrow, 1982.
Rebound Caper (Junior Literary Guild selection), Morrow, 1983.
Tournament Upstart (Junior Literary Guild selection), Morrow, 1984.
Wilderness Peril, Morrow, 1985.
Halfback Tough, Morrow, 1986.
The Rookie Arrives, Morrow, 1988.
Forward Pass, Morrow, 1989.

■ Work in Progress

Sports and adventure novels for young adults.

■ Sidelights

"I was born in Little Rock, Arkansas, a town of about 100,000 people," Dygard told *Authors and Artists for Young Adults (AAYA)*. "Looking back on it, I must have had a horribly 'normal' childhood. I did what most kids did—went to school and played ball. My father, a tailor, died when I was ten. He had been ill for five of those years, so I don't remember very much about him. I was an only child, and, of course, when your father dies, you become worried and frightened, but people have a way of surviving that sort of thing. It probably sounds worse now than it actually appeared to me then." Dygard's mother was a musician who taught the piano and played it, at times, professionally. She died when he was nineteen.

"I was an average student in school, always had trouble with mathematics, and always liked English and history. I've been a voracious reader ever since I first learned how, and I think that's what led me into writing. The idea that I could write something that would interest somebody as much as books had interested me sounded like a very satisfying prospect."

Growing up in Little Rock, Dygard went through the usual set of dream careers. "Army officer, journalist, professional baseball player, novelist, commercial artist, architect, etc., etc. The journalist dream stuck." By age twelve, he was editor of the *Neighbor News*, a neighborhood paper concerned with "local gossip unless something major was happening (like World War II). Then we'd listen to the radio and write our stories."

Dygard's work on his high school's paper led to an apprenticeship with the *Arkansas Gazette*. "I have always been intensely interested in all sorts of writing," he told *AAYA*. "The principal of the high school called me in one day to tell me that the sports editor of the *Gazette* was looking for what they called a junior sports writer. It was night work—from five the afternoon to eleven at night. The *Gazette* was a morning newspaper. The principal asked if I would be interested. I sure was. I went down to talk with the sports editor and he hired me.

"During the first couple of years with the paper in Little Rock, I covered baseball, football, basketball, tennis, golf—just about every sport except jai-lai. I had played football, basketball, and base-

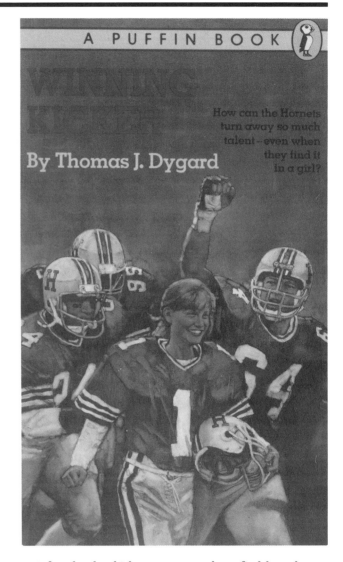

A female placekicker must struggle to find her place on an all-boys' football team.

ball in high school, but was never varsity. Still, I was quite interested in sports, and since it was the area of the news I was covering, I made myself more interested. Of course, a lot of sports writing is talking to coaches and players, trying to find out what's going on in their heads. So I learned as I went along.

"It seemed there were fewer people in the world of sports who took themselves as seriously as people in politics or government. They enjoyed themselves, and, I might add, it was a lot of fun to work with them. I became aware of it after I left sports writing and went into general reporting.

"I was interested in everything I could learn about newspapers, not just reporting and writing, but how the paper was put out, how make-up was handled, how headlines were written, why it was important to do certain things at certain times a certain way. My goal was to be a good newspaper man."

Dygard enrolled at Little Rock Junior College, all the while continuing with his newspaper work. "I covered the football team at school the first year I was there and had a lucky break when they went undefeated to the Little Rose Bowl in Pasadena. I was, after all, going to school with these players and the coach lived on campus, so I got to know them all well. That was a great experience, and a very exciting season to cover."

While Dygard was in school, his mother died. "I was nineteen when she died of cancer. She had been quite ill for about four years and unable to work for two of those years. So it was a pretty frightening time. She was a very courageous woman who was in and out of the hospital all the time but never complained," Dygard related to *AAYA*.

He eventually earned his degree from the University of Arkansas, Fayetteville, "two hundred miles away from Little Rock, but I still worked for the *Gazette*, covering sports and also writing some feature stories. I married a fellow Little Rock Junior College student. Marriage, I found out, will change your life. I'd been living in the fraternity house, and after the marriage, settled in an apartment.

"Suddenly, things like getting through school and getting something out of it seemed a great deal more serious to me. Because I had been very much on my own with no one supporting me for a couple of years, I guess the responsibility of marriage wasn't as jarring a thing for me as it might be for some people.

"After I graduated I went back to Little Rock and worked for the *Gazette*. After about six months, I quit and went to work for the University of Arkansas, Fayetteville, in the editorial division of the Institute of Science and Technology. My main goal was to get a masters degree. I felt that I wasn't making a lot of headway at the newspaper so when I was offered this job, I took the opportunity to work on a Masters in history. I had been there about six months when the Associated Press bureau chief in Little Rock called and offered me a job with the A.P. They were familiar with my work. I was quite excited about working for the A.P. because it was a worldwide news organization.

"The Associated Press is a non-profit, cooperative venture of American newspapers. Nobody owns it. Almost 1800 daily newspapers in the United States are organized into this corporation which main-

Dygard's 1981 novel was a Junior Literary Guild selection.

tains news bureaus all over the world. Each paper pays an assessment based on its circulation. The assessments support the operation. So the bigger papers pay more than the smaller papers. There are around 140 bureaus in the United States, and about eighty overseas. I started out in Little Rock writing some sports and covering the state capital."

Dygard's career with the Associated Press has spanned decades. "I've been a reporter, editor, rewrite man, and now I'm an executive," he explained to *AAYA*. "I've always had that kind of romantic vision of journalism, but it's not all trench coats and beautiful brunettes. There's an awful lot of nitty gritty that goes into it. Fortunately, I've enjoyed the nitty gritty, too.

"I worked in the Birmingham, Alabama, bureau during the time of the Freedom Riders and the Ku Klux Klan. The Blacks, called Negroes then, were

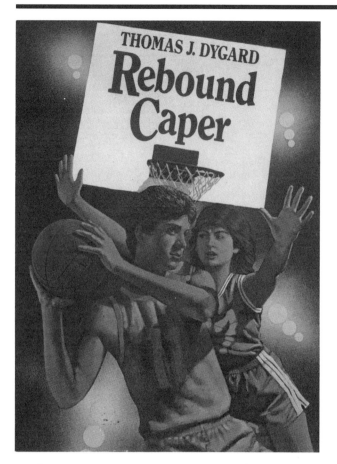

After being benched for clowning around too much on the court, Gary retaliates by joining the girls' basketball team.

trying to integrate places like lunch counters, bus stations, waiting rooms, rest rooms, and water fountains, but the Klan was determined to stop them. There were a lot of bloody riots. I witnessed some of them. They were unforgettable experiences. It was big news at the time—every day you knew you were writing a front-page story.

"You see people at their best, and you see people at their worst, and there was a little bit of both in that situation. Freedom Riders were willing to get their heads caved in trying to win a point. They were certainly very dedicated."

Dygard and his colleagues demonstrated their own courage during this time. "That would have been the only time in my career that I felt physically threatened. The Klan was after the press, and, as a matter of fact, when we knew there was going to be trouble, we would try to disguise ourselves by wearing the Ku Klux Klan uniform—khaki pants and a white T-shirt."

Dygard's career has taken him around the United States as well as around the world. He related these

experiences to AAYA: "I've enjoyed being able to live in different areas—Little Rock, Detroit, Birmingham, New Orleans, Indianapolis, and Chicago. The best place to live and raise a family is Indianapolis. They have nice neighborhoods, good schools, reasonable prices. It has just about everything going for it if you are a young person with children.

"My wife and I started foreign travel as a hobby about twenty years ago and have been to more than thirty countries. Living in Asia, of course, has offered a great opportunity to go to places like China, Bangkok, Hong Kong, and Singapore. We've traveled to Russia and have been to Europe five times. Whether you're going to Europe or Asia, people live in cultures very different from those of us who grew up in the United States. Each country produces different kinds of people, and most of them, I've found, are extraordinarily nice. Even in China, which I had always viewed as big and monolithic and full of terror and horror, people were very nice and friendly. The same was

A young basketball player changes his negative attitude under the guidance of a new coach in Dygard's 1984 novel.

true in Moscow. Every day you read in the news what their governments are doing, but the people are generally nice folks.''

Since 1985, Dygard has been Chief of the Tokyo Bureau of the Associated Press. "One day, the phone rang and the president of the company asked if I would go to Japan. My wife and I decided to go. I enjoy living in Tokyo. Almost everything about it is completely different from the United States: the culture, the language. It's crowded, expensive, noisy, and dirty but there's a fascination about it. The people think differently. 'The company' represents family, and they spend a lot more time at their jobs than they need to (and a lot more time than most people in the world do). Their co-workers are almost like brothers and sisters. It's an attitude I had never seen before. And everything is very, very crowded. They live in very small, cramped quarters and tend to go out instead of having people in.''

Though Dygard's career has provided him with endless experience and satisfaction, it wasn't until 1977 that he was able to accomplish another of his childhood dreams, when he published his first sports novel, *Running Scared.* "I had tried writing a novel a number of times, but always reached a point where I got bored with it. I realized that if the writer is bored, the reader is going to be bored," he explained to *AAYA.* "Then one night in a motel in Champaign, Illinois, where I was left to my own devices, I thought, 'Well I've always said I'll do it—I will start a book and go all the way through to the finish, no matter what.' I wrote the first chapter that night and eventually went all the way through to the finish, telling myself that it may never get published. I finally finished it, which was a scary thing because now I had to do something with it. I let my wife read it; she was less than enthusiastic. 'I've read worse,' said she. (She's not a great sports fan.)

"I went to the library and gathered up about ten books that looked like what I had written, and wrote to their publishers. I heard back from only about half of them, with one or two saying 'Thanks, but no thanks.' The others recommended sending it along and 'we'll take a look at it.' So I started mailing it off. Morrow Junior Books sent my manuscript back with a three-page letter, saying 'We almost took this book, but it's got some flaws.'

"The flaws were things that never would have dawned on me because I'd had no experience in this. Writing fiction was a bigger leap from journalism than I had expected. One problem was point of

In this adventure from 1985, two boys on a wilderness canoe trip find a hijacker's ransom.

view. I would have two characters talking and reading each other's mind. 'That's a "no no,"' according to Morrow. 'You can only see through one set of eyes. If two people are talking, one of them knows what he's thinking, but he should have no idea what the other one is thinking.' I also revealed something at the end of the book that wasn't fair to keep from the reader. You've got to give some hint of it. 'Foreshadowing,' they called it.

"So I took their letter as an invitation and wrote back saying, 'I don't have any arguments with the flaws you cited; I can fix them. Will you look at it again?' They agreed. It did not mean throwing the whole manuscript away and rewriting it. All it involved really was inserting one chapter and rewriting certain portions, which literally took me only one weekend. I sent it back and they bought it. Then they asked if I could do it again.''

Dygard did do it again, writing several popular novels: *Winning Kicker, Outside Shooter, Point Spread, Soccer Duel,* and *Halfback Tough,* dealing with virtually every aspect of sports. He told *AAYA*: "The editors were very good. I was impressed, and always have been, with their suggestions. It's been an education.

"I wrote my first book as an adult novel, but when I finished and reread it, I thought of it more as a book for teenagers. My approach to my readership was from the viewpoint of a fourteen-year-old boy entitled to a story that helps him look ahead to adulthood. I've always tried to keep that in mind as I've written. The books may be called young adult novels, but the reader is entitled to an adult story.

"The number one thing about writing is clarity, which applies to fiction and journalism alike. If the reader doesn't understand something, you've completely missed the boat. The reader can always turn on the television and you will probably lose him. So the writing has got to be abundantly clear,

Joe tries to overcome his delinquent past by becoming a great student and football player.

interesting, and thoughtful, and the basic idea has got to have drama. You present your character in a situation where he 'wants' something, and then you present him with obstacles to be overcome. If it's done correctly, the character will overcome these obstacles only to find more obstacles, which may lead him to change his goal."

Dygard's books contain elements of a deeper nature than the mere pursuit of athleticism, such as the insecurity Joe Atkins, the protagonist of *Halfback Tough*, feels over his bad record in a new school, or the courage of the football star's choice of soccer over football in *Soccer Duel*. Dygard shows great sensitivity for the young adults in his novels. "Well, I used to be one, so I draw rather heavily upon that. I think that a lot of people at fourteen, fifteen, and even twenty, can have a lot of lonely, uncertain moments when they feel like an outsider or feel not as good as they ought to about something. I don't find it difficult to relate to that kind of feeling. It may sound like childishness when a kid says 'I want to do this or that,' but he's actually making important decisions. Joe Atkins felt like an outsider, but he also felt hope about a new beginning and decided that the old way had not been much fun and that maybe he ought to try another approach."

Dygard sees athletics as a healthy aspect of a young adult's life, if it is viewed realistically. Today's youth, he recommends, should not have sport careers as singular goals. "Every kid in the world probably went through some period where he thought he'd like to play shortstop for the Yankees, but I'm sure most of them outgrew it. There are an awful lot of young people these days deciding to make sports a career. Sports can be enjoyable and have real value, as well, but it's all got to be held in perspective. The fact is only a very small percentage of college athletes ever make it in professional sports," he related to *AAYA*.

Notwithstanding, Dygard remains a sports fan. "I still like watching football at the college level. It's better than high school and it's not as automatic as professional football. College ball has a lot more human drama. But I don't really have a least favorite sport. I enjoy them all and always have."

Some of his books required a certain amount of research. "I wrote *Soccer Duel* at the request of Morrow Junior Books. They asked if I could write a book on soccer, but I had never even seen a soccer match. To me, soccer was a game played by Argentines, Italians, and the girls in gym class. I called the soccer coach in my daughter's high school and told him I needed help. He took to it with great enthusiasm. I attended a number of their practice sessions, and a whole season of matches. After the matches, he and I would go out together and he'd tell me why they'd lost. And in the end, I gave him the manuscript of *Soccer Duel* to make sure I hadn't made some horrible technical error. I was quite flattered that he actually picked up a play that I had written and put it in his playbook.

"A lot of my story ideas and happenings, as it is with anybody trying to recreate life-like situations, are certainly reflections of what I have seen, heard, or read. I've been fortunate to be in journalism where my job has been to see and hear those things.

"I do most of my writing from eight until about noon on most Saturday and Sunday mornings. A rather famous writer once said there's nothing to writing, you just sit down and bleed through the pores. Actually, it's not torture for me. I enjoy writing. Of course, an awful lot of it is wadding up pieces of paper and throwing them in the wastebasket. I'm not so much a writer as a rewriter. I tend to write one draft as fast as I can from beginning to end. I'll go back and pick out bits and pieces to revise. Then I'll go back and rewrite the whole thing from page one, then revise again. I outline only in my mind. I tried a written outline once and it fouled me up. My characters would go one way and my outline would go another, so I decided to go 'with the characters.' When I start, I know what the story is about and roughly what's going to happen and where it's going to end, and from there I try to create something. I enjoy the process of seeing a character develop, and come out at the end of a day of writing feeling not exhausted, but like I've had fun. I also get an enormous feeling of satisfaction when a book comes out and I can lay my hands on it for the first time. It's a real upper.

"I try to write one book a year. I've written one outdoor adventure, *Wilderness Peril*, but I guess it's also a sports story. I have toyed with the idea of doing a mystery, but since my writing time is very limited, I continue with sports stories. I'm working on a football story at the moment, called *Backfield Package*, about four boys in a high school backfield who decide to go to college and stick together, but then everything starts falling apart."

Dygard's books have been very popular with his readers. He explained to *AAYA*, "I get one or two letters a week from kids. There are a few questions

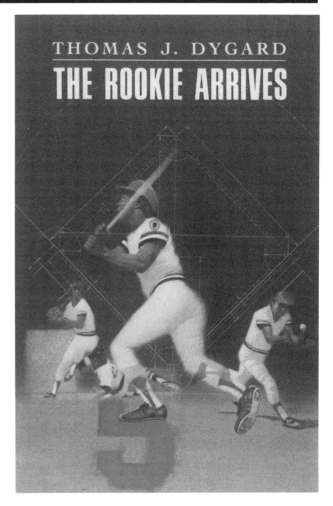

Dygard's 1988 novel tells of a brash young baseball player who learns about himself and the game when he replaces an aging star.

that keep recurring. 'Was this story based on real people?' is one. I say, 'No, not at all.' Another question is, 'Did you ever know anyone who had this problem?' Some of the letters are remarkably thoughtful from kids who are obviously interested in writing themselves. They ask a lot of questions about the mechanics of writing books, such as, 'How long did it take you?'

"The one thing I hope my books do is help make lifetime readers of kids. I think there's something a person can get out of a book that he can't get from movies or television. I'm afraid a lot of people go through life never discovering what that is. A reader is much more apt to think than someone staring at television. Someone who reads a book sometimes slips into real thinking.'"

■ Works Cited

Dygard, Thomas J., in an interview with Dieter Miller for *Authors and Artists for Young Adults*.

■ For More Information See

BOOKS

Contemporary Authors New Revision Series, Volume 15, Gale, 1981.
Something about the Author, Volume 24, Gale, 1981.

PERIODICALS

Bulletin of the Center of Children's Books, June, 1983; July/August, 1986.
Junior Literary Guild, March, 1980; March, 1981; March, 1984.
New York Times Book Review, April 23, 1978.
Publishers Weekly, February 28, 1977.

William Faulkner

◼ Personal

Surname originally Falkner; born September 25, 1897, in New Albany, MS; died of a heart attack, July 6, 1962, in Byhalia, MS; son of Murry Cuthbert (a railroad worker, owner of a cottonseed oil and ice plant, livery stable operator, hardware store employee, and secretary and business manager at University of Mississippi) and Maud (Butler) Falkner; married Lida Estelle Oldham Franklin, June 20, 1929; children: Alabama (died, 1931), Jill (Mrs. Paul Dilwyn Summers, Jr.); (stepchildren) Victoria, Malcolm Argyle. *Education:* Attended University of Mississippi, 1919-1920.

◼ Addresses

Home—Rowan Oak, Oxford, MS.

◼ Career

Writer. First National Bank, Oxford, MS, clerk, 1916; Winchester Repeating Arms Co., New Haven, CT, ledger clerk, 1918; Lord & Taylor, New York City, bookstore clerk, 1921; University of Mississippi, Oxford, postmaster, 1922-24; worked as a roof painter, carpenter, and paperhanger, New Orleans, LA, 1925; deckhand on Genoa-bound freighter, 1925; coal shoveler at Oxford Power Plant, 1929; screenwriter for Metro-Goldwyn-Mayer and Warner Bros., during the 1930s and 1940s; writer-in-residence, University of Virginia, 1957-62. Chairman of Writer's Group People-to-People Program, 1956-57. *Military service:* Royal Air Force, cadet pilot, 1918; became honorary second lieutenant. *Member:* American Academy of Arts and Letters, Sigma Alpha Epsilon.

◼ Awards, Honors

Elected to the National Institute of Arts and Letters, 1939; O. Henry Memorial Short Story Award, 1939, 1940, and 1949; Nobel Prize for Literature, 1950; William Dean Howells Medal from the American Academy of Arts and Letters, 1950; National Book Award, 1951, for *Collected Stories of William Faulkner;* Legion of Honor of the Republic of France, 1951; National Book Award and Pulitzer Prize for fiction, both 1955, both for *A Fable;* Silver Medal of the Greek Academy, 1957; Gold Medal for fiction from the National Institute of Arts and Letters, 1962.

◼ Writings

Marionettes (play), produced at the University of Mississippi, March 4, 1920.
Vision in Spring, privately printed [Mississippi], 1921.
The Marble Faun (poems), Four Seas, 1924.

(With William Philip Spratling) *Sherwood Anderson and Other Famous Creoles: A Gallery of Contemporary New Orleans*, Pelican Bookshop Press, 1926.

Soldiers' Pay (novel), Boni & Liveright, 1926.

Mosquitoes (novel), Boni & Liveright, 1927.

Sartoris (novel; also see below), Harcourt, 1929.

The Sound and the Fury (novel), Cape & Smith, 1929.

As I Lay Dying (novel), Cape & Smith, 1930, new and corrected edition, Random House, 1964.

Sanctuary (novel), Cape & Smith, 1931, published as *Sanctuary: The Original Text*, edited by Noel Polk, Random House, 1981.

These Thirteen (stories), Cape & Smith, 1931.

Light in August (novel), Smith & Haas, 1932.

This Earth, A Poem, Equinox, 1932.

A Green Bough (poems), Smith & Haas, 1933.

Doctor Martino and Other Stories, Smith & Haas, 1934.

Pylon (novel), Smith & Haas, 1935.

Absalom, Absalom! (novel), Random House, 1936, revised edition, 1986.

The Unvanquished (fiction), Random House, 1938.

The Wild Palms (novel), Random House, 1939.

The Hamlet (novel), Random House, 1940.

Go Down, Moses and Other Stories, Random House, 1942.

Three Famous Short Novels: Spotted Horses; Old Man; The Bear, Random House, 1942.

The Portable Faulkner, edited by Malcolm Cowley, Viking, 1946, revised edition, Penguin, 1977.

Intruder in the Dust (novel), Random House, 1948.

Knight's Gambit (stories), Random House, 1949.

Collected Stories of William Faulkner, Random House, 1950.

Requiem for a Nun (novel; also see below), Random House, 1951, revised edition, 1975.

Mirrors of Chartres Streets (stories and sketches), Faulkner Studies, 1953.

A Fable (novel), Random House, 1954.

(And author of foreword) *The Faulkner Reader*, Random House, 1954.

Big Woods (stories), Random House, 1955.

The Town (novel), Random House, 1957.

Requiem for a Nun (play adapted from Faulkner's novel of the same title), produced in London at Royal Court Theatre, November 26, 1957, produced on Broadway at John Golden Theatre, January 30, 1959.

New Orleans Sketches, edited by Carvel Collins, Rutgers University Press, 1958.

The Long, Hot Summer: A Dramatic Book from the Four-Book Novel, The Hamlet, New American Library, 1958.

The Mansion (novel), Random House, 1959.

Faulkner in the University (interviews and conversations), edited by Frederick L. Gwynn and Joseph Blotner, University Press of Virginia, 1959.

Selected Short Stories, Modern Library, 1961.

The Reivers, a Reminiscence (novel), Random House, 1962.

Early Prose and Poetry, edited by Collins, Little, Brown, 1962.

Faulkner at West Point (interviews), edited by Joseph L. Fant and Robert Ashley, Random House, 1964.

Essays, Speeches, and Public Letters, edited by James B. Meriwether, Random House, 1965.

The Faulkner-Cowley File: Letters and Memories, 1944-1962, edited by Cowley, Viking, 1966.

The Wishing Tree (juvenile fiction), Random House, 1967.

Flags in the Dust (unabridged version of *Sartoris*), edited by Douglas Day, Random House, 1973.

A Faulkner Miscellany, edited by Meriwether, University Press of Mississippi, 1974.

Mayday, University of Notre Dame Press, 1976.

Jealousy and Episode, Folcroft, 1977.

Helen, A Courtship [and] *Mississippi Poems*, Yoknapatawpha, 1981.

Faulkner: A Comprehensive Guide to the Brodsky Collection. Volume III: The DeGaulle Story, edited by Lewis Daniel Brodsky and Robert W. Hamblin, University Press of Mississippi, 1984.

Father Abraham, Random House, 1984.

Contributor of poems, short stories, and articles to magazines and newspapers, including Oxford *Eagle*, New Orleans *Times-Picayune*, *New Republic*, *Saturday Evening Post*, *Scribner's*, and *Sports Illustrated*.

SCREENPLAYS

Today We Live (based on short story "Turn About"), Metro-Goldwyn-Mayer, 1933.

(With Josel Sayre) *The Road to Glory*, Twentieth Century-Fox, 1936, published by Southern Illinois University Press, 1981.

(With Nunnally Johnson) *Banjo on My Knee*, Twentieth Century-Fox, 1936.

(With Sam Hellman, Lamar Trotti, and Gladys Lehman) *Slave Ship*, Twentieth Century-Fox, 1937.

(With Sayre, Fred Guiol, and Ben Hecht) *Gunga Din*, RKO, 1939.

Stallion Road, Warner Bros., 1944, published as *Stallion Road: A Screenplay by William Faulkner*, University Press of Mississippi, 1989.

(With Jules Furthman) *To Have and Have Not* (based on Ernest Hemingway's novel of the same title), Warner Bros., 1944, published by University of Wisconsin Press, 1980.

(With Jean Renoir) *The Southerner*, Universal, 1945.

(With Leigh Brackett and Furthman) *The Big Sleep*, Warner Bros, 1946, published by Irvington, 1971.

(With Harry Kurnitz and Harold Jack Bloom) *Land of the Pharaohs*, Warner Bros., 1955.

Faulkner's MGM Screenplays, University of Tennessee Press, 1982.

Country Lawyer and Other Stories for the Screen, edited by Brodsky and Hamblin, University Press of Mississippi, 1987.

Faulkner's papers are collected at the University of Virginia, University of Texas at Austin, Yale University Library, New York Public Library, and Brodsky Collection at Southeast Missouri State University.

■ Adaptations

MOTION PICTURES

Intruder in the Dust, Metro-Goldwyn-Mayer, 1949.

Tarnished Angels (based on *Pylon*), Universal, 1957.

The Long, Hot Summer (based on *The Hamlet*), Twentieth Century-Fox, 1958.

The Sound and the Fury, Twentieth Century-Fox, 1959.

Sanctuary (also includes parts of *Requiem for a Nun*), Twentieth Century-Fox, 1961.

The Reivers, Cinema Center Films, 1969.

Two Soldiers (videocassette; based on short story), Pyramid, 1986.

The Sound and the Fury was adapted for television in 1955 and several of Faulkner's short stories have been adapted for television, including "An Error in Chemistry" and "The Brooch."

AUDIOCASSETTE

William Faulkner Cassette Library (includes teacher's guide), Listening Library, 1977.

"A Rose for Emily" and "Wash," Caedmon, 1979.

"Two Soldiers," Knowledge Unlimited, 1989.

Also available on audiocassette are *William Faulkner Reads the Nobel Prize Acceptance Speech and Selections from "As I Lay Dying," "A Fable," and "The Old Man,"* Caedmon, and *"As I Lay Dying" and Others*, Caedmon.

■ Sidelights

One of the greatest American writers of the twentieth century, William Faulkner authored novels and short stories that address universal concerns although most are set in the South. He created the mythical Yoknapatawpha County and peopled it with characters inspired by those of his native Mississippi, through whose actions he commented on man's place in society, the nature of evil, religious intolerance, and civil rights. Although his artistry was recognized during his lifetime—he received the Nobel Prize for Literature in 1949—Faulkner struggled financially for decades and even resorted to writing Hollywood screenplays to support his family. Yet his fiction, including the novels *The Sound and the Fury, As I Lay Dying, Light in August, Absalom, Absalom!*, and *The Hamlet* and the stories "Barn Burning" and "Go Down, Moses," endures.

Faulkner was born on September 25, 1897, in New Albany, Mississippi, to Murry Cuthbert and Maud Butler Falkner. A great-grandfather had dropped the "u" from the original family name, but after the printer of Faulkner's first book inadvertently added the letter, the author changed it back. Faulkner was a moody child who rarely mixed with his fellows, and he was an indifferent student as well. His younger brother John recalled in *My Brother Bill: An Affectionate Reminiscence* that "It was after Bill's sophomore year in high school that he just sort of quit. Mother and Dad didn't like Bill's refusing to go to school but they didn't force him to go back. They knew it would do no good if he had made up his mind not to study. So Phil Stone guided his reading for the next two years. Phil was a Yale graduate, the only 'up East' man in our community.

"The Stones had a big old Studebaker touring car, a seven-passenger affair. Phil loaded it with books for Bill to read and turned the car over to him. Bill would go out on some country road, a side road where it was quiet, and park the car and spend the day reading. He taught himself French out there and later he actually taught French at the University. Phil's guidance was good, for it put the finishing touches on the reading program that Mother had established in all of us. I think that's the reason she didn't object any more than she did over Bill's quitting school. What Phil picked for Bill to read was pretty much what she would have chosen. Bill read Plato, Socrates, the Greek poets, all the good Romans and Shakespeare. He also read the other good English writers and the French and German classics.

"It was about this time that Bill began to develop an almost foppish taste in clothes," John continued. "He now had a regular monthly income and he spent most of it adorning himself. If pants were tight, he had his tighter. If coats were short, he had his shorter. He began going to the University dances because Estelle [his childhood sweetheart and future wife] was always there."

During the spring of 1918, Estelle Oldham announced her engagement to Cornell Franklin. Faulkner, who had planned to marry her, felt rejected and betrayed, and moved to New Haven, Connecticut, where he worked in a bookstore. His brother recalled: "That's where Bill went so as to get as far away as possible when he found he'd lost Estelle. He must have gone through torment in that strange land with his whole world gone to pot. He counted the days as Estelle's wedding approached, and when that deed was accomplished he joined the Royal Flying Corps. . . . He tried the U.S. Signal Corps first. . . . But the Signal Corps turned Bill down. They said he didn't have two years of college.

"Bill went to the British next. They needed men, and badly. He applied for training with the RFC, the land branch of the British flying service, and they turned him down too. He wasn't tall enough. Bill got mad and told them he was going to fly for someone and he guessed if they didn't need him the Germans would take him. They needed flyers too. He asked them the way to the German embassy and the RFC man said, 'Wait, hold on a minute.' Bill waited and the man went inside an office and pretty soon he came back and told Bill they could use him." World War I ended before Faulkner completed flight training, a great disappointment for one who was seeking an opportunity for heroism.

But Faulkner embellished his own military legend somewhat. His biography sometimes included an item that he served with the Royal Flying Corps in France and was wounded in action. In fact, his commission was made only after he returned home, and his wound consisted of a leg injury incurred when he and a companion got drunk on Armistice Day, flew stunts in a plane, and crash-landed upside down through a hangar roof.

Faulkner's first writings were published during the winter of 1918. His stories about flying school were printed in the *Eagle* in Oxford, Mississippi. Beginning in 1919, with the encouragement of

Stone, Faulkner regularly sent poems to the *New Republic*. All were rejected except "L'Apres-midi d'un faune," a reworking of Stephane Mallarme's work. Future submissions to *New Republic* were, however, rejected.

For a short time in 1921 Faulkner lived the bohemian writer's life in New York City's Greenwich Village. His pieces did not find publication, however, and early the next year he returned to Oxford, where he became postmaster of the University of Mississippi post office. The experience was a disaster; Faulkner did as little work as possible. "The University had its own post office," recalled John Faulkner in *My Brother Bill*. "A small one for professors and students. There were only six hundred students in Ole Miss at the time and about thirty-five or forty professors. All the professors and most of the students had boxes, though a few got their mail by general delivery.

"There really wasn't much to keeping the University post office but Bill didn't attend to that little bit very well. If he was sitting in his chair reading he wouldn't get up to wait on anyone at the window.

"It wasn't too long before they fired Bill. A paragraph from the bill of complaint, signed by a professor, said that the only way he ever got his mail was by digging it out of the trash can at the back door. He said Bill took the sacks as they came in and dumped them there rather than take the time to distribute the letters. One student said that Bill so seldom disturbed his box he had to blow the dust out of it each time he opened the door." After he was fired in 1924 Faulkner exclaimed, "Thank God. I won't ever again have to be at the beck and call of every son of a bitch who's got two cents to buy a stamp," as quoted by Stephen B. Oates in *William Faulkner: The Man and the Artist*.

Faulkner's first book, *The Marble Faun*, was published in 1924. These melancholy poems, linked together by observations on the seasons of the year, are essentially meditations on youth, beauty, love, and nature as voiced by the marble faun himself. Stone, who had underwritten the costs of publishing the edition of one thousand copies, launched a promotional campaign, writing his friends and the Yale alumni magazine that "this poet is my personal property and I urge all my friends and class-mates to buy his book . . . [because I am trying] to help advertise Mississippi and put it on the map artistically," as cited by Oates. Not more than fifty copies were sold.

In 1925 Faulkner moved to New Orleans, where he met the writer Sherwood Anderson, who was to become his friend and literary mentor. Faulkner remarked in an interview, collected by James B. Meriwether and Michael Millgate in *Lion in the Garden: Interviews with William Faulkner, 1926-1962*, that he and Anderson "used to sit around every afternoon with two or three bottles of whiskey, laughing and talking about people. Next morning Sherwood would be in seclusion for about four hours, and next afternoon we'd sit around talking and drinking again. And next morning Sherwood would be in seclusion again. So I thought to myself that was as pleasant a life as was possible to lead. I'd found I liked to write already, so one day I sat down and started writing. After about a week, Anderson came over to my place, which was pretty nice of him, as he'd never done that before. He asked 'What's wrong? You mad at me?' I said I was writing a novel [*Soldiers' Pay*]. He said, 'My God!' and walked off. A few weeks later, I met Mrs. Anderson, who said, 'Sherwood has a message for you. He says if you won't make him

read the book, he'll send it to his publishers with his recommendation.' And when I had it finished in three months, he sent it off."

On July 7, 1925, Faulkner left for Europe on a freighter. Except for brief tours through the French countryside, England, Italy, and Switzerland, Faulkner remained in Paris, where he began and abandoned several novels. To augment his meager revenues, he also wrote stories for the New Orleans *Times-Picayune*. That autumn he received news that Boni & Liveright agreed to publish *Soldiers' Pay*. On the verge of a new literary career, Faulkner decided not to stay in Europe and sailed for New York City and New Orleans in December. Although *Soldiers' Pay*, a pessimistic novel about soldiers returning home disillusioned by World War I, was well received by critics, it did not attract a popular audience.

By January, 1927, Faulkner was home in Mississippi, penniless and living off his parents. He completed *Mosquitoes*, a portrait of the artist in the process of becoming an artist. The novel is based on the

Robert Duvall starred in the 1972 PBS adaptation of *Tomorrow*.

Faulkner claimed that this 1929 classic was the work he felt "tenderest towards."

literary community with which Faulkner associated in New Orleans.

Faulkner then began work on a story about the slow decay of a proud old southern family, clearly modeled on his own. Colonel William Cuthbert Faulkner, his great-grandfather and the founder of the clan, was portrayed as Colonel John Sartoris, "with his bearded, hawklike face and the bold glamor of this dream," Faulkner wrote. Like Colonel Faulkner, Sartoris was the commander of Civil War troops and the founder of a Mississippi railroad. Faulkner's grandfather was represented by the elder Bayard Sartoris, "cemented by deafness to a dead time," who found himself pondering family relics and recalling the history of the Sartoris clan. A whole generation of younger Sartorises came into being. The younger Bayard Sartoris, a man of Faulkner's generation, returns

from World War I bent on self-destruction and incapable of affection.

Introduced in this saga of the Sartoris clan is Yoknapatawpha County, which was closely modeled after Lafayette County, where Faulkner lived nearly his entire life. "I discovered that my own little postage stamp of native soil was worth writing about and that I would never live long enough to exhaust it," Faulkner explained in an interview collected by Meriwether and Millgate, "and by sublimating the actual into apocryphal I would have complete liberty to use whatever talent I might have to its absolute top. It opened up a gold mine of other peoples, so I created a cosmos of my own. I can move these people around like God, not only in space but in time too."

As the Sartoris story grew into a novel Faulkner titled it *Flags in the Dust*, but was unable to find a publisher in that form. After heavy editing—and a substantial reduction in bulk—it was published in 1929 by Harcourt Brace as *Sartoris*. Faulkner did, however, preserve an uncut typescript that was published under the original title after his death.

The critic Robert Coughlan observed in *The Private World of William Faulkner* that "one of the virtues of Faulkner's best work is its sense of the past, so that every event is seen in deep perspective, colored and shaded like a forest floor, where today's growth feeds and blooms on the refuse of the past and will itself become food for the future. This derives from his own sense of the past: the past of the South, of his county and town, and especially of his family. For the Sartoris family, whose exploits and agonies occupy one novel and one volume of short stories and who appear as leading or supporting characters in many of the other works, have a basis of reality. They are, in fact, the Falkners (or Faulkners), as seen from William Faulkner's point of view and as molded by him to suit the needs of fiction."

In June, 1929, Faulkner married his childhood sweetheart, Estelle Oldham Franklin, who, in the intervening years, had divorced Cornell Franklin and had two children. Faulkner and Estelle's marriage was not a happy one, plagued by financial problems and a mutual heavy dependence on alcohol and further undermined by Faulkner's long-term affairs during the 1930s, 1940s, and 1950s.

In October, 1929, *The Sound and the Fury*, which charts the decline and fall of an aristocratic clan through incest, insanity, and greed, was published. With this novel Faulkner began his experiments in narrative technique. For much of *The Sound and the Fury* the narrative voice is taken by three family members, one of whom, quite remarkably, is severely retarded. "[The novel] began with a mental picture," Faulkner was quoted as saying in *Lion in the Garden.* "I didn't realize at the time it was symbolical. The picture was of the muddy seat of a little girl's drawers in a pear tree where she could see through a window where her grandmother's funeral was taking place and report what was happening to her brothers on the ground below. By the time I explained who they were and what they were doing and how her pants got muddy, I realized it would be impossible to get all of it into a short story and that it would have to be a book. And then I realized the symbolism of the soiled pants, and that image was replaced by the one of the fatherless and motherless girl climbing down the rainpipe to escape from the only home she had, where she had never been offered love or affection or understanding.

"I had already begun to tell it through the eyes of the idiot child since I felt that it would be more effective as told by someone capable only of knowing what happened, but not why," Faulkner continued. "I saw that I had not told the story that time. I tried to tell it again, the same story through the eyes of another brother. That was still not it. I told it for the third time through the eyes of the third brother. That was still not it. I tried to gather the pieces together and fill in the gaps by making myself the spokesman. It was still not complete, not until fifteen years after the book was published when I wrote as an appendix to another book the final effort to get the story told and off my mind, so that I myself could have some peace from it. It's the book I feel tenderest towards. I couldn't leave it alone, and I never could tell it right, though I tried hard and would like to try again, though I'd probably fail again.

"[*The Sound and the Fury*] caused me the most grief and anguish, as the mother loves the child who

Joanne Woodward as she appeared in the film version of *The Sound and the Fury.*

$3.95/394-74745-3

Faulkner's sixth novel was written during a period when he shoveled coal at a power station at the University of Mississippi.

became the thief or murderer more than the one who became the priest.''

Faulkner's next novel, *As I Lay Dying*, was written while he worked in the power station of the University of Mississippi, shoveling coal on an overnight shift. Faulkner said, in an interview collected by Meriwether and Millgate, that when writing *As I Lay Dying* he was inspired. ''Sometimes technique charges in and takes command of the dream before the writer himself can get his hands on it. That is *tour de force* and the finished work is simply a matter of fitting bricks neatly together, since the writer knows probably every single word right to the end before he puts the first one down. This happened with *As I Lay Dying*. It was not easy. No honest work is. It was simple in that all the material was already at hand. It took me

just about six weeks in the spare time from a twelve-hour-a-day job at manual labor. I simply imagined a group of people and subjected them to the simple universal natural catastrophes which are flood and fire with a simple natural motive to give direction to their progress. But then, when technique does not intervene, in another sense writing is easier too. Because with me there is always a point in the book where the characters themselves rise up and take charge and finish the job.''

Faulkner later said, as quoted by Linda W. Wagner in a *Dictionary of Literary Biography* article, that while composing *As I Lay Dying*, ''That other quality which *The Sound and the Fury* had given me was absent: that emotion definite and physical and yet nebulous to describe: that ecstasy, that eager and joyous faith and anticipation of surprise which the yet unmarred sheet beneath my hand held inviolate and unfailing, waiting for release. I said, More than likely I shall never again have to know this much a book before I begin to write it.''

Even with the publication of *As I Lay Dying* Faulkner found himself in dire financial straits. *Sartoris* had not sold particularly well, and he had no commercial hope for *The Sound and the Fury* or his latest novel, although they were all praised by critics. Faulkner surmised that the public might take to a sensationalistic story of the roaring twenties. In the introduction to the Modern Library edition of *Sanctuary*, he explains the circumstances of this novel's creation. ''This book was written three years ago. To me it is a cheap idea, because it was deliberately conceived to make money. I had been writing books for about five years, which got published and not bought. But that was all right. I was young then and hard-bellied. . . . I could do a lot of things that could earn what little money I needed, thanks to my father's unfailing kindness which supplied me with bread at need despite the outrage to his principles at having been of a bum progenitive.

''Then I began to get a little soft. I could still paint houses and do carpenter work, but I got soft. I began to think about making money by writing. I began to be concerned when magazine editors turned down short stories. . . .

''I began to think of books in terms of possible money. I decided I might just as well make some of it myself. I took a little time out, and speculated what a person in Mississippi would believe to be current trends, chose what I thought was the right answer and invented the most horrific tale I could imagine and wrote it in about three weeks and sent it to Smith, who had done *The Sound and the Fury* and who wrote me immediately, 'Good God, I can't publish this. We'd both be in jail.' So I told [myself], 'You're damned. You'll have to work now and then for the rest of your life.'

"I think I had forgotten about *Sanctuary*, just as you might forget about anything made for an immediate purpose, which did not come off. *As I Lay Dying* was published and I didn't remember the [manuscript] of *Sanctuary* until Smith sent me the galleys. Then I saw that it was so terrible that there were but two things to do: tear it up or rewrite it. I thought again, 'It might sell; maybe 10,000 of them will buy it.' So I tore the galleys down and rewrote the book. It had been already set up once, so I had to pay for the privilege of rewriting it, trying to make out of it something which would not shame *The Sound and the Fury* and *As I Lay Dying* too much and I made a fair job."

Sanctuary, full of sadistic violence, sexual perversion, and twisted psychology, focuses on Temple Drake, an Ole Miss coed and daughter of a prominent judge. After she is raped by an impotent gangster named Popeye—"a contemporary Satan," according to Faulkner—he installs her in a brothel and serves as her pimp. The plot is long and complicated, but the novel's commercial success finally established Faulkner as a popular literary figure.

Throughout the late 1920s, Faulkner produced short stories at a prodigious rate. His brother John recalled in *My Brother Bill* that "One time Bill called me in. He was standing in front of his opened closet door writing something on a sheet of paper he had tacked there. I walked over and looked over his shoulder to see what he was doing.

"He had a piece of typewriter paper tacked up on the back of the closet door. On it were ruled columns, with lines drawn across them like the pages of a ledger. In a wide column to the left were the names of various stories. The rest of the page was double columns. At the top of each double column was the name of a magazine—the *Post*, *Collier's*, *Atlantic Monthly*, *Scribner's*, etc. When he would send a story to the *Post* he would mark the date down in the first half of the column, then when they'd return it he would mark down that date alongside it. He said he kept a record like that so he wouldn't send the same story to the same magazine twice.

"The page was almost full. Bill must have written and sent out fifty or sixty stories up to that time.

After *Sanctuary* came out the *Post* wrote Bill and said they wanted to apologize for having turned his stories down and if he would send them back they would put in a preferred bracket and buy them at a thousand dollars apiece.

"Bill sent them sixty!"

However gratified he may have been about his increased recognition, Faulkner submitted to interviews and information requests reluctantly and would often provide flippant or blatantly false answers. He once answered a request for biographical information, cited in Joseph Blotner's edition of the *Selected Letters of William Faulkner*, with: "Born male and single at early age in Mississippi. Quit school after five years in seventh grade. Got job in Grandfather's bank and learned medicinal value of his liquor. Grandfather thought janitor did it. Hard on janitor. War came. Like British uniform. Got commission R.F.C., pilot. Crashed. Cost British gov't 2000 pounds. Was still pilot. Crashed. Cost British gov't 2000 pounds. Quit. Cost British gov't $84.30. King said, 'Well done.' Returned to Mississippi. Family got job: postmaster. Resigned by mutual agreement on part of two inspectors; accused of throwing all incoming mail into garbage can. How disposed of outgoing mail never proved. Inspectors foiled. Had $700. Went to Europe. Met man named Sherwood Anderson. Said, 'Why not write novels? Maybe won't have to work.' Did. *Soldiers' Pay*. Did. *Mosquitoes*. Did. *Sound and Fury*. Did. *Sanctuary*, out next year. Now flying again. Age 32. Own and operate own typewriter."

In 1931 Faulkner went to Hollywood, where he was to work off and on until the mid-1940s. "I have the assurance of a movie agent that I can go to California, to Hollywood and make 500.00 or 750.00 a week in the movies," Faulkner wrote in a letter collected by Blotner. "We could live like counts." He formed a particularly close professional and personal partnership with Howard Hawkes at Metro-Goldwyn-Mayer, and his first produced script was *Today We Live*, for Hawkes. The filmmaker found Faulkner's talents as a script doctor particularly useful and often used him to revise scenes in others' screenplays. Faulkner also worked on, in varying measure, *Slave Ship*, *Submarine Patrol*, and *Gunga Din*.

When asked in an interview collected in *Lion in the Garden* if he thought a film script a promising form of literature, Faulkner replied, somewhat more generously than usual: "Well, it's promising, but in my opinion, that's all, just promising.... There's no chance for the individual to make something as he himself thinks it should be made. That it's made by too many people, too many forces comment, not only difference of individual opinions about what's good, but there's the tremendous cost in money which must be considered.

"The good ones apparently emerge by accident, are not the work of anyone, but nobody of the people concerned know, themselves, as to what happened that this turned out to be first rate. They can't be repeated every time, where one does learn something from a book, a poem, in which he himself has worked alone, so at least he can avoid mistakes, but in motion pictures, you can't."

Faulkner began writing *Light in August* in August, 1931. In composing that novel Faulkner had hoped to feel the same exhilaration he experienced while writing *The Sound and the Fury*. "I began *Light in August*," Faulkner said, as quoted by Blotner in his

In 1936, Faulkner wrote this tale of a man whose attempt to create a dynasty ends in disaster.

biography of the author, "knowing no more about it than a young woman, pregnant, walking along a strange country road.... [The rapture] did not return. The story was going pretty well: I would sit down to it each morning without reluctance yet still without that anticipation and that joy which alone ever made writing a pleasure to me. The book was almost finished before I acquiesced to the fact that it would not recur, since I was now aware before each word was written down just what the people would do, since now I was deliberately choosing among possibilities and probabilities of behavior and weighing and measuring each choice by the scale of the Jameses and Conrads and Balzacs. I knew that I had read too much, that I had reached that stage which all young writers must pass through, in which he believes that he had learned too much about his trade."

Light in August received wide and laudatory critical attention. One reviewer, quoted in Blotner's *Faulkner,* called it "a novel of extraordinary force and insight, incredibly right in character studies, intensely vivid, rising sometimes to poetry, and filled with that spirit of compassion which saves those who look at life too closely from hardness and despair."

Faulkner followed *Light in August* with *A Green Bough,* his second collection of poetry. The volume has little cohesion, probably because it includes poems written years prior to its 1933 publication, even some from his teen years. The critical assessment was not positive and Faulkner, with one brief exception, would never publish another poem. He remarked, as quoted by his biographer Blotner: "I've often thought that I wrote the novels because I found I couldn't write the poetry, that maybe I wanted to be a poet, maybe I think of myself as a poet, and I failed at that, I couldn't write poetry, so I did the next best thing."

In 1936 *Absalom, Absalom!* was published. While the reviews were decidedly mixed, those that were favorable were extremely so. *Time* magazine called it "The strangest, least readable, most infuriating and yet in some respects the most impressive novel that William Faulkner has written," as cited by Wagner in her *Dictionary of Literary Biography* piece. *Absalom, Absalom!* is the complex and impossible-to-summarize tale of Thomas Sutpen, a nineteenth-century Faust who sets out to establish a southern dynasty doomed to failure from the moment of its inception—a familiar Faulkner theme. Faulkner uses at least four narrators, none of them reliable, and the reader must piece together the story from fragmentary and highly subjective information.

In December, 1938, Faulkner wrote to his editor at Random House, Robert K. Haas, that he was beginning work on his saga of the Snopes family. "It will be in three books," he explained in the letter, collected in his selected correspondence, "whether big enough to be three separate volumes I dont know yet, though I think it will. The first one I think will run about 80,000 words. I am half through with it. Three chapters have been printed in mags, as short stories, though not in my collections yet. The title is THE PEASANTS. Has to do with Flem Snopes' beginning in the country, as he gradually consumes a small village until there is nothing left in it for him to eat. His last coup gains him a foothold in Jefferson, to which he moves with his wife, leaving his successor kinsmen to carry on in the country.

"The second volume is US IN URBE. [Snopes] begins to trade on his wife's infidelity, modest blackmail of her lover, rises from half owner of back street restaurant through various grades of city employment, filling each post he vacates with another Snopes from the country, until he is secure in the presidency of a bank, where he can even stop blackmailing his wife's lover.

"The third volume is ILIUM FALLING. This is the gradual eating-up of Jefferson by Snopes, who corrupt the local government with crooked politics, buy up all the colonial homes and tear them down and chop up the lots into subdivisions."

The three novels Faulkner sketched out to Haas would be published as *The Hamlet* (1940), *The Town* (1957), and *The Mansion* (1959). While members of the Snopes family had been appearing in various novels and stories, the trilogy provided Faulkner with sufficient breadth for depicting the rise and destruction of a foredoomed clan.

In the early 1940s, Faulkner's financial difficulties were becoming even more acute. He had become the sole supporter of his wife, child, two stepchildren, mother, brother's widow and child, as well as his father's dependents. "Now and then," he wrote in a letter collected by Blotner, "when pressed or worried about money, I begin to seethe and rage over this. It does no good, and I waste time when I might and should be writing. I still hope some day to break myself of it."

Thus, desperate for a job, Faulkner signed a long-term contract with Warner Brothers studio in July, 1942. The terms were quite unfavorable: Jack Warner, who described writers as "schmucks with Underwoods," boasted that he had America's best writer on his payroll at three hundred dollars a week. This was less than even novice screenwriters received—far less than the twelve hundred dollars Faulkner made in his earlier stints in Hollywood. During his stay there he worked on a number of projects, including an unproduced biography of Charles de Gaulle, a drama about wartime aircraft manufacturing called *The Life and Death of a Bomber,* Howard Hawkes's productions of *Air Force, To Have and Have Not,* and *The Big Sleep,* and an adaptation of an Eric Ambler novel, *Uncommon Danger,* retitled *Background to Danger.*

In 1945 Faulkner worked with filmmaker Jean Renoir on *The Southerner,* a motion picture whose themes echoed Faulkner's own. He considered it to be the best of his Hollywood work. Although

First novel in the trilogy that traces the rise and fall of the Snopes family.

Paul Newman, Tony Franciosa, and Lee Remick in the film adaptation of *The Long, Hot Summer.*

Renoir received screen credit for the script, Zachary Scott, the film's star, testified that Faulkner was the author.

The artistic merit of *The Southerner* notwithstanding, Faulkner had reached his nadir. In a letter to his agent, Harold Ober, collected in his *Selected Letters,* he wrote: "I think I have had about all of Hollywood I can stand. I feel bad, depressed, dreadful sense of wasting time, I imagine most of the symptoms of some kind of blow-up or collapse. I may be able to come back later, but I think I will finish this present job and return home. Feeling as I do, I am actually becoming afraid to stay here much longer. For some time I have expected, at a certain age, to reach that period (in the early fifties) which most artists seem to reach where they admit at last that there is no solution to life and that it is not, and perhaps never was, worth the living. Before leaving here, I will try to make what contacts I can in hopes to do work at home, as this seems to be the easiest way I can earn money which I must have or at least think I must have.

"Meanwhile," Faulkner continued, "have you anything in mind I might do, for some more or less certain revenue? My books have never sold, are out of print; the labor (the creation of my apocryphal country) of my life, even if I have a few things yet to add to it, will never make a living for me. I don't have enough sure judgment about trash to be able to write it with fifty per cent success. Could I do some sort of editorial work, or some sort of hack-writing at home, where living won't cost me so much as now, where I support a divided family, that is myself here in hotels, etc., and a house at home whose expenses don't alter whether I am there or not.

"I think mainly though that I am not well physically, have lost weight, etc., though nothing serious that I know of or anticipate."

In 1948 Faulkner published *Intruder in the Dust,* a novel, he explained in a letter, "set in my apocryphal Jefferson. The story is a mystery-murder though the theme is more relationship between Negro and white, specifically or rather the premise being that the white people in the south, before the North or the govt. or anyone else, owe and must pay a responsibility to the Negro. But it's a story; nobody preaches in it.... A Negro in jail, accused of murder and waiting for the white folks to drag him out and pour gasoline over him and set him on fire, is the detective, solves the crime because he goddamn has to to keep from being lynched, by asking people to go somewhere and look at something and then come back and tell him what they found.''

Intruder in the Dust brought Faulkner more attention than anything he had written previously, partly because of the obvious political implications of the story. The white southern press felt that he portrayed white southerners and their society in a decidedly negative light. This controversy was to pre-figure future storms whipped up by Faulkner's pronouncements on civil rights. Nonetheless, Metro-Goldwyn-Mayer bought the film rights for fifty thousand dollars, effectively solving Faulkner's financial problems. The film was shot in Oxford, beginning in the spring of 1949. Faulkner helped scout locations and made minor script revisions but otherwise had little to do with the production.

The 1950s brought Faulkner great public recognition. In November, 1950, Faulkner was notified of his selection for the 1949 Nobel Prize in Literature. Faulkner's acceptance speech, delivered on December 10, 1950, made a powerful impression and brought about renewed interest in his work. The 1950 edition of his *Collected Stories* won the National Book Award and his novel *A Fable*, the story of a World War I French corporal whose life paralleled that of Jesus Christ's, won both the National Book Award and the Pulitzer Prize for fiction in 1955. Two years later Faulkner, who was in increasing demand as a lecturer, was named a writer-in-residence at the University of Virginia.

Beginning in 1959 Faulkner suffered a number of serious injuries as a result from falls from horses. A fall in June, 1962, contributed to his already failing health and he died of a heart attack on July 6, 1962, in Byhalia, Mississippi. A month earlier Faulkner had published his final work, *The Reivers*, a picaresque novel set in Yoknapatawpha County narrated by a grandfather—not unlike Faulkner—relating his boyhood adventures at the turn of the century.

■ Works Cited

Blotner, Joseph, editor, *Selected Letters of William Faulkner*, Random House, 1977.

Blotner, *Faulkner: A Biography*, Random House, 1974.

Coughlan, Robert, *The Private World of William Faulkner*, Harper, 1954.

Faulkner, John, *My Brother Bill: An Affectionate Reminiscence*, Trident, 1963.

Faulkner, William, *Sartoris*, Harcourt, 1929.

Faulkner, "Introduction" to *Sanctuary*, Random House, 1932.

Meriwether, James B., and Michael Millgate, editors, *Lion in the Garden: Interviews with William Faulkner, 1926-1962*, Random House, 1968.

Oates, Stephen B., *William Faulkner: The Man and the Artist*, Harper, 1987.

Wagner, Linda W., "William Faulkner," *Dictionary of Literary Biography*, Volume 9: *American Novelists, 1910-1945*, Gale, 1981.

■ For More Information See

BOOKS

Adams, Richard P., *Faulkner: Myth and Motion*, Princeton University Press, 1968.

Authors in the News, Volume 1, Gale, 1976.

Backman, Melvin, *Faulkner, the Major Years: A Critical Study*, Indiana University Press, 1966.

Bassett, John, editor, *William Faulkner: The Critical Heritage*, Routledge & Kegan Paul, 1975.

Beck, Warren, *Man in Motion: Faulkner's Trilogy*, University of Wisconsin Press, 1961.

Beck, *Faulkner*, University of Wisconsin Press, 1976.

Brooks, Cleanth, *William Faulkner: The Yoknapatawpha Country*, Yale University Press, 1963.

Brooks, *William Faulkner: Toward Yoknapatawpha and Beyond*, Yale University Press, 1978.

Concise Dictionary of American Literary Biography: The Age of Maturity, 1929-1941, Gale, 1989.

Contemporary Literary Criticism, Gale, Volume 1, 1973, Volume 3, 1975, Volume 6, 1976, Volume 8, 1978, Volume 9, 1978, Volume 11, 1979, Volume 14, 1980, Volume 18, 1981, Volume 28, 1984, Volume 52, 1989.

Cowley, Malcolm, editor, *The Faulkner-Cowley File: Letters and Memories*, Viking, 1966.

Cowley, *—And I Worked at the Writer's Trade*, Viking, 1978.

Cullen, John B. and Floyd C. Watkins, *Old Times in the Faulkner Country*, University of North Carolina Press, 1961.

Dictionary of Literary Biography, Gale, Volume 11: *American Humorists, 1800-1950*, 1982, Volume 44: *American Screenwriters, Second Series*, 1986.

Dictionary of Literary Biography Documentary Series, Volume 2, Gale, 1982.

Dictionary of Literary Biography Yearbook: 1986, Gale, 1987.

Falkner, Murry C., *The Falkners of Mississippi: A Memoir*, Louisiana State University Press, 1967.

Faulkner, William, *Essays, Speeches and Public Letters*, edited by Meriwether, Random House, 1965.

Fried, Barbara, *The Spider in the Cup: Yoknapatawpha County's Fall into the Unknowable*, Harvard University Press, 1978.

Gold, Joseph, *William Faulkner: A Study in Humanism from Metaphor to Discourse*, University of Oklahoma Press, 1966.

Hoffman, Frederick J., and Olga W. Vickery, editors, *William Faulkner: Three Decades of Criticism*, Michigan State University Press, 1960.

Hoffman, *William Faulkner*, Twayne, 1961, revised edition, 1966.

Kerr, Elizabeth M., *William Faulkner's Gothic Domain*, Kennikat Press, 1979.

McHaney, Thomas L., *William Faulkner: A Reference Guide*, G. K. Hall, 1975.

Meriwether, James B., *The Literary Career of William Faulkner: A Bibliographical Study*, Princeton University Press, 1961.

Meriwether, *Faulkner and the South*, University Press of Virginia, 1964.

Millgate, Michael, *William Faulkner*, Grove, 1961.

Millgate, *The Achievement of William Faulkner*, Random House, 1966.

Minter, David, *William Faulkner, His Life and Work*, Johns Hopkins University Press, 1980.

Richardson, Harold Edward, *William Faulkner: The Journey to Self-Discovery*, University of Missouri Press, 1969.

Rubin, Louis D., Jr., *Writers of the Modern South: The Faraway Country*, University of Washington Press, 1963.

Short Story Criticism, Volume 1, Gale, 1988.

Thompson, Lawrence Roger, *William Faulkner: An Introduction and Interpretation*, Holt, 1967.

Vickery, Olga W., *The Novels of William Faulkner: A Critical Interpretation*, Louisiana State University Press, 1959, revised edition, 1964.

Volpe, Edmond, *A Reader's Guide to William Faulkner*, Farrar, Straus, 1964.

Wagner, Linda W., *William Faulkner: Four Decades of Criticism*, Michigan State University Press, 1973.

Warren, Robert Penn, editor, *Faulkner: A Collection of Critical Essays*, Prentice-Hall, 1967.

Williams, David, *Faulkner's Women: The Myth and the Muse*, McGill-Queens University Press, 1977.

Wolfe, George H., editor, *Faulkner: Fifty Years after "The Marble Faun,"* University of Alabama Press, 1976.

PERIODICALS

American Literature, May, 1973.

Book Digest, February, 1978.

Christian Science Monitor, January 27, 1955.

Georgia Review, summer, 1972.

Journal of Popular Culture, summer, 1973.

Life, September 28, 1953; October 5, 1953; July 20, 1962.

Modern Fiction Studies, summer, 1973; winter, 1973-74; summer, 1975.

New London Day (CT), June 10, 1983.

New Republic, September 8, 1973.

New York Herald Tribune Book Review, January 31, 1960.

New York Times, March 8, 1958; April 1, 1958; December 30, 1982; July 28, 1987.

New York Times Book Review, November 7, 1948; December 15, 1963.

Sewanee Review, winter, 1970; autumn, 1971.

Southern Review, summer, 1968; autumn, 1972.

Studies in Short Fiction, summer, 1974.

Sunday Mirror, May 15, 1955.

Twentieth Century Literature, July, 1973.

OBITUARIES

New York Herald Tribune, July 7, 1962; July 8, 1962.

New York Post Magazine, July 8, 1962.

New York Times, July 7, 1962.*

Chester Gould

■ **Personal**

Born November 20, 1900, in Pawnee, Okla.; died May 11, 1985, in Woodstock, Ill., of congested heart failure; son of Gilbert R. (a newspaper editor) and Alice (Miller) Gould; married Edna Gauger, November 6, 1926; children: Jean (Mrs. Richard O'Connell). *Education:* Attended Oklahoma A & M College (now Oklahoma State University), 1919-21; Northwestern University, diploma, 1923; also attended Chicago Art Institute.

■ **Career**

Tulsa Democrat, Tulsa, Okla., editorial cartoonist, 1918; *Daily Oklahoman,* Oklahoma City, Okla., sports cartoonist, 1919-21; worked for several Chicago newspapers during early 1920s; *Chicago American,* Chicago, Ill., cartoonist for syndicated comic strips "Fillum Fables" and "Radio Cats," 1924-29; *Chicago Daily News,* Chicago, ad illustrator, 1929-31; Chicago Tribune-New York Daily News Syndicate (now Tribune Media Services Syndicate), Chicago, cartoonist for "Dick Tracy" comic strip, 1931-77. *Member:* National Cartoon-

ists Society, Woodstock Country Club, Lambda Chi Alpha.

■ **Awards, Honors**

American Institute of Men's and Boys' Wear special plaque, 1957; Reuben Award, National Cartoonists Society, 1959, 1978; Special Edgar Award, Mystery Writers of America, 1980, for "Dick Tracy" comic strip; also received numerous awards from law enforcement agencies and police departments, including the Police Athletic League Award, 1949, and the Associated Police Communications Officers Award, 1953.

■ **Writings**

Dick Tracy and Dick Tracy, Jr., and How They Captured "Stooge" Viller, Cupples & Leon, 1933.
How Dick Tracy and Dick Tracy, Jr., Caught the Racketeers, Cupples & Leon, 1934.
Dick Tracy, Ace Detective, Whitman Publishing, 1943.
Dick Tracy Meets the Night Crawler, Whitman Publishing, 1945.
Dick Tracy and the Woo Woo Sisters, Dell, 1947.
The Celebrated Cases of Dick Tracy, 1931-1951, with an introduction by Ellery Queen, edited by Herb Galewitz, Chelsea House, 1970.
Prune Face, Fawcett, 1975.
Snowflake and Shaky, Fawcett, 1975.
Dick Tracy, the Thirties: Tommy Guns and Hard Times, edited by Galewitz, Chelsea House, 1978.

Dick Tracy and the Kidnapped Princess, T. Raiola, 1983.

Dick Tracy: America's Most Famous Detective, edited by Bill Crouch, Jr., Lyle Stuart, 1987.

■ Adaptations

Dick Tracy (film), starring Morgan Conway, RKO, 1945.

Dick Tracy Vs. Cueball (film), starring M. Conway, RKO, 1946.

Dick Tracy Meets Gruesome (film), starring Ralph Byrd and Boris Karloff, RKO, 1947, also released as *Dick Tracy Meets Karloff*.

Dick Tracy's Dilemma (film), starring R. Byrd, RKO, 1947.

Dick Tracy (television series) starring R. Byrd, ABC-TV, September 11, 1950-February 12, 1951.

Dick Tracy Show (animated cartoon), starring Everett Sloane as the voice of Tracy, United Productions of America, syndicated beginning September 7, 1961, broadcast as part of *Archie's TV Funnies*, Columbia Broadcasting System (CBS), September 11, 1971-September 1, 1973.

Dick Tracy (film), starring Warren Beatty, Touchstone Films, 1990.

Dick Tracy (video cassette), Bantam, 1990.

SERIALS; EACH CONTAINS FIFTEEN EPISODES

Dick Tracy, Republic Pictures, 1936.
Dick Tracy Returns, Republic Pictures, 1938.
Dick Tracy's G-Men, Republic Pictures, 1939.
Dick Tracy Vs. Crime, Inc., Republic Pictures, 1941, released as *Dick Tracy Vs. the Phantom Empire*, 1952.

COMIC BOOKS

Dick Tracy comic strips were reprinted in each monthly issue of *Super Comics*, Dell, beginning in May, 1938. *Dick Tracy Comics* was published by Dell in the late 1930s; the title was continued by Harvey Publications until 1961. A *Dick Tracy* comic book was also published by DC Comics in 1976.

RADIO

The *Dick Tracy* radio series was produced by the Mutual Broadcasting System, 1935-37, by the National Broadcasting Company (NBC), 1937-39, by the NBC Blue Network, 1943-44, and by the American Broadcasting Company (ABC), 1944-48.

■ Sidelights

Chester Gould was the creator of the comic strip character Dick Tracy, one of America's most popular fictional detectives. From 1931 until his retirement in 1977, Gould chronicled the square-jawed, hawk-nosed Tracy's heroic battles against a steady stream of wildly surreal underworld villains, always being sure to have his hero strictly follow actual police procedures. By the late 1940s, Tracy was so well known that he was the second-most recognized figure in America, just behind Bing Crosby and ahead of then-president Harry S. Truman. At the peak of the strip's popularity in the late 1950s, *Dick Tracy* was carried in well over one thousand newspapers around the world.

Gould was born in Pawnee, Oklahoma, the son of a printer and newspaper editor. "It was probably that influence which got me into the frame of mind to become a cartoonist," Gould explained in *The Celebrated Cases of Dick Tracy, 1931-1951*. At the age of seven, Gould was asked by his father to draw pictures of the town's local politicians. These pictures were then displayed in the window of his father's newspaper office, where the whole town could see them. "I got considerable attention," Gould said in *The Celebrated Cases of Dick Tracy, 1931-1951*, "and I think it's perhaps the thing that definitely turned me into this business."

Gould's cartooning career took a big step forward when he spent $20 on a mail-order cartooning course, completed the study, and landed a job with a local newspaper while still attending high school. Gould later worked for another newspaper while majoring in commerce and marketing at North-western University in Chicago. (Gould's father, wary of his son becoming an artist, insisted he study business.) During the 1920s he worked a variety of assignments for Chicago's six daily newspapers, landing a job in 1924 as cartoonist on the syndicated comic strip "Fillum Fables," a parody of the silent films of the day. "Radio Cats," a similar strip poking fun at radio, soon followed. Gould later claimed that both strips were "stinke-roo."

While working for the Chicago newspapers, Gould often had the opportunity to accompany reporters on special pieces that took him behind the scenes of the city's Prohibition gangster wars. "Without a doubt," Gould explained in *Dick Tracy: The Thir-ties, Tommy Guns, and Hard Times*, "it was this era that planted the idea of Dick Tracy in my head. The revelations of fixed juries, crooked judges, bribery of public officials and cops who looked the

10-2, I **READ** YOU LOUD AND CLEAR...

2-WAY WRIST TV

NOW **READ** ME!

CHESTER GOULD

Gould's famous detective as he appeared in an animated TV series.

was awesome, especially in the early years, I can say now that I doubt there is any business that can be equally as satisfying over such a long period of time."

The new comic strip debuted in the now-defunct *Detroit Daily Mirror* on October 4, 1931, was picked up by the *New York Daily News* a week later, and was quickly syndicated nationwide. The strip's first adventure introduced young Tracy and his fiancee, Tess Trueheart. Tess's father, a grocer, is murdered during a hold-up at his store, and Tracy is moved by the tragedy to become a police detective. In record time, the rookie is assigned to track down the killers of Mr. Trueheart. Gould broke new ground with the story, which depicted the first murder in comic strip history. He also "invented a hero who was not intended to be humorous," as Albin Krebs noted in the *New York Times.* "Tracy dealt grimly with murderers and racketeers.... Gould's 'Dick Tracy' was the first uncomic comic strip."

Early newspaper editors sometimes objected to Gould's realistic depiction of bloodshed. Wes Smith and Kenan Heise reported in the *Chicago Tribune* that *Dick Tracy* was the first comic strip to "graphically portray bullets spurting from brains and blood gushing from wounds." As Gould recounted in *Comics and Their Creators: Life Stories of American Cartoonists,* "Back in 1931 no cartoon had ever shown a detective character fighting it out face to face with crooks via the hot lead route." But the comic strip's violence only reflected the violence of Prohibition. Gould lived in Chicago where street shootings, underworld battles, and murders were common. In an affectionate parody of Gould, fellow cartoonist Al Capp of *Li'l Abner* fame introduced the detective character Fearless Fosdick in his own comic strip. Fosdick, a square-jawed, steely-eyed copy of Tracy, confronted his criminal adversaries in wild shooting sprees that left villains and bystanders alike riddled with bullets.

To keep Dick Tracy's crime-fighting realistic, Gould took classes in forensics, fingerprinting, and ballistics at Northwestern University. Story ideas were gleamed from actual crimes reported in the newspapers, and a police officer friend reviewed each panel for accuracy before publication. An added feature, the Crimestoppers Textbook, appeared in the upper right-hand corner of each Sunday *Dick Tracy* strip and gave readers useful advice on detecting and deterring crime in their own neighborhoods. Writing in his introduction to *The Celebrated Cases of Dick Tracy, 1931-1951,*

other way showed the crying need for a strong representative of law and order who would take an eye for an eye and a tooth for a tooth. Tracy was that man."

In an effort to secure his own comic strip, Gould spent nearly ten years bombarding "Captain" Joseph Medill Patterson, head of the Chicago Tribune-New York Daily News Syndicate and publisher of the *New York Daily News,* with strip ideas. He offered everything from romances to westerns to comedy without success. At one point, Gould was even sending his daily editorial cartoons to Patterson via the overnight train to New York.

In 1931 the constant effort paid off when Patterson thought Gould's idea for a strip called *Plainclothes Tracy* showed some promise, and the young artist was called in for a meeting. As the two men discussed the idea, Patterson decided that the detective hero's first name was too long. Instead of Plainclothes, he suggested the name Dick, a then-popular slang term for police detectives. ("Tracy" was Gould's pun on a detective's job of tracing criminals.) Patterson also gave Gould an idea for the strip's first adventure. Gould took the advice and the comic strip *Dick Tracy* was born. Writing in *Dick Tracy: The Thirties, Tommy Guns, and Hard Times,* Gould recounted: "Though the work load

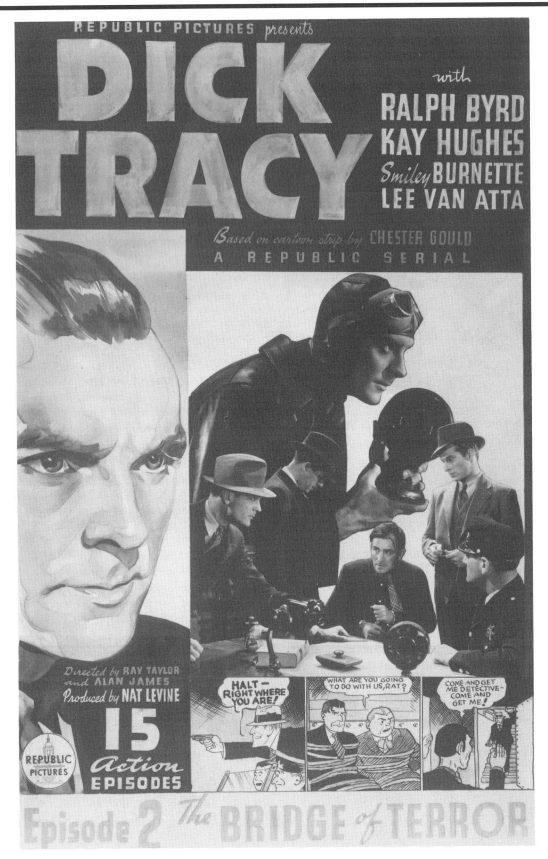

Poster advertising the Republic serial.

Ellery Queen noted Tracy's use of strictly scientific method in solving crimes. Tracy, Queen noted, was "the world's first procedural detective of fiction, in the modern sense."

Because he kept abreast of the latest breakthroughs in crime-fighting technology, sometimes Gould would stray from realism into science fiction. Over the years *Dick Tracy* readers were the first to see such futuristic gadgets as two-way wrist radios (later updated to wrist TVs), closed-circuit television surveillance, and space shuttles. Tracy's eccentric industrialist friend Diet Smith was often the source of such advanced crime-fighting equipment. Many of these devices were later adapted for use by the police, although in somewhat different form than Gould imagined. Tracy's wrist radios, for example, became the police miniature lapel radios of today. In 1963 one of Gould's characters even performed a human heart transplant, four years before that operation was performed in the real world.

Because there was an eight to thirteen week delay between the time when a comic strip was drawn and the time of its publication in newspapers, Gould often worried that his ideas might be stolen before they were published. To protect himself from lawsuits, he dated and signed a copy of any strip showing science-fictional ideas, put it into an envelope and mailed it to himself, the unopened envelope being filed away in his office.

While Gould could stray into science fiction when depicting Tracy's crime-fighting technology, he often strayed from realism into surrealism when depicting criminals. All of his villains were colorful, grotesque figures with pronounced physical abnormalities and matching nicknames. Flattop, for example, had a head as flat as an aircraft carrier. Pruneface was hideously wrinkled; the Mole resembled his animal namesake; and the Brow had deep fissures in his forehead. Writing in *Dick Tracy: The Official Biography*, Jay Maeder referred to Gould's villains as a "great parade of twitching, jittering, limping, squinch-faced, bug-eyed, wrinkle-browed, flat-headed, rat-eared, large-shouldered moral bankrupts." "I wanted my villains to stand out definitely so that there would be no mistake who the villain was...," Gould explained in *The Celebrated Cases of Dick Tracy, 1931-1951*. "I never looked at them as being ugly.... I think the ugliest thing in the world is the face of a man who has killed seven nurses—or who has kidnapped a child. His face to me is ugly."

Maeder pointed out that many of Tracy's villains were played for comedy, a nasty black comedy. One killer was a midget named Jerome Trohs ("short" spelled backward) who was carried around in a suitcase by accomplices. The gangster Shaky (a specialist in the shakedown, of course) was afflicted with a nervous tremor that kept him in constant motion. And the character Laffy laughed so often that his jaws froze open in a terrible grimace. When a punch in the face freed him, his jaws promptly froze shut and Laffy starved to death.

Justice always prevailed in *Dick Tracy*, albeit a bloody and ironic justice. Gould's villains were rarely brought before a court of law; they usually received their due punishment in spectacular and bizarre ways while attempting to flee the police. Nazi spy the Brow was impaled on a flag pole displaying Old Glory; the cop-killer Scardol was buried under two hundred tons of wet concrete; and, according to Krebs, "the nefarious B.B. Eyes met a most timely demise by being smothered under the cargo of a garbage scow."

Tracy, too, was often the victim of violence. In the strip's first 24 years, he was shot some 27 times. In the course of his career he has been beaten, stabbed, run over by cars, dragged from a speeding car, buried alive, tortured, burned, and gassed. No self-respecting villain would simply shoot the noted crimefighter; Tracy was invariably placed in an escape-proof death trap from which, in due course, he would escape. Tess Trueheart, Tracy's fiancee and, beginning in 1949, his wife, was also a frequent target of underworld threats and mischief. But the couple managed to come through all such encounters with no lasting damage, and Tracy always got his man.

Ironically, during World War II, the feisty Tracy stayed at home instead of donning a military uniform for action overseas. Gould believed there were enough comic strip heroes involved in the fight against the Nazis. He kept Tracy in Chicago fighting behind-the-lines villains trying to sabotage the war effort.

With at least one of his villains Gould dropped his usually grim approach and chose to be humorous, creating "the seedy, bewhiskered and odiforous farmer, B. O. Plenty," as Krebs remarked. After marrying the equally malodorous Gravel Gertie, Plenty became a solid citizen, a close friend to Tracy, and the father of Sparkle Plenty, a little girl born with long golden curls. B.O. became one of the strip's most popular characters, and Gould was obliged to bring back the genial rustic time and again. Sparkle also proved popular with Tracy fans; in the first year they were on the market, Sparkle Plenty dolls enjoyed over $3 million in sales. Eventually a half million dolls were sold.

Other endearing characters included Vitamin Flintheart, a hammy stage actor who is notoriously self-absorbed and constantly popping vitamin pills. Flintheart usually wandered into criminal activities unawares, foiling the criminals without meaning to do so. In 1944, kidnapped by Flattop and sharing a cramped hideout with him in a city park's ship replica, Flintheart drove the criminal crazy with his show-biz anecdotes and constant pill-popping. Years later, Flattop's brother Blowtop (so named for his sudden bursts of anger) used Flintheart as an unwitting accomplice in a scheme to fence hot money. He too found the old actor a barely-tolerable ally. In 1950, because of his many years of entertainment experience, Flintheart became Sparkle Plenty's agent.

Another Tracy regular was Junior Tracy, a street waif adopted by the detective in the early 1930s. Junior was eager to do battle at Tracy's side, often tracking criminals by hitching rides on their automobile spare tires. Often referred to as "Kid," Junior aged slowly. From his first appearance in the early 1930s until Tracy's marriage in 1949, the youngster barely reached puberty. During the 1950s, however, Junior became a young man and worked as a police sketch artist. By 1964, he was married to Moon Maid, a curvaceous extraterrestrial with horns atop her head who could disrupt television transmissions with her body's energy forcefield.

Tracy's working partners on the police force included several officers who shared his adventures for many years. Pat Patton worked with Tracy from the earliest days of the strip, beginning as a comic foil who bumbled his way through criminal investigations, then becoming a loyal and dependable companion, and finally working his way up to chief of police. On one occasion, Patton saved Tracy's life with a vital blood transfusion. In the late 1940s, a pug-nosed, freckle-faced police veteran named Sam Catchem appeared on the scene. Based on Gould's agent Al Loewenthal, the new character quickly became Tracy's close friend and loyal sidekick. Other police regulars included Lizz, a judo-wise woman officer prone to tossing criminals through the air.

Gould's drawing style gave *Dick Tracy* a distinctive look quite different from that of other comic strips.

Tracy himself is a square-jawed, hawk-nosed figure who wears a porkpie hat and trench coat; Gould usually drew him in profile to accentuate his facial features. He revealed in *Comics and Their Creators* that he conceived of Tracy as "a modern Sherlock Holmes, if Holmes were a young man living today, dressed as a modern G-man and bearing the traditional characteristics." Several commentators have noted that the early Tracy strips were almost documentaries about police work, while those after 1940 took on a more stylized appearance, telling morality plays in an almost abstracted visual language.

Speaking of Gould's artwork, Jerry Belcher of the *Los Angeles Times* said that the "strong-lined drawings were impressionistic rather than realistic," while a writer for the London *Times* claimed that the strip featured "brutally simple, almost crude graphics." Yet in 1982, when the Graham Gallery in New York held an exhibition of Gould's *Dick Tracy* artwork, the *New York Times* critic John Russell called Gould "a workman of a very high order in a craft that is much harder than it looks. The images survive well as exhibition material, and as tokens of a time when issues were clear-cut, when law was law, order was order, and the best man won out in the end."

Writing in *America's Great Comic-Strip Artists*, Richard Marschall pointed out that Gould's narrative skills made the *Dick Tracy* strip consistently entertaining for several decades. Gould, Marschall explained, "established a style of pacing in his stories that was more breathless than that of other strips; he constantly shifted the reader's point of view from Tracy to the villain to Tracy, splicing a terse narration throughout the panels and employing all manner of cliff-hanging devices. For weeks a villain would elude Tracy's best efforts by means as logical as careful planning or as unlikely as unexpected coincidences, and the result was at once as compelling as crime movies and pulp novels ... and as believable as front-page news stories."

Gould kept himself to a strict work schedule, always writing on Friday and Monday, drawing the Sunday page on Tuesday, and the rest of the week's strips on Wednesday and Thursday. "If you keep to a schedule," he explained in *Cartoonist Profile*, "you can make yourself available, when needed, to your family—that's why I like it." On occasion, Gould worked family members and friends into the comic strip. An architect named Jean Ellen, the designer of the Tracy family's dream house in a 1950 sequence, was inspired by daughter Jean Ellen Gould.

New York Daily News Sunday magazine cover announcing the rerun of Gould's original strips in 1990.

Two-time winner of the National Cartoonists Society Reuben Award, cartooning's highest honor, Gould was also honored with an appearance on the 1960s television program "This Is Your Life," hosted by Ralph Edwards. In April, 1980, the Mystery Writers of America chose him to receive a special Edgar Award—the first cartoonist to be selected for the honor. The organization praised

Gould as the father of the American police procedural story.

According to Krebs, Gould once spoke of the kind of audience reaction he wanted for his comic strip: "I just want them [the strip's readers] to say, 'I wonder what that damned fool Gould did today.'" And for over forty-five years, some 100 million fans wondered just that when they opened their daily newspapers to read the latest *Dick Tracy* episode. After Gould retired on Christmas Day in 1977, the strip was taken over by Richard Fletcher. Since Fletcher's death in 1983, Dick Locher and Max Collins have continued Dick Tracy's adventures.

Tracy has inspired a host of adaptations in other media. The character was featured in serials during the 1930s, a radio series during the 1940s, a television series during the 1950s, and an animated cartoon series in the 1960s. A host of Dick Tracy products, ranging from cap pistols to toy dolls, have been successfully marketed, including a two-way wrist radio sold in the late 1940s which enabled thousands of customers to tune in their favorite radio stations. In addition, many of Gould's original strips have been gathered into book-length collections.

During the 1980s, Dick Tracy's popularity declined until only about 250 newspapers were carrying the comic strip. For most of the decade, media attention focused not on the cartoon but on the complex legal maneuvers and publicity blitzes surrounding a new film adaptation. Originally optioned by director Floyd Mutroy and producer Art Linson in 1977, the project worked its way through Paramount and Universal studios before finally finding a home at Disney's Touchstone Films. Among the directors considered for the project were Diane Keaton, Walter Hill, John Landis, Richard Benjamin, and Martin Scorsese. Vying for the title role were Clint Eastwood and Warren Beatty. Beatty eventually won out, becoming not only the actor portraying Tracy but the film's director as well.

Easily the most popular adaptation of Dick Tracy ever, the 1990 movie version starred Warren Beatty as the detective, Glenne Headly as Tess Trueheart, and Madonna as a nightclub singer named Breathless Mahoney. Featuring such Hollywood stars as Al Pacino, Dustin Hoffman, Dick Van Dyke, James Caan, and Charles Durning in cameo roles, the movie was one of the largest grossing films of the year. One of the film's most striking features was its use of primary colors to recreate the look of the original comic strip.

Speaking to Smith and Heise, Max Collins, current scriptwriter for *Dick Tracy*, explained that Gould "virtually invented the adventure cartoon strip and he popularized the tough, two-fisted American detective." Mark Evenier said in the *Los Angeles Times* that "Gould was a legend" and "Dick Tracy was the greatest detective strip ever." Marschall

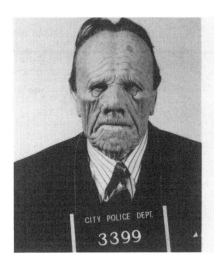  

A rogue's gallery from the 1990 film *Dick Tracy:* (from left) Pruneface, Influence, and Numbers.

Warren Beatty as Dick Tracy offers the Kid some advice about staying out of trouble.

called *Dick Tracy* "a remarkable and sophisticated saga, with fierce integrity and consistency on several levels."

■ **For More Information See**

BOOKS

Crawford, Hubert H., *Crawford's Encyclopedia of Comic Books*, Jonathan David Publishers, 1978.

Gould, Chester, *The Celebrated Cases of Dick Tracy, 1931-1951*, edited by Herb Galewitz, Chelsea House, 1970.

Gould, Chester, *Dick Tracy, the Thirties: Tommy Guns and Hard Times*, edited by Galewitz, Chelsea House, 1978.

Horn, Maurice, *The World Encyclopedia of Comics*, Chelsea House, 1976.

Maeder, Jay, *Dick Tracy: The Official Biography*, Penguin, 1990.

Marschall, Richard, *America's Great Comic-Strip Artists*, Abbeville Press, 1989.

Sheridan, Martin, *Comics and Their Creators: Life Stories of American Cartoonists*, Hyperion Press, revised edition, 1977.

PERIODICALS

American History Illustrated, March-April, 1990.
Antiques and Collecting Hobbies, June, 1990.
Cartoonist Profile, March, 1973.
Coronet, June, 1966.
Holiday, June, 1958.
Newsweek, October 16, 1961, January 14, 1963.
New York Daily News, May 19, 1985.
New York Sunday News, December 18, 1955, April 4, 1971.
New York Times, December 11, 1970.
People, June 18, 1990.
Saturday Evening Post, December 17, 1949.
Video Review, July, 1990.
Washington Post, January 15, 1971.

OBITUARIES

Chicago Tribune, May 12, 1985, May 13, 1985.
Los Angeles Times, May 12, 1985.

Newsweek, May 20, 1985.
New York Times, May 12, 1985.

Time, May 20, 1985.
Times (London), May 14, 1985.°

Bette Greene

Personal

Born June 28, 1934, in Memphis, TN; daughter of Arthur (a store owner) and Sadie (Steinberg) Evensky; married Donald S. Greene (a physician), June 14, 1959; children: Carla, Jordan. *Education:* Attended University of Alabama, 1952, Memphis State University, 1953-54, Alliance Francaise (Paris), 1954, Columbia University, 1955, and Harvard University, 1972. *Politics:* Independent. *Religion:* Jewish.

Addresses

Home and office—338 Clinton Rd., Brookline, MA 02146.

Career

Writer. *Hebrew Watchman*, Memphis, TN, reporter, 1950; *Commercial Appeal*, Memphis, TN, reporter, 1950-52; United Press International, Memphis, reporter, 1953-54; information officer for American Red Cross, 1958-59; Boston State Psychiatric Hospital, Boston, MA, information officer, 1959-61.

Awards, Honors

New York Times outstanding book award, Golden Kite Award from Society of Children's Book Writers, and Notable Book citation from American Library Association, all 1973, and National Book Award nomination for Best Children's Book, 1974, all for *Summer of My German Soldier*; Children's Choice Book Award, *New York Times* outstanding book award, and Notable Book citation from American Library Association, all 1974, and Newbery Honor Book award, 1975, all for *Philip Hall Likes Me. I Reckon Maybe*; *Parents' Choice* Award, 1983, for *Them That Glitter and Them That Don't*.

Writings

Summer of My German Soldier, Dial, 1973.
Philip Hall Likes Me. I Reckon Maybe, illustrated by Charles Lilly, Dial, 1974.
Morning Is a Long Time Coming, Dial, 1978.
Get on out of Here, Philip Hall, Dial, 1981.
Them That Glitter and Them That Don't, Dial, 1983.
The Drowning of Stephen Jones, Bantam, 1991.

Adaptations

Summer of My German Soldier was adapted into a television movie, starring Kristy McNichol, Bruce Davison, and Esther Rolle, broadcast on the National Broadcasting Company (NBC) in 1978; the book has also been released as an audiocassette, as has *Philip Hall Likes Me. I Reckon Maybe*.

■ Work in Progress

The Eyes of Victoria Goldsmith.

■ Sidelights

Bette Greene's books for young adults have earned her critical acclaim and a large readership. She has written serious, gut-wrenching novels as well as lighter, funnier works with equal success. Perhaps her most famous book is her first one, *Summer of My German Soldier,* about a young Jewish girl who becomes friends with a German prisoner-of-war. In both *Summer of My German Soldier* and her later books, which include *Philip Hall Likes Me. I Reckon Maybe* and *Get on out of Here, Philip Hall,* Greene has used her own background to produce compelling stories and realistic characters that her readers can relate to. "When I dig deep and hard enough," Green noted in an interview with Jim Roginski published in *Behind the Covers,* "I can sometimes strike connections with my emotional source. And when I'm writing from those depths, readers respond. They say, 'Hey! I know exactly how that feels. I think you must be writing about me.'"

Greene's early years, which proved to be fertile literary ground, were filled with racial and religious variety. She was born in 1934 in Memphis, Tennessee, but was raised mainly in a small town in Arkansas. From the beginning she was somewhat of an outsider: her family was Jewish, but virtually all of her fellow townspeople were Christian. In addition, her parents were kept busy running the general store they owned, so Greene spent a lot of time with her family's black housekeeper, Ruth. In an interview with *Authors and Artists for Young Adults (AAYA),* Greene commented on her background: "I think the most important aspect of my growing up, the thing that made me, me, was growing up almost counter to my culture. Growing up Jewish in the middle of the Bible Belt. Being white but having, for all practical purposes, a black mother. And not really fitting into the black culture fully because of my skin, but understanding a lot more than most because, in a way, I was part of it. I did go everywhere with Ruth and I think I was accepted as sort of Ruth's girl. So I became part of both the white culture and the black culture."

When she was old enough, Greene began working in her parents' store. "It was really very good for me because I didn't go through the shyness that a lot of people do," she told *AAYA.* "When you're so busy focusing on other people's needs, you don't have time for that. Working in my father's store

gave me a lot of confidence because I liked working with people and I had to sell things to much older people. I learned something about the observation of people."

While Greene enjoyed working in the store, school was more of a struggle. "I was a very poor student and I felt very bad about being a poor student. Friends of mine would have to stay out of school and pick cotton and yet they were doing better in school than I was. But I always knew that I had a capacity to understand things that other people didn't, even adults." Being Jewish and experiencing the black culture around her helped Greene to develop this unique understanding. In particular, she was able to recognize that the world around her was filled with hypocrisy. As she stated in her *AAYA* interview: "What I discovered growing up was how evil some religious people could be. So many would talk about how good they were and

Greene's acclaimed, controversial first novel.

would spend money trying to convert the Africans, and at the same time they were brutalizing the black people who worked in their homes and fields. Because I was Jewish, I could look at it with a little more distance than others."

When Greene entered high school, her family moved from Arkansas back to Memphis. She didn't like her new school, though. "I did not feel as though I fit in. I was looking for people who were willing to talk about more things than the prom." She did begin to cultivate her interest in writing by working for newspapers, but she received little support from her English teachers in school. In fact, she received poor grades in English because she had difficulty with spelling and punctuation. "I always thought that I deserved a better grade than I got," Greene recalled. Once, she entered a city-wide essay contest. She wrote a patriotic essay for the competition, and the judges selected her essay as the winner. Her English teacher, however, refusing to believe that Greene could write such a good essay, accused Greene of copying someone else's work. The judges, the author told *AAYA*, "took me to the office and asked me if I plagiarized, and I kept insisting that I didn't. So they decided that they would give me honorable mention." Greene, however, refused the award. "I told them what they could do with their honorable mention."

Upon graduating from high school, Greene spent a year studying in Paris, France. When she returned to the United States she attended several different colleges, including the University of Alabama and Memphis State University, but she couldn't find a college she liked. Finally, in 1955 she arrived at Columbia University in New York City. "I was very happy when I went to Columbia. There were people there who had a lot of ideas and who were energetic and alive. It was a whole new world for me. I was a general studies student, so I studied whatever I wanted. It was a wonderful opportunity for me and I loved being there." At Columbia Greene focused on two subjects: writing and astronomy. "I took astronomy because I wanted to learn something about how wide the universe was. I wanted to use writing to go the other way, deep within. Astronomy to go as far out as I could go and writing to go inward as far as I could go. They were both very good for me; they gave me some scope as a writer to go deep and yet realize that you're not the only little peanut on the planet. The planet is far bigger and more important than you or me. I'm just a small little cog."

While Greene immersed herself in the writing discipline at Columbia, she managed to avoid a practice that was becoming increasingly popular among her peers: drug use. "I didn't do drugs. I was afraid of becoming addicted. A young man who was studying writing with me at Columbia was angry when I wouldn't smoke the marijuana that was being passed around at a party. He said to me: 'You're never going to be a writer because you don't open up your senses. Marijuana will open up your senses.' He was so positive that I'd never be a writer." Such talk didn't discourage the author, though, as she continued to have confidence in her writing ability.

After Greene left Columbia, she spent several years working as a part-time journalist and a public information officer. Then she met her future husband, Donald. "I don't really believe in love at first sight," she mentioned in the *AAYA* interview. "It was attraction at first sight. I loved his baritone voice. I think that love comes after a lot of understanding." The two were married in 1959. Soon after, they moved to Boston, Massachusetts, where Bette Greene gave birth to her first child.

It was during this period that Greene began writing her first novel, *Summer of My German Soldier*. She wrote the book, she said, "between doing what mothers do with babies. Waiting for her to nap." She continued: "We spent all our money on baby-sitters. As soon as she was a little bit older, a baby-sitter would come and take her to the park. The baby-sitter would take her back and put her to bed for a nap. We didn't have any money, but I did manage to buy time to write." Writing the book took about five years. When she finished, she took a fiction-writing course at Harvard University in order "to test it with as close to a professional group as I could get." As in high school, however, she received negative comments about her writing. The professor of the course refused to read *Summer of My German Soldier* in class and instead gave it to his assistant to read. The assistant wasn't impressed. She told Greene: "It's not a terrible plot, but the problem is you really can't write."

Undeterred by such criticism and confident that *Summer of My German Soldier* was a "great" book, Greene tried to find a company that would publish it. For two years she sent the book to publishers, but none were interested. Some said that the story was too disturbing for young readers, while others maintained that no adult would want to read a book about a twelve-year-old girl. Finally, Greene convinced Dial Press to publish the book. When the

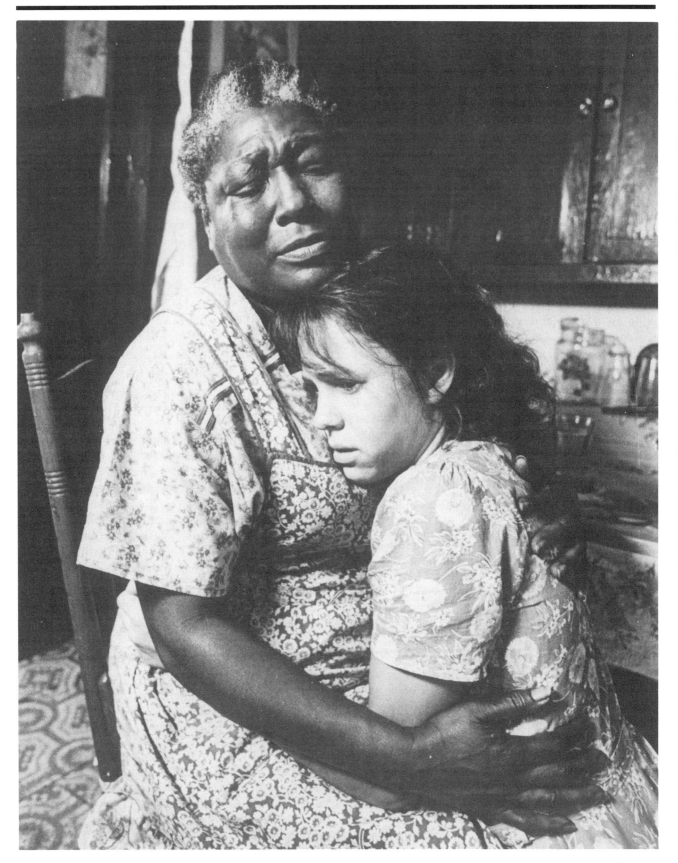

Esther Rolle as Ruth and Kristy McNichol as Patty Bergen in the TV adaptation of *Summer of My German Soldier*.

book appeared in 1973, it caused a stir among readers and critics alike.

Set in a small town in Arkansas shortly after World War II, *Summer of My German Soldier* chronicles the unusual friendship between a lonely, awkward Jewish girl and a polite, soft-spoken German soldier. Patty Bergen is twelve years old during the summer that she meets Anton Reiker, who is a captive in a prisoner-of-war camp near Patty's hometown. They first meet in the store owned by Patty's father. Later, after Patty sees Anton fail in his bid to escape from the camp on a train, she offers to hide him in her house until he can make another escape attempt. Their friendship blossoms, but their happiness doesn't last long; Anton is discovered and killed, and Patty is treated as a criminal by her harsh parents and by the unsympathetic townspeople. Despite these unhappy events, the story offers some hope: thanks to Anton, Patty feels like a "person of value" for the first time in her life.

Summer of My German Soldier deals with a number of serious themes, including prejudice and domestic violence. Despite his gentle nature and his positive effect on Patty, Anton is branded as evil by Patty's parents and by the townspeople because he once was part of Adolf Hitler's German army, which killed millions of European Jews during the "Holocaust" of World War II. Anton, though, is not the only one who becomes a victim of prejudice; because she is Jewish, Patty becomes a target of religious bigotry for the townspeople, all of whom are Christian. In addition to the prejudice is the issue of violence in the novel—Patty's father beats her when she angers him.

These troubling themes, together with a plot filled with tragic events, caused some critics to say that *Summer of My German Soldier* was unsuitable for a young audience. Audrey Laski, for instance, writing in *Times Educational Supplement*, noted that the book would probably "disturb a reader as young as its twelve-year-old heroine, because of the domestic violence and bitterness it records." Other reviewers, however, thought that the book was realistic and honest. *Horn Book* contributor Mary M. Burns praised the author for showing that difficult situations don't always end happily. Noting that the book "consistently maintains a twelve-year-old's perspective," she wrote that *Summer of My German Soldier* "offers no panaceas for loneliness, no easy solutions for problems.... [This is a] moving first novel, unforgettable because of the genuine emotion it evokes." Burns also pointed out that "the conclusion is tragic, but not completely

hopeless," since Patty emerges at the end with newfound self-esteem. Another reviewer, Judy Mitchell, commended the book for showing how a vicious world can damage innocent people. "*Summer of My German Soldier* catches the despair of the holocaust and its aftermath by indicating that one sensitive, loving little girl and one gentle German boy are no match for the times in which they live," wrote Mitchell in *English Journal.*

Summer of My German Soldier also caused controversy in some Jewish circles. A few Jewish critics and writers called the book anti-Semitic, because Greene portrays a Nazi soldier sympathetically while depicting Patty's father—the main male Jewish character in the book—in a negative light. Greene responded to such attacks by noting that, as a Jew herself, she had no intention of writing an anti-Jewish book. "I didn't write Harry Bergen to be a symbol of Jewish men or Jews," she stated in her *Behind the Covers* interview with Roginski. "[I] would hope that ... Jews everywhere, as well as non-Jews, can accept the fact that there might be a Jewish man who can be upset and disturbed and cruel. And if he is the archenemy why can't Patty

Bruce Davison starred as Anton Reiker in the TV version of *Summer of My German Soldier*.

Bergen be viewed as the Jewish archheroine?" The controversy died down, and Greene told Roginski that "the book is now used in a lot of Jewish schools and used as part of Holocaust literature.... And since it's considered important Holocaust literature, I take it as a vindication."

There has been much discussion about how much of *Summer of My German Soldier* is autobiographical. In her interview with Roginski, Greene said only that the book is based on real events. And in a *Philadelphia Inquirer* interview in 1973, Greene told Carroll Stoner that "life is sometimes stranger than fiction, and those events certainly were." Greene did tell Stoner, though, that "I can safely say I am no longer that troubled girl I wrote about in the book."

Summer of My German Soldier won a number of awards, including a Golden Kite Award in 1973, and it was nominated for a National Book Award in 1974. In 1978 the book was turned into a successful television movie starring Kristy McNichol. That same year Greene finished a sequel to the book, titled *Morning Is a Long Time Coming*. The featured character again is Patty Bergen, still alienated from her parents and still consumed with Anton Reiker and the events of her twelfth year. After graduating from high school, Patty angers her parents by using college tuition money to travel to Paris, France. While there, she enjoys the liberating atmosphere of the city and falls in love with a kind Frenchman, Roger Auberon, who asks her to marry him. She declines, instead traveling to Germany to try to find Anton's mother. Her trip is not successful, but the voyage helps her put the memory of Anton behind her and focus her attention on the future. At the end of the novel, she returns to Paris and to Roger.

As with Greene's first novel, reviewers mostly liked *Morning Is a Long Time Coming*. Several critics praised Greene's sensitive portrayal of Patty's search for self-knowledge and contentment. In his *New York Times Book Review* article, for instance, Peter Sourian noted that "Greene excels at depicting the process by which Patty arrives at each moral insight along the way of her literal and figurative journey, first to Paris and then to Germany." Likewise, *Times Educational Supplement* contributor Geoff Fox wrote that "the action of this novel lies within Patty, and she is characterised with subtlety and even tenderness." And a *Horn Book* reviewer, though somewhat critical of the use of emotion in the novel, praised Greene's handling of Patty and Roger's relationship. That reviewer commented, "Patty's scathing realism of observation is combined with an intense, almost hysterical emotionalism; but the scenes with Roger are imbued with a tender romanticism."

In between *Summer of My German Soldier* and *Morning Is a Long Time Coming*, Greene wrote one of her best-loved novels, *Philip Hall Likes Me. I Reckon Maybe*. Like *Summer*, *Philip Hall Likes Me* focuses on a young girl in rural Arkansas, but otherwise the two novels are much different. In *Philip Hall Likes Me*, eleven-year-old Beth Lambert's family is loving and close, and Beth is a well-adjusted young adult who is one of the best students in her class. Beth's life is complicated when she develops a crush on her rival, Philip Hall, a boy who finishes first in everything he tries. Though she is captivated by Philip's good looks, Beth eventually realizes that her crush on Philip is keeping her from beating him in school and in life. By the end of the novel, Beth realizes her dream of becoming the top student in her class.

Once again, critics praised Greene's work. In the *New York Times Book Review*, Betsy Byars called *Philip Hall Likes Me. I Reckon Maybe* "charming and fresh." She added, "There is a nice sort of timelessness about the book too, perhaps because the author has caught something unchanging in young people, and I think the book will retain its warm appeal for a long while." Likewise, a reviewer for *Booklist*, who termed the book "pleasant reading," noted that Greene "has caught the warm atmosphere of rural Arkansas and the spunky personality of a black sixth-grade girl possessed by an affection for her class rival Philip Hall."

Despite such praise, *Philip Hall Likes Me. I Reckon Maybe* did cause some controversy. When Greene first gave the book to her publishers, they wanted her to make the main characters white, not black. "It would have been very easy to do," Greene told Roginski, "because all that was necessary was to remove two references to race. Then it would have been a white book. It was an anguishing decision." Ultimately, though, Greene refused to change the book, because "*Philip Hall* is really a black book. It's black in spirit." Once the book was published, it prompted a cry of racism from one critic. In one scene a black character eats watermelon, a practice that has been the source of anti-black stereotypes. Greene had anticipated such criticism but chose to include the scene anyway, because, she told Roginski, eating watermelon is a Southern tradition. Greene's instincts about the book were richly rewarded in 1975, when *Philip Hall Likes Me. I Reckon Maybe* received a prestigious Newbery Honor Book award.

A DELL YEARLING BOOK   45755-6 •U.S. $3.25
CAN. $3.95

A Newbery Honor Book

Philip Hall likes me.
I reckon maybe.

by BETTE GREENE
Pictures by Charles Lilly

Greene's second novel was a Newbery Honor Book in
1975.

In the book's 1981 sequel, *Get on out of Here,
Philip Hall*, Greene confronts her heroine with an
unusual situation: failure. As the book opens, Beth
Lambert is sure that she will be given her school's
leadership award. She is, after all, the top student.
The award, however, goes instead to Philip Hall.
Stunned and angry, Beth attempts to regain her
winner's status by organizing a relay race between
the Pretty Pennies Girls Club—of which she is
president—and Philip's Tiger Hunters Boys Club.
Beth again is frustrated, though, when the boys
beat the girls in the race. Humiliated by her loss
and replaced as president of the Pretty Pennies,
Beth flees to her grandmother's house in a different town. Gradually, she learns to cope with her
failure by realizing that being a leader is risky but
rewarding. And by the end of the book, she and
Philip have developed a rewarding friendship.

"This wise and original novel makes us cry as we
laugh, even at its beautifully resolved happy ending," praised Cynthia King in the *New York Times
Book Review*. Sue Ellen Bridgers, writing in the
Washington Post Book World, also was enthusiastic

about *Get on out of Here, Philip Hall*. She commented that Beth's "journey back to self-confidence is a valid one for young readers who are just
beginning to experience baffling defeats in school
elections, clubs and athletic competitions."

As with her previous books, Greene set her 1983
book *Them That Glitter and Them That Don't* in
rural Arkansas. The book's protagonist is Carol Ann
Delaney, a senior in high school who has tremendous musical talent. Like Patty Bergen in *Summer
of My German Soldier*, though, Carol Ann is
alienated from her peers and troubled by an
unhappy home life. Her father is an alcoholic, her
mother is a Gypsy fortune-teller, and the family
lives in a run-down shack. In order to fulfill her
dreams of a music career, Carol Ann decides she
must leave her family and move to Nashville,
Tennessee. Here, she hopes to become a country-
and-western singer. Her journey is a difficult one,
however, and she has to call upon all of her survival
instincts—the same qualities that she hated in her
mother—in order to achieve her goal. Having
endured hardship, Carol Ann emerges stronger and
tougher at the end of the novel. Mary M. Burns,
again writing in *Horn Book*, termed *Them That
Glitter and Them That Don't* "persuasively real,"
while *School Library Journal* contributor Susan F.
Marcus noted that Carol Ann "will keep her
readers turning the page (pulling for her) as she
honestly faces, and overcomes, her painful situation."

Though some of her work, especially *Summer of
My German Soldier*, has been criticized for being
too depressing and troubling for young readers,
Greene says she only tries to portray reality as she
sees it. "I think that if you are an artist you have to
see all sides," Greene commented in her *AAYA*
interview. "You have to see light anywhere it
plays, not just sunshine. You have to see shadows,
too." And she told Carroll Stoner of the *Philadelphia Inquirer* that readers can identify with her
characters' problems. "Scratch a success and you'll
see insecurity. Every teenager goes through stages
when they either have acne or are fat or have no
breasts or think they're ugly and unpopular. And if
they don't have any of these problems they invent
them."

While Greene's own childhood has given her
valuable material for most of her books, she notes
that as she ages she is becoming more interested in
exploring other themes besides teenage angst. "I
think as you get older you get less interested in
your own life," she stated in her *AAYA* interview.
"I am interested in the world and the evil that is

done by 'good people.' I'm never interested in the evil done by evil people, because that's sort of boring to me. We all know that the Hell's Angels are out there making the world tough for the rest of us.''

This interest in ''the evil done by 'good people''' is evident in Greene's attitude toward religion and religious leaders. She exhibits skepticism and cynicism when discussing religion. ''The world is filled with clergy telling others that the only way to reach God is through them,'' she told *AAYA*. ''They're the only conduit. Elie Wiesel, a famous Jewish writer who won the 1986 Nobel Peace Prize, spoke words that chilled me: 'The road to Hitler's extermination camps was paved with Christian theology.'''

Greene's skepticism toward religious groups was an issue as she wrote her most recent book, *The Drowning of Stephen Jones*. Based on a real event, the book tells about a young gay man who died after he was thrown off a bridge by three youths. While researching the book, Greene became intrigued by the religious background of the three killers. ''The three young men who did it came from religious homes, particularly the one who was the leader. So I really tried to find out how it could be that people who are followers of the Prince of Peace could do such evil things, like murder people,'' Greene told *AAYA*. ''I didn't do my book to prove something. I was just fascinated that a man could be drowned because he's gay. I don't quite understand it.'' When Greene questioned leaders from national gay and lesbian groups, she discovered that ''there's a high correlation between fundamental Christians and the [gay] people who are getting bashed. Wouldn't it be wonderful if these people really were Christians? Because if they were they'd keep sacred what Jesus begged his followers the day before his death: 'Love thy neighbor as thy self.'''

As part of her research for *The Drowning of Stephen Jones*, Greene conducted over three hundred interviews in places like Bangor, Maine, and Eureka Springs, Arkansas. During her research she found people who didn't want the book published. ''When I was working on the book I had all kinds of harassments and had my life threatened by a right-wing religious group.'' Nevertheless, she was able to finish the book, though she admits that ''sometimes I fear that the right-wing haters who murdered Jewish talk-show host Allan Berg will come after me.''

Future projects, she says, will be like *Stephen Jones*—based less on her own life and more on events happening in the world. When she's working on a book, it consumes most of her time. ''I try to write six to eight hours a day. Sometimes ten. So many things come up—life and people—that it's very hard, but I try to write six hours a day,'' she commented in her interview with *AAYA*. She continued: ''I write. I don't do it as a hobby. I don't write letters. I write a grocery list, maybe. That's about it. I have a studio in New Hampshire. I do a little canoeing, and I take walks and go to the diner every morning. I never cook breakfast. And I read the newspapers. I think about things and then I go back to work.'' Greene characterizes the writing profession as ''a harsh business,'' adding, ''I wouldn't encourage anybody to be a writer. People should be writers who feel that it's the only thing that makes them happy.''

Greene continues to live with her husband in a suburb of Boston. The couple has two grown

The rivalry between Beth Lambert and Philip Hall continues in Greene's 1981 novel.

children, Carla and Jordan. "This sounds like a bouquet to myself, but I think I was a more loving and more concerned parent than my parents were," she mentioned to *AAYA.* Of her own life, she told Roginski: "I've certainly been through bad times but I've always come through. I've enjoyed the ride. I've been lucky. I guess what I'm trying to say is that I've been ahead of the game. And any day or anything I get after that is a plus. I've reached the point where I'm adding up all the pluses and minuses. There are a lot of minuses. But there are many more pluses, too." In her interview with the *Philadelphia Inquirer,* she highlighted the message that she hopes to send to young adults: "I hope that I convey one thing to young people. Failure is not the worst thing. The worst thing is not to try."

■ Works Cited

Bridgers, Sue Ellen, "Stories of Rural Childhood," *Washington Post Book World,* May 10, 1981, pp. 15-16.

Burns, Mary M., review of *Summer of My German Soldier, Horn Book,* February, 1974, p. 56.

Burns, Mary M., review of *Them That Glitter and Them That Don't, Horn Book,* August, 1983, p. 453.

Byars, Betsy, review of *Philip Hall Likes Me. I Reckon Maybe, New York Times Book Review,* December 8, 1974, p. 8.

Fox, Geoff, "Parents and Lovers," *Times Educational Supplement,* November 24, 1978, p. 48.

Greene, Bette, interview with Chris Hunter for *Authors and Artists for Young Adults,* August, 1990.

King, Cynthia, review of *Get on out of Here, Philip Hall, New York Times Book Review,* February 21, 1982, p. 35.

Laski, Audrey, "Partridge in a Pear Tree," *Times Educational Supplement,* December 9, 1977, p. 21.

Marcus, Susan F., review of *Them That Glitter and Them That Don't, School Library Journal,* April, 1983, pp. 122-23.

Mitchell, Judy, "Children of the Holocaust," *English Journal,* October, 1980, pp. 14-18.

Review of *Philip Hall Likes Me. I Reckon Maybe, Booklist,* March 15, 1975, p. 760.

Roginski, Jim, *Behind the Covers,* Libraries Unlimited, Inc., 1985, pp. 94-102.

Sourian, Peter, "The Nazi Legacy, Undoing History: *Morning Is a Long Time Coming,*" *New York Times Book Review,* April 30, 1978, p. 30.

Stoner, Carroll, "Love Story: A Jewish Girl and a Captured Nazi," *Philadelphia Inquirer,* December 28, 1973, pp. 1G, 6G.

■ For More Information See

BOOKS

Children's Literature Review, Volume 2, Gale, 1976.

Contemporary Literary Criticism, Volume 30, Gale, 1984.

Something about the Author, Volume 8, Gale, 1976.

PERIODICALS

Boston Evening Globe, December 28, 1973.

New York Times Book Review, November 4, 1973.

Washington Post Book World, May 8, 1983.

—*Sketch by Neil R. Schlager*

Constance C. Greene

1969, and listed as an American Institute of Graphic Arts Children's Book, 1970; *A Girl Called Al* and *Beat the Turtle Drum* were named American Library Association Notable Books.

■ Writings

A Girl Called Al, illustrated by Byron Barton, Viking, 1969.

Leo the Lioness, Viking, 1970.

The Good-Luck Bogie Hat, Viking, 1971.

Unmaking of Rabbit, Viking, 1972.

Isabelle the Itch, illustrated by Emily McCully, Viking, 1973.

The Ears of Louis, illustrated by Nola Langner, Viking, 1974.

I Know You, Al, illustrated by Barton, Viking, 1975.

Beat the Turtle Drum, illustrated by Donna Diamond, Viking, 1976.

Getting Nowhere, Viking, 1977.

I and Sproggy, illustrated by McCully, Viking, 1978.

Your Old Pal, Al, Viking, 1979.

Dotty's Suitcase, Viking, 1980.

Double-Dare O'Toole, Viking, 1981.

Al(exandra) the Great, Viking, 1982.

Ask Anybody, Viking, 1983.

Isabelle Shows Her Stuff, Viking, 1984.

Star Shine, Viking, 1985.

Other Plans (adult novel), St. Martin's, 1985.

The Love Letters of J. Timothy Owen, Harper, 1986.

Just Plain Al, Viking, 1986.

Isabelle and Little Orphan Frannie, Viking, 1988.

■ Personal

Born October 27, 1924, in New York, NY; daughter of Richard W. (a newspaper editor) and Mabel (a journalist; maiden name, McElliott) Clarke; married Philip M. Greene (a radio station owner), June 8, 1946; children: Sheppard, Philippa, Stephanie, Matthew, Lucia. *Education:* Attended Skidmore College, 1942-44. *Politics:* Democrat. *Religion:* Roman Catholic.

■ Addresses

Home—East Hampton, Long Island, NY 11937. *Agent*—Marilyn Marlow, Curtis Brown Ltd., 575 Madison Ave., New York, NY 10022.

■ Career

Associated Press, New York City, began as mailroom clerk, became reporter, 1944-46; writer, 1968—.

■ Awards, Honors

A Girl Called Al was named a *Washington Post Book World*'s Spring Book Festival Honor Book,

Monday I Love You, Harper, 1988.
Al's Blind Date, Viking/Kestrel, 1989.
Funny You Should Ask (short story collection), Delacorte, in press.

Contributor to periodicals, including New York *Daily News.*

■ Adaptations

Beat the Turtle Drum was presented as "Very Good Friends" on *ABC Afternoon Special,* 1976; "Very Good Friends" and *A Girl Called Al* are available on audiocassette, both distributed by Listening Library, both 1985.

■ Sidelights

Since both of her parents worked for the New York *Daily News,* children's and young adult fiction writer Constance C. Greene was born with the "tools" of her trade readily accessible. "I grew up with typewriters, newspapers, books, magazines,

Greene's first novel about an independent, nonconformist young teen.

and conversation all around," Greene related in an interview for *Authors and Artists for Young Adults (AAYA).* "So while it wasn't inevitable that I'd become a writer, that background certainly influenced me.

"My father was a long-time editor of the paper, and my mother reviewed movies for them. The *Daily News* was much more powerful in those days and had the largest circulation in the country. They didn't call themselves journalists back then; they were newspaper people. I've always thought that newspaper work was the best possible profession because it led to a very interesting life. A friend of mine whose father was a businessman said that she used to be so impressed because my family talked about all kinds of ideas and things that weren't discussed at her house."

Greene grew up in the suburbs, but her family eventually moved to the city. "I lived in Larchmont, and that was about twenty-five minutes from New York," she recalled in her *AAYA* interview. "But shortly after I turned fifteen, the *Daily News* made my father their managing editor. He began to work all night long, which was why we moved into the city. This was just before World War II, so New York City was still comparatively safe, but exciting."

Greene completed her secondary schooling in Manhattan, but then left Skidmore College after only two years. She explained to *AAYA:* "Not a serious student, I tired of wasting my time and my father's money. I really wanted to get a job in newspapers. I tried the *Sun, World Telegram,* and *Time,* but nobody would hire me. I finally asked the Associated Press [AP] if they needed help and they put me to work in the mailroom—the bottom rung of the ladder, a very lowly job, indeed. I worked nights for $16.50 a week. At midnight, I would go home by myself on the subway. Always nervous, my mother gave me a whistle to wear around my neck. Fortunately, I had a rapid climb at the AP.

"Since all the young men had gone off to war by 1945, I worked hard and finally got onto the City Desk, which had to be the most exciting job anyone of my age ever had. I did a lot of interviews and went out to Staten Island to meet the incoming troopships. Since the *Baltimore Sun* papers were big AP clients, I would ask the troops where they were from and write about those from Baltimore. I even interviewed Frank Sinatra once. He had just returned from a U.S.O. tour. I saw him at the Paramount in the midst of a shrieking, screaming, and fainting crowd. The famous bad-tempered boy of all times, he always shot his mouth off or misbehaved in some way.

"There were also the tiresome things, like interviewing 4-H Club members from Iowa. I can't be thankful enough for the year and a half at AP. The job taught me a lot. Working for a wire service, you learn to cram as much as you can into the smallest space possible. I rarely have to cut anything. Some people prefer Henry James; I don't. I've just been trying to get through Jane Austen for the eighteen thousandth time."

Greene left the Associated Press after she married in 1946 to move to Connecticut and concentrate on raising her family. "It's very difficult to write when you have a bunch of kids around," she revealed to *AAYA*. "With so many interruptions, I found myself putting a lot of things on hold. I wrote short stories because I could do those in one sitting. My mother suggested that I write a book for children, but that was the furthest thing from my mind at that time. I didn't believe that I could sustain the interest of a reader throughout a book, and really wanted, most of all, to write my short stories. I published a series of these one-page short stories in the *Daily News*. I wrote a lot about little kids, especially one named Charlie, but always from an adult's point of view. They were very easy for me.

"When we were living in Connecticut and the children were still growing up," Greene recalled in an article in *50 Plus*, "I joined a short-story writing group at the Darien Community Association. Everyone was very serious about their writing and a few had even been published. I got so tired of the rejection slips that our teacher—who, by the way, was excellent—suggested that I try for the juvenile market. I started writing my first book, *A Girl Called Al*, and it felt right from the beginning. When I showed the teacher the first few chapters, she said, 'This is what you should do.'"

"I should forget all the other stuff, and that my book was good, she told me," Greene continued her story with *AAYA*. "So I sent it to a publisher where a friend's daughter was a reader. The daughter wrote back and said that although they liked my book, they didn't think that it was complete. 'The heck with this,' I decided, and wrote Phyllis McGinley, a friend of my mother's. McGinley had written a lot of children's books and had won a Pulitzer Prize for her poetry. I asked her if there were any agents who handled just children's books. She gave me the name of her agent,

Marilyn Marlow, one of the foremost children's book agents in New York. I sent Marilyn my material. She returned my manuscript and said that she also didn't think it was complete, but was interested in my writing. If I finished the book off a little, she would send it out.

"The first publisher to receive it suggested that I make so many changes that I left saying, 'Oh my God, I don't know what to do.' Marilyn advised we try someone else. She sent it to Velma Varner at Viking, who called me in and said, 'You've got the bones, just flesh them out.' That did it for me. I went home absolutely exhilarated to flesh out the bones. It was the best piece of advice I've ever heard. It demonstrated the differences between those two publishers: the first was too wordy and left me discouraged; Velma had the right touch. She said simply, 'Just do this.' It is the same advice that I now give."

A Girl Called Al was published in 1968. Greene discussed the character of Al in her *AAYA* interview: "The special thing about Al is that she

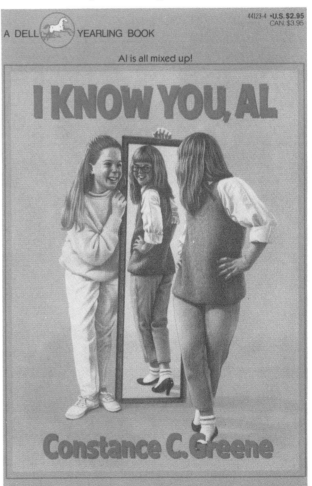

The second book in the "Al" series appeared in 1975.

describes herself. She has a high I.Q. but doesn't work to capacity. She's also very nonconformist. At the time I invented her, the terminology of a 'latch-key' kid hadn't been created, but that's what Al was. Her mother and father were divorced and she came home every day to an empty place because her mother worked. Those kids, who often have to take care of younger brothers and sisters, have a great weight of responsibility on their shoulders, but Al's nonconformity is what made her different. The narrator of the book is the opposite of Al; she's really the straight man. Her family has a mother, father, and little brother, and she is relatively unsophisticated. Al has traveled to a lot of places and has done all kinds of things like riding on airplanes. The narrator's family can't afford to do all those things, so she and Al make a nice contrast. The narrator is about as close to me as anything I've done, or maybe I just remember myself being like that."

Greene's 1982 story about the enduring friendship of two seventh-grade girls.

Louise Fitzhugh's *Harriet the Spy* provided Greene with the needed inspiration that led to the "Al" series. "I'm almost positive that I started writing *Al* after reading that book," Greene explained to *AAYA*. "It opened doors for me. I set out to write about a city kid because they have such a different life from suburban or country kids, and I enjoyed the idea of moving those two kids around the city.

"I think there were two mistakes I made in *A Girl Called Al*. First, I killed one of the best characters at the end of the story that I have ever created. I could have used him a couple of times, and don't really know why I let him die. My second mistake was that I didn't give the narrator a name. I don't know why. Nobody really thought about it. By some quirk of my imagination, it doesn't bother me that she doesn't have a name. I tell the kids that if it really bothers them, they should just make one up.

"I really had no intention of writing the sequel, *I Know You, Al*. I wrote the second one only after about five years of receiving letters which requested another book. Writing a sequel is a difficult thing because a good one should stand on it's own. Writing that second book was a pleasure. The fact that the series has turned into six books amazes me. I find it surprising as well as rewarding that kids still read all of them.

"Al was thirteen when I started out and after six books, I've reluctantly made her fourteen. Maybe I should not have tampered with her age at all. Although Al and her friend have wandered all over New York City, they have remained relatively unsophisticated. I have always expected somebody to call me out on that fact, but, so far, nobody has."

Throughout the "Al" series, as well as in the rest of her writings, Greene has tried to keep her prose and ideas fresh and enduring. "I read the newspapers and that still gives me a feeling for language," she told *AAYA*. "I also listen to kids." Indeed, "eavesdropping—in the nicest possible way—can be very productive," she wrote in a *Writer* magazine article. Greene admits that while window-shopping she heard one young friend say to another "Have a weird day." She was intrigued by the play on the common "Have a good day" and later used its slangy form in *I Know You, Al* and other "Al" books. Now she receives letters from young fans who sign off with "Have a weird day."

Greene also points out that there is a difference between "current" and "superficial" information in books. "I hate young adult books in which the authors talk about the kinds of jeans, sneakers, sweatshirts the characters wear," she complained

Katy Kurtzman and Melissa Sue Anderson in *Very Good Friends*, an ABC Afterschool Special based on Greene's *Beat the Turtle Drum*.

to *AAYA*. "In five or ten years, people will read it and say, 'Do you remember Guess jeans? I remember way back when I wore those.' I find those things to be very irritating. I try not to include anything that might possibly date the book. Al will wear red, clunky shoes. I've worn red, clunky shoes in the past, and think they're here to stay."

Greene tries to entertain rather than instruct in her books about Al and her other novels: "I am not an educator, I am a writer," she declared in a *Something about the Author Autobiography Series (SAAS)* article. Greene added in that piece that children feel the same emotions that adults feel—and often more intensely than adults. "Children ... are very sharp, very aware. They know far more than grown-ups give them credit for." "Don't talk down to them," she also advises in *Writer*. "Books extend their knowledge, expose them to thoughts, ideas, emotions they might not otherwise explore."

Greene tries to keep her work light despite the shift in young adult literature toward "heavy" themes. She told her *AAYA* interviewer: "Children's books have changed radically from my day. Drugs or sex would never have been touched. Take Nancy Drew as she was when I knew her in the 1930s. I understand that she's been considerably beefed-up or modernized in order to get kids to read her. I'm not so sure that's such a good idea. Books today for the junior high to high school level dwell too much on the heavy stuff. There's enough heavy stuff in kid's daily lives already. All they have to do is read the newspapers or watch TV to be assailed by all sorts of graphic things that I don't think are good for them. It's incredible that they can get away with the graphic sex and cruelty in song lyrics. But if it makes money, it's in.

"I've really written only two books that I would call young adult, for kids over twelve, and they illustrate an interesting point. The first was called *The Love Letters of J. Timothy Owen*, a lighthearted

A shy sixteen-year-old's first crush is the focus of this 1986 book.

look at a boy's problems growing up, and *Monday I Love You,* about a girl with low self-esteem. I actually based this on a girl I knew with large breasts who suffered ridicule at the hands of her peers because of it. In one incident in the bathroom, girls tried to tear off her clothes. Although *Monday I Love You* has been more successful, *The Love Letters of J. Timothy Owen* was a heck of a lot more fun to write. I recognize that life is not a bowl of cherries, but in my books for younger readers, I'd really prefer to make them laugh."

Elaborating on the importance of good humor in children's literature, Greene noted in *SAAS* that "whenever feasible, I try to write happy endings. This is not always possible. The ending must fit. The ending is very important, perhaps the most important part of the book.... The perfect ending leaves the reader satisfied, content. Wishing the book had not ended. A child's book should end on a hopeful note even though lots of children in this country lead lives devoid of it."

Additionally, Greene told *AAYA,* "I try to avoid subjects such as drug abuse or alcoholism. It's been done to the nines. I think that young adult books have also plumbed the depths of 'terminal illness of the week' story, as well as just about everything else. In the past five years, I think young adult books have changed for the better in that respect. I also try to avoid graphic sex. A librarian once told me that she used Judy Blume's book *Forever* as sort of a textbook for kids about contraception. I thought to myself, 'Dear, sweet Jesus, if I ever wrote a book that could be used as a textbook for contraceptive use by kids, I'd like to jump out of the highest window I could find.'

"I like to think of myself as a humorous writer, but there are times when serious elements creep into the work. The best thing to do is to combine laughter with a little bit of real life. Divorce is a constant in my work because it seems to be here to stay. When kids ask why there is so much of it in my books, I answer that I see it everywhere, although kids seem to be accepting and rising above it. I write realistic fiction, but try to work around the heavy stuff. There are many other writers, like Robert Cormier, who can do that much better than I. Cormier was very much against marketing his books as young adult, and I don't blame him. Many people don't like his work because evil sometimes wins. But I like him despite his heaviness. He is a very good writer."

Greene has based many of the ideas for her other books on her own children. For instance, *Leo the Lioness* was inspired by her daughter Lucia. She told *50 Plus:* "[When] our youngest was a teenager, she was an astrology freak. She was always studying the signs and talking about how Leo was the best sign, the lion, the king! So I built a story around it."

Other people and events have also inspired her, as well, but Greene interprets those with a writer's eye. The character of Gran in *The Unmaking of Rabbit* is modeled on her own mother-in-law. *Double-Dare O'Toole* was based on an phase in her son-in-law's life when he couldn't resist a dare. He consequently found himself in dangerous or humorous situations because of that. "Don't be afraid to use bits and pieces of anything you have lying around in your head," she wrote in *Writer.* "A pinch of this, a pinch of that, never mind whether it really happened or not. It *could* have happened."

Getting Nowhere was based on the true story of a young boy who took the family car out for a drive while his parents were away. He totalled the car;

then, fearful of his parents retribution, committed suicide. "I tried to imagine what had driven this real boy to such a tragic act," Greene recalled in *Writer.* "I tried to reconstruct in my mind his relationships with his parents, his siblings, his peers. What had this boy been like in life? What went on inside his head? What had made him take his own life?" She rewrote the story for *Getting Nowhere,* giving her novel a less tragic ending. "It is not without hope. I try to leave a promise of better things to come, a taste of hope."

Despite Greene's distaste for heavy fiction, one of her most popular books remains *Beat the Turtle Drum,* the story of her older sister's death at age thirteen. She wrote the book after the death of her parents. "That is the only book that I have taken directly from my own life," she explained to *AAYA.* "I wrote that story of two sisters many, many years after in order to try and recreate what had happened. I was only eleven at the time and couldn't remember much about how my mother or father felt, or how people reacted. It was difficult in the beginning but, as with most of my books, I started with a real idea and character and then let my imagination take over. *Beat the Turtle Drum* might have been a better story if I'd recited everything exactly the way it happened, but oftentimes I don't remember it that way. Though I'm not sure that everything in the story actually happened, writing it did make me feel a little better. When I go to schools, this is the book all kids seem to want to talk about. I would really rather not have it be the one thing that I'm known for."

Beat the Turtle Drum was eventually adapted as "Very Good Friends" for an *ABC Afterschool Special* in 1976. Also in the mid-1970s, Greene moved from Connecticut to Maine, where her husband owned a radio station. The sudden peace and quiet disturbed her concentration, she told *AAYA.* "All my kids were in or through with college and I didn't have any friends. Although I could never understand how anyone could write with little kids around, I could do so once mine were reasonably grown up. Having been used to telephones ringing, people coming and going, and lots of friends, I found that serenity was not really good for me."

Several of Greene's children have followed her example, she informed *AAYA.* Her son, Sheppard, wrote the young adult novel *The Boy Who Drank Too Much,* while her daughter, Philippa, writes young adult novels as well. "I also have one daughter who is an advertising copywriter. She and her husband had worked on Madison Avenue but moved to New Hampshire where she now free-lances. She's trying to write a book but has a little boy, and that's tough. My other daughter has three kids and is a reporter for *People.* All I can tell them is to wait until their children get into school. Then, at least they have a framework around which to work in earnest from nine to three."

Greene and her husband sold their radio station after six years of living in Maine and settled happily in East Hampton, Long Island. "Now we live on North Main Street, smack in the middle of town with the fire engines, the ambulances, and never mind the tourists," she informed her *AAYA* interviewer. "I used to be fairly rigid in my writing hours, but either I've changed, or I was doing it wrong all the time. I've found that I work better if I'm not too rigid. I write a little in the afternoon, maybe do something else, and then go back to it.

"I like writing for the middle-grade kids, ages nine to twelve. I think that those kids have changed less from when I or my children were their age than

Greene examines the pain of a young girl suffering from low self-esteem in this poignant 1988 novel.

any of the others. The publishers have been wanting funny books for boys that age, so I've been working on that. I've written a couple of books already that have been popular with boys, such as *Double Dare O'Toole. The Love Letters of J. Timothy Owen* was the ideal situation of a lighthearted book with serious overtones.

"I would like to write another adult book. My first was published in 1986 and was called *Other Plans*. It was a story about a boy who didn't get along with his father and although it got some good reviews, it didn't do very well. If I had that one to do all over again, I probably would have written it as a young adult and it probably would have been a heck of a lot more successful. But I have written another adult novel that I started a long time ago that had a very good plot. I used to think that if you had a good plot, the rest was easy, but the book didn't turn out to be saleable. I'd like to go back to it, which is sometimes harder than starting afresh, but the book still intrigues me. It is a murder mystery—the sort I like to read, so it might be fun to do. Writing should not be all drudgery.

"I've also thought of writing some short stories for children and putting them into a collection. The big stumbling block there is that publishers may not want to publish a collection of short stories because they're afraid it won't sell. But every now and then, I still write an adult short story which is absolutely perfect for *The New Yorker*. I have finally established a relationship with one of the editors there who sends me very nice rejection letters."

■ Works Cited

Greene, Constance C., in an interview with Marc Caplan for *Authors and Artists for Young Adults*.

Greene, Constance C., "What You Can Make Live," *Writer*, August, 1982, pp. 23-26.

Something about the Author Autobiography Series, Volume 11, Gale, 1991, pp. 129-147.

Whitcomb, Meg, "Connie Greene's Kids Taught Her Well," *50 Plus*, June, 1981, pp. 74-75.

■ For More Information See

PERIODICALS

Horn Book, August, 1969; February, 1971; April, 1973; February, 1974; April, 1975.

New York Times Book Review, January 21, 1973; November 15, 1975; February 15, 1981.

Saturday Review, April 19, 1969.

Teacher, April, 1975.

Judith Guest

Personal

Born Judith Ann Guest, March 29, 1936, in Detroit, MI; daughter of Harry Reginald (in business) and Marion Aline (Nesbit) Guest; married Larry Lavercombe (an executive), August 22, 1958; children: Larry, John, Richard. *Education:* University of Michigan, B.A., 1958.

Addresses

Home—4600 West 44th St., Edina, MN 55424.

Career

Writer. Elementary teacher in public schools in Royal Oak, MI, 1964, and Birmingham, MI, 1969; writer for *Palatine Press*, Palatine, IL, and *Daily Herald*, Arlington Heights, IL, during early 1970s; teacher in continuing education program, Troy, MI, 1974-75. *Member:* P.E.N. American Center, Authors League of America, Detroit Women Writers.

Awards, Honors

Janet Heidinger Kafka Prize, University of Rochester, 1977, for *Ordinary People; Ordinary People* was selected one of New York Public Library's Books for the Teen Age, 1980, 1981, and 1982; *Second Heaven* was selected one of *School Library Journal*'s Best Books for Young Adults, 1982.

Writings

NOVELS

Ordinary People, Viking, 1976.
Second Heaven, Viking, 1982.
(With Rebecca Hill) *Killing Time in St. Cloud*, Delacorte, 1988.

OTHER

Judith Guest: 'Second Heaven' (sound recording), New Letters, 1984.
Rachel River, Minnesota (TV adaptation; based on stories by Carol Bly), PBS-TV, 1989.

Author of an essay, *The Mythic Family*, Milkweed, 1988. Also author of screen adaptation of *Second Heaven.* Contributor to periodicals, including *Writer.*

Adaptations

Ordinary People was adapted for a filmstrip released by Center for Literary Review, 1978, for a feature film released by Paramount, 1980, and for a cassette released by Recorded Books, 1986; *Second Heaven* was adapted for a cassette released by Recorded Books, 1983.

■ **Work in Progress**

A novel, tentatively titled *Errands;* two original screenplays.

■ **Sidelights**

In her blockbuster debut novel, *Ordinary People*, Judith Guest established herself as a perceptive chronicler of adolescent problems and emotions. Both *Ordinary People* and her follow-up novel, *Second Heaven*, focus on likeable, sensitive teenage boys who face personal and family crises. "[Adolescence is] a period of time ... where people are very vulnerable and often don't have much experience to draw on as far as human relationships go," she told Barbara Holliday of the *Detroit Free Press*. "At the same time they are making some pretty heavy decisions ... about how they're going to relate to people and how they're going to shape their lives." In an interview with *Contemporary Authors New Revisions* (CANR) Guest said that she can relate to young adult characters because she still sees vestiges of adolescence in herself: "I'm sure there are things in my own adolescence that I have not completed yet, things that I haven't thought through or put to rest. So there's a lot of me in those kids—a *lot* of me."

Guest was born in 1936 in Detroit, Michigan. She began writing at the age of twelve, but kept her efforts private. "I never showed anybody anything that I had done," she told *CANR*. "It's easy to look back with hindsight and say, well, yes, I was heading in that direction from the time I was twelve. I don't think that's necessarily true. You could be distracted by many things. I'm fairly creative on a lot of levels, and if I'd had a certain amount of success with some of the other endeavors I tried, I might have concentrated more on them—say, painting. I painted for a long time, and I just wasn't a good painter. I got frustrated. For some reason, I think writing was the creative endeavor that suited my temperament and my abilities best." Yet she felt too intimidated to take any writing courses at the University of Michigan, where she earned a degree in education. She graduated in 1958 and got married that summer.

During the 1960s Guest taught in Michigan elementary schools and began raising a family. Not until she was in her mid-thirties, when her three sons were of school age, did she begin devoting a lot of time to writing fiction. She told Carol Kleiman in the *Houston Post* that she regards her time spent as a homemaker valuable: "I don't believe all those years of parenting, PTA, driving,

committees were wasted. They were not unproductive years. I was serving my apprenticeship. In my mind, I was writing, preparing." In her *CANR* interview she remarked, "I think there's a certain process that has to be gone through, and it doesn't matter when you start it. I know that there are people like John Updike, who published his first novel at age twenty-eight. But it's hard for me to believe that most people have lived long enough and garnered enough experience and have known what to do with that experience. You have a lot more to write about when you get to age forty."

Guest gained experience writing for newspapers when the family moved to Illinois, but disliked the constraints of journalism. "I learned about the discipline of writing—having to meet a deadline and having to conform a piece of writing to the limits of a certain space," Guest commented in *CANR*. "And I also learned that I don't like to do either one of those things!" A writing seminar encouraged her to start taking her fiction seriously. She decided to expand one of her early short stories because she remained interested in the characters and desired to complete a larger project. "I pretty much made a decision that I was going to finish a novel, and then get some outside opinions as to whether or not it was interesting to anyone other than myself," she commented in *CANR*. The finished product became *Ordinary People*—a moving novel about how a teenage boy and his family respond after he attempts suicide.

Guest sent the manuscript to Viking Press without the customary letter of introduction or outline. Beating considerable odds, the manuscript was rescued from the glut of uninvited manuscripts known as the "slush pile" to become the first unsolicited book published by Viking in twenty-seven years. In an article by Andrea Wojack of the *Detroit News*, Guest described her visit to Viking after the book was accepted: "When I walked into the office of Mimi Jones, my editor, I saw a few books stacked in the corner. I asked if that was the famous slush pile. Mimi shook her head and opened a nearby door. There it was, just stacks and stacks and piles of envelopes, boxes, all sizes and shapes imaginable! ... I probably would have thought twice about sending mine in if I had known what all I had to compete with."

In choosing to write about an average suburban family, Guest opposed the idea that a book should focus on unusual or extraordinary characters or settings. "I always grew up with the feeling that a majority of the people in the world were like me and the people I know," she remarked in *Family*

Circle. "And so, maybe at the beginning of my writing career, I thought, 'This old stuff. Nobody wants to read about this.'" She came to the conclusion, though, that people do enjoy reading about characters like themselves. Prior to publication, Viking expressed reservations about the book's title. Guest tenaciously defended her original choice in letters to her editor and the publisher—remarks which were later quoted in *Publishers Weekly*. "It says exactly what I want to say about these people. It is not meant ironically at all; these are ordinary people to whom something extraordinary happened—as it does to people every day."

Ordinary People relates the ordeal of the Jarrett family after seventeen-year-old Conrad attempts suicide. Plagued by guilt for surviving a boating accident which took his brother's life a year earlier, Conrad had become crippled by depression and anxiety. Opening with Conrad's return from an eight-month stay in a mental hospital, the book goes on to chronicle Conrad's counseling sessions with his warmhearted psychiatrist and his gradual progression toward health. Meanwhile, Conrad's desperate act forces his father to recognize the absence of communication in the family and the severity of his son's depression. Conrad's mother Beth, by contrast, seems angry with her son, perhaps viewing his suicide attempt as an effort to make her miserable. Beth's aloof character remains mysterious and incomprehensible to many. Dorothea D. Braginsky, for example, wrote in *Psychology Today* that Beth's views are "barely articulated.... Guest has given her no voice, no platform for expression. We never discover what conflicts, fears, and aspirations exist behind her cool, controlled facade." Her inability to openly share in her husband's grief and concern—and her refusal to admit that their lives are not entirely under control—leads to the breakup of the Jarretts' marriage. "Failure is finally what *Ordinary People* is about," asserted Melvin Maddocks in *Time*. "It may be Guest's ultimate irony that the older brother's drowning and Conrad's attempted suicide are only symbols for spiritual death—for a thousand subtle methods of neglect and undernourishment by means of which loved ones kill and are killed within the family circle." In spite of this, the book's ending has a positive side because Conrad comes to understand and forgive himself and his mother.

New York Review of Books contributor Michael Wood deemed the conclusion improbable. "Here the family is broken up, but everyone is on the way to emotional health, because they have understood

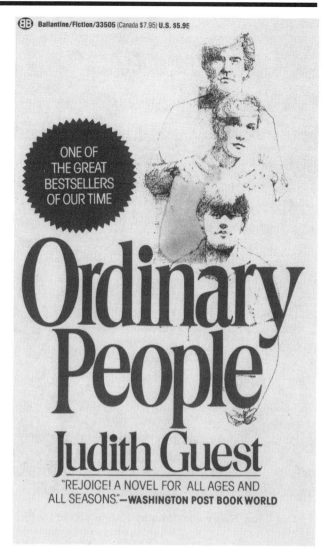

Guest's 1976 novel about a dysfunctional family was chosen one of the New York Public Library's Books for the Teen Age.

their weaknesses," the critic remarked. "But then the whole novel is subtly implausible in this sense, not because one doesn't believe in the characters or in Conrad's recovery, but because problems just pop up, get neatly formulated, and vanish.... 'I think I just figured something out,' Conrad says to his psychiatrist, and he has. It's a milestone on the road to reason."

Many critics found much to praise in the novel. Lore Dickstein commended Guest in the *New York Times Book Review* for her "passionate honesty and sensitivity." Other critics appreciated Guest's restraint. Considering the book's somber subject, Sandra Salmans remarked in the *Times Literary Supplement* that the novel "could easily turn maudlin, and Judith Guest is to be congratulated for avoiding that trap." Reviewers' most glowing

Mary Tyler Moore and Timothy Hutton played mother and son in the acclaimed film adaptation of *Ordinary People*.

remarks, though, concerned Conrad. Many considered him a most attractive and credible character. Salmans called him "unusually likeable," and Dickstein asserted, "Guest portrays Conrad not only as if she has lived with him on a daily basis—which I sense may be true—but as if she had gotten into his head. The dialogue Conrad has with himself, his psychiatrist, his friends, his family all rings true with adolescent anxiety."

Guest views writing as a process of discovery and means to explore problems. "I write because I have to," she told *English Journal*. "I'm not really sure why I have to. I have a quotation by Herbert Gold on my wall. He said, 'I write to master my experience,' and I thought, 'Yes, right on, Herbert!' and I do think that's part of it. I think that it's a feeling of 'I'm going to set up this situation and I'm going to make it turn out the way I want it to turn out in real life.' Although, to tell you the truth, I really don't write much about actual experiences. *Ordinary People*, for example, is not based on any experience I had or anyone that I

know had. It's just a fiction. It's really a vehicle for all the feeling that I was trying to work out, and it's a vehicle of craft. You set up the situation, then you can fool around, and ideally I would like to just work on the feelings and not have this plot."

In *Ordinary People* Guest's main interests were communication and depression. Guest herself has suffered from depression and following *Ordinary People* she sought psychological help. "In my own life, therapy's been *really* important," she told Bruce Cook in *Chicago Tribune Magazine*. "I had some *tough* sessions after 'Ordinary People'—after all that happened to me. It helped me out of that state I got into. The way I feel about therapy is that all of us are working with inadequate tools to help ourselves. So it's great to be able to go to someone and get the right tools to help. That's what a therapist does. In my case, he showed me how I was working against myself."

Guest had to adjust to the pressures of fame as a result of the phenomenal success of *Ordinary People*. A private person, she finds interviews draining and intrusive, and she is uncomfortable with the notion of celebrity. "I don't see myself as a celebrity, and I feel very annoyed and irritated and put-upon when people try to put me into that category," she commented in *CANR* in 1985. "My youngest son was telling me that when he applied to the school he'll be attending next year, the guy who processed his form and interviewed him said, 'I hear you're Judith Guest's son. That must make life pretty exciting for you.' I said to my son, 'How did you feel when he said that?' He said, 'Well, I didn't know what to say, because I never think of you that way.' Well, I never know what to say, because I never think of me that way either, and every once in a while it brings you up short when somebody tells you that. So I think basically it's a phenomenon of my life that I have dealt with as little as possible. And whenever I deal with it, I get very uncomfortable and don't know how to react."

She did, however, enjoy collaborating on a film version of *Ordinary People* with actor and director Robert Redford, even though the project thrust her further into the limelight. "I was advised by a lot of writer friends to stay as far away from the project as I could," Guest told Blades in the *Detroit News*. "They said, 'It'll just break your heart—take the money and run.' But I like to experience things first hand, and I figured the first time I got burned I'd back away." Redford chose *Ordinary People* for his first film directing venture. He sent Guest a note complimenting the book and requested her input in making a feature film. "I received the letter and was absolutely thrilled with his comments. Naturally, I told my friends and family about it. My mother wanted to know if the letter was for real," Guest was quoted by Wojack in the *Detroit News*. "Anyway, when we visited Viking recently, one of the editors there told me Robert Redford had come into the office in person to comment on the book and asked 'Do you think it would be gauche to send her a note?' Gauche! Can you imagine?" In the *Los Angeles Times* she described her part in the filming process. "Bob kept me very involved all the way through the movie. I saw all the drafts of the script and was invited to make any comments on the script that I wanted to. And I did, and most of the comments that I made, he and Alvin (Sargent, the screenplay writer) worked with and used."

Guest, in turn, appreciated Redford's suggestions. In a *Redbook* article she cited an instance where Redford asked for a scene showing Beth attempting to connect with her son, and being rejected by him. "After Bob read my third try he said, 'You

know, you love this kid too much. You won't let him do anything stupid. And you *have* to, because that's what will make him human. Now go back and let him do something really dumb—let someone else win, for a change.' Wasn't that sharp."

She was also very pleased with Mary Tyler Moore's portrayal of Beth Jarrett. "She just knocks me out. She's a terrific actress, a very complex person, and she brought a complexity to the character that I wish I'd gotten into the book," Guest told Blades in the *Detroit News*. "I fought with that character for a long time, trying to get her to reveal herself, and I finally said this is the best I can do. When I saw Mary in the movie, I felt like she'd done it for me."

Ordinary People appeared in movie theaters in September, 1980, and won the Academy Award for best film of that year. Asked for her opinion of the film, Guest continued in the *Detroit News* article, "I . . . think it's a damned good movie. I've seen it three times now, and I intend to see it 300. I expect to see it upside down. Then maybe I'll

SIGNET · 451-AE2499 · (CANADA $4.95) · U.S. $3.95

NATIONWIDE BESTSELLER!
FROM THE AUTHOR OF
ORDINARY PEOPLE

JUDITH GUEST
SECOND HEAVEN

A POWERFUL, DEEPLY INVOLVING NOVEL ABOUT THREE PEOPLE WHO DISCOVER LOVE'S POWER TO HEAL..."GREAT TENDERNESS AND INSIGHT... A SUSPENSEFUL CLIMAX."
—THE NEW YORK TIMES

The personal crises faced by a sensitive teenage boy are at the center of Guest's 1982 novel.

A quiet town is caught up in the circumstances surrounding a young girl's violent death.

watch it under water. I can't imagine that I'll ever get tired of watching it."

The enormous success of her first novel made writing the second a daunting undertaking, as she related in *CANR:* "It's so tenuous, so scary, right at the beginning, that you have a lot of trouble getting yourself to go in the room and start. You think, God, what if you don't like it? There you are with no idea again.... You look for any excuse you can to avoid doing it." Eventually she overcame her fear and completed *Second Heaven*, which was published in 1982. As in *Ordinary People*, the novel focuses on a teenage boy confronting serious problems. In this case, Gale Murray adopts an apathetic manner to hide the pain inflicted by his abusive, self-righteously religious father. After a brutal beating, Gale leaves home and finds shelter with the newly divorced Catherine (Cat) Holzman.

Gale enlists the aid of her divorce lawyer Michael Atwood, who is himself divorced. He accepts Gale's case partly as a favor to Cat. In surmounting their own problems in order to help Gale, Cat and Mike begin to fall in love.

The subject of religion, particularly the harmful fanaticism of Gale's father, pervades the novel. "I'm curious to know why some people who see themselves as religious people are really at bottom very self-righteous, intolerant people," Guest explained in *Family Circle*. "In some ways, this book is about my feeling of organized religion versus your own personal religion—about people forcing truths on you that you really have to learn for yourself."

Before actually writing *Second Heaven*, Guest visited a juvenile detention center and discussed child abuse with a family court judge. According to Peter S. Prescott in *Newsweek*, her research paid off. "Guest has done her homework and got the legal aspects of the problem right. More important, she understands precisely the victim's psychology," asserted Prescott. Once again, Guest won lavish praise for her main character. In a review of *Second Heaven* in the *Detroit News*, Anne Tyler wrote: "Gale is one of the most believable adolescents in recent fiction—surly, touching, tough, desperate to make some sense of his life, but so guarded that if you ask politely what classes he's taking, he manages to imply that 'this was not information you simply give away to strangers on the street.'" Tyler continued, "There are elements in his characterization that are positively brilliant—little quirks that first surprise us and then, on second thought, seem absolutely right." Similarly, *Chicago Tribune Magazine* contributor Cook declared that the "characters are so true to life that at times they seem to jump right up from the page."

Washington Post critic Jonathan Yardley considered the novel very similar to *Ordinary People*, but somewhat more artificial than that novel. Yardley decided that "neither contrivance nor familiarity can disguise the skill and most particularly the sensitivity with which Guest tells her story.... She is an extraordinarily perceptive observer of the minutiae of domestic life, and she writes about them with humor and affection."

In her next book, *Killing Time in St. Cloud*, which she coauthored with Rebecca Hill, Guest began to focus more closely on adult characters. Michael Dorris commented in *Tribune Books* that the novel "represents a true blend of skills and voices; a product of subtle, generous effort, it is a departure from any of Guest or Hill's previous work." *Killing Time in St. Cloud* is a suspenseful murder mystery set in a small town in Minnesota. When young Molly is killed, the townspeople assume that a local n'er-do-well, Nick Uhler, had a hand in the crime until he, too, turns up dead. Eventually Molly's uncle Simon, a highly respected physician, is revealed to be the culprit for Molly's death as well as a host of other unsavory events. Critics deemed the plot exciting and Simon a chilling villain. Reviewers also praised the authors' deft delineation of the intolerance and lack of privacy that are aspects of small-town life. In his review, Dorris called the book "a first-rate, beautifully written novel." Dorris continued, "The authors have forged a believable, gritty sense of place."

Guest drew on her own familiarity with suburban and small-town existence in order to capture the flavor and implications of life in St. Cloud. But much of her writing is inspired by her imagination, rather than personal experience. She discussed the subject at a writers conference in 1982, and her words were later released as part of the University of Missouri's "New Letters on the Air." "I think probably the question that I've been asked about most ... is whether or not I write from personal experience," Guest began. "I always say no, but of course that's a lie, because what else do you have to write from other than personal experience? But I think what I mean by that is that the people and the situations in my novels are not real people or real situations that I've experienced. What is real are the feelings that I am trying to explore; the emotional content of my work is my own. And the plot situations and the characters are vehicles to carry and work out these emotional things that I'm exploring."

In a similar vein, she was quoted by Hilary Devries in the *Houston Post:* "Society teaches people and especially men to 'be afraid of their feelings.' There is no substitute for 'self-knowledge. You have to keep looking inside yourself for answers. You just have to be brave and do it.'"

■ **Works Cited**

Blades, John, "The Writer Blessed from the Start," *Detroit News*, November 9, 1980.

Braginsky, Dorothea D., *Psychology Today*, August, 1976, p. 84.

Contemporary Authors New Revision Series, Volume 15, Gale, 1985.

Cook, Bruce, "No Ordinary Person," *Chicago Tribune Magazine*, October 17, 1982, p. 45.

Devries, Hilary, "No Ordinary Person," *Houston Post*, November 14, 1983, p. 6F.

Dickstein, Lore, review of *Ordinary People* in *New York Times Book Review*, July 18, 1976, p. 14, 18.

Dorris, Michael, "Dazed by School," *Tribune Books*, November 20, 1988, p. 5.

Farley, Ellen, "Cinderella Novelist: Tears of Joy," *Los Angeles Times*, September 21, 1980, p. 32.

Guest, Judith, *Judith Guest: Second Heaven*, New Letters, 1984.

Hirshey, Gerri, "A Visit with the Novelist Next Door," *Family Circle*, September 16, 1982, pp. 4, 24.

Holliday, Barbara, *Detroit Free Press*, October 7, 1982.

Janeczko, Paul, "An Interview with Judith Guest," *English Journal*, March, 1978, p. 18-19.

Jones, Mimi, "Ordinary People—the Redford Way!," *Redbook*, November, 1980, p. 136, 188, 190, 192.

Kleiman, Carol, "A Child of Suburbia," *Houston Post*, October 13, 1977, p. 2BB.

Maddocks, Melvin, "Suburban Furies," *Time*, July 19, 1976, pp. 68-69.

Prescott, Peter S., "Unsweet Sixteen," *Newsweek*, October 4, 1982, p. 73.

Salmans, Sandra, "Going Straight," *Times Literary Supplement*, February 4, 1977, p. 121.

"Story behind the Book: 'Ordinary People,'" *Publishers Weekly*, April 19, 1976, p. 44.

Tyler, Anne, "Bad News, Good News," *Detroit News*, September 26, 1982.

Wojack, Andrea, "Ed Guest's Kin Writes a Hit Novel," *Detroit News*, August 17, 1976, p. 7H.

Wood, Michael, "Crying for Attention," *New York Review of Books*, June 10, 1976, p. 8.

Yardley, Jonathan, "Heaven and Earth: Judith Guest's Encore to 'Ordinary People,'" *Washington Post*, September 22, 1982, pp. B1, B15.

■ **For More Information See**

BOOKS

Contemporary Literary Criticism, Gale, Volume 8, 1978, Volume 30, 1984.

PERIODICALS

Chicago Tribune, November 4, 1980.

Christian Science Monitor, November 6, 1982.

English Journal, March, 1978.

Family Circle, September 6, 1982.

Los Angeles Times Book Review, October 30, 1982.

Ms., December, 1982.

New Statesman, February 4, 1977.

Newsweek, July 12, 1976.

New York Times, October 22, 1982.

New York Times Book Review, October 3, 1982; October 25, 1982.

Village Voice, July 19, 1976.°

Jamake Highwater

■ Personal

Full name is Jamake Mamake Highwater; given name is pronounced "Ja-*mah*-ka"; actual birthdate and location unknown, though many sources say February 14, 1942(?), in Montana; son of Jamie (a rodeo clown and movie stuntman) and Amana (Bonneville) Highwater; adopted at or about age of seven by Alexander and Marcia Marks. *Education:* Attended a community college and a university in California.

■ Addresses

Office—Native Lands Foundation, Little River Farm, Rt. 97, Hampton, CT 06247. *Agent*—Alfred Hart, Fox Chase Agency, Ledger Bldg., Philadelphia, PA.

■ Career

Writer. Choreographer in San Francisco, CA, beginning in 1954; Contemporary Center, San Francisco, founder of modern dance troupe, 1950s and 1960s; lecturer at various universities in United States and Canada, 1970s; senior editor, Fodor's travel guides, 1971-75; New York University, New York City, graduate lecturer at School of Continuing Education, 1982; Columbia University, Graduate School of Architecture, New York City, adjunct assistant professor, 1984, visiting scholar, 1985. Host of television shows for Public Broadcasting Service (PBS), 1977, *Indian America* for WHET-TV, New York City, 1982, and of the documentaries *The Primal Mind*, PBS, 1985, and *Native Land*, PBS, 1986; guest on television shows, including *Six Great Ideas* and *Red, White, and Black: Ethnic Dance in America*, both for PBS, 1982. Co-moderator and organizer of "Indian America: Past, Present and Future," Aspen Institute's art festivals and seminars, 1982-83; general director of Native Arts Festival, Rice University, 1986; general director of "Festival Mythos: A Celebration of Multicultural Mythologies in the Arts," Philadelphia, 1991. Member of President Carter's art task force, Commission on Mental Health, 1977-78; member of task force on the individual artist, New York State Arts Council, 1981-82; founding president of Native Lands Foundation; founding member and past president of American Indian Community House, New York City; member of National Support Committee of the Native American Rights Fund; nominator for awards in the visual arts for the Rockefeller Foundation and the National Endowment for the Humanities. *Member:* PEN American Center (executive board, 1984-86), American Federation of Television and Radio Artists, Authors Guild, Dramatists Guild, Business Music, Inc.

■ Awards, Honors

Honorary Citizen of Oklahoma, 1977; Newbery Honor Award, 1978, Boston Globe/Horn Book Award, and Best Book for Young Adults award from American Library Association, 1978, all for *Anpao: An American Indian Odyssey;* named "Eagle Son" by Blood Band of Blackfeet Nation of Alberta, Canada, 1979, for achievements on behalf of Indian culture; Jane Addams Peace Award, 1979, for *Many Smokes, Many Moons;* Best Book for Young Adults award from *School Library Journal,* 1980, for *The Sun, He Dies;* Anisfield-Wolf Award from the Cleveland Foundation, 1981, and citation as one of three hundred books chosen by the American Publishers Association to represent America at the Moscow International Book Fair, both for *Song from the Earth;* Virginia McCormick Scully Literary Award, 1982, for *The Primal Mind;* Notable Children's Book award, Best Books for Young Adults award from American Library Association, and citation as one of the best books of 1984 from *School Library Journal,* all 1984, all for *Legend Days;* honorary doctor of fine arts, Minneapolis College of Art and Design, 1986; Best Book for Young Adults award from American Library Association, 1986, for *Legend Days* and *The Ceremony of Innocence;* best film of the year, National Educational Film Festival, 1986, and ACE Award, National Cable Television Association, 1990, both for *The Primal Mind.*

■ Writings

(Under pseudonym J Marks) *Rock and Other Four Letter Words: Music of the Electric Generation,* Bantam, 1968.
(Editor under name J Marks-Highwater, with Eugene Fodor) *Europe under Twenty-Five: A Young Person's Guide,* Fodor's, 1971.
(Under pseudonym J Marks) *Mick Jagger: The Singer Not the Song,* Curtis Books, 1973, published under name J Marks-Highwater as *Mick Jagger,* Popular Library, 1974.
Fodor's Indian America, McKay, 1975.
Song from the Earth: American Indian Painting (Literary Book Club Selection), Little, Brown, 1976.
Ritual of the Wind: North American Indian Ceremonies, Music, and Dances, Viking, 1977.
Anpao: An American Indian Odyssey, Lippincott, 1977.
Journey to the Sky: A Novel about the True Adventures of Two Men in Search of the Lost Maya Kingdom, Crowell, 1978.

Many Smokes, Many Moons: A Chronology of American Indian History through Indian Art, Lippincott, 1978.
Dance: Rituals of Experience, A & W Publishers, 1978.
Masterpieces of American Indian Painting, two folios, limited and signed edition, Folio/Bell Editions, 1979-83.
The Sun, He Dies: A Novel about the End of the Aztec World, Lippincott, 1980.
The Sweet Grass Lives On: Fifty Contemporary North American Indian Artists, Harper, 1981.
The Primal Mind: Vision and Reality in Indian America (also see below), Harper, 1981.
Moonsong Lullaby (poems), Morrow, 1981.
Eyes of Darkness (novel), Morrow, 1983.
Leaves from the Sacred Tree: Arts of the Indian Americas, Harper, 1983.
Words in the Blood: Contemporary Indian Writers of North and South America, Meridian, 1984.
Legend Days (first book of "Ghost Horse" cycle), Harper, 1984.
The Ceremony of Innocence (second book of "Ghost Horse" cycle), Harper, 1984.
The Primal Mind (television script; broadcast by PBS, 1985), Cinema Guild, 1985.
I Wear the Morning Star (third book of "Ghost Horse" cycle), Harper, 1986.
Native Land: Nomads of the Dawn (television script; also see below; broadcast by PBS, 1986), Cinema Guild, 1986.
Native Land: Sagas of American Civilizations (based on PBS program), Little, Brown, 1986.
Shadow Show: An Autobiographical Insinuation, Alfred Van der Marck, 1986.
Myth and Sexuality, New American Library, 1990.
Songs for the Seasons (poems), Morrow, 1991.
The World of 1492: "The Americas," Holt, in press.
Kill Hole (fourth book of "Ghost Horse" cycle), Harper, in press.

AUTHOR OF INTRODUCTION

Bear's Heart, Lippincott, 1976.
Charles Eastman, *Indian Boyhood,* Rio Grande Press, 1976.
One Hundred Years of American Indian Painting, Oklahoma Museum of Art, 1977.
Master Pueblo Potters, ACA Galleries, 1980.

OTHER

Music critic and contributor to *New Grove Dictionary of American Music.* Contributor of articles and critiques to literary journals, including *New York Times, Chicago Tribune, Archaeology, Commonweal, Esquire, Dance Magazine, Saturday Review,* and *American Book Review*. Contributing editor, *Stereo Review*, 1972-79, *Indian Trader*, 1977-80, *New York Arts Journal*, 1978-86, and *Native Arts/West*, 1980-81; classical music editor, *Soho Weekly News*, 1975-79, and *Christian Science Monitor*.

■ Adaptations

Anpao: An American Indian Odyssey was adapted into a sound recording, Folkways Records, 1978.

■ Work in Progress

Athletes of the Gods: The Ritual Life of Sport; I Took the Fire: A Memoir; The Magi's Ring, a novel.

■ Sidelights

Jamake Highwater is a leading commentator on American Indian culture. A descendent of Blackfeet and Cherokee Indians, Highwater is widely regarded as a masterful storyteller who uses books to relate tales that for centuries have been told through the spoken word. Though his writings hold appeal for all age groups, he has been especially popular among young adults. "I value young readers," Highwater wrote in *Contemporary Authors Autobiography Series (CAAS)*. "But I cherish them as readers and not as children, because I strongly reject the notion that writers create good books for specific, 'target audiences.'" Highwater's approach has won him a broad readership and several literary awards, including the prestigious Newbery Honor Award, which he received in 1978 for his first novel, *Anpao: An American Indian Odyssey*. In addition to *Anpao*, Highwater has written several other novels and nonfiction works on Indian life, art, dance, and history.

Highwater's success as an adult came after experiencing a troubled childhood. Because his natural parents were too poor and unstable to care for him, Highwater was placed in an orphanage while they were still alive. When he was adopted by Alexander and Marcia Marks, a California Anglo family, they insisted on keeping secret many of the details of his early life. Carl R. Shirley quoted Highwater in *Dictionary of Literary Biography Yearbook: 1985*: "I was adopted between the age of six and ten when adoption was a highly secretive matter— to such an extent that the state in which I was adopted permanently sealed all records of my birth and adoption. I have no original birth certificate. Since my adoption as a child I was put in the position of keeping my origins secret at my foster

family's insistence. It is often difficult to know the difference between what I personally remember and what I was told." According to his autobiographical portion in *Children's Literature Review*, Highwater knows only that he "was born in the early forties and was raised in northern Montana and southern Alberta, Canada."

Though he does not know the exact date and place of his birth, Highwater is certain that his natural mother and father had strong ties to the Indian community. His mother, for instance, had mixed blood but was most influenced by the Blackfeet tribe. In *CAAS*, Highwater noted the impact his mother had on his life and work. "Despite her complex blend of French Canadian and Blackfeet (Blood) ancestry, the woman who raised me retained much of the special mentality of her tribal background. She taught me something of the language and customs of both her French and Blackfeet parents. And she placed in my heart the fragile faith in the world that has informed my entire life. She was a marvelous storyteller; and it was undoubtedly from her that I attained my gifts of the imagination.... From her I learned to stay alive by dreaming myself into existence—no matter how many persons attempted to negate or to repudiate my sense of identity and pride. From her I learned that *everything* is real. And that single idea has been the most important lesson in my life as a creative artist and as an individual."

Highwater's mother also had a tough life. Both of her parents starved to death during the Depression, and life with her husband was economically and emotionally difficult. Highwater's father was a rodeo clown and a Hollywood stuntman who had a drinking problem and spent much of his time on the road. Despite an unreliable husband and financial hardship, Highwater's mother still managed to give her son positive values. "She gave me a rare and splendid freedom which allowed me to discover myself," he proclaimed in *CAAS*. "I remember little else about her, but I do vividly recall the warmth of her encouragement and approval. I doubt that I could have survived without the memory of her love."

Highwater's memories of his father are less fond. He recalls feeling a great deal of bitterness toward him for not keeping the family together. His resentment reached a peak when his father visited him at the orphanage to tell him that a friend of his would take care of him. "As he spoke," Highwater wrote in *CAAS*, "it gradually occurred to me that my own father was giving me away to another man. I hated him for doing that to me. I angrily turned

ANPAO

Highwater's story of an Indian boy's emergence into adulthood was a Newbery Honor Book in 1978.

from him and then I wept. He pleaded with me not to hate him. But I did hate him. But I also wanted him to love me and to take me home with him. When I turned to embrace him and beg him not to abandon me, he was already gone. I never saw my father again." Shortly thereafter Highwater's father died in a traffic accident while intoxicated.

With the passage of years, however, Highwater has come to an understanding and appreciation of his father's life. In a 1978 interview with Jane B. Katz published in *This Song Remembers: Self-Portraits of Native Americans in the Arts*, Highwater reflected on the positive and negative aspects of his father. "My father was a ... member of the American Indian Rodeo Association. He was a very good rider. He was also an alcoholic who often fell off his horse. He got a reputation for being very funny, so he became a rodeo clown. My father was a handsome, brave and wise man, without any education in the traditional Western sense.... But in some strange way he was poisoned with a deep sense of rage about his situation and blamed most of his failures on the fact that he wasn't given chances." Although he understands his father's

frustrations of being an Indian in twentieth-century America, Highwater still feels anger well up inside him when he sees him in old movies on late-night television. "For a moment, that ghostly shadow on the screen evokes a terrible bitterness in me," he observed in *CAAS*. "Then he is gone. And once again I am abandoned in the dark."

Life changed drastically when Highwater moved in with his foster family in San Fernando Valley, California. The Marks told him that there would be no discussion of his life before adoption. To make matters worse, his foster parents did not get along with his mother and father, so visiting them was only possible if done secretly. His new house was comfortable, but he was made to feel like a stranger in it and was never given a key. After school he would have to wait outside until his foster parents came home. He also had to adjust to a name change. "While most children found comfort and a sense of belonging in their family names, I was haunted by the falseness of mine," he recalled in *CAAS*. "Names became a problem. I was supposed to call my foster parents 'Mother' and 'Father,' but I always insisted upon calling them Marcia and Al, despite their disapproval. I myself was variously called 'J,' 'Jake,' 'Jack,' 'Corky,' and 'John' during these formative years."

Perhaps one of the biggest adjustments Highwater faced was getting used to being around white people at home and at school. The change was not easy, and soon Highwater developed a reputation for starting fights with white children. In a *Publishers Weekly* interview, Highwater told Sarah Crichton that he was "a real lousy kid—aggressive, with lots of negative energy, really killer energy and hostility toward non-Indians. White kids would call us names, and for a long time I guess I took it—I don't really remember that part. Finally, I got to be a real ringleader, and we'd beat the hell out of any kids who did that to us."

Life with his foster family was not all bad. At least Highwater could now count on receiving the basics of life, including food, shelter, clothing, and education. He also had new siblings, and the youngest daughter became his close friend. They shared a love of music, dance, and books. She had a wonderful sense of humor and would do all sorts of things to make them laugh. In his *CAAS* entry Highwater described the significance of his relationship with her. "For many years this youngest of my sisters was the single most important person in my life. My love for her and my need for her were so massive that they were painful. Then, one day, not very long after I had become her brother, she went away. Her marriage and departure from our home devastated me. I took my resentment out on everyone.... Today I can joke about the old breach between us, but at the time it seemed like ultimate abandonment. Even during that debacle, I doggedly persisted in my affection for my sister. She was the only person whose approval I sought. It took me years to recognize that as a child without a history or life of my own, I had wanted to live out my existence through my sister's life."

In addition to his sister, Highwater had two other early positive influences. The first were the Dorrs, neighbors who gave Highwater a key to their house so he could come in when he was locked out of his foster family's house. While there Highwater would listen to classical music, read novels, and dance around the living room. He would also go there on Sunday mornings to listen to gospel music on the radio. The other positive influence was a teacher named Alta Black, who helped him through his troubles at school. "I was not liked, and so I took no delight in living," Highwater recollected in CAAS. "I didn't have a single friend or a moment of happiness in school, until a social studies teacher, named Alta Black, made me feel as if she cared about me. Once I felt her approval, I did anything to keep her good opinion of me. And the effort to please her gave me the motivation to become one of the most accomplished students in school.... And it was also Alta Black who gave me an old Royal portable typewriter and an instruction book, telling me that one night she had dreamed that I was going to be a writer."

Highwater has maintained his close association with his sister, the Dorrs, and Alta Black throughout his life. In fact, he spoke with Black when she was in her nineties, just before she died. He recounted the conversation in CAAS: "'All my life,' she murmured sadly, 'I thought that we would win and that cruelty and greed and prejudice would disappear. I thought that the voices of the great prophets would finally be heard. But now, I am not so sure. Now I suspect that the world is dying with me.' 'As long as I am alive,' I promised her, 'you too will live. And as long as my books survive, you will survive with them. That I swear. I will breathe life into you with every word I write.'"

During junior high and high school Alta Black continued to help Highwater with his schoolwork. After graduating he wanted to go on to college, but financing his education was a problem. During the 1950s there were few scholarships available and no guaranteed student loans. At first he attended a small, affordable community college, but he left when he realized he was not being challenged intellectually. Next he tried a major state university that required Reserve Officers Training Corps (ROTC) training, but this arrangement soon ended after Highwater decided he "absolutely could not endure this bristling, militant, and macho bullshit that was supposed to make a man out of me," he explained in CAAS. He further noted, "I did what I had to do, and eventually I managed to get the education I wanted. Under the circumstances, however, I always decline to make formal mention of my education in resumes and entries in various biographical directories. Even when I was appointed a lecturer at New York University and an [adjunct] assistant professor at Columbia University, I was hired without providing educational data."

In 1954, while finishing his schooling, Highwater moved to San Francisco and began a career in dance. This early career choice seemed natural because he enjoyed dancing in the Dorr's living room and because dance is an integral part of the Indian way of life. (Highwater even proclaimed to Katz, "All dancers are 'Indians.'") He worked as a dance instructor and later co-founded a dance troupe at a small local theater called the Contemporary Center. The troupe was only moderately successful in the Bay area, but they found more receptive audiences when they performed on the road.

As a citizen of San Francisco for more than a decade, Highwater was able to view the cultural revolution of the 1960s from the city on the cutting edge of change. Participants of the cultural revolution were typically young adults in their teens and twenties who rebelled against the conservative values of their parents. They antagonized the older generation by growing long hair, protesting against the Vietnam War, listening to rock music, and experimenting with sex and drugs. But they also had a positive impact by bringing attention to issues such as individual liberty, peace, and the environment. Highwater began his writing career during this period. "I witnessed the rise of a counter-culture in San Francisco which struck me as remarkably similar to Native American values in some of its viewpoints and visions," he recalled in Something about the Author (SATA). "The result of that encounter with the Hippie and Rock movement was a series of articles for various 'underground' newspapers which were being founded at the time, as well as two experimental books: Rock and Other Four Letter Words and Mick Jagger: The Singer Not the Song." These early books, both published under his adoptive name, J Marks, discuss the culture and music of the 1960s. Commenting on *Mick Jagger,* Alice K. Turner wrote in *Publishers Weekly* that it "is a book less about Jagger than about Jagger's vibes. Man, you're supposed to *know* something about Jagger before you read this book because if you don't you're *lost.*" David Jackson, however, claimed in *Village Voice* that *Mick Jagger* ranks "among the most perceptive and imaginative writing about '60s pop culture."

At the beginning of his writing career Highwater felt himself to be part of both the Indian and Anglo cultures. His Indian heritage, however, exerted a greater influence on him after 1969, the year Indians took over Alcatraz island and claimed ownership. He reflected on the impact of the incident in *SATA*: "With the Alcatraz takeover I was fired with a sense of visibility and courage as an Indian person. It was in 1969 that I began work on my first 'Indian' book which would bear my name, Jamake Highwater. It was called *Indian America: A Cultural and Travel Guide.*" Since 1969 Highwater has focused much of his writing on Indian ideas, some of which he explained to Crichton: "To the Indian mentality, dead people walk and things go backward and forward in time, and these are absolutely real and vivid ideas to my head. . . . And more than that, the Indian world is one of the few worlds where human identity is not a major issue. In this society, you're not permitted any kind of personal transformation. In ours, it is expected. We can even change gender if we want."

Between 1971 and 1975 Highwater worked as senior editor of Fodor Travel Guides, living in countries such as Turkey, Switzerland, Belgium, France, and Germany. "Fodor not only gave me my first chance to write about my own heritage, he also gave me the marvelous opportunity to see myself in relationship to the peoples of the whole world," Highwater said in *SATA*. "He appointed me editor and writer of a student guide to Europe which gave me virtually unlimited access to the entire world, all expenses paid!"

While living in Zurich, Switzerland, Highwater began his first novel, *Anpao: An American Indian Odyssey.* The inspiration came suddenly, and he completed the book in only six weeks. He sent the manuscript to an American publisher. In his *CAAS* sketch Highwater recounted his lunch with an editor from Lippincott. "I chatted nervously while awaiting coffee and dessert, when the editor would surely bring up the subject of my book. On cue, she said; 'About your remarkable novel . . .' *My*

remarkable novel! My little novelist's heart sang so loudly at those words that I couldn't hear what else she had to say . . . except the phrase 'ideal for the young-adult market.' How dare she! My novel! For kids! The fact of the matter is that *Anpao* was regarded as 'fantasy,' and in the mysterious world of American publishers, fantasy is usually kid stuff."

Anpao tells the story of an Indian boy's entrance into adulthood. At the beginning Anpao meets a beautiful girl named Ko-ko-mik-e-is who refuses all offers of marriage until she meets Anpao. She says she will marry him if he can get permission from the Sun. This prompts Anpao to begin his journey. He travels with his brother Oapna, who says everything in reverse. Oapna dies during their travels, but by the story's end Anpao sees that Oapna is actually the contrary side of his own personality. Anpao gains experience and wisdom as he travels the earth and encounters a variety of creatures, eventually obtaining permission from the Sun to marry Ko-ko-mik-e-is. Highwater says at the end of the book in "The Storyteller's Farewell" that the novel is a combination of old and new Indian legends. "But old or new, the stories have no known authors. They exist as the river of memory of a people, surging with their images and their rich meanings from one place to another, from one generation to the next—the tellers and the told so intermingled in time and space that no one can separate them."

Anpao was a literary success, winning the Newbery Honor Award in 1978. Although critical response to *Anpao* was largely favorable, Jane Yolen claimed in the *New York Times Book Review* that the book read more like a series of Indian tales rather than as a coherent novel. Still, Yolen affirmed: "I applaud Highwater's effort. His retelling of the tales is fluid and in many instances compelling. The book cries to be read aloud." In addition, *Washington Post Book World* contributor Virginia Haviland praised "the author's gift for using the poetic, dignified language required of tellers of great epics." Haviland concluded that the novel is an "enduring book" that holds appeal for all age groups. Shirley expressed a similar sentiment: "The fact that *Anpao* [was a Newbery Honor Book] and thus has frequently been characterized as a children's work has probably prevented many adults from savoring the richness of its language and the magic of its story. It is a fine novel that can be enjoyed by all readers."

Highwater's writing career blossomed in the 1970s after finishing his European travels and settling in

New York City. Though he has had homes in Montana, Switzerland, and Turkey, Highwater spends a good deal of his time in Connecticut and New York. There he enjoys an accepting artistic community that encourages his creative abilities. In *CAAS*, Highwater recalled the pleasure he experienced when he first came to New York. "In New York I discovered something utterly remarkable. I was no longer perceived as an eccentric. My gifts, that had always been regarded as risky or useless, suddenly became assets in New York. I was no longer isolated. Instead, I found myself in the company of novices as well as renowned people in the arts. When I spoke about my ideas, these artists fully understood what I was trying to say. It was the most liberating encounter with people, almost as if I had finally discovered a world in which everyone was an Alta Black or a Virginia Dorr. Now I could make art the central belief of my life without being told that art is just an elaborate fiction."

During the 1970s Highwater began writing extensively on Indian history and art. Some of the nonfiction books he produced include *Song from the Earth: American Indian Painting,* which traces the increasing interest in Indian art from the nineteenth century to the 1960s and features interviews with nine contemporary Indian artists; *Ritual of the Wind: North American Indian Ceremonies, Music, and Dances,* which contains Highwater's descriptions of Indian rituals; and *Many Smokes, Many Moons: A Chronology of American Indian History through Indian Art,* a book that focuses on Indian art from 3,500 B.C. to modern day and details some of the destructive effects whites have had on Indians over the centuries. In his interview with Katz, Highwater reflected on the close connection between Indians and art. "For the Indian, art is not reserved for a leisure class, as it is in Anglo society. It is part of our fundamental way of thinking. We are an aesthetic people. Most primal people are. We represent a constant chord that's been resounding ever since man began. . . . This idea of life as art is part of being Indian. It's not quaint or curious or charming. It's fundamental, like plowing a field. There's great beauty in plowing a field."

Writing about the Indian way of life has been a dream come true for Highwater. In 1978 he told Crichton, "For so long there was no expressive outlet, no recognition. Now people are saying, 'Wow, we want a book from you; we want this, we want that!' It's marvelous. It's super. I can finally write what I want to write about: Native America.

Because, this is really what I know about; this is what I feel; this is what I'm at home with; this is what I'm best at." In March of 1979 Highwater's contribution to Indian culture was recognized by the Blackfeet tribe when he was given a new Indian name. Shirley quoted Highwater's view of the ceremony: "It is a ceremony usually reserved for a *minipoka,* a 'favored child' of the Blackfeet Nation. My new name is Piitai Sahkomaapii, meaning 'Eagle Son.' This name-ceremony was the vindication of my mother's constant efforts to keep my heritage alive within me." Highwater has since called the ceremony one of the high points of his professional and personal life.

During the late 1970s Highwater also distinguished himself as a music and art critic. He published reviews in publications such as *Stereo Review, New York Arts Journal,* and *New Grove Dictionary of American Music.* In addition, he was founding editor of *Soho News,* serving as classical music editor from 1975 to 1979.

The historical perspective of Native American author Charles Alexander Eastman influenced Highwater's 1983 novel.

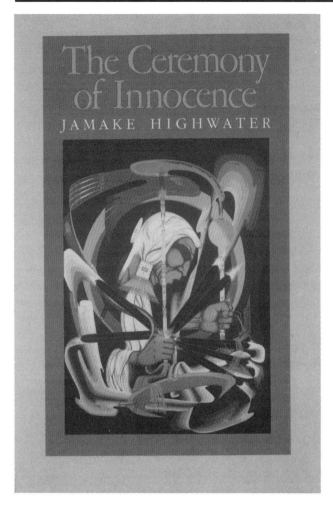

The second volume in Highwater's acclaimed "Ghost Horse" cycle.

In 1980 Highwater published *The Sun, He Dies: A Novel about the End of the Aztec World*, which some have called his best work. Before writing this historical novel, Highwater conducted extensive background research. The narrator of the story is Nanautzin, an Aztec Indian who becomes the spokesperson of Montezuma, the Aztec leader. Through Nanautzin the reader is able to gain insight into the development and destruction of the Aztecs, whose history covered more than two thousand years before Hernando Cortes destroyed it in six. Kurt Vonnegut, Jr., who is quoted by Shirley, called *The Sun, He Dies* a "historical novel of a very high order . . . a stunning revelation to all who have never before glimpsed the history of this hemisphere through a Native American's eyes." Not all reviews were favorable—some thought Nanautzin was not fully developed—yet John Adams commented that although the story is not new, "never has it been told with the eloquent, progressively angry Indian voice Highwater has created."

Highwater continued his prolific output during the 1980s, writing nonfiction works, novels, a book of poems entitled *Moonsong Lullaby,* and television scripts for the Public Broadcasting Service, including *The Primal Mind* and *Native Land.* One of the most notable works to come out of this period is the "Ghost Horse" cycle. This award-winning quartet of novels consists of *Legend Days,* 1984, *The Ceremony of Innocence,* 1984, *I Wear the Morning Star,* 1986, and *Kill Hole.*

The focus at the beginning of the "Ghost Horse" series is on Amana, who in the opening of *Legend Days* is an eleven-year-old Indian girl who loses her parents to a smallpox epidemic. At this young age Amana "becomes" a man; that is, she takes on the characteristics of a man. (Identity changes like this are accepted and even praised in Indian culture.) An inward spiritual guide, grandfather fox, teaches her the ways of the warrior with the condition that she keep her powers a secret and use them only when necessary. Amana also learns traditionally feminine roles—such as cooking and sewing—from her grandmothers and sister. Thus Amana experiences life as both a man and a woman, realizing as she grows up the vast differences between the two roles—she once exclaims, "How free men are!" Much of Amana's early life is dedicated to caring for her sister and her sister's husband, both of whom die before the end of *Legend Days.* The novel closes with Amana alone but reunited with the fox, her spiritual guide. "The book is written in powerful, rhythmic prose," affirmed Kate M. Flanagan in *Horn Book Magazine.* "Layered with symbolism and the supernatural, the story reveals the spiritual richness of the Indian people even as their culture hovered on the brink of annihilation."

In *The Ceremony of Innocence* Amana marries a French trader and gives birth to a daughter, Jemina, who lives and is educated in the Anglo world. Set in the first half of the twentieth century, this second novel in the "Ghost Horse" cycle depicts the disintegration of the Indian world. Reflecting on Jemina's immersion into white culture, Amana thinks her daughter "was born into a dead land. There is no center. The world in which we once lived and into which we brought our children is gone." Jemina later marries Jamie Ghost Horse, an Indian rodeo rider and stuntman, and together they have two sons. The younger, Sitko, shows a trace of Indian vision. At the end of the novel Amana places her hope for the future of Indians in Sitko. As with *Legend Days,* *The Ceremony of Innocence* was warmly received by critics, including Evie Wilson, who in *Voice of Youth Advocates* called the novel "a beautiful, moving rendering of the ties that bind us in our age to generations past and future."

Sitko pursues his vision in *I Wear the Morning Star*, but he encounters several obstacles: Jemina abandons him in a foster home and his brother Reno urges him to give up his Indian vision and learn to fit into the white world. At school, however, Sitko receives tremendous encouragement from a teacher named Mrs. Blake, who introduces him to art and literature. As Sitko is increasingly fascinated by these subjects, he is distanced from his family. Years pass and those close to Sitko die off, leaving him alone with his imagination. Though somewhat gloomy, *I Wear the Morning Star* was praised by critics. Hazel Rochman, for example, proclaimed in *Booklist* that the novel "powerfully dramatizes the modern Indian conflict about identity and acceptance."

The "Ghost Horse" cycle, which also includes *Kill Hole*, contains several autobiographical elements. Like Highwater, Sitko had a mother of French and Indian ancestry who married a rodeo clown and movie stuntman. Sitko's similarly unstable home life resulted in placement in a foster home, and he faced a constant struggle to maintain his Indian vision. There is also Mrs. Blake who, like Alta Black, inspired Sitko's interest in arts and letters.

Highwater's writings have been generally well received over the years, but like most authors, he has his critics. Criticisms have often centered on the Indian issue. Some have complained that he has exploited his heritage for profit, a few have challenged whether his ancestry is indeed Indian, and some reviewers charge that his condemnation of whites is too bitter. In *Interracial Books for Children Bulletin*, Doris Seale questioned Highwater's ability to capture authentic Indian sentiment: "The work of Jamake Highwater has always been something of a problem for me. With the exception of *Anpao*, ... none of his books 'feels' very Indian to me. For me, they lack some balance, a certain pattern of thought—something—that keeps them ... from delivering that instantaneous whap! that comes with the recognition of *kin*."

Many, however, find considerable merit in Highwater's works. Nellvena Duncan Eutsler averred in *Dictionary of Literary Biography, Volume 52: American Writers for Children since 1960* that "Jamake Highwater's metaphors are meaningful; his symbols are vivid; his imagery is awe-inspiring. Highwater creates for the reader an awareness of

In this 1986 continuation of the "Ghost Horse" cycle, young Sitka pursues his visions despite suffering personal setbacks.

the earth and its wonders." Shirley also holds a high opinion of Highwater, calling him "a storyteller whose tales of Native Americans are splendid stylistic re-creations of the oral literature of his ancestors. His novels ... stand as successful examples of modern efforts to capture the Indian legender's voice that has endured the centuries—the songs, the recitals of history, the tales and chants passed from storyteller to storyteller, from generation to generation."

One reason critics misunderstand his books, according to Highwater, is that they fail to appreciate the "multiversal" outlook that pervades his life and writings. Rather than being simply universal, Highwater sees himself as "multiversal" in that he accepts many different viewpoints, some of which may appear to contradict one another. Jackson explained Highwater's artistic perspective in *Village Voice:* "Since the late '60s, when Indians occupied Alcatraz and inspired many young Native

Jamake Highwater in 1988.

Americans to seek out their heritage, Highwater has been involved in an encyclopedic undertaking to interpret Native American and Mesoamerican history, and find a basic metaphor for the values lacking in much of Western civilization. The notion he has sought is the primal mind—analogous, in his writing, to 'Indian' and 'artist.' It is also analogous to 'multiverse,' the abiding principle of tribal people which makes them see both nature and society as places for absolutely everything and everybody." Highwater's view of reality is thus inclusive rather than exclusive: he attempts to include many different cultural perspectives in his work.

Highwater credits his Indian heritage for giving him his broad outlook. Indeed, as he told Katz, he takes very little personal credit for his success. "All I've done is carry out my instructions. All I really am is what I was made to be. The talent is in me—I don't know where it came from. When I write, I go away for hours at a time. I don't know where I've been or who does the writing. I have to give myself up to it entirely. I'm a technician. I use a typewriter. But I can't take credit for my work. In some way I feel I'm just a conduit."

Highwater told *AAYA*: "Because of the range of subject matter in my writing and because of my decade of concentration upon Native American studies, I suspect that readers often miss the driving force behind my work. From the beginning, I have been more interested in the subterranean streams that flow beneath the surface of things: dreams, intuition, the irrational, spiritual, and visionary impulses that stir our imaginations. I have focused upon the rituals and myths that make the ineffable momentarily visible in art and in religion. I have never been much concerned with the great currents of prosaic facts that some of us mistake for history. I have always preferred the night and the shadow side of existence, because I believe that the unknown is knowable and that the real effort of the artist is to describe the fragile place where the inner and outer worlds meet. My dear friend, the late Joseph Campbell, often complained that people confuse the meal with the menu and end up munching on cardboard. I have devoted my career to the meal, and I have left the menu to others."

■ Works Cited

Adams, John, review of *The Sun, He Dies* in *School Library Journal*, October, 1980, p. 167.

Children's Literature Review, Volume 17, Gale, 1989.

Crichton, Sarah, "PW Interviews: Jamake Highwater," *Publishers Weekly*, November 6, 1978, pp. 6-8.

Eutsler, Nellvena Duncan, "Jamake Highwater," *Dictionary of Literary Biography*, Volume 52: *American Writers for Children since 1960*, Gale, 1986, pp. 185-192.

Flanagan, Kate M., review of *Legend Days* in *The Horn Book Magazine*, June, 1984, pp. 336-37.

Haviland, Virginia, "Tales of the Tribes," *Washington Post Book World*, February 12, 1978, p. G4.

Highwater, Jamake, in comments provided to James F. Kamp for *Authors and Artists for Young Adults*.

Highwater, Jamake, *Legend Days*, Harper, 1984.

Highwater, Jamake, *The Ceremony of Innocence*, Harper, 1984.

Highwater, Jamake, "I Took the Fire," *Contemporary Authors, Autobiography Series*, Volume 7, Gale, 1988, pp. 69-83.

Jackson, David, "Jamake Highwater's Native Intelligence," *Village Voice*, May 3, 1983, pp. 38-40.

Katz, Jane B., editor, *This Song Remembers: Self-Portraits of Native Americans in the Arts*, Houghton, 1980, pp. 171-177.

Rochman, Hazel, review of *I Wear the Morning Star* in *Booklist*, March 1, 1986, p. 973.

Seale, Doris, review of *Legend Days* in *Interracial Books for Children Bulletin*, Volume 16, number 8, 1985, pp. 18-19.

Shirley, Carl R., "Jamake Highwater," *Dictionary of Literary Biography Yearbook: 1985*, Gale, 1986, pp. 359-366.

Something about the Author, Volume 32, Gale, 1983, pp. 92-96.

Turner, Alice K., review of *Mick Jagger: The Singer Not the Song* in *Publishers Weekly*, June 25, 1973, p. 75.

Wilson, Evie, review of *The Ceremony of Innocence* in *Voice of Youth Advocates*, August, 1985, p. 184.

Yolen, Jane, review of *Anpao* in *New York Times Book Review*, February 5, 1978, p. 26.

■ For More Information See

BOOKS

Contemporary Literary Criticism, Volume 12, Gale, 1980.

PERIODICALS

America, September 26, 1981.
Catholic Library World, December, 1977.
Horn Book, February, 1978.
Language Arts, February, 1978.
Los Angeles Times Book Review, October 18, 1981.
New York Times Book Review, December 4, 1977; July 17, 1980.
Publishers Weekly, November 6, 1978; November 12, 1982.
Washington Post Book World, August 5, 1980; December 7, 1986.

—Sketch by James F. Kamp

John Hughes

■ Personal

Born ca. 1950 in Michigan; married Nancy Ludwig, ca. 1970; children: two. *Education:* Attended Arizona University.

■ Addresses

Home—Chicago, IL. *Agent*—Bill Haber, Creative Artists Agency, Inc., 1888 Century Park East, Los Angeles, CA 90067.

■ Career

Writer, 1970—; screenwriter, director, and producer of motion pictures, 1979—. Has also worked as an advertising copywriter for Needham Harper & Steers, Chicago, IL, and Leo Burnett & Co. Founder of John Hughes Co., 1985.

■ Writings

SCREENPLAYS

National Lampoon's Class Reunion, Twentieth Century-Fox, 1982.
(With David Odell) *Nate and Hayes,* Paramount, 1983.

National Lampoon's Vacation (adapted from Hughes's story "Vacation '58," first published in *National Lampoon,* 1975), Warner Brothers, 1983.
Mr. Mom, Twentieth Century-Fox, 1983.
(And director) *Sixteen Candles,* Universal, 1984.
(And director) *The Breakfast Club,* Universal, 1985.
(With Robert Klane) *National Lampoon's European Vacation,* Warner Brothers, 1985.
(And director) *Weird Science,* Universal, 1985.
Pretty in Pink, Paramount, 1986.
(And director) *Ferris Bueller's Day Off,* Paramount, 1986.
Some Kind of Wonderful, Paramount, 1987.
(And director) *Planes, Trains, and Automobiles,* Paramount, 1987.
She's Having a Baby, Paramount, 1988.
The Great Outdoors, Universal, 1988.
(And director) *Uncle Buck,* MCA, 1989.
Home Alone, Twentieth Century-Fox, 1990.
Career Opportunities, Universal, 1991.

OTHER

Contributor of parodies and short stories to periodicals, including *Playboy* and *National Lampoon.* Former editor of *National Lampoon.*

■ Sidelights

John Hughes is a filmmaker with a magic touch. Since the early 1980s Hughes has been turning out hit movies every year with stunning regularity. His long list of profit-turning comedies includes *Sixteen Candles, Ferris Bueller's Day Off, Uncle Buck,* and

Home Alone, stories featuring suburban families in familiar—but funny—situations. A *Library Journal* reviewer notes that a typical John Hughes comedy "makes you laugh out loud over the little day-to-day inanities we all identify with as part and parcel of humankind's lot."

Hughes is primarily a screenwriter, but he also directs and produces movies. Some of his biggest hits have been those he wrote and then directed—*Sixteen Candles, The Breakfast Club,* and *Planes Trains, and Automobiles,* to name a few. His work has proven so successful that Hollywood now bills his features as "John Hughes comedies," banking on the ready recognition of his name. Hughes told *Film Comment* that he tries above all to be honest in his work, "to reach deep into myself and pull out things that other people [are] also thinking."

The best John Hughes films portray children or teens in realistic, everyday situations. His characters "are likely to be teen-aged, free-spirited, more than a little afflicted with adolescent angst, and very popular with young audiences," according to *New York Times* reporter Thomas O'Connor. From the outset of his career Hughes rebelled against the stereotyped notion of a teen film, creating instead in-depth character studies that allowed teens to be human as well as funny. "Young people support the movie business, and it's only fair that their stories be told," Hughes said in *Seventeen* magazine. "I think it's wrong not to allow someone the right to have a problem because of their age. People say, 'Well, they're young. They have their whole lives ahead of them. What do they have to complain about?' They forget very quickly what it's like to be young."

The secret of Hughes's success is just that: he has never forgotten what it is like to be young.

Hughes's own teenage years were far from perfect. He described himself in *Seventeen* as "kind of quiet," a boy who "spent a lot of time by myself, imagining things." He was born in Michigan, but his family moved frequently—often he was barely in a school long enough to make friends. "Life just started to get good in seventh grade, and then we moved to Chicago," he remembered. "I ended up in a really big high school, and I didn't know anybody." Hughes added that his lack of athletic ability only increased his unpopularity. To this day, he identifies most with teens who are outsiders, who rebel against notions of peer pressure and conformity.

During his high school years, Hughes had a number of heroes. He told *Seventeen* that the Beatles "changed my whole life." He added: "And then Bob Dylan's *Bringing It All Back Home* [album] came out and *really* changed me. Thursday I was one person, and Friday I was another. My heroes were Dylan, John Lennon, and Picasso, because they each moved their particular medium forward, and when they got to the point where they were comfortable, they always moved on." Hughes spent his late teens with his family in a comfortable North Shore suburb of Chicago, an area that he regularly revisits when making films.

Hughes attended Arizona University briefly, but as early as twenty he discovered that he had a flair for comedy. He turned to free-lance writing and sold material to such noted comedians as Henny Youngman and Rodney Dangerfield. For some time during his early twenties he worked as an advertising copywriter for various firms in Chicago, but that sort of work was not a suitable outlet for his talents. In 1979 he quit his regular job and turned to writing humor full time. His early parodies appeared in *Playboy* and *National Lampoon,* and eventually he became an editor at *National Lampoon.*

Hughes joined the staff of *National Lampoon* just as the company was moving into filmmaking on a large scale. The 1979 comedy *National Lampoon's Animal House* was just the sort of runaway success that the entertainment industry loves—it was made on a small budget, with relatively unknown actors, and it quickly became one of the top-grossing comedies in the history of film. *Animal House* offered a standard *National Lampoon* parody of a stuffy university with a rowdy fraternity house, and its success spawned a whole series of similar movies under the Lampoon name. Hughes was drafted as a screen writer for some of these sequels, most notably *National Lampoon's Vacation.*

National Lampoon's Vacation is a slapstick story of a cross-country trek by a dotty suburban family called the Griswolds. Every imaginable mishap afflicts the poor Griswold family as they journey toward an amusement park in their battered station wagon. Hughes based his screenplay on a story he had written for *National Lampoon* magazine about some of his own memories of nightmare family vacations. The movie—one of the first starring vehicles for comedian Chevy Chase—was a major success at the box office during the competitive 1983 summer season. *New York Times* reviewer Janet Maslin complimented the work for its "tou-

Five diverse high-school students find out how much they have in common when they serve Saturday detention together in *The Breakfast Club.*

ches of the ordinary ... presented with cleverness.''

Hughes's next screenplay went into production as the film *Mr. Mom.* Once again the writer based his story on his own experiences as a ''house husband'' raising young children. The movie, starring Michael Keaton, did brisk box office business late in 1983, but Hughes was never satisfied with the final product. He told *Film Comment* that his original script ''was pretty badly butchered. I just got raped on that project.'' Fortunately for Hughes, the film critics seemed to agree that the faults in *Mr. Mom* lay in its production and direction. *Washington Post* reviewer Gary Arnold, for instance, wrote: ''John Hughes' screenplay sets up a potentially effective parallel situation that is then undermined by scatterbrained execution.''

At that point Hughes decided to try his hand as a director. He did not specifically plan to make movies about teenagers, but once he turned his attention to those difficult adolescent years, he found a veritable gold mine of material at his fingertips. His first film as a writer-director was *Sixteen Candles,* a work many critics consider the most endearing and sophisticated teen comedy ever made.

Sixteen Candles centers on what high school sophomore Samantha considers the worst day of her life: her sixteenth birthday. Amidst hasty preparations for her older sister's wedding, her parents have forgotten Samantha's important milestone completely. To make matters worse, she is hounded on the school bus by a gangly freshman known as ''the Geek,'' while the object of her devotion—a handsome senior named Jake Ryan—ignores her completely. Samantha endures humiliation at a school dance and embarrassing moments at home among her loving but dimwitted grandparents. Throughout, the winsome Samantha—brought to life by actress Molly Ringwald—elicits sympathy from even the hardest-hearted viewer.

Matthew Broderick wheels and deals in *Ferris Bueller's Day Off*, a film written and directed by Hughes.

Critics have hailed *Sixteen Candles* as a breakthrough in teen comedy: a film that portrays high school students as thoughtful, emotional people with dreams and daring. Hughes made two important decisions that affected the outcome of the movie. First, he cast teenaged actors and actresses in all the parts, rather than using slightly older people who just *looked* young. Second, he paid careful attention to the speech patterns of modern teens, using popular expressions and occasional swearwords as most high school students do. These careful preparations drew the praise of *New Yorker* columnist Pauline Kael. The critic praised Hughes's "feeling for verbal rhythms" and wrote: "He knows how kids toss words around, especially the words that set them apart from their elders. What gives 'Sixteen Candles' its peppiness is his affection for teenagers' wacko slang—phrases carrying such strong positive and negative charges that they have a dizzy immediacy."

With its happy ending for all and its giddy party scenes, *Sixteen Candles* is a pure comedy. Hughes turned to a more serious vein for his follow-up film, *The Breakfast Club*, another that he wrote and directed. *The Breakfast Club* follows five students through a long Saturday morning spent in detention in a suburban school library. Hughes's five characters are high school archetypes: a macho athlete, an academic overachiever, a popularity queen, an angry rebel, and an introverted eccentric. Sitting together and charged with the task of writing essays, the students ignore one another at

first. Then gradually—as boredom sets in—they begin to communicate, learning deep secrets about one another in the process.

Chicago Tribune film critic Gene Siskel called *The Breakfast Club* one of "the very best teenage movies ... a thoroughly serious picture." Siskel added: "'The Breakfast Club' is a breath of cinematic fresh air, taking on a very real adolescent problem and offering, in a dramatic way, a possible solution." Once again the movie generated a significant profit, and it helped to launch the careers of Judd Nelson, Emilio Estevez, and Ally Sheedy. In his *Washington Post* review of the film, Joe Brown concluded: "The searching, often awkward monologues really sound like kids learning that there are other kinds of people out there, that there's something beyond high school's soul-crushing popularity race."

After *The Breakfast Club*, Hughes found his scripts in high demand. In just two years he wrote six films and directed four of them. *Sixteen Candles*, *The Breakfast Club*, and *Ferris Bueller's Day Off* all became major hits, while two other comedies, *Weird Science* and *National Lampoon's European Vacation*, were only modestly successful. In *Seventeen*, Hughes credited his success to a streak of romanticism, an attitude starkly different from that of many teen film producers. "Most of my characters are romantic rather than sexual," he said. "I think that's an essential difference in my pictures. I think they are more accurate in portraying young people as romantic—as wanting a relationship, an understanding, with a member of the opposite sex more than physical sex."

This romantic streak is evident in *Pretty in Pink*, a Hughes film released in 1986. Directed by Howard Deutch, *Pretty in Pink* tells the story of Andie Walsh, a bright but financially disadvantaged high school student. Andie faces a crisis when a member of her school's wealthy crowd develops a crush on her. Once again Hughes tapped actress Molly Ringwald for the leading role and drew another spirited character for her. *Los Angeles Times* critic Patrick Goldstein found *Pretty in Pink* a "delightful new comedy" and called Hughes "one of the few filmmakers in Hollywood who remembers high school." The columnist continued: "What makes 'Pretty in Pink' such a satisfying, big-hearted film is the way it lets us watch kids through their own eyes, exploring feelings instead of making caricatures of them."

Ferris Bueller's Day Off, also released in 1986, has been called "Hughes's most beguiling high-school fantasy yet" by *Newsweek* critic David Ansen. Ferris Bueller leads a charmed life—he fools his parents, outwits his high school principal, infuriates his stuffy sister, and leads his girlfriend and best pal on a merry all-day romp through downtown Chicago. Feigning sickness, Ferris wrangles a day off school from his doting parents. He then uses computers to answer the telephone and the door when school officials come snooping. Not only does he free himself for the day, he also craftily excuses his girlfriend and his comrade, whose father's prized Ferrari is used to roam Chicago. Ansen described the movie as "a kind of daydream of adolescent omnipotence: an account of a high-school hero's perfect day of playing hooky."

One of the top-drawing films of the 1986 Christmas season, *Ferris Bueller's Day Off* proved the perfect vehicle for its star, Matthew Broderick. As Ferris, Broderick makes confident and witty asides to the audience as he charms his way through throngs of admirers. "Here is a dream as old as adolescence," wrote Richard Schickel in *Time*, "and it is fun to be reminded of its ageless potency, especially in a movie as good-hearted as this one."

A number of actors and actresses have found their careers boosted by an appearance in a John Hughes film. One such performer is John Candy, a portly, outgoing comic who had received few choice movie roles before teaming with Hughes. Candy has starred in two Hughes films, *Planes, Trains, and Automobiles* and *Uncle Buck.* In *Newsweek*, Ansen writes that as a lovable boob, Candy makes a perfect Hughes character—a grownup child. "Under Hughes's sympathetic eye," the critic concludes, "this often misused comic actor finally gets to show his unique colors."

In *Planes, Trains, and Automobiles*, Candy and co-star Steve Martin portray businessmen trying to travel—via airplane, bus, rental car, and train—to their homes in Chicago for the Thanksgiving holiday. Thrown together by chance, the mismatched men struggle to retain their sanity as flights are cancelled, cars break down, and every sort of travel problem imaginable besets them. The movie was released just before Thanksgiving in 1987, and it became one of the biggest hits of that Christmas movie season. *Washington Post* correspondent Hal Hinson praised Hughes for creating a "weirdly inventive, off-kilter comedy out of the

A shy teenage artist (Eric Stoltz) finally meets his dream girl (Lea Thompson) in 1987's *Some Kind of Wonderful.*

horrors of modern travel.'' The critic added that *Planes, Trains, and Automobiles* provided ''a riotously springy holiday knock-about.''

Candy also stars in *Uncle Buck*, yet another Hughes comedy that highlights the suburban family. In *Uncle Buck*, Candy appears as a ''sweet sleazeball slob,'' to quote Ansen, a last-minute babysitter for an ordinary family of three. Sloppy Uncle Buck is certainly not an ideal caretaker for two youngsters and a bratty, spoiled teen, but gradually he wins his charges over because he cares so deeply about them. A comedy with a serious message about family love and understanding, *Uncle Buck* was Hughes's sixth film as a writer-director.

Hollywood's executives always pray for a ''sleeper hit''—a small-budget movie that draws vast crowds and huge profits just on the strength of its story. Hughes provided just that with *Home Alone*, a Christmas, 1990 release. Twentieth Century-Fox put little money into promoting *Home Alone*, fearing it would not fare well against its competitors. Almost everyone was taken by surprise when the movie outpaced every rival to become perhaps the biggest hit of 1990. In fact, since its release, *Home Alone* has moved into the top ten most

profitable films of all time, passing such megahits as *Jaws* and *Return of the Jedi.*

The idea for the movie hit Hughes all of a sudden, as he was packing for a vacation. ''I was going away on vacation, and making a list of everything I didn't want to forget,'' he told *Time*. ''I thought, 'Well, I'd better not forget my kids.' Then I thought, 'What if I left my 10-year-old son at home? What would he do?''' Taking a break from his packing, Hughes jotted some notes for a script. A full-length screenplay was quickly completed, and *Home Alone* was directed by Chris Columbus.

In *Home Alone*, young Kevin McCallister (played by Macaulay Culkin) wakes up alone in his comfortable suburban house. His parents and siblings have rushed off to Europe, forgetting him in their haste. Free to do as he pleases, Kevin indulges in every forbidden treat: he eats as much ice cream as he wants, he jumps on his parents' bed, and he ogles *Playboy* magazine. His joy turns to anxiety as the day advances, however, and soon he finds himself in a desperate battle to outwit two bungling burglars. Against all odds, Kevin's creative booby traps save him time after time as his mother tries frantically to return home to him.

Kevin Bacon (center) starred as an expectant father with an active fantasy life in *She's Having a Baby*.

Macaulay Culkin faces a couple of would-be burglars in the 1990 Hughes smash *Home Alone*.

Time reporter Elizabeth L. Bland called *Home Alone* the "breakaway hit of the season." The movie earned more than fifty million dollars in its first three weeks in the theatres and has since grossed more than $260 million. "Nearly every year, it seems, John Hughes gives moviegoers a surprise Christmas present: an amiable, unassuming film that blossoms into a smash entertainment," wrote Bland. With *Home Alone*, she concluded, "Hughes and his colleagues have succeeded again in reminding Hollywood that though audiences like to be scared and occasionally shocked, they like most of all to feel good."

A Hughes film will certainly warm the soul, but it might also remind the viewer to be caring, considerate of others, and tolerant of human error. Many of Hughes's movies deal with the very dawning of these qualities in a youngster or a teen—the filmmaker says he has learned many lessons from listening to what his own children and the nation's high school students have to say. Hughes told the *Chicago Tribune:* "Many filmmakers portray teenagers as immoral and ignorant with pursuits that are pretty base.... They seem to think that teenagers aren't very bright. But I haven't found that to be the case. I listen to kids. I respect them."

Hughes feels that his phenomenal success stems from his sensitivity to both the joys and sorrows that young people experience growing up. "I don't think of kids as a lower form of the human species," he told the *New York Times.* "... What turned things around for me is remembering how serious I was [as a teen]. It's the point in your life where you're most serious, yet, due to conditions beyond your control, you're also at your geekiest.... I write about other people's lives, filtered through my life."

■ **For More Information See**

BOOKS

Contemporary Authors, Volume 129, Gale, 1989.
Contemporary Theatre, Film, and Television, Volume 5, Gale, 1987.

PERIODICALS

Chicago Tribune, July 29, 1983; February 15, 1985; February 17, 1985; August 14, 1985; March 12, 1986; June 11, 1986; February 27, 1987; June 20, 1988.
Detroit Free Press, August 15, 1987.
Film Comment, June, 1984.
Glamour, April, 1988.

Library Journal, February 1, 1990.

Los Angeles Times, July 22, 1983; November 18, 1983; November 23, 1983; May 4, 1984; February 15, 1985; February 20, 1985; July 30, 1985; August 2, 1985; February 28, 1986; June 11, 1986; February 27, 1987; April 7, 1987; November 25, 1987; December 15, 1987; February 5, 1988; June 17, 1988; August 16, 1989.

Maclean's, May 14, 1984.

Newsweek, August 12, 1985; June 16, 1988; September 4, 1989; December 3, 1990.

New Yorker, May 28, 1984; August 7, 1986.

New York Times, October 30, 1982; July 29, 1983; August 26, 1983; May 4, 1984; February 15, 1985; July 27, 1985; August 2, 1985; February 28, 1986; March 9, 1986; March 17, 1986; June 11, 1986; February 27, 1987; March 15, 1987; November 25, 1987; June 17, 1988.

People, February 22, 1988; September 4, 1989.

Philadelphia Inquirer, April 1, 1991.

Premiere, October, 1989; October, 1990.

Rolling Stone, September 7, 1989.

Seventeen, March, 1986.

Time, March 3, 1986; June 23, 1986; November 30, 1987; February 22, 1988; December 10, 1990.

Times (London), February 13, 1987.

Village Voice, May 8, 1984.

Washington Post, July 29, 1983; August 20, 1983; February 15, 1985; July 27, 1985; August 2, 1985; February 28, 1986; June 12, 1986; February 27, 1987; February 28, 1987; November 25, 1987; November 27, 1987.

—Sketch by Anne Janette Johnson

W. P. Kinsella

■ Personal

Born William Patrick Kinsella, May 25, 1935, in Edmonton, Alberta, Canada; son of John Matthew (a contractor) and Olive (a printer; maiden name, Elliott) Kinsella; married Myrna Salls, 1957 (divorced, 1963); married Mickey Heming, September 10, 1965 (divorced, 1978); married Ann Knight (a writer), December 30, 1978; children: (first marriage) Shannon Leah, Erin Irene; (second marriage) Lyndsey Denise (stepdaughter). *Education:* University of Victoria, B.A., 1974; University of Iowa, M.F.A., 1978. *Politics:* "Rhinoceros Party." *Religion:* Atheist.

■ Addresses

Office—14881 Marine Dr. #201, White Rock, British Columbia, Canada V4B 1C2; Box 2162, Blaine, WA 98230. *Agent*—Nancy Colbert, 55 Avenue Rd., Toronto, Ontario, Canada M5R 3L2.

■ Career

Government of Alberta, Edmonton, clerk, 1954-56; Retail Credit Co., Edmonton, manager, 1956-61; City of Edmonton, account executive, 1961-67; Caesar's Italian Village (restaurant), Victoria, British Columbia, owner, 1967-72; student and taxicab driver in Victoria, 1974-76; University of Iowa, Iowa City, instructor, 1976-78; University of Calgary, Calgary, Alberta, assistant professor of English and creative writing, 1978-83; writer, 1983—. Founder of the Calgary Creative Reading Series. *Member:* American Amateur Press Association, Society of American Baseball Researchers, American Atheists, Enoch Emery Society.

■ Awards, Honors

Award from *Canadian Fiction,* 1976, for story "Illianna Comes Home"; honorable mention in *Best American Short Stories 1980,* for "Fiona the First"; Houghton Mifflin Literary Fellowship and *School Library Journal*'s Best Books for Young Adults, both 1982, Books in Canada First Novel Award and Canadian Authors Association prize, both 1983, all for *Shoeless Joe;* Writers Guild of Alberta O'Hagan novel medal, 1984, for *The Moccasin Telegraph;* Alberta Achievement Award for Excellence in Literature, 1987; Stephen Leacock Award for Humor, 1987, for *The Fencepost Chronicles;* named Author of the Year by Canadian's Booksellers Association, 1987-88; Vancouver Award for Writing, 1987.

■ Writings

Dance Me Outside: More Tales from the Ermineskin Reserve (stories), Oberon Press, 1977, David Godine, 1986.
Scars (stories), Oberon Press, 1978.

Shoeless Joe Jackson Comes to Iowa (stories; also see below), Oberon Press, 1980.

Born Indian (stories), Oberon Press, 1981.

Shoeless Joe (novel; based on title story in *Shoeless Joe Jackson Comes to Iowa*), Houghton, 1982.

The Ballad of the Public Trustee (chapbook), William Hoffer Standard Editions, 1982.

The Moccasin Telegraph (stories), Penguin Canada, 1983, David Godine, 1984.

The Thrill of the Grass (chapbook), William Hoffer Standard Editions, 1984.

The Alligator Report (stories), Coffee House Press, 1985.

The Iowa Baseball Confederacy (novel), Houghton, 1986.

Five Stories (chapbook), William Hoffer Standard Editions, 1986.

The Fencepost Chronicles (stories), Collins, 1986, Houghton, 1987.

Red Wolf, Red Wolf (stories), Collins, 1988.

The Further Adventures of Slugger McBatt (stories), Houghton, 1988.

The Rainbow Warehouse (poetry), Pottersfield, 1989.

The Miss Hobbema Pageant (stories), Harper, 1990.

The Spirits Soar: The Art of Allen Sapp (art book), Stoddard, 1990.

Box Socials (novel), Harper, 1991.

Contributor to numerous anthologies, including *Best Canadian Stories: 1977, 1981, 1985, Aurora: New Canadian Writing 1979, Best American Short Stories 1980, More Stories from Western Canada, Oxford Anthology of Canadian Literature, Pushcart Prize Anthology 5, The Spirit That Moves Us Reader, Introduction to Fiction, The Temple of Baseball, Penguin Book of Modern Canadian Short Stories, The Armchair Book of Baseball, Small Wonders, Illusion Two, West of Fiction, Anthology of Canadian Literature in English,* Volume II, *Contexts: Anthology 3, Aquarius, New Worlds, The Process of Writing, A Sense of Place, The Anthology Anthology, New Voices 2, 3, Rainshadow,* and *Here's the Story.* Also contributor of more than two hundred stories to American and Canadian magazines, including *Sports Illustrated, Arete: Journal of Sports Literature, Story Quarterly, Matrix,* and *Canadian Fiction Magazine.* The novel *The Iowa Baseball Confederacy* has been recorded on audio cassette by Kinsella and released by New Letters, 1989.

■ Adaptations

The novel *Shoeless Joe* was adapted to film as *Field of Dreams,* starring Kevin Costner, Burt Lancaster, Amy Madigan, and James Earl Jones, Universal, 1989; *Dance Me Outside* has been optioned for film by Norman Jewison.

The stories "The Thrill of the Grass," "Valley of the Schmoon," and "The Night Manny Moto Tied the Record" were produced as plays at the Waterfront Theater, Vancouver, 1988, and performed at the Quad Cities Arts Festival, Davenport, IA, 1991; "The Thrill of the Grass" and "Valley of the Schmoon" were produced as one-man shows at White Rock Theater, British Columbia, 1990.

■ Work in Progress

The novels *The Winter Helen Dropped By, Magic Time,* and *Conflicting Statements.*

■ Sidelights

W. P. Kinsella, a Canadian author of stories and novels, has attracted fans internationally with his imaginative and humorous fictions. Many of Kinsella's short stories follow the daily escapades of characters living on a North American Indian reservation, while his longer works mix magic and the mundane in epic baseball encounters. The 1989 movie *Field of Dreams,* about an Iowa farmer who builds a baseball diamond in his cornfield, is based on his bestselling novel *Shoeless Joe.* Though Kinsella is not an Indian and does not play baseball, critics often praise his ability to create realistic people and places in his work. "I've mixed in so much, I'm not sure what's real and what's not," Kinsella told *Publishers Weekly,* "but as long as you can convince people you know what you're talking about, it doesn't matter. If you're convincing, they'll believe you."

A determined writer who didn't publish his first story collection until reaching forty-two, Kinsella spent his childhood in relative isolation in northwestern Canada. For the first ten years of his life he was actually raised in a log cabin. "There aren't too many of us can claim that distinction anymore," Kinsella reflected in *Contemporary Authors Autobiography Series.* "Our log cabin was located in an isolated area of central Alberta. Although it was only sixty miles from Edmonton, the capital, it might as well have been six hundred. Our only transportation was horse and buggy in summer, and horse-drawn sleigh in winter. I was an only child, and the nearest neighbors with children were several miles away."

Since Kinsella found few companions his own age, he spent much of his childhood with adults. "Having no contact with children, I considered myself a small adult," Kinsella admitted. "Consequently, I claim to have been suffering from culture shock ever since." Despite some deprivations, he considers himself fortunate that his upbringing exposed him to literature: "My parents and my aunt Margaret were highly intelligent people, and though none had gone much beyond eighth grade, all three were readers, and all read aloud to me, especially my father. He would read what few novels we possessed, and as I grew, a weekly novel that appeared in the weekend edition of a Toronto newspaper. Some of the novels I heard read aloud many times over were *The Valley of Silent Men* by James Oliver Curwood, *The Call of the Wild* by Jack London, *A Girl of the Limberlost* by Gene Stratton Porter, *The Desert of Wheat* by Zane Grey, and *Tarzan's Great Adventure* by Edgar Rice Burroughs."

Kinsella claims the combination of reading and loneliness stirred his creativity: "I believe being raised in isolation had a good deal to do with my becoming a writer, for in order to entertain myself ... I had to create my own entertainment. That meant I created fictional companions.... And I created elaborate fantasies involving my stuffed animals.... I'm one of these people who woke up at about age five knowing how to read and write, and I did my first fiction writing then, little, one-page, hand-printed stories, some of which my mother still has, with titles like 'The Little Lost Pansy.' Our farmhouse had large beds of those velvety purple-and-yellow flowers outside the kitchen door."

In 1945 Kinsella's family moved to Edmonton so that he could attend school. He had completed the first five years of his education by correspondence, but his mother did not feel qualified to teach him further. Kinsella regrets that his formal schooling did not recognize his budding talent as a writer, and, in fact, seemed to discourage creative ventures altogether. "Creative writing was not encouraged at Eastwood High School, in fact nothing creative was encouraged," he explained. "Our parents and teachers had survived, and been scarred by, the Great Depression; what was pounded into us was, get a job with security, learn a trade, acquire a profession, attend university. My high-school counselor, whom I will never forgive, after I had scored 98 percent on the writing section of an aptitude test, and 0 percent on the mechanical section, discouraged me from considering writing as a profession. He suggested instead that I become an accountant or an engineer, and write as a hobby, once I was established professionally."

Though Kinsella concedes that his study habits were not ideal, he managed to retain the information that would be important to his later career: "I graduated with 90 percent in English and 51 percent in each of seven other subjects, the nature of which I immediately forgot. I would get up at 4:00 a.m. the morning of an exam and cram enough vital information to pass, then let that information float away as the exam finished, knowing I would never use it again. I have never regretted my approach to learning."

During his school days, Kinsella began to develop an interest in baseball that would later blossom into a lifelong passion. He first heard about the game from his father, Johnny Kinsella, who travelled around the United States as a semi-pro third baseman for several years after World War II. Admitting that he is not athletically inclined, Kinsella recalled his first, comical attempt to play the game: "During my first spring in a regular school ... during a pickup game at recess, I suddenly had a bat thrust into my hands and was

Dance Me Outside

MORE TALES FROM THE
ERMINESKIN RESERVE

by W. P. Kinsella

Kinsella's 1977 collection of short stories about life on a reservation was noted for its balanced view of Indian culture.

The power of dreams can make you come alive...

SHOELESS JOE

"A LYRICAL, SEDUCTIVE, AND ALTOGETHER WINNING CONCOCTION."
THE NEW YORK TIMES BOOK REVIEW

WINNER OF A HOUGHTON MIFFLIN LITERARY FELLOWSHIP AWARD

W. P. KINSELLA

Author of *The Iowa Baseball Confederacy*

Ballantine/Fiction/34256 (Canada $6.50) U.S. $4.95

Kinsella's 1982 mythical baseball fable drew on the author's long-term love of the game.

told I was 'up.' I had witnessed enough play to know I was supposed to hit the ball, and I did hit the first pitch somewhere deep into the outfield, but I hadn't witnessed enough of the game to understand that I was supposed to run the bases *after* I hit the ball. I stood at home plate and watched the proceedings, while my playmates screamed at me, 'Run! Run!' 'To where?' I said, as I was pulled along by the arm toward first base. Unfortunately, by the time I had been dragged to first, the ball had been retrieved and I was out.''

After high school Kinsella held a variety of jobs in Edmonton, Alberta, and Victoria, British Columbia. He was a clerk for the Alberta government, a collector for a finance company, an investigator for a credit bureau, a taxicab driver, and the owner and operator of a pizza restaurant. "No matter what I did, I always thought of myself as a writer,"

he told *Publishers Weekly.* "You're born with a compulsion to write." In 1957 he married Myrna Salls, and they had two daughters, Shannon Leah and Erin Irene. The marriage ended in 1963, and in 1965 he married Mickey Heming and acquired a stepdaughter, Lyndsey Denise.

Kinsella continued his education in 1970, enrolling in a creative writing course at the University of Victoria. He graduated in 1974 with a degree in creative writing and a major in play writing. One particular instructor, Kinsella said, set him on the road to publishing success: "I had published a number of poems, plus three or four stories in minor, minor markets, but, even though I knew my stories were good, there was something lacking. In the fall of 1974, a writer named W. D. Valgardson came to teach at U-Vic. He was a writer I admired very much, so I enrolled in his Advanced Fiction Workshop, a step that changed my life. I knew my stories were 90 percent publishable, but I couldn't get that last 10 percent. Billy Valgardson looked at my work, and he would tear off my first page, then tear off the last page, and scissor off half of the second from last page, and say, 'Look! You warmed up for a page before you started your story, and you wound down for a page and a half after it was over. Don't do that!' I took that advice from Valgardson, and my work suddenly started to catch on. In one *week* I had five stories accepted by magazines, as many as had been accepted in the previous five years. And I've sold every story I've written since—over two hundred of them."

Though he would eventually find literary success, while studying at the University of Victoria neither Kinsella nor his mentor Valgardson entertained the possibility that Kinsella could ever make a living from storytelling. At Valgardson's suggestion, Kinsella enrolled in the Iowa Writers' Workshop to earn an M.F.A. in creative writing, a degree that would enable him to teach at the university level. "The week before I left for Iowa," Kinsella told *CAAS*, "I packaged up eighteen of my Indian stories and mailed them to Oberon Press, Billy Valgardson's publisher, a small, quality press, located in Ottawa, Ontario. Earlier, Valgardson had submitted a sampling of my stories to Oberon. Their reaction was, 'These are very good, but so diverse they sound like they've been written by at least three different authors,' which was true, since they saw two Indian stories plus 'Fiona the First,' 'The Grecian Urn,' and 'Waiting for the Call.' Soon after I arrived in Iowa, I received word that my collection of stories had been accepted. *Dance Me*

Outside was due for publication in the spring of 1977."

Dance Me Outside is a collection of short stories about life on a North American reservation narrated by a young, self-conscious Cree Indian. Unlike the many biased books of Indian fiction—guilt-ridden works written by whites, and finger-pointing prose by Indians—*Dance Me Outside* is a balanced depiction of the North American Indians and reveals a variety of ways in which they are conditioned to resign themselves to victimization.

Most critics agreed that the book is an authentic and sensitive handling of the Cree culture. "Kinsella is not an Indian," wrote *Praire Schooner* contributor Frances W. Kaye, "a fact that would not be extraordinary were it not for the stories Kinsella writes about ... a Cree world. Kinsella's Indians are counterculture figures in the sense that their lives counter the predominant culture of North America, but there is none of the worshipfully inaccurate portrayal of 'the Indian' that has appeared from James Fenimore Cooper through Gary Snyder." In the *Wascana Review*, George Woodcock likewise praised Kinsella for an approach that "restores proportion and brings an artistic authenticity to the portrayal of contemporary Indian life which we have encountered rarely in recent years."

Dance Me Outside's success has been attributed in large measure to Kinsella's handling of Silas Ermineskin, the book's endearing narrator. In *Contemporary Authors Autobiography Series*, Kinsella recalled his search for a successful narrative voice: "I thought of a couple I knew casually; the young woman was Indian and her husband was white. I thought, 'There must be a story there about the clash of the cultures.' My immediate idea was to write from the young man's point of view, theorizing, 'What kind of problems would *I* have bringing an Indian girl home to meet my immediate family,' which at that time consisted of my mother and aunt, now living in retirement in Edmonton, and not having seen an Indian for many years, and with no plans to meet one. Then I said, 'No, *Guess*

Kevin Costner and James Earl Jones at the ballpark in the movie *Field of Dreams*, based on Kinsella's novel *Shoeless Joe*.

Who's Coming to Dinner has already been written; so, *what would happen if* (a phrase fiction writers bandy about from dawn to dusk) I told the story from the Indian girl's kid brother's point of view? A boy who had been possibly to sixth grade, but wrote by intuition, not in white man's syntax.'

"I was getting a lot of crap in the class I was taking about my sentence structure, and I thought, 'The hell with you, I'll show you. I'll write something from the point of view of someone who's had a grade five education, and then you can't yap about sentence structure. . . .' I left the story in a drawer until 1975, when I got several more ideas I felt could be told by the same voice." Kinsella found more than a few ideas for his Ermineskin character. So convincing was his initial portrayal of the Cree Indian and the reservation where he lived, that Ermineskin has since narrated nearly one hundred of Kinsella's Indian stories, collected in such books as *Scars, Born Indian, The Moccasin Telegraph,* and *The Fencepost Chronicles.*

With a successful first book to his credit, Kinsella adapted quickly to his new surroundings in Iowa. Admittedly, he fell in love with the state, a sentiment no doubt bolstered by two occurrences: meeting Ann Knight, a woman Kinsella would eventually marry in 1978, and discovering the Iowa City Creative Reading Series, a writing group that so inspired Kinsella that he founded the Calgary Creative Reading Series after moving there from Iowa. Despite these benefits, however, Kinsella expressed misgivings about the University's writing program: "I discovered quickly that the quality of the writing program at Iowa, though supposedly at graduate level, was not nearly as difficult as the undergraduate program at University of Victoria. . . . Being used to straightforward, honest, but hard-hitting criticism of my work, I found the students' comments useless, uninformed, and in many cases detrimental, while the instructors I studied with were unwilling to offer their criticism for fear of offending their students. For me, the total lack of supervision was not a major problem; I wrote *Scars,* [and] a good part of the collection *Shoeless Joe Jackson Comes to Iowa.*"

Shoeless Joe Jackson Comes to Iowa marked a considerable change for Kinsella. Suspending the Indian perspective, he placed these tales in such varied locales as Disneyland, Iowa, urban Canada, and San Francisco. The title story was selected to appear in *Aurora: New Canadian Writers 1979* and attracted the attention of a Houghton Mifflin editor, Larry Kessenich, who contacted Kinsella about expanding the story into a novel. In a

Publishers Weekly interview Kinsella recalled his reaction to the prospect of writing a novel: "It was something that hadn't occurred to me at all, but Larry sounded so enthusiastic. He said, 'If you have a novel, we'd like to see it.' I told him, 'I've never written anything longer than 25 pages, but if you want to work with me, I'll try it.' This is usually the kind of response that brings a great silence from editors." Much to Kinsella's surprise, however, the editor agreed. Kinsella set to work expanding "Shoeless Joe Jackson Comes to Iowa," but he decided instead to leave the story intact as the first chapter and build on the plot with a variety of other material. "I enjoyed doing it very much," he said. "They were such wonderful characters I'd created, and I liked being audacious in another way. I put in no sex, no violence, no obscenity, none of that stuff that sells. I wanted to write a book for imaginative readers, an affirmative statement about life."

Shoeless Joe, a novel-length baseball fable set on an Iowa farm, won Kinsella the Houghton Mifflin Literary Fellowship in 1982. The story follows a character named Ray Kinsella in his attempts to summon the spirits of the tarnished 1919 Chicago White Sox by building a ballpark in his cornfield. Among the ghostly players lured to Kinsella's perfectly mowed grass is Shoeless Joe Jackson, the White Sox star player who fell in scandal when it was revealed that his team threw the World Series. As the story progresses, the same mysterious loudspeaker voice that suggested construction of the ballpark says, "Ease his pain," and Ray Kinsella sets off to kidnap author J. D. Salinger for a visit to Fenway Park. The novel blends baseball lore with legend, and historical figures with fictional characters.

One of the fictional characters, narrator Ray Kinsella, earned his name from an old Salinger story. W. P. Kinsella explained in *Books in Canada:* "Salinger wrote a story that I discovered in the archives at Iowa. It's in a 1947 issue of *Mademoiselle,* a story called 'A Young Girl in 1941 with No Waist at All.' It's one of Salinger's quite bad uncollected stories, but the character's name is Ray Kinsella. And then of course in *The Catcher in the Rye* there's a character named Richard Kinsella, so the narrator develops a twin brother named Richard who doesn't come in until later on in the story."

Most critics were impressed with the stable blend of fantasy and realism in *Shoeless Joe. Detroit News* writer Ben Brown claimed: "What we have here is a gentle, unselfconscious fantasy balanced perilous-

Father and son meet in a climactic moment from *Field of Dreams.*

ly in the air above an Iowa cornfield. It's a balancing act sustained by the absolutely fearless, sentimentality-risking honesty of the author. And it doesn't hurt a bit that he's a master of the language." Similar acclaim was given the book by Alan Cheuse, who wrote in the *Los Angeles Times,* *Shoeless Joe* "stands as fictional homage to our national pastime, with resonances so American that the book may be grounds for abolishing our northern border." *Washington Post* reviewer Jonathan Yardley had quite a different view of the work, however, calling it "a book of quite unbelievable self-indulgence, a rambling exercise the only discernible point of which seems to be to demonstrate, ad infinitum and ad nauseum, what a wonderful fellow is its narrator/author." Nevertheless, most reviewers deemed the book praiseworthy. *Christian Science Monitor* contributor Maggie Lewis wrote: "The descriptions of landscape are poetic, and the baseball details will warm fans' hearts and not get in the way of mere fantasy lovers. This book would make great reading on a

summer vacation. In fact, this book *is* a summer vacation."

When *Shoeless Joe* was published, Kinsella and wife Ann set out on a tour that would combine the book's promotion with Kinsella's yearly visit to baseball parks nationwide. He told *CAAS:* "Since *Shoeless Joe* was a first novel, Houghton Mifflin had not planned much of a promotion tour (in fact they had planned only a printing of 10,000, but the sales department loved the book so much the figure was raised to 25,000), but when we told them we planned to tour a number of baseball stadiums on our own, they agreed to pay our hotel expenses and kick in a little gas money."

The book tour proved both fruitful and taxing for Kinsella, who said he returned from the circuit tired, irritable and ill. "I recognized the symptoms, for I'd known for over twenty years I was a borderline diabetic. I consulted a physician and was diagnosed as having adult-onset diabetes. Becoming diabetic has given me even more of a sense of urgency about my writing. I have more ideas in my head than I could write in three lifetimes. My father died young, and few of the males on the Kinsella side of the family have lived past sixty. By careful diet, exercise, and oral medication I keep my diabetes under control, but it takes a toll in time; I have to walk briskly for a half hour after each meal, in order to slow the digestive process and the entry of sugar into my blood."

In 1983 Kinsella started to earn enough money writing books to quit his teaching post at the University of Calgary, a place he not-so-fondly refers to as "Desolate U." That summer, his fourth book of Indian stories narrated by Silas Ermineskin, *The Moccasin Telegraph*, was published. Like those in his previous Indian collections, the stories in *The Moccasin Telegraph* avoid romanticizing native traditions, relating instead the restless reconciliation of surviving customs with contemporary technology and bureaucracy. Jodi Daynard wrote in the *New York Times Book Review:* These stories "include possibly some of the most funny writing of recent times. Silas Ermineskin, 18, a born storyteller and Huck Finnian scamp, narrates tales about his Indian reservation in Alberta. There's his troublemaking buddy, Frank Fence-post, presenting himself as the chief of the Onagatihies (sometimes Onadatchies) to suburban hunters looking for a guide; Mad Etta, a 400-pound medicine woman whose office is a tree-trunk chair; the unanimously despised Chief Tom and his wicked girlfriend, Samantha Yellowknees; and other ne'er-do-wells whose lives we come to cherish. Bound together by a common history of official mistreatment, these people have a finely tuned instinct for silence, mutual help and deadpan trickery.... Not all the stories are funny, though, and some, like 'Strings,' 'Green Candles' and 'Nests,' seem to challenge the limits of human rage, jealousy and sanity. Unsentimentally poignant, full of the energy and drama of folk tales, these marvelous stories go far in dispelling many lingering myths and misconceptions about the North American Indians—none greater, perhaps, than the one that says they have no sense of humor."

By the time *The Moccasin Telegraph* was published in 1983, Kinsella had begun to garner a reputation as one of Canada's leading Indian authors. Consequently, most readers were surprised to learn that such vivid tales of the Cree world were the imaginative creations of an author who was not in fact Indian. "That is what fiction writing is all about," he told *Strong Voices.* "Imagination. Imagination is my stock in trade. I have to keep coming up with new things. That's my occupation. We are storytellers. Fiction exists to entertain and for no other reason. If you want to write something preachy or autobiographical, you should write nonfiction."

Kinsella went on to describe his Indian stories in the following way: "I write about people who just happen to be Indians. It's the oppressed and the oppressor that I write about. The way that oppressed people survive is by making fun of the people who oppress them. That is essentially what my Indian stories are all about. Silas and his friends understand the absurdity of the world around them. They survive by making fun of the bureaucrats and the do-gooders and the churches and all these idiots who have absolutely no idea what is going on in the world but who are in positions of power. Nine out of ten people in positions of power are hopelessly incompetent. It's that one person out of ten that keeps the country running. Silas sees the absurdity of all this. And that's what I have always done. I know the mentality of the oppressed minority. As a writer I am certainly an oppressed minority."

The mid 1980s saw Kinsella produce several more books of short stories and a second novel, *The Iowa Baseball Confederacy.* As in *Shoeless Joe,* Kinsella blends elements of fantasy and realism in this novel to create his youthful vision of baseball. The plot revolves around a game that lasts forty days in a continual rain between the all-stars of the mystical Iowa Baseball Confederacy and the 1908 Chicago Cubs. Of his tendency to fuse magic with baseball, Kinsella wrote in the introduction to his short story collection *The Thrill of the Grass:* "I feel it is the timelessness of baseball which makes it more conducive to magical happenings than any other sport. There are forays into magic, but I also realize baseball players are very ordinary mortals with the same financial, and domestic problems as Joe Citizen. As well, they suffer unique problems because of the short and ephemeral nature of their careers. Every player, no matter his talent, is only one beanball or one torn rotator-cuff away from the past tense.

Kinsella's second novel generally received favorable reviews, and in some cases, greater praise than his first novel. "*The Iowa Baseball Confederacy* contains bigger magic, larger and more spectacular effects, than anything attempted in *Shoeless Joe,*" wrote Jonathan Webb in *Quill and Quire.* "Kinsella is striving for grander meaning: the reconciliation of immovable forces—love and darker emotions—on conflicting courses." Time travel and a ballgame that lasts in excess of 2,600 innings are two of the supernatural events in the story; characters as diverse as ex-president Teddy Roosevelt and renaissance man Leonardo da Vinci make brief appearances. Contributor Roger Kahn wrote in the *Los Angeles Times Book Review:* "We are reading a writer here, a real writer, Muses be praised. But we are also adrift in a delicate world of fantasy, weird deaths and, I suppose, symbolism. Sometimes the work is confusing, as Kinsella adds a fantasy on top of an illusion beyond a mirage. But I never lost my wonder at how the ballgame would turn out; any author who can hold you for 2,614 innings deserves considerable praise."

In 1987, Twentieth Century-Fox's option to produce *Shoeless Joe* as a movie expired, and the script was subsequently picked up by screenwriter Phil Robinson, who took the idea to Universal Pictures. The script was retitled and filmed in 1989 as the highly successful *Field of Dreams.* In the film's preliminary production notes Robinson noted: "Everything good about the film is from the book. . . . It's an extraordinary vision. It's about the power of love to make dreams come true."

Field of Dreams, starring Kevin Costner as Ray Kinsella, earned an Oscar nomination for Best Picture. Though the film essentially follows Kinsella's original text, Robinson did make one major change in his adaptation: protagonist Ray Kinsella kidnaps author Terence Mann instead of J. D. Salinger. "Legal issues aside," explained Robinson, "J. D. Salinger has moved me to tears with his writing, and I feel great pain for him not being allowed his privacy. Why hurt him? He's somebody I respect and admire. So, I decided to create a character as far away from Salinger as I could but still keep the story intact."

Kinsella attended filming of the movie for a day as an extra and came away from the experience with something less than admiration for the film industry. He related his impressions to his wife, Ann Knight, in an interview for *American Film:* "The movie business is all waiting. And I don't have the patience for that. I like to think things through carefully and then put them down. Everybody has to be present, it seems, while they think things through. They could set up a scene and then call everybody in, instead of having everybody there for 10 hours to get in one hour of work.

"And then, when they work, they do things 19 or 20 times. As a writer, I essentially do things in one-and-a-half takes. If I were the director, I wouldn't do more than three takes on anything, ever. If they

don't get it right the first time, then they damn well better get it right the second—that would be my attitude. You can see why I'm cut out to work alone."

Since the film success of *Field of Dreams,* Kinsella has continued to entertain readers with his magical fictions and, more recently, stage adaptations of his baseball stories and a book of poetry. Unable to get his work published until he was forty-two years old, success did not come easy for W. P. Kinsella. He revealed his formula for achievement in *Contemporary Authors Autobiography Series:* "To be a success, a writer needs five things: *ability,* the skill to write complete sentences in clear, straightforward standard English; *imagination,* which involves having a story to tell; *passion,* which is a nebulous quality that can't be taught, it is what makes a reader fall in love with a character, it is what keeps readers turning pages; *stamina,* which I define as sitting down to write your fiftieth short story knowing that the previous forty-nine have been

Fantasy and realism meet in Kinsella's 1986 novel about a baseball game that lasts for forty days.

failures and that the fiftieth will also be a failure, but that it will be 1 percent better than the previous forty-nine; and finally *luck*, for if Billy Valgardson hadn't come to Victoria to teach, I might still be driving a cab and writing on weekends. If a British Columbia poet named Cathy Ford hadn't had a poem published in a magazine called *Three Cent Pulp* in the early 1970s, I would never have written the story 'Dance Me Outside.' If Larry Kessenich hadn't read a review of an obscure anthology and decided to write me, I would never have written *Shoeless Joe*. If Nancy Colbert hadn't taken me on as a client, I wouldn't be enjoying such financial success. And if Ann Knight hadn't decided to invite a Canadian author who sat across the table from her in a free-lance workshop at the University of Iowa to hear the London Symphony at Hacher Auditorium in Iowa City, I wouldn't be the happy man I am today."

■ Works Cited

Contemporary Authors Autobiography Series, Volume 7, Gale, 1988.
Dahlin, Robert, "Publishers Weekly Interviews: W. P. Kinsella," *Publishers Weekly*, April 16, 1982.
Daynard, Jodi, "Review of *The Moccasin Telegraph*," *New York Times Book Review*, September 2, 1984.
Kinsella, W. P., "Introduction," *The Thrill of the Grass*, Penguin, 1984.
Knight, Ann, "Baseball Like It Oughta Be," *American Film*, May 1989.
McGoogan, Kenneth, "W. P. Kinsella on the $10,000 Trade That Took Him from the Indians to the Chicago Cubs," *Books in Canada*, October 1981.
"Preliminary Production Notes for 'Shoeless Joe'," Universal Pictures, 1989.
Twigg, Alan, *Strong Voices: Conversations with Fifty Canadian Authors*, Harbour, 1988.

■ For More Information See

BOOKS

Contemporary Authors Autobiography Series, Volume 7 Gale, 1988.
Contemporary Authors New Revision Series, Volume 21, Gale, 1987.
Contemporary Literary Criticism, Gale, Volume 27, 1984, Volume 43, 1987.

PERIODICALS

Books in Canada, April 1983; February 1984; November 1984.
Canadian Literature, summer 1982.
Chicago Tribune Book World, April 25, 1982; March 30, 1986.
Christian Science Monitor, July 9, 1982.
Detroit Free Press, May 4, 1986.
Detroit News, May 2, 1982; May 16, 1982.
Fiddlehead, fall 1977; spring 1981.
Globe and Mail (Toronto), November 17, 1984; April 27, 1985; April 12, 1986.
Library Journal, February 1, 1982.
Los Angeles Times, August 26, 1982.
Los Angeles Times Book Review, May 23, 1982; July 6, 1986.
Maclean's, May 11, 1981; April 19, 1982; July 23, 1984.
New Republic, May 8, 1989.
Newsweek, August 23, 1982.
New York Times Book Review, July 25, 1982; September 2, 1984; January 5, 1986; April 20, 1986.
Prairie Schooner, spring 1979.
Publishers Weekly, April 16, 1982; February 28, 1986; April 3, 1987.
Quill and Quire, June 1982; September 1984; April 1986.
Saturday Night, July 1983.
Village Voice, December 4, 1984; April 1, 1986.
Wascana Review, fall 1976.
Washington Post, March 31, 1982.
Western American Literature, February 1978.
Writer's Digest, Volume 67, April 4, 1987.

Robert Lipsyte

■ Personal

Full name, Robert Michael Lipsyte; born January 16, 1938, in New York, NY; son of Sidney I. (a principal) and Fanny (a teacher; maiden name, Finston) Lipsyte; children: Sam, Susannah. *Education:* Columbia University, B.A., 1957, M.S., 1959.

■ Addresses

Home—New York, NY. *Agent*—Theron Raines, Raines & Raines, 71 Park Ave., Suite 4A, New York, NY 10016.

■ Career

New York Times, New York City, copyboy, 1957-59, sports reporter, 1959-67, sports columnist, 1967-71 and 1991—; *New York Post*, New York City, columnist, 1977; Columbia Broadcasting Service, Inc. (CBS-TV), New York City, sports essayist for program *Sunday Morning*, 1982-86; National Broadcasting Company, Inc. (NBC-TV), New York City, correspondent, 1986-88; Public Broadcasting Service (PBS-TV), New York City, host of program *The Eleventh Hour*, 1989-90; writer. Has also worked as a journalism teacher and radio commentator. *Military service:* U.S. Army, 1961.

■ Awards, Honors

Dutton Best Sports Stories Award, E. P. Dutton, 1964, for "The Long Road to Broken Dreams," 1965, for "The Incredible Cassius," 1967, for "Where the Stars of Tomorrow Shine Tonight," 1971, for "Dempsey in the Window," and 1976, for "Pride of the Tiger"; Mike Berger Award, Columbia University Graduate School of Journalism, 1966; Wel-Met Children's Book Award, Child Study Children's Book Committee at Bank Street College of Education, 1967, for *The Contender*; *One Fat Summer* was named an outstanding children's book of the year by the *New York Times* and was selected as one of the American Library Association's best young adult books, both 1977; New Jersey Author citation, New Jersey Institute of Technology, 1978; Emmy Award for on-camera achievement, Academy of Television Arts and Sciences, 1990, as host of the television program *The Eleventh Hour*.

■ Writings

(With Dick Gregory) *Nigger*, Dutton, 1964.
The Masculine Mystique, New American Library, 1966.
The Contender, Harper, 1967.
Assignment: Sports, Harper, 1970, revised edition, 1984.
(With Steve Cady) *Something Going*, Dutton, 1973.
Liberty Two, Simon & Schuster, 1974.

SportsWorld: An American Dreamland, Quadrangle, 1975.

That's the Way of the World (screenplay; also released under title "Shining Star"), United Artists, 1975.

One Fat Summer, Harper, 1977.

Free to Be Muhammad Ali, Harper, 1978.

Summer Rules, Harper, 1981.

Jock and Jill, Harper, 1982.

The Summerboy, Harper, 1982.

The Brave, Harper, 1991.

Scriptwriter for *Saturday Night with Howard Cosell;* contributor to periodicals, including *TV Guide, Harper's Magazine, Nation, New York Times, New York Times Book Review,* and *New York Times Sports Magazine.*

Lipsyte's works are housed in the De Grummond Collection, University of Southern Mississippi and the Kerlan Collection, University of Minnesota.

■ Sidelights

Robert Lipsyte, a journalist who left the medium to write books, spent fourteen years covering sports for the *New York Times*, from the late 1950s to the early 1970s. Lipsyte gained national attention as a result of his sports columns, and Paul D. Zimmerman, in a *Newsweek* review of Lipsyte's book *SportsWorld: An American Dreamland*, called the author "the most original and elegant writer on the sports staff" of the *New York Times* during his tenure. However, frustrated by the periodical's space limitations that adversely affected his ability to depict his subjects, Lipsyte began writing books while still on staff at the paper. His seven publications for young adults have been praised as unsentimental books featuring characters who experience a transformation through a combination of hard work and adherence to ethics. Not surprisingly, the majority of the author's books also involve aspects of athletics and, because of his experience as a sportswriter, Lipsyte is considered an authority in the field of children's sports stories. Offering advice in an article for *Children's Literature in Education*, the author commented, "I don't think we have to make any rules for sports books for children beyond asking that they present some sense of truth about the role of sports in our lives."

For Lipsyte, this means providing realistic portraits of athletes who do not lead idyllic lives solely because of their physical abilities, but must contend with ordinary problems in other areas of their lives. The author also believes the importance of physical ability should be downplayed because many people, especially youngsters who haven't had the time to develop skills in other areas, may be humiliated when they are unable to display athletic prowess. In an article for *Children's Literature in Education*, Lipsyte commented, "Sports is, or should be, just one of the things people do—an integral part of life, but only one aspect of it. Sports is a good experience. It's fun. It ought to be inexpensive and accessible to everybody." He added, "In our society, sports is a negative experience for most boys and almost all girls.... They're required to define themselves on the basis of competitive physical ability." And, according to Lipsyte, sports programs are elitist because individuals with only average ability are quickly weeded out of the system.

These problems, evident in organized sports, have led Lipsyte to refine his own philosophy regarding athletic involvement and question the appropriateness of the nation's fixation with all levels of athletic competition. The author maintains that a subculture exists in American society based on the myth that such practices as obeying a screaming coach, suppressing individualism for the team's sake, and playing through pain are noble pursuits. He alleges that media coverage of sporting events promotes this myth and invites spectators to triumph vicariously through the exploits of their favorite superstars instead of participating in sports themselves. As a sportswriter, Lipsyte was an integral part of this subculture he has christened "SportsWorld," and his disillusionment with certain athletic conventions has thus been deemed noteworthy. In his work *SportsWorld: An American Dreamland*, Lipsyte recapitulates his career as a sportswriter, using encounters with athletes in baseball, football, basketball, boxing, and tennis to give examples of and validate his philosophy.

Explaining his displeasure with "SportsWorld," Lipsyte elucidated in his book, "Sometime in the last fifty years the sports experience was perverted into a SportsWorld state of mind in which the winner was good because he won; the loser, if not actually bad, was at least reduced, and had to prove himself over again, through competition.... SportsWorld is a grotesque distortion of sports.... It has made the finish more important than the race." The author is disconcerted that such maxims have been readily accepted by the American public. He argues that "very few people seem to be questioning SportsWorld itself, exploring the possibility that if sports could be separated from SportsWorld we could take a major step toward liberation from the false values, the stereotypes, the idols of the arena that have burdened us all since childhood."

Statements such as these in *SportsWorld* prompted reviewers to categorize Lipsyte as a disenchanted writer harboring an intense dislike of sports. Disappointed with the book's emphasis on the negative aspects of sports, Roger Kahn, writing in the *New York Times Book Review*, admitted "I admired his column and I wanted to like his book. But 'SportsWorld' lacks a sense of joy." In a review of *SportsWorld* in the *New York Review of Books*, Garry Wills reasoned, "If you take Lipsyte's advice and cease to care about professional sports, there is nothing much left to care about in his book." Lipsyte, however, foresaw such criticism and proclaimed at the conclusion of the book: "I am no hater of athletes and my book is not antisports, although these will be the reflex charges." Instead, the author claims he questions athletic procedures and policies because of his affinity for sports. Noting the contentious nature of the work, Zimmerman deemed *SportsWorld* "a persuasive volume of dissent," and added, "Read him, and you will never look at a sports event in quite the same way again."

In the opening chapter of *SportsWorld*, Lipsyte exposes his childhood association with athletics. He remarked: "I was never an avid spectator sports fan. Although I grew up in New York while there were still three major league baseball teams in town, I didn't attend my first game until I was 13 years old. I was profoundly disappointed.... I went to only one more game as a paying customer. The third one I covered for *The New York Times*. I attended few sports events as a child, but there was no escaping SportsWorld. That's in the air. I grew up in Rego Park, in Queens, then a neighborhood of attached houses, six-story apartment buildings, and many vacant jungly lots. We played guns in the lots, Chinese handball against the brick sides of buildings, and just enough stickball in the streets and schoolyard to qualify ... as true natives. There was no great sporting tradition in the neighborhood."

Apparently no precedent of athletic participation existed in Lipsyte's family. Instead, intellectual pursuits were stressed due to the fact that both of his parents were teachers and the family's house contained many books. The young Lipsyte spent hours reading and decided early on to become a writer. He received an undergraduate degree in English from Columbia University in New York and planned to continue his education by attending graduate school. Yet, unpredictably, his career as a

Lipsyte's 1967 novel chronicles the metamorphosis of an aimless teen into a disciplined young man.

sports reporter began. In *SportsWorld* he recalled, "In 1957, a few days after graduation from Columbia, I answered a classified ad for a copy boy at *The Times*. I wanted a summer job to pay my way out to graduate school in California.... The job was at night, from 7 to 3, and it was in the sports department, filling paste-pots, sharpening pencils, and fetching coffee for the nights sports copy desk." Despite his decidedly unglamorous entrance into the sports department, Lipsyte opted to stay and eventually graduated from his gopher status. He continued in *SportsWorld*: "I moved from copy boy to statistician to night rewrite reporter. I wrote high school sports and occasional features, often on my own time, and I was sometimes let out to catch a celebrity passing through town or make a fast grab between editions for a quote to freshen up someone else's limp story."

Lipsyte seemed enamored with the newsroom's colorful figures and hectic pace and was eager to test his writing skills. He earned his first major assignment for the paper in 1962, covering the New York Mets in that baseball team's first year of existence. The author also learned to write within space constraints while heeding deadlines. In the 1984 edition of his book *Assignment: Sports* Lipsyte explained, "Writing under deadline is often exhilarating, and if you're lucky and the event has moved you, a rhythm develops and the story just flows out of the typewriter." However, he noted the drawback that "at night in a chilly arena, with the clock moving toward the deadline, that moment comes when even the best story in the world, finished too late, is worthless."

Lipsyte recalled that the 1960s were an excellent time to break into the sportswriting field because of the surge in the appeal of sports as family entertainment and the exposure of athletic contests on television. These developments generated a change in the configuration of articles in the sports page. Previously, stories were essentially game summaries, written for the benefit of those who had not attended the competition. As television gained popularity and more people were able to watch various sporting events, fans looked to newspaper articles to give them unique information about a team or athlete. As Lipsyte acknowledged in *SportsWorld*, this meant that "the sportswriter had to offer his reader fact and opinion unavailable elsewhere, and that meant controversy, bold speculation, and outspoken second-guessing."

In addition to the evolution of reporting, the social conflicts of the 1960s, beginning with the civil rights movement and continuing in the wake of the Vietnam War, profoundly influenced athletes and thus sports stories. Lipsyte chronicled the exploits of many sports figures and tried to demythicize his subjects by reporting about their successes on the field as well as the troubles they faced in their everyday lives. The author was deemed controversial because of his tendency to infuse social and political issues in his sports column. Defending this approach in his book *Assignment: Sports,* an edited collection of his columns, Lipsyte argued, "Politics, race, religion, money, the law—all play roles in sports. . . . sports is no sanctuary from reality." Yet, his philosophy had some supporters in the newspaper industry. In *SportsWorld* he admitted, "My age-group counterparts on other papers seemed pleased when I started covering . . . the growing discontent of athletes, racism, sexism,

In this controversial 1978 biography, Lipsyte recounts episodes from Ali's life and presents examples of his charismatic nature.

distorted nationalism, the sports-politics interface. By appearing in *The Times,* these stories got instant credibility. It became easier for other writers to get such stories past their own editors. Such is the power-by-default of *The Times."*

Lipsyte's most controversial columns inevitably involved the boxer Muhammad Ali, previously named Cassius Clay. In the 1960 Rome Olympics Clay won a gold medal and publicly credited the United States with progress in race relations. As a professional boxer in 1964, however, he converted to the Islamic religious denomination called the Black Muslims, a black separatist sect which adheres to strict rules and seeks to limit contact of its members with whites. As part of his religious conversion, the boxer subsequently changed his name to Muhammad Ali. Some members of the American public viewed his involvement with the Black Muslims as a rebuke against the United States—the country that had afforded Ali the opportunity to become a champion. Many periodicals, including the *New York Times,* initially refused to address the boxer by his newly adopted Islamic name. Ali's religious beliefs came to the forefront again in 1967 when he refused to serve in the Vietnam War, complying with a Black Muslim precedent. This act resulted in the rescindment of his boxing title and a forced three-year hiatus from fighting. In addition, Lipsyte recalled in *Sports-World* that *The Ring*, a boxing magazine, "refused to designate a Fighter of the Year in 1967 because 'most emphatically is Cassius Clay of Louisville, Ky. not to be held up as an example to the youngsters of the United States.'"

Lipsyte, who began covering the boxing beat for the *New York Times* in 1964 and followed Ali's career for more than three years, witnessed the controversy firsthand. Yet, in contrast to the negative perception some members of the American public had of Ali, Lipsyte viewed Ali's expressions of individuality with respect. In his biography of the boxer titled *Free to Be Muhammad Ali*, the author categorized Ali as "far and away the most interesting character in that mythical kingdom I call SportsWorld." Ali's outspokenness—manifested in snappy, original sayings—also offered the author plenty of material with which to write stories. In *SportsWorld*, the author recalled, "Every time I wrote about Ali in those days I would get a flood of letters praising me for being courageous or liberal or irreverent, attacking me for being un-American or a nigger-lover or a fool. The letters more or less neutralized each other. But sometimes [in reference to the ongoing Vietnam War] I would get a sad, thoughtful letter reminding me of all the young Americans coming home in rubber bags while Ali and I were free to prattle."

The title *Free to Be Muhammad Ali* relates to an incident that occurred after the young Clay had defeated Sonny Liston in 1964 to assume the heavyweight championship. After reporters questioned his lifestyle, values, and religious philosophy, Ali replied, according to Lipsyte in *SportsWorld*, "I don't have to be what you want me to be, I'm free to be who I want." Lipsyte remembered that the remark "was very simple, but at that time, coming from a brand-new heavyweight champion of the world, it was profound and revolutionary. A declaration of independence from SportsWorld." In *Free to Be Muhammad Ali*, Lipsyte recounts episodes of the fighter's life and supplies illustrations of his charismatic nature. Mel Watkins, writing in the *New York Times Book Review*, categorized the work as "a thoughtful, complex portrait of one of America's greatest athletes" and added that the reader derives a sense

of Ali's personality and "the affection and respect the author feels for him as an athlete and as a man."

Lipsyte drew upon his experiences as a boxing writer to produce his first novel for young readers, *The Contender*. The protagonist, Alfred Brooks, is an orphaned seventeen-year-old boy living in Harlem. A recent high school dropout, Alfred lives with his aunt and works as a stock boy in a grocery store. The work chronicles the metamorphosis of the aimless Alfred into a disciplined young man with long-term goals. He achieves this change by applying principles he learns while training to be a boxer. Offering universal advice in one of these training sessions, his manager Donatelli insists, "Everybody wants to be a champion. That's not enough. You have to start by wanting to be a contender.... It's the climbing that makes the man. Getting to the top is an extra reward." After months of training, Alfred enters the ring and wins several matches as an amateur. Donatelli, sensing that Alfred does not have the killer instinct required to be a top boxer, advises him to quit fighting competitively. Alfred insists on fighting once more against a worthy opponent to see if he has the requisite courage to be a contender. Although ultimately losing the contest, Alfred discovers an inner resolve that will help him in everyday life. At the book's conclusion, Alfred has plans to go back to school and open a recreation center for the children of Harlem.

The novel was commended for its trendsetting treatment of athletic participation. Unlike the common theme of sports as a vehicle out of the ghetto, Lipsyte's *Contender* presents sports involvement as a form of discipline that will help his protagonist survive and be productive in his same environment. Approving of this realistic approach, John S. Simmons, writing in *Elementary English*, remarked that "tribute to the author lies in the fact that in his search for himself, Alfred has scaled no Matterhorn peaks at the novel's conclusion." Instead, Simmons noted, the protagonist's "gains are modest and his successes frequently tainted with fear, reproach, and self-depreciation." Nat Hentoff, writing in the *New York Times Book Review*, remarked that "whenever Lipsyte writes about boxing itself he indicates how intensely evocative he can be," but hastened to add that "when he leaves the gym and the ring ... Lipsyte is too often content to map the road to salvation" for Alfred. Edward B. Hungerford, writing in *Book World*, concluded by calling *The Contender* "a fine book in

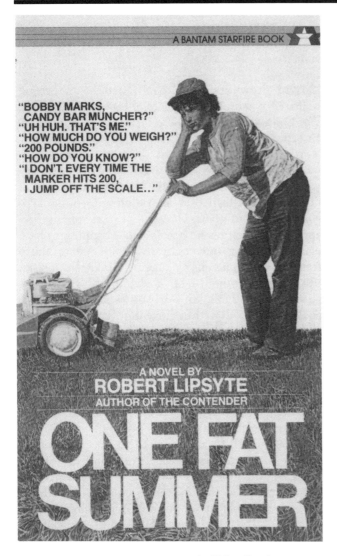

"BOBBY MARKS,
    CANDY BAR MUNCHER?"
"UH HUH. THAT'S ME."
"HOW MUCH DO YOU WEIGH?"
"200 POUNDS."
"HOW DO YOU KNOW?"
"I DON'T. EVERY TIME THE
    MARKER HITS 200,
    I JUMP OFF THE SCALE..."

A BANTAM STARFIRE BOOK

A NOVEL BY
ROBERT LIPSYTE
AUTHOR OF THE CONTENDER

ONE FAT SUMMER

This first installment in Lipsyte's "fifties" trilogy was named an ALA Best Book for Young Adults in 1977.

which interest combines with compassion and enlightenment."

In the fall of 1967, Lipsyte left the boxing beat to begin writing a general sports column for the *New York Times*. In *SportsWorld* he remarked, "It was an exciting time to be writing a column, to be freed from the day-to-day responsibility for a single subject or the whims of the assignment desk. For me, after more than three years with Ali, the newly surfaced turmoil in sports seemed a natural climate." Responsible for three columns a week for the *New York Times*, Lipsyte had the freedom to choose his topics, but was still forced to adhere to stringent space limitations. He continued in *SportsWorld*, "Professionally, there is a challenge, for a while at least, to creating within formalized boundaries. Over an extended period of time, however, it's a poor way to transmit information." The

author also confessed, "As that second year slipped into a third year, as the column became progressively easier to write, . . . I found I was less and less sure of what I absolutely knew."

Lipsyte's columns became the source for his 1970 work titled *Assignment: Sports*, in which he edited his writings from the *New York Times* to appeal to a younger audience. In 1984, he revised the first edition to incorporate the changes in sports, specifically the emergence and acceptance of the female athlete. As with *SportsWorld*, *Assignment: Sports* serves as a historical guide of American athletics. The author provides an account of the Black Power protests in the 1968 summer Olympics and offers portraits of sports figures, including football's Joe Namath, boxing's Ali, and baseball manager Casey Stengel. Sam Elkin, writing in the *New York Times Book Review*, credited Lipsyte "with the skill of a fine fiction writer for nuance" and added the "readers meeting him for the first time, regardless of age-group, have a rare treat in store."

Despite the acclaim his columns received, Lipsyte left the *New York Times* in the fall of 1971. In his book *Assignment: Sports* he remarked, "I knew I'd miss the quick excitement of deadline journalism.... But I wanted more time to think about what I had seen during the past fourteen years, and more space to shape those thoughts into characters and stories." During the next eleven years he wrote books, taught journalism at college, visited schools to talk about his books, wrote jokes for a television show called *Saturday Night with Howard Cosell*, and spent nine months at the *New York Post* writing a column about the people of that city. Although Lipsyte admitted to sometimes missing his old job at the *New York Times* he reasoned, "Mostly I enjoyed a deeper, richer creative challenge. It was a wonderful time. I remember with pleasure the months of traveling slowly through the back roads of my imagination."

In the late 1970s and early 1980s, Lipsyte wrote what he deemed a fifties trilogy consisting of the books *One Fat Summer*, *Summer Rules*, and *The Summerboy*. The author shares similarities with his protagonist, Bobby Marks, who also comes of age in the fifties and conquers an adolescent weight problem. Each book is set in a resort town in upstate New York called Rumson Lake where Bobby's family spends each summer. Lipsyte presents the maturation process of his protagonist from the age of fourteen to eighteen. In the trilogy, Bobby faces problems, but overcomes them by relying on determination, hard work, and positive values. Critics have endorsed the novels for tackling adolescent dilemmas in a realistic manner and for offering believable first-person narration.

The first installment, *One Fat Summer,* depicts the protagonist as a fourteen-year-old nicknamed the "Crisco Kid" because he weighs more than two hundred pounds. Wishing to hide his flabby body beneath baggy winter clothes, Bobby dreads the family's annual migration to Rumson Lake. The protagonist must also contend with Willie Rumson, a town bully who dislikes "summer people" such as the Marks family, and takes out his frustrations by subjecting Bobby to public humiliation. During this particular summer Bobby must also endure the snide comments of Dr. Kahn, who employs the youngster as a landscaper. Despite the aching muscles and blisters he is afflicted with during his stint of manual labor, Bobby loses fifty pounds over the summer and, more significantly, gains the self-esteem necessary to stand up to Willie and Dr. Kahn. When describing the protagonist, Stephen Krensky, writing in the *New York Times Book Review,* commented that "refreshingly, he is neither precocious nor off-beat ... but simply a normal boy in abnormal circumstances."

The second book of the trilogy, *Summer Rules,* chronicles Bobby's adventures as a sixteen-year-old. Although eagerly looking forward to socializing during the summer, Bobby is forced by his father to work as a counselor at the Happy Valley Day Camp. Here the protagonist meets Sheila, his first real girlfriend. Unfortunately, she is also the cousin of Harley, a spoiled nine-year-old who has experienced emotional problems since his mother's death. The book recounts Bobby's budding romance with Sheila and his tribulations as a counselor. A building fire nearly kills some of the campers and, based on his past record, Willie Rumson, Bobby's nemesis from *One Fat Summer,* is falsely arrested on the suspicion of arson. Bobby knows that Harley actually set the fire, but struggles with his conscience to determine if telling the truth will cause the boy more distress and alienate Sheila. Several critics approved of the sophisticated subject and praised Lipsyte's writing style.

Bobby returns as an eighteen-year-old in the novel *The Summerboy.* The protagonist begins his summer job at Lenape Laundry thinking that the town girls will be impressed by his new status as a college student. Instead, his coworkers shun him because he is an affluent "summerboy." The owner of the laundry, Roger Sinclair, allows his workers to toil in unsafe working conditions and will fire anyone who complains. Bobby, who wants to be accepted by the other workers, must decide whether to side with the boss and keep his job, or stand up for the other employees. After a serious accident at the laundry, Bobby leads a protest and is fired, but the demonstration forces Sinclair to improve conditions.

Lipsyte was forced to battle his own problems beginning in the summer of 1978 when he was diagnosed as having testicular cancer. In his book *Assignment: Sports* he recalled, "Like most people, we regarded cancer as one of the most dread words in the language; if not a death sentence, we thought, at least it meant the end of a normal, productive life. We knew very little about cancer, but we learned quickly. After surgery, I underwent two years of chemotherapy. I was sick for a day or two after each treatment, and I lost some strength and some hair, but we were amazed as how normally my life continued: I wrote, I traveled, I swam and ran and played tennis. After the treatments were over, my strength and my hair re-

The sequel to *One Fat Summer* continues the adventures of Bobby Marks, now sixteen and a camp counselor.

turned. There was no evidence of cancer. I was happy to be alive, to be enjoying my family, to be writing."

Lipsyte's next book, *Jock and Jill,* involves themes of social responsibility and the use of pain-killing drugs in athletics. In the book, Jack Ryder, a high school pitching ace, breaks up with his girlfriend of two years to date Jill, a socially aware girl who has taken therapeutic drugs for emotional problems. He then joins Jill's coalition with Hector, a Hispanic gang leader, to lobby for better conditions in the housing projects of New York City's ghettos. Early in the work it appears that Jack has a perfect life, but it is gradually revealed that his younger brother is mentally retarded and his father cannot afford Jack's college tuition. Consequently, the protagonist, though receiving cortisone shots to relieve the pain in his arm, must rely on his pitching skills for a scholarship. As Jack prepares to pitch for his high school team in the Metro Area Championship in Yankee Stadium, he ponders his varying responsibilities to his father, coach, teammates, and the girl he has fallen in love with. Jack has the chance to be a hero in the game, but instead decides to use his platform to benefit Jill and Hector. The protagonist selflessly interrupts his no-hitter game in the seventh inning to protest the false arrest of Hector. Critics generally considered that Lipsyte skillfully handled the numerous elements in the story. John Leonard, writing in the *New York Times Book Review,* commented that the author "has a number of pitches to make in this engaging and didactic novel" and added, "On the big game, Mr. Lipsyte is superb."

Following the publication of *Jock and Jill,* Lipsyte began another career as a television correspondent. In *Assignment: Sports* he recalled, "One day in the spring of 1982, Shad Northshield and Bud Lamoreaux, the executive producers of the CBS 'Sunday Morning' show, asked me if I'd like to appear on television. It would mean hitting the road again and writing on deadline, learning a new field and meeting new people. . . . [It] would be like starting all over again." Lipsyte took the challenge and, after leaving *Sunday Morning,* worked as a correspondent for NBC-TV and became the host of *The Eleventh Hour* PBS program, a combination talk and interview show.

Despite his detour into broadcasting, Lipsyte continues to observe and comment upon college athletics. Serving as a senior fellow at the Center for the Study of Sport in Society at Northeastern University, the author has studied the alienation of college and professional athletes from the general public as well as the problems this isolation causes when an athlete's career is finished. He wrote in the *New York Times Magazine,* "I have begun to understand the problems of the temporarily rich and famous trying to become ordinary people." Lipsyte believes that once athletes retire, they experience difficulty adjusting to a lifestyle that lacks the structure and discipline of a sports team.

For Lipsyte, these issues serve as another indication of the dangers of mythicizing athletic involvement. The author wishes sports to once again be popular recreation instead of an industry that offers false hopes of stardom to millions of youngsters. As a writer, Lipsyte has attempted to present athletic participation in a proper perspective for young readers. In an article for *Children's Literature in Education,* Lipsyte concluded, "If we write more truthfully about sports, perhaps we can encourage kids to relax and have fun with each other—to challenge themselves for the pleasure of it, without self-doubt and without fear."

Although Lipsyte took an eight-year break from composing books, the urge to write never left him. In 1991, he published *The Brave,* a sequel to *The Contender,* his best-selling book. The author had received numerous letters in the years since *The Contender*'s publication all posing a common question—"what happened next?" to Alfred. Lipsyte told *AAYA:* "I began to wonder what happened to Alfred too. In the psychosis that is writing, you begin to think that some of your characters really lived." The idea for *The Brave*'s plot was formed while Lipsyte was on a journalism assignment at an American Indian reservation. There he met and talked with a young man who described his fear of being stuck on the reservation where there were high levels of disease, alcoholism, and unemployment. At the same time, he was also afraid of leaving the reservation and facing the "white" world and possible rejection and prejudice. Nonetheless, he ran away to New York City for a few days. Although he was caught and forced to return home, the action was one of personal triumph. Lipsyte admired the boy's bravery and told *AAYA:* "The idea of this runaway meeting Alfred Brooks marinated in my mind for a few years."

Lipsyte was able to act on this potential plot after the PBS television program he hosted was suddenly canceled. Ironically this happened in June, which Lipsyte told *AAYA* was his "lucky month for starting books." In *The Brave,* Sonny Bear, a seventeen-year-old half-Indian runaway, meets Alfred Brooks in New York City. Alfred is now a forty-year-old police sergeant who seeks to curtail

Both a love story and an expose on the use of painkillers in athletics, Lipsyte's 1982 novel was praised for its realism.

drug trafficking in the city. Sonny unwittingly becomes a pawn in the drug war, yet he has a friend in Alfred. Explaining the police officer's urge to help out the youngster, Lipsyte told *AAYA*, "Alfred wanted to pass on what he learned from Donatelli" his old boxing manager who gave advice that changed the course of Alfred's life when he was a teenager.

During the same year that *The Brave* was published, Lipsyte returned to the *New York Times* to write one sports column a week. The author told *AAYA* that his comeback as a sportswriter was "all part of the return to writing, the recommitment. I wanted to see how the world had changed—how I had changed. It was a terrific challenge; people might tell me that 'anything you had to say, you said twenty years ago.'" As for the changes in sports and the sportswriting field since his first stint in 1957, Lipsyte added, "The stakes are higher in sports now, but *I'm* more different than

sports are. The writers are much better—they are better educated and sharper in perception." The author also pointed out that when he began, most writers were white males. "Now there are more women and blacks. There is beginning to be a representation of America" in the sports department.

■ Works Cited

Elkin, Sam, review of *Assignment: Sports, New York Times Book Review*, May 31, 1970, p. 14.

Hentoff, Nat, review of *The Contender, New York Times Book Review*, November 12, 1967, p. 42.

Hungerford, Edward B., review of *The Contender, Book World*, November 5, 1967, p. 43.

Kahn, Roger, "No Tears for Namath," *New York Times Book Review*, November 8, 1975, p. 5.

Krensky, Stephen, review of *One Fat Summer, New York Times Book Review*, July 10, 1977, p. 20.

Leonard, John, review of *Jock and Jill, New York Times Book Review*, April 25, 1982, p.34.

Lipsyte, Robert, *Assignment: Sports*, revised edition, Harper, 1984, pp. 137-138.

Lipsyte, R., "Forum: Robert Lipsyte on Kids/Sports/Books," *Children's Literature in Education*, spring, 1980, pp. 43, 44, 45, 47.

Lipsyte, R., interview with Mary Ruby for *Authors & Artists for Young Adults*, conducted May 17, 1991.

Lipsyte, R., *SportsWorld: An American Dreamland*, Quadrangle, 1975, pp. x, xiv, 4, 5, 7, 8, 26, 43, 88, 120, 126, 129, 133, 183, 192, 195, 206.

Lipsyte, R. "The Athlete's Losing Game," *New York Times Magazine*, November 30, 1986, p. 59.

Lipsyte, R. *The Contender*, Harper, 1967, p. 27.

Simmons, John S., "Lipsyte's *Contender*: Another Look at the Junior Novel," *Elementary English*, January, 1972, p. 117.

Watkins, Mel, review of *Free to be Muhammad Ali, New York Times Book Review*, March 4, 1979, p. 32.

Wills, Garry, "The Sporting Life," *New York Review of Books*, October 30, 1975, p. 6.

Zimmerman, Paul D., "Cold Shower," *Newsweek*, November 24, 1975, pp. 120-121.

■ For More Information See

BOOKS

Contemporary Literary Criticism, Volume 21, Gale, 1982.

PERIODICALS

English Journal, December, 1980.
Harper's Magazine, September, 1985.
Nation, May 25, 1985.
New York Times, November 7, 1988.

New York Times Magazine, February 16, 1986; November 30, 1986; May 22, 1988.
New York Times Sports Magazine, March 31, 1985.
People Weekly, March 25, 1985.
TV Guide, August 4, 1984; April 13, 1985.

—*Sidelights by Mary K. Ruby*

Monty Python

■ Personal

Collective pseudonym for British comedy troupe comprised of writers and performers Graham Chapman, John Cleese, Terry Gilliam, Eric Idle, Terry Jones, and Michael Palin.

Graham Chapman: Born January 8, 1941, in Leicester, England; died of throat and spinal cancer, October 4, 1989, in Maidstone, Kent, England; son of Walter (a policeman) and Edith (Towers) Chapman; children: (adopted) John Tomiczek. *Education:* Emmanuel College, Cambridge, M.A., 1962; St. Bartholomew's Medical School, M.B., B.Chir., 1966.

John Cleese: Full name John Marwood Cleese; born October 27, 1939, in Weston-super-Mare, Somerset, England; son of Reginald (an insurance salesman) and Muriel (an acrobat; maiden name, Cross) Cleese; married Connie Booth (an actress and writer), February 20, 1968 (divorced, 1978); married Barbara Trentham (a director and artist), February 15, 1981 (divorced, 1990); children: (first marriage) Cynthia; (second marriage) Camilla. *Education:* Downing College, Cambridge, M.A., 1963. *Politics:* Social-Democrat Liberal.

Terry Gilliam: Full name Terry Vance Gilliam; born November 22, 1940, in Minneapolis, MN; came to England, 1967; son of James Hall (a carpenter) and Beatrice (Vance) Gilliam; married Margaret Weston (a makeup artist), 1974; children: Amy Rainbow, Holly du Bois, one son. *Education:* Occidental College, B.A., 1962.

Eric Idle: Born March 29, 1943, in South Shields, Durham, England; son of Ernest (a Royal Air Force sergeant) and Norah (a health visitor; maiden name, Sanderson) Idle; married Lyn Ashley (an actress), July 7, 1969 (divorced, 1978); married second wife, Tania (a model), 1981; children: (first marriage) Carey (son). *Education:* Graduated from Pembroke College, Cambridge, 1965.

Terry Jones: Full name Terence Graham Parry Jones; born February 1, 1942, in Colwyn Bay, North Wales; son of Alick George Parry (a bank clerk) and Dilys Louisa (a homemaker; maiden name, Newnes) Jones; married Alison Telfer (a botanist), 1970; children: Sally, Bill. *Education:* Graduated from St. Edmund Hall, Oxford, 1964.

Michael Palin: Full name Michael Edward Palin; born May 5, 1943, in Sheffield, Yorkshire, England; son of Edward (an engineer) and Mary Palin; married Helen M. Gibbins, 1966; children: Tom, William, Rachel. *Education:* Brasenose College, Oxford, B.A. (second class honors), 1965. *Hobbies and other interests:* Reading, running, railways.

■ Addresses

Office—c/o Python Pictures Ltd., 68A Delancey St., London NW1 7RY, England.

■ Career

Writers and performers, beginning 1969, in television series *Monty Python's Flying Circus*, BBC-TV, 1969-74, in motion pictures *And Now for Something Completely Different*, 1972, *Monty Python and the Holy Grail*, 1975, *Monty Python's Life of Brian*, 1979, *Monty Python Live at the Hollywood Bowl*, 1982, and *Monty Python's The Meaning of Life*, 1983, and in concert tours in England, Canada, and the United States. Founders of Prominent Features, a production company.

■ Awards, Honors

British Academy of Film and Television Arts (BAFTA) special award for production, writing and performance, 1969, Silver Rose, Montreux Television Festival, 1971, and BAFTA Award for light entertainment program, 1972, all for *Monty Python's Flying Circus*; Grand Prix Special du Jury award, Cannes Film Festival, 1983, for *Monty Python's The Meaning of Life*; BAFTA Michael Balcon Award For Outstanding British Contribution to Cinema, 1987.

■ Writings

MONTY PYTHON SCREENPLAYS

And Now for Something Completely Different (adapted from the television series), Columbia, 1972.
Monty Python and the Holy Grail (also see below), Cinema 5, 1975.
Monty Python's Life of Brian (also see below), Warner Brothers, 1979.
Monty Python Live at the Hollywood Bowl, Handmade Films/Columbia, 1982.
Monty Python's The Meaning of Life (also see below), Universal, 1983.

MONTY PYTHON BOOKS

Monty Python's Big Red Book, Methuen, 1972, Warner Books, 1975.
The Brand New Monty Python Bok, edited by Idle, illustrations by Gilliam (under pseudonym Jerry Gillian) and Peter Brookes, Methuen, 1973, published as *The Brand New Monty Python Papperbok*, Methuen, 1974.
Monty Python and the Holy Grail (also published as *Monty Python's Second Film: A First Draft*), both by Methuen, 1977.
Monty Python's Life of Brian [and] *Montypython-scrapbook*, Grosset, 1979.

The Complete Works of Shakespeare and Monty Python: Volume One—Monty Python (contains *Monty Python's Big Red Book* and *The Brand New Monty Python Papperbok*), Methuen, 1981.
Monty Python's The Meaning of Life, Grove Press, 1983.
The Complete Monty Python's Flying Circus: All the Words, two volumes, Pantheon, 1989.

MONTY PYTHON RECORDINGS

Monty Python's Flying Circus, BBC Records, 1970.
Another Monty Python Record, Charisma, 1971.
Monty Python's Previous Record, Charisma, 1972.
Monty Python Matching Tie and Handkerchief, Charisma, 1973, Arista, 1974.
Monty Python Live at the Theatre Royal, Drury Lane, Charisma, 1974.
The Album of the Soundtrack of the Trailer of the Film of Monty Python and the Holy Grail (film soundtrack; includes additional material), Arista, 1975.
Monty Python Live at City Center, Arista, 1976.
The Worst of Monty Python, Kama Sutra, 1976.
The Monty Python Instant Record Collection, Charisma, 1977.
Monty Python's Life of Brian (film soundtrack), Warner Brothers, 1979.
Monty Python's Contractual Obligation Album, Arista, 1980.
Monty Python's The Meaning of Life (film soundtrack), CBS Records, 1983.
Monty Python's the Final Ripoff (compilation), Virgin Records, 1988.

OTHER MONTY PYTHON WORKS

Monty Python's Flying Circus (television series), BBC-TV, 1969-74, televised in the United States, PBS-TV, 1974.
Pythons in Deutschland (television movie), Batavia Atelier, c. 1972.

BY CHAPMAN

(With Bernard G. McKenna) "Idle at Work" (teleplay), *Comedy Playhouse*, BBC-TV, 1972.
(With McKenna and Douglas Adams) *Out of the Trees* (teleplay), BBC-TV, 1976.
The Odd Job (screenplay; based on a teleplay by McKenna), Columbia, 1978.
A Liar's Autobiography: Volume VI, Methuen, 1980.
(With McKenna and Peter Cook) *Yellowbeard* (screenplay), Orion, 1983.

BY CHAPMAN AND CLEESE

(And with Peter Sellers, Terry Southern and Joseph McGrath) *The Magic Christian* (based on Southern's novel), Grand/Commonwealth, 1970.

(And with Cook and Kevin Billington) *The Rise and Rise of Michael Rimmer*, Seven Arts/Warner Brothers, 1970.

Rentadick (screenplay), Virgin Films, 1972.

Also authors of various episodes of the London Weekend Television series *Doctor in the House*, *Doctor at Large*, and *Doctor in Charge*, 1969, 1972-73.

BY CHAPMAN AND IDLE

No, That's Me over Here (television series), ITV, 1967.

BY CLEESE

(With Connie Booth) *Fawlty Towers* (television series), BBC-TV, 1975 and 1979, published by Futura, Volume 1, 1977, Volume 2, 1979, published in one volume as *The Complete Fawlty Towers*, Pantheon, 1989.

(With Jack Hobbs and Joe McGrath) *The Strange Case of the End of Civilisation as We Know It*, London Weekend Television, 1977, published by Star Books, 1977.

(With Robin Skynner) *Families and How to Survive Them*, Methuen, 1983.

(With others) *The Golden Skits of Wing-Commander Muriel Volestrangler, FHRS and Bar*, Methuen, 1984.

A Fish Called Wanda (screenplay), Metro-Goldwyn-Mayer, 1988, published by Applause Book Publishers, 1988.

Also author, with Connie Booth, of short film *Romance with a Double Bass*, 1974. Author of numerous business training films for Video Arts, Ltd.

BY GILLIAM

(Compiler with Harvey Kurtzman) *Harvey Kurtzman's Fun and Games*, text by Charles Alverson, Fawcett, 1965.

(With Joel Siegel) *The Cocktail People* (cartoons), Pisani Press, 1966.

(With Alverson) *Jabberwocky* (screenplay), Umbrella/Cinema 5, 1977, published by Pan Books, 1977.

(With Lucinda Cowell) *Animations of Mortality* (cartoons), Methuen, 1978.

(With Tom Stoppard and Charles McKeown) *Brazil* (screenplay), Universal, 1984.

(With McKeown) *The Adventures of Baron Munchausen* (screenplay; also see below), Columbia, 1989, published as *The Adventures of Baron Munchausen: The Screenplay*, Applause Book Publishers, 1989.

(With McKeown) *The Adventures of Baron Munchausen: The Novel* (based on their screenplay), illustrated by James Victore and Joyce L. Houlihan, Applause Book Publishers, 1989.

BY GILLIAM AND PALIN

Time Bandits, Avco Embassy, 1981, published as *Time Bandits: The Movie Script*, Doubleday, 1981.

BY IDLE

Hello Sailor (novel), Weidenfeld & Nicolson, 1974.

Rutland Weekend Television (television series), BBC-TV, 1975-76.

Rutland Dirty Weekend Songbook (recording), BBC Records, 1975.

The Rutland Dirty Weekend Book, Methuen, 1976.

All You Need Is Cash (television movie), NBC, 1978 (televised in Britain as *The Rutles*, BBC-TV, 1978).

Pass the Butler (play; produced in London, 1982), Methuen, 1982.

Also author of scripts for *Nearly Departed*, NBC, 1989.

BY JONES

Chaucer's Knight: The Portrait of a Medieval Mercenary (nonfiction), Louisiana State University Press, 1980.

Fairy Tales (for children), Schocken, 1981, published as *Terry Jones' Fairy Tales*, Puffin, 1986.

The Saga of Erik the Viking (for children), Schocken, 1983.

Nicobobinus (for children), Viking Kestrel, 1985.

Labyrinth (screenplay), Tri-Star, 1986.

The Goblins of Labyrinth (adapted from the film *Labyrinth*), illustrated by Brian Froud, Pavilion, 1986.

The Curse of the Vampire Socks (poetry for children), Pavilion, 1988.

Attacks of Opinion (essays), Penguin, 1988.

Erik the Viking (screenplay), Orion, 1989, published as *Erik the Viking: The Screenplay*, Applause Book Publishers, 1989.

BY JONES AND PALIN

The Complete and Utter History of Britain (television series), London Weekend Television, 1969.

Secrets (teleplay), BBC-TV, 1973.

Bert Fegg's Nasty Book for Boys and Girls, Methuen, 1974, new revised edition published as *Dr. Fegg's Encyclopaedia of All World Knowledge*, Peter Bedrick, 1985.

Their Finest Hours (two short plays, *Underhill's Finest Hour* and *Buchanan's Finest Hour*), produced in Sheffield, England, 1976.

Ripping Yarns (television series; also see below), BBC-TV, 1976-77, 1979.

Ripping Yarns (stories; adapted from the television series), artwork by Walter Junge, photographs by Amy Lune and Bertrand Polo, Methuen, 1978, Pantheon, 1979.

More Ripping Yarns (stories; adapted from television series *Ripping Yarns*), Methuen, 1978, Pantheon, 1980.

BY PALIN

Small Harry and the Toothache Pills (for children), Methuen, 1981.

The Missionary (screenplay), Handmade Films, 1982, published by Methuen, 1983.

"Confessions of a Train-Spotter," *Great Railway Journeys of the World*, BBC-TV, 1983, published by Dutton, 1983.

Limericks (for children), Hutchinson, 1985, Random House, 1987.

(With Richard Seymour) *The Mirrorstone: A Ghost Story with Holograms* (for children), illustrations by Alan Lee, Knopf, 1986.

Cyril and the House of Commons (for children), Pavilion, 1986.

Cyril and the Dinner Party (for children), Pavilion, 1986.

East of Ipswich, BBC-TV, 1987.

Number 27, BBC-TV, 1988.

Around the World in Eighty Days? (travel documentary), BBC-TV, 1989, companion volume published by BBC Books, 1989.

■ Adaptations

The film *Consuming Passions*, produced by Samuel Goldwyn and Euston Films in 1988, was based on the teleplay *Secrets* by Palin and Jones; some of Jones's *Fairy Tales* were adapted for television.

■ Sidelights

"Pythons—they have a singular genius for making nonsensical fun of all who are pompous, pretentious, humorless, or boring, or who take themselves too seriously," Thomas Meehan says in the *New York Times Magazine*. Featuring the talents of Graham Chapman, John Cleese, Terry Gilliam, Eric Idle, Terry Jones, and Michael Palin, the Monty Python comedy troupe first appeared on British television in 1969 and since then has become a popular favorite with young people around the world, with numerous books, records, and films to their credit. Meehan added that "unlike almost all other comedians these days, on TV or elsewhere, the Pythons are shamelessly willing to go in for absolute nonsense—to dress up in women's clothes, to talk in non sequiturs, and to be not only utterly silly but often in outrageously bad taste.... Yet part of their infinite charm is that they're willing to try almost anything and to lampoon just about anyone." As a result, Monty Python has become "a transatlantic cult phenomenon, a virulent force whose rude and relentless explorations of television comedy changed that medium forever," as Laurence Shames observes in *Esquire*. In addition, Pythons have been responsible—as a group and as individuals—for such popular films as *Monty Python and the Holy Grail*, *Monty Python's Life of Brian*, *Time Bandits*, *Monty Python's Meaning of Life*, *Brazil*, and *A Fish Called Wanda*.

As children, many of the Pythons found comedy fascinating and even useful. Cleese recalled that as an only child, he was "rather solitary, not a particularly good mixer," he told Frank Lovece in the *New York Post*. "Then I found I could get laughs saying funny things like my father used to." Palin also remembered using humor to cope during his childhood; of his days at boarding school, he remembered that they were "great ... for elaborate practical jokes," as he told George Perry in *Life of Python*. "Even the masters would play practical jokes on each other. Our house was a very happy one, largely due to a wonderful housemaster who was very silly, full of jokes. He kept us full of laughter, and enabled us to cope with the awful food and waking up in winter with six inches of snow on our beds." Chapman had an early interest in comedy as well as medicine, he similarly related to Perry: "From the age of about eight or nine I had been an avid listener to the radio, to all things comedic, and later I became a television watcher.... Then around about the age of fourteen I saw an excerpt on TV of a Footlights Show, I think that

The "How to Hit People over the Head" sketch from *Monty Python's Flying Circus*, featuring (from left) Palin, Idle, Cleese, Gilliam, Chapman, and Jones.

Jonathan Miller may have been in it. So that slipped into my subconscious, and I thought that if I'm to do medicine then Cambridge is the university to go to."

Chapman did go to Cambridge, where he ended up joining the Footlights Society, a theatre group; there he met and began collaborating with Cleese. Idle also became involved in the Footlights at Cambridge, while Jones and Palin joined the theatrical troupe at Oxford. Palin related his particular experience to Chris Chase of the *New York Times:* "There were people writing scripts for little college reviews and setting up groups to go around doing cabaret. I spent as much time as possible doing that. So at the end of three years, I was totally unqualified to teach history to anybody except inanimate objects. But through Oxford contacts, I got my first job for a television company." The other British Pythons similarly found jobs with the British Broadcasting Corp. (BBC) in radio and television after completing their educations.

Gilliam, who attended college in California, came to the BBC in a more roundabout fashion. After graduation, he traveled to New York, where he found a job illustrating for the humor magazine *Help!* At this time, he met Cleese, who was in

America with Chapman and the touring company of *Cambridge Circus*, and when Gilliam moved to England he contacted Cleese for help in finding a job. "I was really low—it seemed impossible to get anywhere with magazines, so I called John Cleese and asked him how I could get into television," he related to Perry. Cleese put him in contact with BBC director Humphrey Barclay, who "was only mildly amused by my written sketches, but when I mentioned I was a cartoonist he was interested." Gilliam was hired for *Do Not Adjust Your Set*, a comedy program that also had Palin, Jones, and Idle among its cast.

The Pythons were initially enlisted separately to write and appear on various BBC programs during the 1960s, including *The Frost Report, Do Not Adjust Your Set*, and *At Last, the 1948 Show*. But writing for other performers proved unsatisfying, as Chapman related to Perry: "We often felt when we were doing things for *The Frost Report* that some items that we knew were funny would not get done because it was felt that they were too rude or too silly. And with other people performing what we had written they also injected a lot of themselves into our material and changed it away from what we intended. We thought that apart from enjoying performing we would be able to do it how we wanted—we didn't have to worry about performers because we were going to do it ourselves. We could approach the thing as writers. We had much more control." In addition, Jones told Russell Miller of *Radio Times*, Spike Milligan's program *Q5* inspired them with the desire to create a new, unconventional kind of television show. "We suddenly realised we had been writing in complete cliches," Jones said. "What [Milligan] was doing to comedy was amazing and so from that moment we started breaking out of the traps."

In 1969, Cleese made good on the BBC's standing invitation to do his own program. As Gilliam related in an interview with *Contemporary Authors,* "[Cleese] took the opportunity and said, 'There's five other people and myself who want to do a show. We don't know exactly what it's going to be, but it'll be funny.' That was it. Literally the six of us from the start decided that we wanted to do a show together. From that we developed whatever style there is to it." The group would write sketches individually and in pairs, with the entire group voting on which bits should make the show. The Pythons wrote to please themselves; "We don't really care [about what the fans want]," Gilliam said in an *Aquarian* interview with Tony DeSena. "It sounds arrogant but it's also honest. We don't know or care about demographics. We write totally for ourselves, what *we* think is funny. We never take into consideration anyone else." Palin, for instance, prefers "making connections about things which people normally wouldn't," as he remarked to John Fitzgerald of the Toronto *Globe and Mail.* "I conjure surreal images and I don't like comedy which is forced."

The Pythons' democratic method of choosing material proved very helpful in developing it, as Idle related to Kim Howard Johnson in *The First 200 Years of Monty Python:* "If it worked and we got laughs, there it was—it was obviously funny. And if it didn't get laughs, or if it only got a few laughs, then we had immediate advice: 'I can help this sketch go here,' or 'What it needs is this.' And we could do it in a rewrite, or someone else could take it on." "I think there's an advantage to the six of us being together," Gilliam told DeSena. "People on their own are very vulnerable and often have to put up facades. We're a group of people who give *each other* a bad time. We take care not to allow each other to think too highly of himself so we're reasonably confident and not worried about exposing ourselves."

The result of all this cooperation and collaboration was *Monty Python's Flying Circus*, an offbeat comedy series that indulged in silliness and rudeness, trampling the taboos that had restricted other television series. Punctuated by Gilliam's bizarre animations, the shows presented a series of sketches that followed no set form—sketches would transform into "something completely different," end in the middle, or even be interrupted by other sketches. A favorite method was to use explosions, a sixteen-ton weight, a knight with a rubber chicken (played by Gilliam), or an animated foot to obliterate obnoxious characters. "They were convenient ways of getting rid of characters, and they livened up the shows a bit," Palin told Johnson. "It was the slightly destructive side of Python, getting rid of characters as they would in a cartoon, but doing it live." The show's title and closing credits were similarly unpredictable, appearing at various points during the show.

Although the shows followed a stream-of-consciousness, almost shapeless format—only one of the forty-five *Flying Circus* programs actually featured a single sketch for the entire show—each episode had a specific comic structure. Gilliam explained that in certain episodes "things kept referring back to themselves, people went back on television whom we had seen earlier," as Hendrik Hertzberg quoted him in the *New Yorker.* In one episode, "at one point, we saw the ladies watching themselves on television watching a television set showing the beginning of the film.... Our shows tend to be very strong on form. We think of each one as a show, try to interrelate all these things; so the form is as important to the name of Monty Python as the laughs." Continuity of *humor,* rather than form, provided each show's focus. "What we were after," Cleese told Shames in *Esquire,* "was something less linear and more abstract than anything we'd seen. We wanted to satirize attitudes rather than individuals; we were more interested in a web of comic logic than a string of separate jokes."

The Pythons lampooned a variety of subjects each episode. The humor, however, was not blatantly social or political; this was the intent of the Pythons. As Chapman told Johnson in *The First 200 Years of Monty Python:* "Since we came along fairly closely after *Beyond the Fringe* [a British comedy revue of the early 1960s], and the social consciousness and satirical label that they'd gotten—somewhat unfairly—we wanted to avoid being bracketed as being another offshoot of their methods. More importantly, however," he continued, "a very practical reason was repeats. We'd written in TV for a few years, so we'd obviously realized at this stage that if we wrote something in a show that got repeated, then we would get another fee for it without having to do any extra work! Now, that looked like a good idea, and as the BBC didn't pay us very much in the first place, it was almost essential to have the thing repeated. Obviously, topical things were not favored, because they wouldn't work in a couple of years' time, so we did tend to avoid them."

Instead, the Pythons targeted a broad range of people and institutions. Authority figures and government bureaucracy were mocked in sketches such as the "Ministry of Silly Walks" and "Police Station." The upper class was skewered in the "Upper-Class Twit of the Year" contest, while the lower and middle classes were unflatteringly portrayed in such recurring characters as the Pepperpots—Pythons in drag as loud, middle-aged ladies in housecoats and curlers—and the Gumbies, perpetually puzzled men who dressed in gumboots, rolled-up pants and shirts, and handkerchiefs on their heads. The Pythons were particularly fond of poking fun at television; interviewers would have to deal with bizarre guests—or vice

versa—and there were also game shows such as "Blackmail" and contests such as "The All England Summarize Proust Competition." Other trademarks were absurd arguments, such as in the "Dead Parrot" and "Fish License" sketches; unusual cases of cross-dressing, as in the "Lumberjack Song"; and just plain strange happenings, including the "Fish-Slapping Dance" and "Spam" sketches.

With their irreverent attitudes towards everyone and everything, the Pythons frequently offended the sensibilities of various groups, sometimes sparking letters and protests. But Cleese insisted that Python was never deliberately insulting: "The overall thing is whether it's fundamentally good natured or not," he said in an *Aquarian* interview with Lewis Archibald. "It's a very simple kind of thing to say but if you feel that there's basically a lot of *joie de vivre* and good nature behind it all, then somehow that kind of stuff's okay. I hope that if anybody finds something in the Python [work] that's a bit offensive, they will find that all the rest of it isn't. It's so very much to do with people's individual repressions. That's what it comes down to. We've all got certain areas where we're more or

A publicity photo featuring favorite characters from the TV series: Cleese with dead parrot, Gilliam in Nude Organist "costume," Jones as a Pepperpot, Chapman as the Colonel, Palin as a Gumby, and Idle in Master of Ceremonies dress.

Gilliam's animation for the "Legendary Black Beast of Arrrghhh" from *Monty Python and the Holy Grail.*

less comfortable and they vary wildly from person to person."

Although the show's outrageous humor regularly flaunted conventions, the Pythons initially had free rein to write and perform whatever they wanted. As Jones related in a *Contemporary Authors* interview, "We had total latitude, absolutely, the first season of 'Monty Python's Flying Circus. . . .' The whole organization was geared to give the artist a free hand under the producers. Nobody checked any scripts or looked at the shows before they went out." But after the first two seasons, the BBC came under new management, which paid more attention to the increasingly popular show. The group was subjected to attempts at censorship, with sketches mentioning cannibalism and masturbation receiving particular attention. Even one of Gilliam's animations, concerning a cancerous black spot which eats its owner, came under BBC scrutiny.

Nevertheless the series, after initially languishing in a late-night spot, became Britain's highest-rated show. The show eventually crossed the Atlantic and aired on PBS, who agreed to present the programs uncut and uncensored. The *Flying Circus* also proved popular in the States, becoming the network's most popular entertainment program, despite the doubts of critics who felt the show's humor wouldn't translate to an American audience. But "the impact of the Pythons' approach depended . . . [more] on absurd juxtapositions and pure silliness" than on specific British references, Hertzberg explained in the *New Yorker*. Therefore, "one doesn't have to know very much about parliamentary government to recognize that it is funny when a Cabinet minister on a bogus news interview falls through the crust of the earth, or wears a tutu, or addresses his remarks to a small patch of brown liquid, possibly creosote."

Palin offered another reason for the program's American success to Sally A. Lodge of *Publishers Weekly:* "We got across to a lot of kids who were quite fed up with the standard American telly. Python seemed to open a few doors, and that's what we want to see television doing. People are drawn to something that breaks a few rules and moves into taboo areas—like those areas that [comedian] Lenny Bruce broke into on stage. I think that Python has done something similar in the TV age." Gilliam suggested a similar cause: "What has happened with Monty Python in the States is that there are a lot of people who have come to believe in Python as a form of honesty, as opposed to what is normally presented on television,"

Hertzberg quoted him as saying. "Here is a show that is outspoken, says what it wants to say, does extraordinary things, takes all sorts of chances, is not out to sell corn plaster, or anything. It is out to entertain, surprise, enlighten even, the people that are viewing it."

Critics as well as audiences found much to praise in *Monty Python's Flying Circus. Image* contributor Laurence Bergreen, for instance, calls the Pythons "masters of the television medium, arch-parodists of every device the tube conditions us to accept. They are the first comedy group to break all the rules of TV, to mock it and us, and to get away with it. The grotesque and disturbing elements slyly injected into the stream of their patter steal our attention," the critic elaborates, "creating a unique comic language more dangerous and subversive than anything else on TV—and also funnier." "'Monty Python's Flying Circus' has a kind of compact hilarity going for it," *Village Voice* writer Richard Goldstein asserts. "That is, it comes across as a much more intimate entertainment than anything on American television: zany, childish, but also terribly witty, so that your cerebral zone laughs right along with your silly zone, and your fairy-tale zone isn't left behind." *New York Times* critic Clive Barnes, reviewing a Python stage show, similarly describes the group as "vulgar, sophomoric, self-satisfied, literate, illiterate, charmless, crass, subtle, and absolutely terrific. They are the funniest thing ever to come out of a television box. . . . The humor is occasionally raunchy, but for sheer irreverence, impertinence and spaced-out zaniness there has been nothing to beat it since Genghis Khan."

The troupe took many different approaches to humor. "Much of Python comedy is simple reversal," former BBC producer Barry Took told Perry in *Life of Python*. "Take Hell's Grannies. That's straight out of the Child's Book of How to Write Comedy. Thugs beating up old ladies? Why not have old ladies ganging up, roaming the streets looking for thugs to bash, young people to bully? But it's the way they do it that's so good." But the Pythons also had an educated edge to their comedy, frequently using literary and historical figures and references in their sketches. "Their literacy put them on a different plane from the smutty comedians in men's clubs," Perry suggested. "In many respects they were commenting on and mocking the very permissiveness for which they were thought to be crusading. Sketches such as . . . those aimed at Oscar Wilde, wife-swapping and dirty vicars, somehow span the entire spectrum of

Sunday newspaper reading, and do so with enough original wit and sharpness of observation to neutralise such topics."

"The Pythons were pretty much dedicated to silliness, but our satire had a sort of root subject that made it not wholly frivolous," Cleese similarly explained to Hal Hinson in the *Washington Post.* "Some of Python was exquisitely silly and magnificent. Like the fish dance. There's no way you can say this was a comment on the human condition. It was just stupid. But our best stuff, we always used to say, was about something." Even Gilliam's animations had deeper meanings, as he told Leslie Bennetts in the *New York Times:* "A lot of the cartoons I did for 'Python' were very disturbing. There's a lot of anger, anarchy and nihilism along with the bright colors and silly pictures. . . . You hope you can reach people on different levels. There's the odd dodo out there who just likes color and noise, and if people want to look at the surface, it's an entertaining surface, but if they want to look deeper there are other things going on."

The *Flying Circus*'s most popular skits from the first two seasons formed the basis for Monty Python's first motion picture, 1971's *And Now for Something Completely Different.* The film was produced in an attempt to court the American market, but didn't perform very well since the group was not yet well known. In addition, Palin told Perry, "Unfortunately [the series] didn't expand on to the big screen very well. You can get away with very tatty sets on telly—it's all part of it—but you can't do the same apologies for quality on film." Nevertheless, *New York Times* critic John Simon praised the film for daring "to offend in . . . the pursuit of comic truth. Moreover," continues Simon, it "is indeed different from the usual movie satire, whose eye is bleary, whose teeth are made of rubber, and whose heart has sunk to its heels."

After the third season of shows, Cleese declined to do any more episodes; the remaining members completed six more shows under the title *Monty Python* before retiring from television. Palin explained the reasoning behind the group's decision to Lodge in *Publishers Weekly:* "It was constantly challenging to surmount various barriers, forms and conventions. But we couldn't go on with that much longer, for in the end the challenge becomes a cliche in itself. We felt as though the audience began to expect things like showing the credits in the middle of the show, or putting 'The End' up five minutes into the program, and we feared *that* would become convention." Although there would be no more *Flying Circus* episodes, the group

agreed to reunite to write and act in their own movies. Meanwhile, the Pythons began working on their own pet television and film projects.

Shortly after leaving *Flying Circus,* Cleese founded Video Arts, Ltd., a company specializing in business training films. Cleese, who writes and stars in many of the films, brings a sense of humor to such topics as meetings, organizing time, and balance sheets. Marvin Kitman observes in *Newsday,* "the humor is understated Cleese, used to drive home points about good performance or bad. You know, nothing to scare off executives." But the humor must "grow out of the teaching points," Cleese observed in *People.* "It's absolutely no good just writing a straight script and then sticking half a dozen jokes in, because people would just remember the jokes and forget the teaching points." The humorist continued: "If the audience is laughing at somebody doing it wrong, then the next time they start doing it wrong themselves, that starts a little bell ringing in the back of their minds." Cleese's films have proved so successful that today his company achieves yearly revenues in the millions of dollars.

In 1974, Cleese rejoined the other Pythons to work on their first independent feature film. "We'd all been convinced that we'd make a lot of money out of *And Now for Something Completely Different,*" Jones told Perry in *Life of Python,* "but it came to about a thousand pounds, if it was anything at all. We still wanted to make a film and about the time of the third series we started writing a screenplay. We'd liked an idea of Mike's about King Arthur, and our first version was a mixture of old and new, with the Holy Grail being found in Harrod's [a London department store]. Harrod's, of course, had got everything! Then we took a year off from it. I'd got very heavily into the Middle Ages by then, and I thought it would be great to set it in one period so that we could give it an overall look." With this format, Palin related to Gordon Gow of *Films and Filming,* "we've still got the range to develop little Python characters who would normally be in present-day garb—and yet it has the unity of being an historical film." The result was *Monty Python and the Holy Grail,* a satirical saga of the Round Table's search for the sacred cup from which Christ drank at the Last Supper. Arthur and his knights overcome many obstacles in their quest, including the Knights Who Say Ni, a castle full of seductive young women, taunting Frenchmen, and a killer rabbit, only to be hauled away by a modern policewagon before achieving their goal.

The Pythons in costume for *Holy Grail:* Chapman as King Arthur, Idle as Sir Robin the Not-So-Brave, Palin as Sir Galahad, Gilliam as the loyal Patsy, Jones as Sir Bedevere the Wise, and Cleese as Sir Lancelot the Brave.

Because the Pythons wanted more control in producing their work than with *And Now for Something Completely Different,* Gilliam and Jones were appointed to direct the film. "The filming was a nightmare," Jones recalled to Perry. "Everybody was underpaid, including us, and doing it half for love.... We had this loony schedule—scenes that should take a week were shot in a day." But the lack of a big budget didn't restrain the Pythons' creativity; as Palin observed to Johnson, "We never said 'We can't do this.' We wrote it, then pared it down if someone said we couldn't do it.... Rather than make economics that ruin sketches or scenes, we write the scenes first, then find a way of doing them." This need for improvisation inspired some of the film's best moments; because the team couldn't afford horses for Arthur and his knights, they came up with the rattling coconut halves that the squires used to imitate the sound of hoofbeats.

Holy Grail opened and reviews of the film were generally favorable. "We saw it last week," a *New Yorker* critic relates in "The Talk of the Town," "and it's our very deep, very personal privilege to report that during the entire length of 'Monty Python and the Holy Grail,' the audience was either laughing or getting ready to laugh." "The whole film, which is often recklessly funny and sometimes a matter of comic genius, is a triumph of errancy and muddle," *New Yorker* critic Penelope Gilliatt remarks. "Its mind strays like an eye, and it thrives on following false trails. The Monty Python people have won a peculiar right to be funny even when they make a mess of things, because their style accepts floundering as a condition of life." Although *New Republic* reviewer Stanley Kauffmann believes the film has "hits and misses," he adds that "soon the picture reaches the good leg-pull level, mostly sustained and just moves along in a comic temperament without much actual laughter."

Richard Schickel, however, sees a deeper edge to *Holy Grail*'s comedy. "*Grail* is as funny as a movie can get," he states in *Time*, "but it is also a tough-minded picture—as outraged about the human propensity for violence as it is in its attack on that propensity." While "there are the usual sillies— phrases repeated endlessly, nonsense syllables, and sight gags plentiful enough to warm the cockles of a hitter's heart," Goldstein similarly comments in the *Village Voice*, there is also "a great deal of gratuitous cruelty, much of it occasioned by the presence of poverty and plague. The film's anger at these occurrences adds dimension to its anarchy, and makes it matter more than the tv show." Chapman told Gow in *Films and Filming* that this emphasis on blood and brutality was intentional: "This terrible-or-marvelous King Arthur figure goes through the lot, with terrible things happening in the background. To a large extent, he's immune from it. . . . So a lot of that is in the film. And a lot of the violence of the age is in the film."

During the filming of *Holy Grail*, Chapman had resolved to stop drinking. Due to his medical training, Chapman was well aware of the medical effects of alcohol abuse; nevertheless he had become an alcoholic, drinking three to four pints of gin a day. "I remember on the first day of filming *Holy Grail*, seven o'clock in the morning on a Scottish hillside, and nothing to drink—I suddenly had DTs [delirium tremens]," Chapman revealed to Perry in *Life of Python*. "I was playing King Arthur in a cold drizzle, and I realised I was letting my friends down. I stayed more or less on a even keel, not drinking too much, but I resolved to stop as soon as I could." Chapman eventually overcame his addiction in 1977, a struggle that he recounted in his 1980 book *A Liar's Autobiography: Volume VI*.

One of Cleese's goals when he left the *Flying Circus* was to create a series with his then-wife, actress Connie Booth. Because Cleese plays "with devastating effect seething, angry, mentally volcanic characters who if they are pushed just one more inch will erupt in a ranting, fist-shaking, quavering rage—and then, of course, are pushed that one inch," as Bill Bryson describes in the *New York Times Magazine*, Cleese and Booth created this type of character in innkeeper Basil Fawlty. In their BBC series *Fawlty Towers*, which aired for two seasons in 1975 and 1979, the two "struck genius when they hit on the basic premise of having their Torquay resort hotel run by a man who hates people," Hinson declared in the *Washington Post*. The critic explained: "Fawningly obsequious to his betters and abusive to everyone else, Fawlty was the archetypal British misanthrope and fool, and the show itself was a study in the hilarity of humiliation." The show was an instant hit in Britain, in places surpassing the popularity of Python, and also became popular when it aired on PBS in the United States.

Idle, in the meantime, persuaded the BBC to air his program *Rutland Weekend Television*, a parody of a small independent television station. The show only ran for two seasons, but provided the idea for the "Rutles," a takeoff of the Beatles. With the assistance of Neil Innes, who regularly contributed music to Python projects, Idle constructed a thorough "re-creation" of a pop music group's trials and triumphs. After the group appeared with Idle on an episode of *Saturday Night Live* in 1977, NBC offered Idle the chance to make a Rutles television movie. *All You Need Is Cash* had cameos by such recording stars as Mick Jagger, Paul Simon, and even former Beatle George Harrison. "The growth of the ersatz quartet's career and ultimate breakup is followed in a take-off of that you-are-actually-making-history-this-very-moment approach to documentary reporting," *Village Voice* writers Howard Smith and Leslie Harlib stated. The reviewers found the program had a "sneaky power" to its satire and praised in particular its "fifteen slyly brilliant parody songs of well-known Beatles tunes."

In directing his first solo project, Gilliam returned to the time of the Middle Ages with his 1977 film *Jabberwocky*. Palin stars as Dennis, a naive country apprentice whose first trip to the city involves him in a quest to slay a horrible monster (inspired by the famous Lewis Carroll poem). The film is filled with scenes of blood, muck, and filth, and brings a somber edge to its humor. As Gilliam told William Wolf of *Cue*, "We're very serious about our comedy. It's rubbish to think that you can't do serious comedy. . . . In 'Jabberwocky' we are taking a look at the Middle Ages and show that even violence can be funny." As with *Holy Grail*, *Time*'s Schickel observes, "the medieval world is seen as all ignorance, blood and excrement. Once again chivalry and romance are viewed as aristocratic conceits designed to make an ugly epoch palatable to the more delicate sensibilities of the time—and to latter-day observers of history."

Nevertheless, Schickel faults the film for a lack of "consistent comic tone"; Judith Crist likewise feels that despite "intermittent moments of wild satire and inventive comedy" the film "becomes wearing," as she states in *Saturday Review*. *New Yorker* critic Gilliatt, however, believes that Lewis Carroll, creator of the original Jabberwocky monster, "would have rejoiced in [the film's] nincompoop wit and the blue-sky reaches of its nonsense. Not often has the rude been so recklessly funny." And Robert Berkvist of the *New York Times* praises Palin's character in particular: "Muddling through it all, his only defense a beamish smile, Mr. Palin manages to create one of the most likable movie dunderheads to come along since the heyday of Danny Kaye." *Jabberwocky,* falsely marketed as a Python film, proved an ambivalent success with audiences; its serious, darker tone proved dissatisfying to fans who expected the usual Python lunacy. A subsequent release, more accurately targeted, fared better with the public.

After working with Gilliam on film, Palin collaborated with Jones on the television series *Ripping Yarns.* Described by Palin as a series of "Edwardian English folkstories," the tales followed such events as a mountain crossing by amphibian; a murder where four different suspects insist on their guilt, not innocence; and the flight of two parents who run away from their boring son. *Ripping Yarns* was "a deliberate attempt to capture the atmosphere of a period in which life seemed extremely genteel and smooth, though underneath some bizarre disruptive forces were at work," Palin told Lodge in his *Publishers Weekly* interview. The series was

successful in Britain, winning a critics' award, and was subsequently turned into two books. "At first we didn't think of the yarns as a book," Palin continued. "But then they were filmed for the series, and the response from the editors at BBC made us realize that the scripts *read* rather well. The editors told us that they couldn't wait to see what was on the next page, and we felt that was a very telling sign."

After reuniting for an Amnesty International benefit show in 1976, the Pythons decided the time was ripe for another film together. They finally settled on the biblical era, with its possibilities for sending up religion and overblown biblical movie epics, as their subject. Weeks of hammering out ideas resulted in a script for *Monty Python's Life of Brian,* the story of a mild-mannered fellow who, born the next manger over from Christ, is continually mistaken for the messiah throughout his life. After production began, however, the Pythons experienced financial difficulties when EMI Films got wind of the controversiality of the script and

Chapman as Brian and director Jones as his mother, Mandy, in *Monty Python's Life of Brian.*

canceled their backing. The production was saved by former Beatle George Harrison, however, a Python fan who helped raise money to complete the project by creating the company Handmade Films.

EMI correctly foresaw *Life of Brian's* controversiality, for the film opened to protests from various religious groups who saw the film as a blasphemous attack on Christ and religion. Attempts to prevent the film's screening occurred in Britain and the United States, and were sometimes successful. But these protests misinterpreted the targets of the film, as Jones explained to New York *Daily News* writer Bruce Smith: "Christ's ideas and what Christ was saying weren't what we wanted to make fun of. You *couldn't* make fun of them. Our target was the way human beings have interpreted Christ's ideas." "I actually think 'The Life of Brian' was a very religious film," Cleese similarly told the *New Yorker's* Gilliatt. "What it was sending up was the way people usually follow religious leaders by rapidly discarding what the religious leaders really meant—so that religion ends up by serving the purpose of making people feel more righteous than others they disagree with." *Punch* contributor Barry Took concurs with this assessment, noting that in *Life of Brian,* "true religion, being unmockable, is not mocked, but bogus, catchpenny and lunatic fringe religion *is*." The reviewer further states that the targets in the film are not religious figures but rather "a puzzled and anxious proletariat, incompetent rulers, ineffective revolutionary committees, property developers, snobbism and bigotry, a mass of minorities jockeying for their own petty advantage. In short, civilisation as we know it today."

"Jesus isn't singled out for ridicule," Gene Siskel of the *Chicago Tribune* similarly observes; "'Life of Brian' is simply the Python response to such pompous pictures as 'King of Kings.'" The critic adds that "the protests of religious groups against the film, however well-intentioned, are simply missing the point of the picture." Schickel, however, believes that "this is no gentle spoof, no good-natured satire of cherished beliefs." Nevertheless, the critic adds, *Life of Brian* "is a richer, funnier, more daring film [than another youth favorite, *Animal House*]—too good to be left solely to kids." John Hind and Stephen Mosco concur, concluding in *Face* that *Life of Brian* is "a technically crisp work, a finely tuned statement in favour of originality, and also an all-time classic comedy in the bargain." Audiences agreed, for *Life of Brian* became a popular success, earning the Pythons

enough money to continue with their individual projects.

Jones, for instance, now had the freedom to devote more time to a study of Chaucer he had been planning since his Oxford days. In 1980 he published *Chaucer's Knight,* and in 1981 he came out with *Fairy Tales,* a volume of children's stories that he had written for his daughter. Unsatisfied with many traditional fables that "deal with violence in a way I don't approve of," as Jones told Andrea Chambers of *People,* the comedian turned his imagination to a series of satirical yet light-hearted tales. Giving equal time to his son, Jones later created *The Saga of Erik the Viking,* which follows the hero on a search for "the land where the sun goes at night." Critics have praised these works for their imagination; *Times Literary Supplement* writer Andrew Wawn, for instance, calls *The Saga of Erik the Viking* "an intriguing sequence of tales, . . . full of wit and invention." And Carol Van Strum praises the author in a *New York Times Book Review* article for "adding new color and his own whacky sense of humor to the classic style and form of the fairy tale. As a story teller, Mr. Jones is a wizard." Jones has since published three more books for kids, and plans to continue; as he said in his *Contemporary Authors* interview, "I love writing the children's books; it's the thing that gives me the most pleasure."

Palin and Gilliam also directed their efforts towards children, teaming up in 1981 to write the screenplay for *Time Bandits.* According to *New York Times* critic Vincent Canby, *Time Bandits* is "a cheerfully irreverent lark" about a young boy who, accompanied by six dwarfs, embarks on a trip through time in search of riches and adventure. This fantasy, says *Newsweek's* David Ansen, "is a teeming and original stew that stirs in many genres and moods. There are giants and escapes that recall 'The Thief of Baghdad,' a childlike innocence out of Tom Swift, an earthy, satirical edge closer to Jonathan [Swift], and a strong dose of absurdist surrealism derived from the European theater." This darker edge to the film was the writers' intent, as Gilliam told Jerene Jones of *People:* "Fairy tales used to frighten kids. They were wonderful to experience—and come out alive. I don't like *Sesame Street*—too bland and nice. We're correcting the balance a little."

Time Bandits was backed by Handmade Films, and proved the surprise hit of 1981, becoming one of the top-grossing films in the United States that year. Critical response has also been enthusiastic; Gary Arnold of the *Washington Post* finds the film

Cleese's Robin Hood surrounded by the six time-travelers in *Time Bandits*, a film written by Palin and Gilliam and directed by Gilliam.

"a sumptuous new classic in the tradition of time-travel and fairy-tale adventure," while *Film Comment* writer Anne Thompson calls it "the closest thing to a delicious fairy tale since *The Wizard of Oz*." "*Time Bandits* is true invention, a fecund imagination at play," Ansen concludes. The film "is at once sophisticated and childlike in its magical but emotionally cool logic.... 'Time Bandits' is a wonderful wild card in the fall movie season."

Palin ventured out on his own in 1982, writing, producing, and starring in *The Missionary*, "a sly comedy of manners in which a young Edwardian idealist dispenses religion—and sex—with equal fervor," as Pat H. Broeske describes in the Hollywood *Drama-Logue*. Palin plays Charles Fortescue, a naive missionary returning from duty in Africa who hopes to settle in the country and finally wed his fiance. His bishop has other ideas, however,

The book adaptation of the Pythons' last film.

and Fortescue is dispatched to establish a mission among the "fallen women" of London. The character, Palin told Berkvist in the *New York Times*, fits in with the type he likes to play: "[Not] a dominating kind of character but one for whom life always becomes rather complicated. I have a fairly heightened sense of the absurd, which colors my writing and performing, and I like *reacting* to absurd things." As a result, the innocent Fortescue finds himself trading "favors" with rich women to finance the mission and sleeping with poor women to "save" them. "His adventures in raising the funds and raising the women are often keenly, slyly funny," Kauffmann observes in the *New Republic*. "The only complaint is not the usual one about such scripts, that some of the humor falls flat: the trouble is that from time to time it wanders away from wildness."

New York Times critic Canby likewise finds that *The Missionary* "gets bogged down in plot from time to time," but adds that "that isn't too often." The reviewer further explains that the film "is not a laugh-riot from beginning to end, but even when it isn't, it's still a pleasure to watch the cockeyed misbehavior of Mr. Palin." David Denby of *New*

York magazine also finds *The Missionary* a pleasure to watch: "Here we have ... a calm, beautifully photographed movie, an aesthetically pleasing object that is also very funny." "Palin's roundabout comedy," states *Newsweek*'s Ansen, finally "reveals itself as a sunny attack on the upper classes, a happily unfashionable tribute to downward mobility and a sort of backhanded love story." The film, adds the critic, "is that rare comedy that never strains for a laugh."

To make his film *Yellowbeard* in 1983, Chapman enlisted the aid of Cleese and Idle, among other British and American comic actors. Starring scriptwriter Chapman as the pirate Yellowbeard, the film "attacks the pirate genre with a mad comedic thrust," *New York Times* writer Stephen Farber comments. "The story stirs memories of many other adventure films: A group of greedy characters fight to discover the buried treasure secreted on an island in the Spanish main." Nevertheless, Chapman remarked that the film was not intended to be satire. "There are elements of parody, but this is not really a spoof of the genre," he told the reporter. "It has a story that, although ludicrous, hopefully sweeps you along with it. The characters are slightly larger-than-life but not incredible." The production suffered a blow, however, when actor Marty Feldman—whom Chapman had known since his early days with the BBC—suffered a heart attack and died during production in Mexico City. The pall over the production extended to generally lackluster reviews and audience response upon its release.

Chapman soon had other pursuits to occupy him, for in 1983, the Pythons reunited to film *Monty Python's The Meaning of Life*. The film almost didn't get made, for the Pythons, long accustomed to working on solo projects, found it difficult to write together again. As Gilliam explained to Hind and Mosco in *Face*, "the whole mechanical, chemical relationship isn't quite as it was—everybody has their own projects, diversions, companies, families. It's a real love/hate relationship, a terrible marriage. We're always fighting, but we all really admire each other a lot." Idle pointed out to Perry in *Life of Python* that the group's self-criticism was essential, however: "I think it's the important thing—we do all keep a strong critical eye on what everyone else is doing. It's healthy, and if you're reading scripts out to everyone and something doesn't work, it's better to get that sort of criticism while you're still making the film than when it is out—at least you have a chance to make it better."

But in this instance the criticism almost derailed the project. Unlike the last two Python movies, *The Meaning of Life* didn't begin with a central character, and so it took several months of brainstorming to come up with the idea to bring the film together. "There was one point in the writing where we all thought, 'This is it, we'll never do anything else again,'" Jones told Johnson in *The First 200 Years of Monty Python.* "We had a format and sixty percent of the material, and couldn't get it into a shape.... I'd always gone on about it being a life story, only nobody could agree about whose life story it was going to be. At this point, I thought everybody was going to go 'Oooh, Terry's going on about it,' because that's what I'd been saying for the last two years. But suddenly Eric or John—I can't remember who—said 'It could be *anybody*'s life story.' And Eric came up with 'It's the meaning of life!' Over that breakfast, it just returned from the brink of disaster."

The several sections of *The Meaning of Life* address the different stages of human existence, from birth to death. The scenes range from a song-and-dance number "Every Sperm Is Sacred" lampooning the Catholic stance on birth control to a depiction of a live organ donation to the vomit-drenching explosion of a gluttonous restaurant diner. "Actually, it doesn't feel like a sketch film," Jones said to Johnson. "It has this weird feeling, this momentum that keeps one hoping it's all about the same thing.... It has a continuity of progress in it. While it's not a conventional story, it *is* a story." Siskel concurs, noting in his *Chicago Tribune* review that "the subject matter of the title of the film is ... not avoided as much as one might suspect. By making a mockery of much of life, the six English Python comedians are saying that the real meaning lies elsewhere."

Time's Schickel, however, finds that the sketch structure of the film "provides a convenient place to measure how far the group has come.... As it turns out, the distance is huge. By now the writer-performers of the Python troupe have become a true flying circus, engaged in savage aerial combat

Schoolmaster Cleese reprimands Palin and Jones while Idle and Chapman look on in *The Meaning of Life*.

Jonathan Pryce as Sam Lowry in fantasy combat armor from Gilliam's acclaimed, controversial film *Brazil*.

with the institutionalized madness and hypocrisy of the age, performing their comic loops and turns dangerously close to a battleground that, they insist on reminding us with every low-swooping pass, is a sea of muck, blood and offal." *The Meaning of Life* "is a high-water mark in the group's progress," concurs the *Los Angeles Times*'s Sheila Benson. "This is social satire of a very high order, not quite Swift, perhaps, but very fast indeed, and pungently and acidly observed."

Calling *The Meaning of Life* "the best movie to date from England's satirical sextet," *Newsweek* reviewer Katrine Ames likewise praises the group's humor as "never ... more incisive—they've become savagely hilarious observers of the human condition." But Canby faults the film for excess, writing in his *New York Times* review that "as often as it evokes laughs, it overwhelms them by the majesty of its production and special effects." "Not all the jokes in the film work, but in what recent film do they?" counters Siskel. "'Monty Python's the Meaning of Life' is fresh and original and delightfully offensive. What more can you ask of a comedy?" And Schickel believes that *The Meaning of Life* overcomes its flaws: "In their assaults on conventional morality, [the Pythons] generate a ferocious and near Swiftian moral gravity of their

own," the critic concludes. "It is this quality that distinguishes their humor from the competition, rescues it from its own excesses and makes braving it an exhilarating experience."

The success of *The Meaning of Life*, coupled with his own past achievement with *Time Bandits*, finally gave Gilliam the leverage he needed to work on a pet project he had planned for years. When Gilliam's film *Brazil* finally had its American premiere in late 1985, it was the culmination of a long struggle with financial backers and distributors. Set in a drab, totalitarian society, *Brazil* focuses on Sam Lowry, a government clerk who toils away unambitiously at work; off-duty, however, he indulges in a rich fantasy life in which he is a flying warrior rescuing a beautiful woman from evil forces. When he finds a real-life counterpart of his dream girl, Sam becomes involved in terrorist activities until he is eventually captured and imprisoned by the government. The film concludes with Sam in the hands of a torturer (played by Palin), escaping once again into the fantasies of his own mind.

The American distributor, Universal, was disturbed by the lack of a "happy" ending and refused to release the movie unless Gilliam cut it and reworked the ending. A heated public battle over the film ensued, with Universal finally capitulating when the Los Angeles Film Critics Association, having arranged to see the film, awarded *Brazil* best picture, best director, and best screenplay distinctions. The film, with its mixture of comedy, satire and horror, subsequently opened to much critical praise and respectable box office receipts.

Brazil is a "brilliant, exhausting, savagely funny post-Orwellian satire," Benson of the *Los Angeles Times* observes. "Gilliam's targets are the usual Monty Python concerns: modern technology and the men who run it, terrorists, repairmen, bureaucrats, the plastic surgery industry, the ad game and sticklers for detail, wherever they are." Janet Maslin of the *New York Times* likewise finds that the film, "a jaunty, wittily observed vision of an extremely bleak future, is a superb example of the power of comedy to underscore serious ideas, even solemn ones." This was the director's intent, as he explained to *Chicago Tribune* writer Larry Kart: "The comedy was the spoonful of sugar that helps the medicine go down, a way of drawing people's attention to some of the horrors of life. You raise people up with laughter, and then when you pull the rug out from under them, the fall is that much greater and it hurts that much more."

The basic plot and concerns of *Brazil* are very familiar, echoing past works such as George Orwell's *1984;* "within that well-used theme, however, Gilliam and his writing and design colleagues have created some brilliant riffs," Richard Christiansen comments in the *Chicago Tribune.* "The movie is always exciting to see, even when its plot is moving over well-traveled territory; and, with the aid of his fellow screenwriters ... Gilliam has put some dazzling, dark comic spins on his shopworn material." *Brazil* is "a remarkable accomplishment for Mr. Gilliam, whose satirical and cautionary impulses work beautifully together," Maslin writes. "His film's ambitious visual style bears this out, combining grim, overpowering architecture with throwaway touches.... For all it's fancifulness, 'Brazil' and its characters seem substantial and real."

After his turn as the smiling torturer in *Brazil*, in 1986 Palin published *The Mirrorstone*, a book for children unique in that it is illustrated with holograms. Palin began writing for younger readers in 1981, with *Small Harry and the Toothache Pills*, and has also penned a volume of limericks. He explained his interest in juvenile literature to Broeske of the Hollywood *Drama-Logue:* "I've got three kids of my own. I'm also fairly childlike in my

attitudes. I don't regard myself as a total grownup at all." In *The Mirrorstone* Palin brings this feeling to the story of a young boy who falls through his bathroom mirror and is captured by an evil wizard. "The book is quite good enough not to need its gimmick [of the holograms]," *Times Literary Supplement* reviewer Lachlan Mackinnon remarks, adding that the boy's journey and rescue is both "engrossing" and "emotionally engaging."

In 1988 Palin once again lent his talents to a fellow Python's project. The fruit of several years' planning by writer and star Cleese, *A Fish Called Wanda* "is a convulsively funny affair," Benson of the *Los Angeles Times* writes. The film "pretends to be a caper movie about a smooth London jewel heist and its infinitely complex aftermath," Benson continues. "Actually, it's a smart farce about ingrained cultural differences, playing the clenched respectability of the Brits against the hearty spontaneity—some might call it vulgarity—of the Yanks." Cleese plays Archie Leach, a proper London barrister who is defending Cockney George, the leader of a ring of jewel thieves. Because George hid the loot before his arrest, one of his cohorts, a sexy American named Wanda (played by Jamie Lee Curtis), attempts to seduce Archie in order to obtain information. The remaining gang members, played by Palin and Oscar-winner Kevin Kline, try to find the missing diamonds as well, and along the way they victimize three dogs, an old woman, and each other. Meanwhile Archie falls in love with Wanda, who may ruin his marriage and career to get what she wants—or may genuinely return his affections.

Cleese completed thirteen revisions of the script, working in particular on the character of Archie. He made the role "more real, simply using quite a lot of stuff from my own life and my own attitudes about being British," he told *Newsweek*. He added: "I think my comedy is a lot more interesting and varied than it was ten years ago. I feel much freer to play a straight, more romantic role in 'Wanda.' I couldn't have put that vulnerability on the screen a few years ago—I thought it was unacceptable." Cleese's new strategy worked, for *A Fish Called Wanda* became a popular hit and earned critical praise as well.

For instance, *Newsweek* writer Cathleen McGuigan remarks that *A Fish Called Wanda* "is a weird kettle of you-know-what, and Cleese's unlikely casting of himself is a triumph. After years of creating wacky caricatures, Cleese gives a funny, touching performance that's more than skin deep." Benson likewise praises the romantic angle of the movie: "Comedy this outrageous needs a soft spot at its heart, to offset its lust, brutality and cheerful disregard for propriety. Fortunately for all concerned, not one of these needs seems to go unmet." *A Fish Called Wanda* "is dark and strange, even sadistic," Rita Kempley observes in the *Washington Post.* Cleese's "inventive, happily demented script," the critic concludes, creates a film that is "a breakthrough for Britain and a deftly directed and wonderfully acted sex farce for consenting adults."

In 1989, Cleese took a break from writing and made a brief appearance in Jones's film *Erik the Viking.* Different from Jones's book for children, the film relates the saga of a viking who discovers that raping and pillaging isn't all it's cracked up to be. After accidentally killing the woman he loves, Erik voyages in search of a way to bring her back to life. "Terry Jones is most adept at historical-based movies," a *Variety* critic notes, "and with 'Erik the Viking' he has wonderfully recreated the time of Norse sagas and written a funny script packed with typically weird and wonderful characters." Although the occasional gag falls flat, remarks the *New York Times's* Canby, the film "consistently entertains," as well as "looks terrific and has some very nice, magical special effects."

Another consistently interesting piece was Palin's 1989 television special *Around the World in 80 Days?* Palin's interest in travel provided the inspiration for this unique project. In the early 1980s, he had filmed a travel piece for BBC's *Great Railway Journeys of the World,* and he later expressed to Perry in *Life of Python:* "I'd like to organise a project where I could go to all the places I dreamed about when I was a child. That's why *Great Railway Journeys* was such a good idea." Palin realized that dream when the BBC offered him the opportunity to recreate the travels of Phileas Fogg from Jules Verne's classic novel *Around the World in Eighty Days.* A television crew accompanied Palin as he attempted to trace the nineteenth-century voyager's journey through Europe, Africa, the Middle East, Asia, and America—without using air travel. Palin's trip generated a lot of suspense, due to irregular shipping schedules, government red tape, and other unforeseen circumstances. *Around the World in Eighty Days?* was a popular hit, both in the United States and Britain. Palin produced a book version of his journey as well, and it became Britain's top seller of 1989.

1989 was a productive year for the Pythons, for it also saw Gilliam bring another of his fantastic visions to the screen with *The Adventures of Baron Munchausen.* Set in the eighteenth century during the siege of a walled city, the film follows the surprise appearance of the real Baron Munchausen during a play about his exploits. Accompanied by a young girl, the Baron sets out to find his friends (one is played by Idle) and rescue the city. Bolstered by the little girl's faith in him, the Baron travels to the moon, visits Olympian gods, escapes from the belly of a sea monster, and rescues the city. With *Baron Munchausen,* Gilliam "has created another brilliantly inventive epic of fantasy and satire," Desson Howe states in the *Washington Post.* The film "is full of moments that dazzle, just for the fun of seeing the impossible come to life on the screen," the *New York Times's* Canby likewise notes. "Ironically, [Gilliam] has harnessed the most advanced side of movie technology to make poetry, not hard-edged hardware," Benson observes in her *Los Angeles Times* review.

Some critics, however, found the movie's story overwhelmed by its extraordinary imagery. London *Times* contributor David Robinson, for instance, says that while Gilliam's "vision is dynamic, . . . somehow the script and the ideas seem to buckle and collapse under the weight of spectacle." Gilliam himself admitted to Johnson in *Starlog* that "if this film suffers from anything, it's too much of everything!" But Benson admires the abundant imagery in *Munchausen,* as she notes in another *Los Angeles Times* article: "In the same way that 'Time Bandits' and, to a greater degree, 'Brazil' were carelessly rich with their images, 'The Adventures of Baron Munchausen' is Gilliam's whole bag of favorite toys, spilled open for us to pick through."

The ideas and images in his films provide their focus, Gilliam remarked to Matthew Flamm in the *New York Post:* "The narrative is just a skeleton to hang this stuff on. It's the individual bits that are important. In many ways it's like a variety show. I try to make sense of it so it looks like there's a narrative. All my films are that way. The story part is just a device to connect all the things I'm really interested in: the visuals, the ideas within each scene." But *Baron Munchausen* contains more than a visual spectacle; it also expresses "Gilliam's familiar face-off between good (magic, creativity, imagination, hope) and bad (Age-of-Reason logic, mediocrity and cynicism)," Howe remarks. Benson believes that this theme, "that in the face of logic and reason, there is still a place for the imagination, . . . is its greatest gift."

Despite his individual success as a filmmaker, Gilliam told Perry in *Life of Python* that "I cannot visualise a time when [the Pythons] wouldn't do something together. We're tied in so many ways, not just in business." As Palin explained to Johnson in *The First 200 Years of Monty Python,* "I regard Python as something I can only do with the five other Pythons. It brings something out in me as a writer/performer, a satisfaction I can't get in the same way from doing my own stuff. For me, it's terrific if Python keeps going. However successful anything I do, I would love to have the fact that I can go back to Python." Cleese dissents, however, noting to Johnson in another *Starlog* article that "I've never felt more fond of them all, and I would happily work with any one of them, but I'm damned if—right now—I can see that I would ever want to work with a committee again, even if it was those guys." Individual preferences notwithstanding, it is highly unlikely there will be any more projects under the Python banner. In 1989, one day before *Monty Python's Flying Circus* was to celebrate its twentieth anniversary, Graham Chapman died after a long battle with throat and spinal cancer.

Perhaps it was inevitable that the group would never reunite following the difficulties of making *The Meaning of Life.* "Right from the start, I always felt Python was a centrifugal thing," Palin remarked in Johnson's book; "it wasn't six people who wanted to work together for the rest of their lives. It was six people getting together as a stroke of genius on somebody's part.... For a while, for maybe thirty-nine shows—some people say only twenty shows—we actually held it together so well that we got the combined fire of six people working on all cylinders. That's what was so good about Python, but we just couldn't keep that up." He continued: "That sort of burst of creativity is like a sunspot. It flares up, very intensely and brilliantly, for a very short period. If it lasted any longer, it would never have been as brilliant in the first place." Nevertheless, the Pythons have left behind an abundant treasury of comic works. As Palin continued, "I think the shows still stand up today because they're so *rich.* Not because they're so good—there's a lot of tedious stuff in there sometimes. Some things go on too long, some don't really work, and they certainly can be improved technically. But they're so rich! I always found that twenty minutes into a Python show, I'd think 'This must be the end,' yet there's more and more! So it's like a thick, well-filled comic book. People are always finding new things in Python."

The book version of Gilliam's 1989 fantasy-adventure film.

"The funny thing about all this is that it was just written in two or three peoples' little houses," Cleese told Johnson in *The First 200 Years of Monty Python.* "Then we suddenly find it's successful with the BBC, we hear they like it in Australia, and then they're selling it in Germany and Denmark. The next thing we hear, it's beginning to catch on in America.... These little things were all so private when we wrote them—just two people up in a room in London. When we finish up doing them to eight thousand in California [for the Hollywood Bowl stage show], there's something slightly strange about it." Idle similarly expressed surprise at the enduring popularity of the group in a 1989 *People* article: "It's astounding. Here we are twenty years on, and people are still watching the same silly stuff. They're fascinated by the program."

"I think the great thing about Python is that it was funny in a way that was really about the way people actually are," Cleese told Kevin Haynes in *Women's Wear Daily.* "We must have had some sort of insight into certain types of people that transcended boundaries.... It must be some kind of archetype. Otherwise we couldn't have been so popular around the world." Gilliam assessed the Pythons' influence in his *Contemporary Authors* interview: "I think we might have made it possible for people to do more outrageous things more easily. I don't see much that really is a copy of Python, but I do see a lot of stuff that probably wouldn't have been allowed before because it was considered too silly and stupid. Somehow we made silliness respectable." Perry, however, sees a larger consequence to the Pythons' work: "What [the Pythons] are really setting out to do, apart from providing a sometimes sublimely crazy level of entertainment, is to open our eyes a little wider, forcing the questioning and close scrutiny of those aspects of life which are generally simply accepted," he concludes. "Through their silliness and absurdity they lead us on to a consideration of ourselves and the state of human existence."

"Twenty years on and the best of Monty Python still outshines its imitators in sheer comic inventiveness," Andrew Clifford comments in the *New Statesman and Society.* "No other comedians have inspired such a devoted, indeed virtually addicted following. But it should not be forgotten that this is by no means the only way in which they can claim to have achieved something completely different," the critic concludes, for "Python's cultural significance stretches far beyond the 'comic.'" "*Monty Python's Flying Circus* is not harmless fun," Bergreen explains in *Image.* "It proceeds from the idea that laughter is cathartic, that it expresses our darker impulses and ridicules them in hope of reducing them to ashes. The program will never lull us to sleep or impart a sense of well-being, but it does provide the thrill of walking on dangerous ground and the release of repressed instincts into hoots of laughter. In the end, they aim to offend all of us, and in the logic of comedy, we love them for it." And while the members of the Monty Python troupe will forever be known as "Pythons," they have proven themselves as individual entertainers as well. "The six individual careers that have emerged during recent years have given us an embarrassment of riches, comedic or otherwise, in virtually all media," writes Johnson in *The First 200 Years of Monty Python.* The Pythons have built on and surpassed their work with the *Flying Circus,* and their legions of fans eagerly await the new books, films, and television programs to come.

■ Works Cited

Ames, Katrine, "Montyphysics," *Newsweek,* April 4, 1983, p. 71.

Ansen, David, "A Merry, Scary Chase," *Newsweek,* November 9, 1981, p. 92.

Ansen, David, "Missionary Position," *Newsweek,* November 8, 1982, p. 90.

Archibald, Lewis, "An Interview with John Cleese," *Aquarian,* March 30, 1983, pp. 6-7.

Arnold, Gary, review of *Time Bandits, Washington Post,* November 6, 1981.

Barnes, Clive, "Screaming and Intact, 'Monty Python Live!,'" *New York Times,* April 16, 1976, p. 11.

Bennetts, Leslie, "How Terry Gilliam Found a Happy Ending for 'Brazil,'" *New York Times,* January 19, 1986, section 2, pp. 15-16.

Benson, Sheila, "Python's 'Life' Funny but Raunchy," *Los Angeles Times,* March 31, 1983.

Benson, Sheila, "A Look Ahead, A Look Back," *Los Angeles Times,* December 25, 1985.

Benson, Sheila, "'Wanda' Stuffed to Gills with Laughs," *Los Angeles Times,* July 15, 1988.

Benson, Sheila, "In Defense of Watchdogs of the Imagination," *Los Angeles Times,* March 5, 1989, p. 23.

Benson, Sheila, "The Magical Treasure of 'Baron Munchausen,'" *Los Angeles Times,* March 10, 1989.

Bergreen, Laurence, "Who Are a Monty Python?," *Image,* February, 1975, pp. 8-9, 20.

Berkvist, Robert, "A Benighted Jouster Tilts the Dragon," *New York Times,* May 6, 1977, p. C4.

Broeske, Pat H., "Monty Python's Michael Palin," *Drama-Logue* (Hollywood), December 9-15, 1982, p. 17.

Bryson, Bill, "Cleese Up Close," *New York Times Magazine,* December 25, 1988, pp. 14-25.

Canby, Vincent, review of *Time Bandits, New York Times,* November 6, 1981, section 3, p. 8.

Canby, Vincent, "'The Missionary' Played by Michael Palin," *New York Times,* November 5, 1982.

Canby, Vincent, "Monty Python, 'The Meaning of Life,'" *New York Times,* March 31, 1983.

Canby, Vincent, "How a Notorious Liar Might Have Lived," *New York Times,* March 10, 1989.

Canby, Vincent, "A Viking Antihero Runs Amok with Idealism," *New York Times,* October 28, 1989.

Chambers, Andrea, "The Mad, Mad World of Monty Python's Terry Jones Is Not for Adults Only," *People,* February 6, 1984, p. 103.

Chase, Chris, "Why Python Star Turned 'Missionary,'" *New York Times,* November 12, 1982.

Christiansen, Richard, "Old Theme Gets New Riffs in a Cartoonish 'Brazil,'" *Chicago Tribune,* January 17, 1986.

Clifford, Andrew, "Caught in the Act," *New Statesman and Society,* September 20, 1989, pp. 42-43.

Contemporary Authors, Volume 113, Gale, 1985, pp. 181-186.

Contemporary Authors, Volume 116, Gale, 1986, pp. 238-242.

Crist, Judith, "Middle-aged Adolescence and the Seven-Year Itch," *Saturday Review,* June 11, 1977, pp. 44-45.

Denby, David, "Sweet as Sin," *New York,* November 8, 1982, pp. 62-63.

DeSena, Tony, "An Interview with Graham Chapman and Terry Gilliam," *Aquarian,* July 21-28, 1982, pp. 19, 28.

Review of *Erik the Viking, Variety,* September 6-12, 1989, p. 22.

Farber, Stephen, "Ahoy! Just Over the Horizon, a Fleet of Pirate Movies," *New York Times,* January 9, 1983, section 2, p. 15.

Fitzgerald, John, *Globe and Mail* (Toronto), December 13, 1986.

Flamm, Matthew, "Adventures of Terry Gilliam," *New York Post,* March 21, 1989.

Gilliatt, Penelope, "The Current Cinema: Light-Years Ahead of the Cuckoo Clock," *New Yorker,* May 5, 1975, pp. 115-117.

Gilliatt, Penelope, "The Current Cinema: Humbug," *New Yorker,* May 9, 1977, pp. 124-126.

Gilliatt, Penelope, "Height's Delight," *New Yorker,* May 2, 1988, pp. 41-56.

Goldstein, Richard, "I Am Monty Python, King of the Goons," *Village Voice,* May 5, 1975, pp. 1, 79-80.

Gow, Gordon, "'He Said with Incredible Arrogance...,'" *Films and Filming,* December, 1974, pp. 12-17.

Haynes, Kevin, "Arts & People," *Women's Wear Daily,* October 10, 1986, p. 20.

Hertzberg, Hendrik, "Naughty Bits," *New Yorker,* March 29, 1976, pp. 69-87.

Hind, John, and Stephen Mosco, "Something Completely Different," *Face,* March, 1985, pp. 56-59.

Hinson, Hal, "The Ex-Python on Wigs, 'Wanda' and All Matter of Seriously Funny Things," *Washington Post,* July 31, 1988.

Howe, Desson, "Red-Hot 'Baron,'" *Washington Post,* March 24, 1989.

Johnson, Kim Howard, "John Cleese: 'Why Is *Starlog* Interviewing Me?,'" *Starlog,* July, 1985, pp. 88-90.

Johnson, Kim Howard, "Terry Gilliam's Marvelous Travels and Campaigns," *Starlog,* April, 1989.

Johnson, Kim Howard, *The First 200 Years of Monty Python,* St. Martin's, 1989.

Jones, Jerene, "The Only Yank in Monty Python Stares Down Critics as His 'Time Bandits' Steals $24 Million," *People,* December 21, 1981, p. 50.

Kart, Larry, "'Brazil' Director's Struggle Mirrors Scenes in His Film," *Chicago Tribune,* January 17, 1986, section 5, pp. 1-2.

Kauffmann, Stanley, review of *Monty Python and the Holy Grail, New Republic,* Mary 24, 1975, pp. 20, 34.

Kauffmann, Stanley, review of *The Missionary, New Republic,* November 29, 1982, pp. 23-24.

Kempley, Rita, "The Wild, Wild 'Wanda,'" *Washington Post,* July 29, 1988.

Kitman, Marvin, "There's Nothing Fawlty about These Films," *Newsday,* May 20, 1984, p. 7.

Lodge, Sally A., "Michael Palin," *Publishers Weekly,* March 26, 1979, pp. 6-7.

Lovece, Frank, "Cleese's 'Wanda' Lust," *New York Post,* July 18, 1988, p. 27.

Mackinnon, Lachlan, "Exotic Excursions," *Times Literary Supplement,* December 26, 1986, p. 1458.

Maslin, Janet, "The Screen: 'Brazil,' from Terry Gilliam," *New York Times,* December 18, 1985.

McGuigan, Cathleen, "Help Help Me, Wanda," *Newsweek,* August 8, 1988, pp. 68-69.

Meehan, Thomas, "And Now for Something Completely Different," *New York Times Magazine,* April 18, 1976, pp. 34-36.

Miller, Russell, "Now for Something Entirely Similar," *Radio Times,* October 26-November 1, 1974, p. 6.

"Monty Python's John Cleese Pursues a Not-So-Silly Walk of Life—Making Business-Training Films," *People,* September 26, 1983, pp. 83-84.

Perry, George, *Life of Python,* Little, Brown, 1983.

"Puzzling out His Post-*Python* Life Leaves Eric Idle with Hands Full," *People,* April 24, 1989, p. 59.

Robinson, David, "Going for Broke," *Times* (London), March 16, 1989.

Schickel, Richard, "Legendary Lunacy," *Time,* May 26, 1975, p. 58.

Schickel, Richard, "Gilliam the Questionable," *Time,* May 9, 1977, p. 89.

Schickel, Richard, "Bright Side: 'Monty Python's Life of Brian,'" *Time,* September 17, 1979, p. 101.

Schickel, Richard, "A Fine Kettle of Fish," *Time,* March 28, 1983, p. 62.

Shames, Laurence, "God Save John Cleese," *Esquire,* April, 1984, pp. 60-67.

Simon, John, "And Now for Something Truly Funny," *New York Times,* September 10, 1972, section 2, pp. 1, 19.

Siskel, Gene, "'Brian' a Clever Sendup of Biblical Films," *Chicago Tribune,* September 21, 1979, p. 13.

Siskel, Gene, "Python 'Meaning of Life' Tingles with High-Voltage Shocks," *Chicago Tribune,* April 1, 1983.

Smith, Bruce, "A Matter of Interpretation, So They Say," *Daily News* (New York), September 25, 1979, p. 43.

Smith, Howard, and Leslie Harlib, "New Hash on 'Cash' Flash," *Village Voice,* March 20, 1978, p. 16.

"The Talk of the Town," *New Yorker,* May 12, 1975, pp. 35-36.

Thompson, Anne, *Film Comment,* November-December, 1981, pp. 49-54.

Took, Barry, "Python Preview," *Punch,* November 29, 1978, p. 970.

Van Strum, Carol, "Children's Books," *New York Times Book Review,* January 16, 1983, p. 22.

Wawn, Andrew, "Excalibur and Exocet," *Times Literary Supplement,* November 25, 1983, p. 1310.

Wolf, William, "Filmcues," *Cue,* May 14-27, 1977, p. 10.

■ **For More Information See**

BOOKS

Contemporary Literary Criticism, Volume 21, Gale, 1982.

Hewison, Robert, *Monty Python: The Case Against,* Eyre Methuen, 1981.

Hewison, Robert, *Footlights!,* Eyre Methuen, 1983.

Mathews, Jack, *The Battle of Brazil,* Crown Books, 1987.

PERIODICALS

American Film, September, 1985.

Chicago Tribune, November 5, 1982; June 24, 1983; November 2, 1986; July 29, 1988.

Christian Science Monitor, January 7, 1982; February 3, 1986.

Daily News (New York), March 9, 1989.

Films and Filming, October, 1988.

Globe and Mail (Toronto), March 11, 1989.

Interview, April, 1985.

Los Angeles Times, October 25, 1987; August 4, 1988; March 12, 1989; November 1, 1989.

Nation, May 21, 1977.

New York Times, November 10, 1974; December 29, 1974; April 6, 1975; May 1, 1977; March 25, 1983; June 10, 1983; June 24, 1983; July 17, 1988; February 14, 1989.

People, October 29, 1979; March 17, 1986.

Radio Times, October 12, 1972.

Saturday Review, May 31, 1975.

Spin, April, 1986.

Starlog, January, 1982; January, 1986; May, 1986; May, 1989.

Times (London), March 4, 1983.

US Magazine, April 3, 1989.

Village Voice, January 21, 1986; June 28, 1988.

Washington Post, March 31, 1983.

Washington Post Weekend, September 21, 1977.°

—Sketch by Diane Telgen

Flannery O'Connor

Personal

Given name, Mary; born March 25, 1925, in Savannah, GA; died of lupus erythematosus, August 3, 1964, Milledgeville, GA; daughter of Edward Francis (a real estate broker and appraiser) and Regina (Cline) O'Connor. *Education:* Georgia State College for Women (now Georgia College), A.B., 1945; State University of Iowa, M.F.A., 1947. *Religion:* Roman Catholic. *Hobbies and other interests:* Raising chickens, ducks, geese, and peafowl; painting.

Addresses

Home—Milledgeville, GA. *Agent*—McIntosh, McKee & Dodds, 22 East 40th St., New York, NY 10016.

Career

Writer. Resident at Yaddo writers' colony, Saratoga Springs, NY, 1948-49.

Awards, Honors

University of Iowa Writers' Workshop fellow, 1945-47; *Kenyon Review* fellowship in fiction, 1953 and 1954; National Institute of Arts and Letters grant in literature, 1957; first prize, O. Henry Memorial Awards, 1957, for "Greenleaf," 1963, for "Everything That Rises Must Converge," and 1965, for "Revelation"; Ford Foundation grant, 1959; Brenda Award, Theta Sigma Phi, 1960; Georgia Writers' Association Scroll, 1962, for *The Violent Bear It Away*; Litt.D. from St. Mary's College, 1962, and Smith College, 1963; Henry H. Bellaman Foundation special award, 1964; National Book Award, 1972, for *The Complete Short Stories*; National Book Critics Circle Board Award and *Library Journal* notable book citation, both 1980, for *The Habit of Being*.

Writings

Wise Blood (also see below; novel), Harcourt, 1952.

A Good Man Is Hard to Find (stories; contains "A Good Man Is Hard to Find" [also see below], "The River," "The Life You Save May Be Your Own," "A Stroke of Good Fortune," "A Temple of the Holy Ghost," "The Artifical Nigger," "A Circle in the Fire," "A Late Encounter with the Enemy," "Good Country People," and "The Displaced Person"), Harcourt, 1955 (published in England as *The Artificial Nigger*, Neville Spearman, 1957).

(Contributor) Granville Hicks, editor, *The Living Novel: A Symposium*, Macmillan, 1957.

The Violent Bear It Away (also see below; novel), Farrar, Straus, 1960.

(Editor and author of introduction) *A Memoir of Mary Ann*, Farrar, Straus, 1961 (published in England as *Death of a Child*, Burns & Oates, 1961).

Three by Flannery O'Connor (contains *Wise Blood*, "A Good Man Is Hard to Find," and *The Violent Bear It Away*), Signet, 1964.

Everything That Rises Must Converge (stories; contains "Everything That Rises Must Converge," "Greenleaf," "A View of the Woods," "The Enduring Chill," "The Comforts of Home," "The Lame Shall Enter First," "Revelation," "Parker's Back," and "Judgement Day"), Farrar, Straus, 1965.

Mystery and Manners: Occasional Prose, edited by Sally Fitzgerald and Robert Fitzgerald, Farrar, Straus, 1969.

The Complete Stories, introduction by Robert Giroux, Farrar, Straus, 1971.

The Habit of Being (letters), selected and edited with an introduction by S. Fitzgerald, Farrar, Straus, 1979.

The Presence of Grace and Other Book Reviews by Flannery O'Connor, compiled by Leo Zuber, edited by Carter Martin, University of Georgia Press, 1983.

Collected Works (contains *Wise Blood, A Good Man Is Hard to Find, The Violent Bear It Away*, and *Everything That Rises Must Converge*), Library of America, 1988.

Work represented in many anthologies including *Eight Great American Short Novels*, edited by Philip Rahv, Berkeley; *The American Short Story*, Volume 1, edited by Calvin Skaggs, Dell, 1985; and *Stepping Stones*, edited by Robert Gold, Dell, 1986. Contributor to periodicals, including *Accent, Mademoiselle, Critic*, and *Esquire*.

O'Connor's writings have been translated into French, Italian, Portuguese, Spanish, Greek, Danish, and Japanese. An annual, *The Flannery O'Connor Bulletin*, was established in 1972 and is devoted to articles about O'Connor and her work.

O'Connor's papers are part of the permanent collection of the Georgia College Library.

■ Adaptations

"The Displaced Person" was adapted for stage by Cecil Dawkins, first produced at American Place Theatre, New York City, in 1966; a filmstrip and cassette package based on the story was released by Random House in 1986. *Wise Blood* was adapted for a film of the same title, directed by John Huston, starring Brad Dourif, Ned Beatty, and Harry Dean Stanton, New Line Cinema, 1979.

■ Sidelights

Flannery O'Connor ranks among the most important American fiction writers of the twentieth century. A Roman Catholic who grew up in the predominantly Protestant South, she infused her stories with a dual sense of evil and divinity, capturing both the reality of human weakness and the redemptive power of God's grace. O'Connor's works are almost always set in the southern United States and feature bizarre, often deformed characters. Written in simple, unadorned language, her writings are noted for their unique blend of dark humor, violence, tragedy, and religious philosophy. Although she published only two novels and about thirty short stories before her death in 1964, O'Connor continues to attract a remarkable degree of critical attention and is regarded throughout the world as a timeless and insightful literary figure.

O'Connor was born in 1925 in Savannah, Georgia, and lived there with her family until she was thirteen. In 1938, the O'Connors moved to Milledgeville, a small Georgia farming town. A few years later, her father, Edward, died of a disease of the immune system known as lupus erythematosus. After graduating from Peabody High School in 1942, O'Connor attended Georgia State College for Women, where she provided illustrations for the school newspaper and yearbook and edited *The Corinthian*, a literary magazine. This college experience figured largely in her receiving a fellowship to the University of Iowa Writers' Workshop after earning her B.A. from Georgia State. Her first short story, "The Geranium," was published in *Accent* in 1946, and she received her master's degree from Iowa the following year. O'Connor further refined her writing skills at Yaddo writers' colony in upstate New York in the late 1940s.

In the fall of 1949, O'Connor moved to Connecticut as a boarder at the country home of her friends Sally and Robert Fitzgerald. "Flannery was out to be a writer on her own and had no plans to go back to live in Georgia. Her reminiscences, however, were almost all of her home town and countryside, and they were told with gusto," recalled Robert Fitzgerald in his introduction to O'Connor's *Everything That Rises Must Converge*. O'Connor would subsequently credit her capacity for writing stories to her Southern heritage. "The South is a story-telling section," she told C. Ross Mullins, Jr., in an interview for *Jubilee*. "The Southerner knows he can do more justice to reality by telling a story than he can by discussing problems or proposing abstractions. We live in a complex region and you have to tell stories if you want to be anyway truthful about it."

Over the next year, O'Connor worked laboriously on the novel that would later be published as *Wise Blood*. She and the Fitzgeralds grew closer, and she became godmother to the couple's third child in May of 1950. By December, recounted Robert Fitzgerald, "just after the long labor of typing out her first draft [of *Wise Blood*], Flannery told us with amusement of a heaviness in her typing arms." Her condition worsened rapidly. While in Georgia for Christmas, she was diagnosed as having lupus, the same disease that killed her father a dozen years earlier. O'Connor underwent months of treatment at Emory Hospital in Atlanta. After being discharged in the summer of 1951, she went to live with her mother, Regina, at Andalusia, a dairy farm near Milledgeville, where she would spend the last thirteen years of her life.

While convalescing at Andalusia, O'Connor developed a regular writing schedule, dabbled in painting, and raised ducks, geese, and peafowl. (Peacocks became a prominent symbol in her works and are featured on the dustjackets of several of her books.) By the mid-1950s, according to Robert Fitzgerald, "either her disease or the drug [adrenocorticotropic hormone or ACTH] that controlled it, or both, caused a softening or deterioration of the bones, her jaw bones and also her leg bones at the hip.... The doctor put her on crutches." Shortly thereafter, O'Connor began treatment with a new medication. Her condition improved enough to allow her to give talks and lectures at various colleges and universities in the United States. Still, writing drained O'Connor of much of her energy. "I write from nine to twelve and spend the rest of the day recuperating from it," she told Granville Hicks in a *Saturday Review* interview. A highly disciplined individual, O'Connor insisted on adhering to her daily writing schedule, even during unproductive periods. In a letter published in *The Habit of Being*, she explained, "I'm a full-time believer in writing habits, pedestrian as it all may sound.... Sometimes I work for months and have to throw everything away, but I don't think any of that was time wasted."

Even after the publication of her first novel, *Wise Blood*, in 1952, O'Connor maintained that she had enjoyed only one true moment of fame in her life. "When I was six," she told Betsy Lochridge in an interview for the Atlanta *Journal and Constitution Magazine*, "I had a chicken that walked backward and was in [New York's] *Pathe News*. I was in it too with the chicken. I was just there to assist the chicken but it was the high point in my life. Everything since has been anticlimax." Throughout her writing career, though, O'Connor became the object of intensive critical scrutiny and was often called upon by leading periodicals for interviews and photographs. Shy and unassuming by nature, she expressed her distaste for the fanfare in a 1963 letter, later published in *The Habit of Being*: "I hate like sin to have my picture taken and most of them don't look much like me, or maybe they look like I'll look after I've been dead a couple of days.... I hate to deliver opinions. On most things I don't deserve an opinion and on a lot of things I simply don't have an opinion."

Labeled by critics as both a "Southern writer" and a "Catholic writer," O'Connor strove to clarify her vision and intent as an author. "I see from a standpoint of Christian orthodoxy," she wrote in an essay titled "The Fiction Writer and His Country" for *The Living Novel: A Symposium*. "This means that for me the meaning of life is centered in our Redemption by Christ and that what I see in the world I see in its relation to that." Publisher Robert Giroux is one of several observers who contended that much of the commentary on O'Connor's writings fails to regard her stated worldview. Reflecting in his introduction to her *Complete Stories* on the critical reaction to *Wise Blood*, Giroux wrote: "I was disappointed by the reviews more than she was; they all recognized her power but missed her point."

"She kept going deeper," ventured Robert Fitzgerald, "until making up stories became, for her, a way of testing and defining and conveying that superior knowledge that must be called religious.... Bearing hard upon motives and manners, her stories as moralities cut in every direction and sometimes go to the bone of regional and social truth. But we are not likely to state what they show as well as they show it."

Many critics agree that the intensity of O'Connor's works derive from their simplicity of style. Her writings apparently mirrored her demeanor. "She is a quiet person except when she has something to say, and what she says is generally to the point and often spiked with dry humor," observed interviewer Margaret Turner in the Atlanta *Journal and Constitution*. With a sharp eye for detail and an extraordinary ear for Southern dialect, O'Connor used straightforward language and concrete images

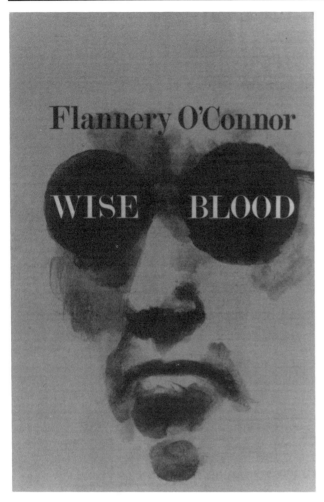

Flannery O'Connor

WISE BLOOD

O'Connor's 1952 novel about a mysterious faith healer brought her wide critical acclaim.

to create a powerful body of bizarre and grotesque literature. As David Eggenschwiler noted in his book *The Christian Humanism of Flannery O'Connor*, the author "repeatedly warned students that stories do not begin with problems or issues that the writer feels a need to illustrate in some way; they begin with concrete situations, and the author's beliefs will determine *how* he sees the situation but they should not determine *what* he sees."

"Fiction operates through the senses," wrote O'Connor in an essay that was published posthumously in the collection *Mystery and Manners*, "and I think one reason that people find it so difficult to write stories is that they forget how much time and patience is required to convince through the senses. No reader who doesn't actually experience, who isn't made to feel, the story is going to believe anything the fiction writer merely tells him. The first and most obvious characteristic of fiction is that it deals with reality through what can be seen, heard, smelt, tasted, and touched."

O'Connor also expressed her feelings on the critical interpretation of literature. "In most English classes," she noted in a reading delivered at Hollins College in Virginia in 1963 and later collected in *Mystery and Manners*, "the short story has become a kind of literary specimen to be dissected. Every time a story of mine appears in a Freshman anthology, I have a vision of it, with its little organs laid open, like a frog in a bottle. I realize that a certain amount of this what-is-the-significance has to go on, but I think something has gone wrong in the process when, for so many students, the story becomes simply a problem to be solved, something which you evaporate to get Instant Enlightenment.

"A story really isn't any good unless it successfully resists paraphrase, unless it hangs on and expands in the mind. Properly, you analyze to enjoy, but it's equally true that to analyze with any discrimination, you have to have enjoyed already, and I think that the best reason [for] a story [to be] read is that it should stimulate that primary enjoyment."

In the same reading, O'Connor discussed an essential element in her fiction: "I often ask myself what makes a story work ... and I have decided that it is probably some action, some gesture of a character that is unlike any other in the story, one which indicates where the real heart of the story lies. This would have to be an action or a gesture which was both totally right and totally unexpected; it would have to be one that was both in character and beyond character; it would have to suggest both the world and eternity. The action or gesture I'm talking about would have to be on the anagogical level, that is, the level which has to do with the Divine life and our participation in it. It would be a gesture that transcended any neat allegory that might have been intended or any pat moral categories a reader could make. It would be a gesture which somehow made contact with mystery." She went on to clarify the epiphanic function of violence in her writings: "With a serious writer, violence is never an end in itself. It is the extreme situation that best reveals what we are essentially.... The man in the violent situation reveals those qualities least dispensable in his personality, those qualities which are all he will have to take into eternity with him.... There is a moment in every great story in which the presence of grace can be felt as it waits to be accepted or rejected, even though the reader may not recognize this moment."

Most of O'Connor's stories center on an act of destruction that leads to the revelation of God's grace and the possibility of redemption. In *Wise Blood*, for instance, protagonist Hazel Motes—founder of a religion of despair known as "The Church without Christ"—is able to see the way of Christ clearly only after blinding himself with quicklime. As Andre Bleikasten put it in an essay included in *Les Americanistes: New French Criticism on Modern American Fiction*, "Not until the soul has reached that ultimate point of searing self-knowledge does salvation become a possibility."

O'Connor's first collection of short fiction, the 1955 volume *A Good Man Is Hard to Find*, further explores the idea that cataclysmic events can lead to insight. The title story—one of O'Connor's best known—involves a grandmother, her son and daughter-in-law, and their children, and the tragedy they encounter en route to Florida for a family vacation. The self-absorbed grandmother, who would rather have gone to Tennessee, convinces her reluctant son to make a detour down a back road in Georgia to search for an old plantation she had visited in her youth. Only after they become lost does the grandmother realize that the house in question had actually been located in Tennessee, not Georgia. Embarrassed by the thought of her error, she inadvertently causes her son to lose control of the car, resulting in an accident. Stranded in a ditch, the family encounters a murderous Misfit who first kills the son, then the daughter-in-law and children, and finally the grandmother. At gunpoint, the grandmother no longer views herself as the center of her own universe, but instead acknowledges the Misfit as her own child. After shooting her to death, the Misfit muses, "She would of been a good woman if it had been somebody there to shoot her every minute of her life."

In a letter to novelist John Hawkes published in *The Habit of Being*, O'Connor dispels the popular notion that the grandmother in the story is entirely evil and explains that the character's blatant imperfection makes her an ideal vehicle for grace. "It's interesting to me," wrote O'Connor, "that your students naturally work their way to the idea that the Grandmother in 'A Good Man' is not pure evil and may be a medium for Grace.... Old ladies [like her] exactly reflect the banalities of the society and

Brad Dourif and Harry Dean Stanton in the 1979 film adaptation of *Wise Blood*.

the effect is of the comical rather than the seriously evil. But [some critics insist] that she is a witch. . . .

"Grace, to the Catholic way of thinking, can and does use as its medium the imperfect, purely human, and even hypocritical. Cutting yourself off from Grace is a very decided matter, requiring a real choice, act of will, and affecting the very ground of the soul. The Misfit is touched by the Grace that comes through the old lady when she recognizes him as her child, as she has been touched by the Grace that comes through him in his particular suffering. His shooting her is a recoil, a horror at her humanness, but after he has done it and cleaned his glasses, the Grace has worked in him and he pronounces his judgment: she would have been a good woman if *he* had been there every moment of her life."

The other stories in *A Good Man Is Hard to Find* are regarded as equally disturbing. In "The Life You Save May Be Your Own," a man's physical deformity mirrors the spiritual deformity of his soul. And in "The Displaced Person," the author illustrates the revelatory power of death among traditional folk in the deep South. Many reviewers focused on the bleaker aspects of the pieces in the collection as a whole, failing to perceive O'Connor's notion of redemption through violence. Her response to such criticism, as cited in *The Habit of Being*, reflects her devotion to Christian philosophy: "I am mighty tired of reading reviews that call *A Good Man* brutal and sarcastic. The stories are hard but they are hard because there is nothing harder or less sentimental than Christian realism."

"The Artificial Nigger" is reportedly among O'Connor's favorite pieces from *A Good Man Is Hard to Find*. Critics have generally regarded the story as an allegory depicting the sin of pride and the destructive effects it can have on those possessed by it. In "The Artificial Nigger," a backwoods grandfather named Mr. Head, who has raised his grandson, Nelson, from infancy, decides to take the boy "to see everything there is to see in a city so that he would be content to stay at home for the rest of his life." Nelson considers the upcoming trip by train to be his second journey to town, since he was born in the city of Atlanta. Furious over what he perceives as his grandson's insolence, Mr. Head resolves to prove that the boy has no knowledge of the city by showing that Nelson cannot recognize a black person when he sees one. Once off the train in the city, the grandfather, who has been out of his element only twice before, loses his way. The old man's stubborn

refusal to admit that they are lost—coupled with the grandson's unwillingness to overlook his elder's navigational incompetence—results in a searing cycle of confrontation, denial, and betrayal that nearly severs their relationship. But Mr. Head's sighting of a battered statue of a black man—an "artificial nigger"—reunites them. It stands as a "monument . . . that brought them together in their common defeat. They could both feel it dissolving their differences like an action of mercy."

During an interview for the Vanderbilt University periodical *Vagabond*, Randall Mize asked O'Connor about the origin of the title "The Artificial Nigger." "Well," she replied, "I never had heard the phrase before, but my mother was out trying to buy a cow, and she rode up the country a-piece. She had the address of a man who was supposed to have a cow for sale, but she couldn't find it, so she stopped in a small town and asked the countryman on the side of the road

A Harvest/HBJ Book

Considered excessively violent by some critics, this 1955 collection explores the relationship between disaster and redemption.

Published posthumously, this collection of stories deals with the issue of racial discrimination.

where this house was, and he said, 'Well, you go into this town and you can't miss it 'cause it's the only house in town with a artificial nigger in front of it.' So I decided I would have to find a story to fit that." The author met with some resistance over her choice of title, though. When negotiating a publication deal with the *Kenyon Review*, John Crowe Ransom, editor of the periodical, suggested it would be prudent for her to call the story by a different name. But O'Connor stood behind her title, refusing to change it.

According to Sally Fitzgerald in her introduction to *The Habit of Being*, O'Connor felt that "The Artificial Nigger" "contains more than she herself understood." In a letter to writer-professor Ben Griffith, reprinted in *The Habit of Being*, the author stated: "What I had in mind to suggest with the artificial nigger was the redemptive quality of the Negro's suffering for us all."

O'Connor wrote at a time when racial segregation dominated life in the South. Even though she died prior to the full emergence of the civil rights movement in the United States, the author is credited with conveying through her works both a penetrating awareness of racial issues and a fresh portrait of black Americans. "She destroyed the last vestiges of sentimentality in white Southern writing," proclaimed Alice Walker in *Ms.*, adding, "She approached her black characters—as a mature artist—with unusual humility and restraint." In the title story of her posthumously published collection *Everything That Rises Must Converge*, O'Connor illuminates the issue of race discrimination with stunning clarity. Through a mortifying confrontation with a black woman, a bigoted white woman is faced with the stark realization that black people occupy a larger place in the world than her narrow, insulated view of life allowed.

O'Connor frequently admitted to having mixed emotions towards her chosen profession of writing. "I think you hate it, and you love it, too. It's something—when you can't do anything else you have to do that," she mused in a conversation with Harvey Breit for a *Galley Proof* telecast. Her second and final novel, *The Violent Bear It Away*, took a full seven years to complete. The story concerns a fourteen-year-old boy's resistance to his calling as a prophet. Orphaned as a young child, Tarwater has been raised in the Southern wilderness by his great uncle, a prophet. Rayber—a nephew of the great uncle and, therefore, an uncle to Tarwater—discounts the supernatural elements of religion and believes that Tarwater should be schooled in modernism and rationalism. In an interview with Joel Wells for the *Critic*, O'Connor explained her intent in the story: "I wanted to get across the fact that the great Uncle (old Tarwater) is the Christian—a sort of crypto-Catholic—and that the school teacher (Rayber) is the typical modern man. The boy (young Tarwater) has to choose which one, which way, he wants to follow. It's a matter of vocation." But young Tarwater does not choose to preach redemption until he experiences evil firsthand.

With each of her stories, O'Connor strove to provide the members of her audience with a jolting literary experience that would stimulate their powers of imaginative thinking. She was especially concerned with arousing the imaginations of those readers who failed to share her Christian vision. In "The Fiction Writer and His Country," she described her use of violence and the grotesque as vital to the reader's attainment of insight: "The novelist with Christian concerns will find in modern life distortions which are repugnant to him, and his problem will be to make these appear as

O'Connor's personal letters are collected in this 1979 volume.

can no more be dissociated from the supernatural than evil can be separated from the mysteries of faith. The grotesque has the power of revelation; it manifests the irruption of the demonic in man and brings to light the terrifying face of a world literally *dis-figured* by evil. The derangement of minds and deformity of bodies point to a deeper sickness, invisible but more irremediably tragic, the sickness of the soul." Speculating on the overall significance of the grotesque in the author's stories, Bleikasten asserted, "Even though O'Connor defended her use of the grotesque as a necessary strategy of her art, one is left with the impression that in her work it eventually became the means of a savage revilement of the whole of creation.... Her work," he continued, "is not content with illustrating Christian paradoxes. It stretches them to the breaking point, leaving us with Christian truths gone mad, the still incandescent fragments of a shattered system of belief."

The magnitude of O'Connor's faith and spiritual reserve is probably best illustrated by her acceptance of her illness and impending death. "Sickness before death is a very appropriate thing and I think those who don't have it miss one of God's mercies," she wrote in a note included in *The Habit of Being*. Fifteen months before she died, the writer composed a cogent and distinctive treatise on Christian faith. Following a lecture she gave to an English class at Atlanta's Emory University, O'Connor had received a letter from a timid young man named Alfred Corn who had been in the audience. Corn claimed to have lost his faith. As reprinted in *The Habit of Being*, O'Connor offered comfort and advice to the youth during his crisis: "I think that this experience you are having of losing your faith, or as you think, of having lost it, is an experience that in the long run belongs to faith; or at least it can belong to faith if faith is still valuable to you, and it must be or you would not have written me about this....

"As a freshman in college you are bombarded with new ideas, or rather pieces of ideas, new frames of reference, an activation of the intellectual life which is only beginning, but which is already running ahead of your lived experience. After a year of this, you think you cannot believe. You are just beginning to realize how difficult it is to have faith and the measure of commitment to it, but you are too young to decide you don't have faith just because you feel you can't believe. About the only way we know whether we believe or not is by what we do, and I think from your letter that you will not take the path of least resistance in this matter

distortions to an audience which is used to seeing them as natural; and he may well be forced to take ever more violent means to get his vision across.... You have to make your vision apparent by shock—to the hard of hearing you shout, and for the almost blind you draw large and startling figures." According to Robert Drake in *Studies in Short Fiction*, "Miss O'Connor's Christian concerns did ultimately lose her some part of her potential audience.... [Readers] sometimes have difficulty with her explicitly Christian frame of reference." The critic stressed, however, that "in the narrow, constricted world of her one story she goes down just about as deep as one can go."

In the decades following her death from lupus in 1964, some critics have attempted to expand upon O'Connor's own commentary on her use of the grotesque in literature. Bleikasten, for instance, stated: "O'Connor used the grotesque very deliberately, ... because she thought it fittest to express her vision of reality.... In her eyes, the grotesque and simply decide that you have lost your faith and that there is nothing you can do about it.

"One result of the stimulation of your intellectual life that takes place in college is usually a shrinking of the imaginative life. This sounds like a paradox, but I have often found it to be true.... You can't fit the Almighty into your intellectual categories...."

"Even in the life of a Christian, faith rises and falls like the tides of an invisible sea. It's there, even when he can't see it or feel it, if he wants it to be there. You realize, I think, that it is more valuable, more mysterious, altogether more immense than anything you can learn or decide upon in college. Learn what you can, but cultivate Christian scepticism. It will keep you free—not free to do anything you please, but free to be formed by something larger than your own intellect or the intellects of those around you."

Many critics regard O'Connor as one of America's most talented and enigmatic writers of the century. A. L. Rowse, writing in *Books and Bookmen*, praised her literary gift as "pure genius, which, in a short life, achieved absolute expression in art; an unflinching view of life which revealed alike its tragedy and its poetry, penetrated by the sense of the mystery behind it all.... She realized that character reveals itself in extreme situations: it is the strange encounters that appeal to the deeper levels of imagination of the real writer.... For her the mystery of the human personality expressed itself in the concrete, the character in the action and the words."

Commenting in the *New York Times Book Review* on the power of O'Connor's writing, Alfred Kazin remarked, "For her, people were complete in their radical weakness, their necessary human incompleteness. Each story was complete, sentence by sentence. And each sentence was a hard, straight, altogether complete version of her subject: human deficiency, sin, error—ugliness taking a physical form.... She was a genius.... Her people were wholly what they were, which wasn't much in 'humane' terms. But they were all intact of themselves, in their stupidity, their meanness, their puzzlement, their Southern 'ruralness.' The South was her great metaphor, not for place but for the Fall of Man." Robert McCown expressed a similar opinion in *Catholic World*, stating, "Her stories, the characters that live in them, the excellencies of her style, are not ends in themselves but rigorously subordinated means of showing us reality, the quality of goodness and the subtle malice of sin,

either of which have power to determine our destiny."

■ Works Cited

Bleikasten, Andre, "The Heresy of Flannery O'Connor," in *Les Americanistes: New French Criticism on Modern American Fiction*, edited by Ira D. Johnson and Cristiane Johnson, Kennikat, 1978, pp. 55-57, 62, 65-66, and 69-70.

Breit, Harvey, transcript of "A Good Man Is Hard to Find," an episode of the television program *Galley Proof*, National Broadcasting Co., May, 1955, published in *Conversations with Flannery O'Connor*, edited by Rosemary M. Magee, University Press of Mississippi, 1987, p. 7.

Drake, Robert, "The Paradigm of Flannery O'Connor's True Country," *Studies in Short Fiction*, summer, 1969, pp. 441-442.

Eggenschwiler, David, *The Christian Humanism of Flannery O'Connor*, Wayne State University Press, 1972, pp. 12-14.

Fitzgerald, Robert, introduction to *Everything That Rises Must Converge* by Flannery O'Connor, Farrar, Straus, 1965, pp. vii-xxv.

Fitzgerald, Sally, introduction to *The Habit of Being*, Farrar, Straus, 1979, p. xviii.

Giroux, Robert, introduction to *The Complete Stories*, by Flannery O'Connor, Farrar, Straus, 1971, p. xii.

Hicks, Granville, "A Writer at Home with Her Heritage," *Saturday Review*, May 12, 1962, pp. 22-23.

Kazin, Alfred, *New York Times Book Review*, November 28, 1971, pp. 1 and 22.

Lochridge, Betsy, "An Afternoon with Flannery O'Connor," *Journal and Constitution Magazine* (Atlanta), November 1, 1959, pp. 38-40.

McCown, Robert, "Flannery O'Connor and the Reality of Sin," *Catholic World*, January, 1959, pp. 285-291.

Mize, Randall, "An Interview with Flannery O'Connor and Robert Penn Warren," *Vagabond*, February, 1960, pp. 9-17.

Mullins, C. Ross, Jr., "Flannery O'Connor: An Interview," *Jubilee*, June, 1963, pp. 32-35.

O'Connor, Flannery, "The Fiction Writer and His Country," *The Living Novel: A Symposium*, edited by Granville Hicks, Macmillan, 1957.

O'Connor, Flannery, *Mystery and Manners: Occasional Prose*, edited by Sally Fitzgerald and Robert Fitzgerald, Farrar, Straus, 1969, pp. 91, 108, 111, 113-114, and 118.

O'Connor, Flannery, *The Habit of Being*, selected and edited with an introduction by Sally Fitzgerald, Farrar, Straus, 1979, pp. 78, 389, 476-478, and 524-525.

O'Connor, Flannery, "A Good Man Is Hard to Find," *A Good Man Is Hard to Find*, Harcourt, 1983, p. 29.

O'Connor, Flannery, "The Artificial Nigger," *A Good Man Is Hard to Find*, Harcourt, 1983, p. 128.

Rowse, A. L., "Flannery O'Connor—Genius of the South," *Books and Bookmen*, May, 1972, pp. 38-39.

Turner, Margaret, "Visit to Flannery O'Connor Proves a Novel Experience," *Journal and Constitution* (Atlanta), May 29, 1960, p. G-2.

Walker, Alice, "Beyond the Peacock: The Reconstruction of Flannery O'Connor," *Ms.*, December, 1975, p. 106.

Wells, Joel, "Off the Cuff," *Critic*, August-September, 1962, pp. 4-5.

■ For More Information See

BOOKS

Allen, Walter, *The Modern Novel*, Dutton, 1964.

Asals, Frederick, *Flannery O'Connor: The Imagination of Extremity*, University of Georgia Press, 1982.

Browning, Preston M., Jr., *Flannery O'Connor*, Southern Illinois University Press, 1974.

Coles, Robert, *Flannery O'Connor's South*, Louisiana State University Press, 1980.

Contemporary Literary Criticism, Gale, Volume 1, 1973, Volume 2, 1974, Volume 3, 1975, Volume 6, 1976, Volume 10, 1979, Volume 13, 1980, Volume 15, 1980, Volume 21, 1982.

Dictionary of Literary Biography, Volume 2: *American Novelists since World War II*, Gale, 1978.

Dictionary of Literary Biography Yearbook: 1980, Gale, 1981.

Drake, Robert, *Flannery O'Connor*, Eerdmans, 1966.

Driskell, Leon V., and Joan T. Brittain, *The Eternal Crossroads: The Art of Flannery O'Connor*, University Press of Kentucky, 1971.

Farmer, David, *Flannery O'Connor: A Descriptive Bibliography*, Garland, 1981.

Feeley, Kathleen, *Flannery O'Connor: Voice of the Peacock*, Rutgers University Press, 1972.

Fickett, Harold, and Douglas R. Gilbert, *Flannery O'Connor: Images of Grace*, Eerdmans, 1986.

Friedman, Melvin J., and Lewis A. Lawson, *The Added Dimension: The Art and Mind of Flannery O'Connor*, Fordham University Press, 1966.

Friedman, Melvin J., and Beverly Lyon Clark, editors, *Critical Essays on Flannery O'Connor*, G. K. Hall, 1985.

Gentry, Marshall Bruce, *Flannery O'Connor's Religion of the Grotesque*, University Press of Mississippi, 1986.

Getz, Lorine M., *Nature and Grace in Flannery O'Connor's Fiction*, Edwin Mellen Press, 1982.

Golden, Robert E., and Mary C. Sullivan, *Flannery O'Connor and Caroline Gordon: A Reference Guide*, G. K. Hall, 1977.

Gossett, Louise Y., *Violence in Recent Southern Fiction*, Duke University Press, 1965.

Grimshaw, James A., Jr., *The Flannery O'Connor Companion*, Greenwood, 1981.

Hendin, Josephine, *The World of Flannery O'Connor*, Indiana University Press, 1970.

Hyman, Stanley Edgar, *Flannery O'Connor*, University of Minnesota Press, 1966.

Kazin, Alfred, *Bright Book of Life: American Novelists and Storytellers from Hemingway to Mailer*, Atlantic-Little, Brown, 1973.

Martin, Carter W., *The True Country: Themes in the Fiction of Flannery O'Connor*, Vanderbilt University Press, 1968.

May, John R., *The Pruning Word: The Parables of Flannery O'Connor*, University of Notre Dame Press, 1976.

McFarland, Dorothy Tuck, *Flannery O'Connor*, Ungar, 1976.

Montgomery, Marion, *Why Flannery O'Connor Stayed Home*, Sherwood Sugden, 1981.

Muller, Gilbert H., *Nightmares and Visions: Flannery O'Connor and the Catholic Grotesque*, University of Georgia Press, 1972.

Orvell, Miles, *Invisible Parade: The Fiction of Flannery O'Connor*, Temple University Press, 1972.

Reiter, Robert E., editor, *Flannery O'Connor*, Herder, 1968.

Short Story Criticism, Volume 1, Gale, 1988.

Shloss, Carol, *Flannery O'Connor's Dark Comedies: The Limits of Inference*, Louisiana State University Press, 1980.

Waldmier, Joseph J., editor, *Recent American Fiction: Some Critical Views*, Houghton, 1963.

Walters, Dorothy, *Flannery O'Connor*, Twayne, 1973.

Westling, Louise, *Sacred Groves and Ravaged Gardens: The Fiction of Eudora Welty, Carson McCullers, and Flannery O'Connor*, University of Georgia Press, 1985.

PERIODICALS

America, March 30, 1957; October 17, 1964; September 8, 1979.

American Literature, March, 1974; May, 1974.

Arizona Quarterly, autumn, 1976.

Catholic Library World, November, 1967.

Censer, fall, 1960.

Chicago Tribune, April 15, 1979.

Christian Century, September 30, 1964; May 19, 1965; July 9, 1969.

College English, December, 1965.

Commentary, November, 1965.

Commonweal, March 7, 1958; July 9, 1965; December 3, 1965; August 8, 1969; April 13, 1979.

Contemporary Literature, winter, 1968.

Critic, October-November, 1965.

Detroit News, March 25, 1979.

English Journal, April, 1962.

Esprit, winter, 1964.

Esquire, May, 1965.

Georgia Review, summer, 1958; summer, 1968; summer, 1977.

Hollins Critic, September, 1965.

Kansas Quarterly, spring, 1977.

Mississippi Quarterly, spring, 1975.

Modern Age, fall, 1960.

Modern Fiction Studies, summer, 1970; spring, 1973.

Ms., December, 1975.

Nation, April 28, 1979.

New Republic, July 5, 1975; March 10, 1979.

New Statesman, December 7, 1979.

Newsweek, May 19, 1952.

New York Herald Tribune Book Week, May 30, 1965.

New York Review of Books, October 8, 1964; May 3, 1979.

New York Times, May 13, 1969; March 9, 1979.

New York Times Book Review, June 12, 1955; February 24, 1960; May 30, 1965; March 18, 1979.

Renascence, spring, 1964; spring, 1965; autumn, 1969.

Saturday Review, December 16, 1962; May 29, 1965; May 10, 1969; November 13, 1971; April 14, 1979.

Sewanee Review, summer, 1962; autumn, 1963; autumn, 1964; spring, 1968.

Shenandoah, winter, 1965.

Southern Humanities Review, winter, 1968; spring, 1973.

Southern Literary Journal, spring, 1970; spring, 1972; spring, 1975.

Southern Review, summer, 1968; July, 1978.

Southwest Review, summer, 1965.

Spectator, August 30, 1968.

Studies in Short Fiction, spring, 1964; winter, 1964; summer, 1969; winter, 1973; spring, 1975; winter, 1976; fall, 1985.

Time, June 6, 1955; May 30, 1969; February 14, 1972; March 5, 1979.

Times Literary Supplement, September 12, 1968.

Washington Post, December 1, 1971.

Western Humanities Review, autumn, 1968.°

—Sketch by Barbara Carlisle Bigelow

Judith St. George

■ Personal

Born February 26, 1931, in Westfield, NJ; daughter of John H. (an attorney) and Edna (Perkins) Alexander; married David St. George (an Episcopal minister), June 5, 1954; children: Peter, James, Philip, Sarah Anne. *Education:* Smith College, B.A., 1952. *Religion:* Episcopalian.

■ Addresses

Home and office—290 Roseland Ave., Essex Fells, NJ 07021. *Agent*—Marilyn Marlow, Curtis Brown Ltd., 10 Astor Place, New York, NY 10003.

■ Career

Suburban Frontiers (relocating service), Basking Ridge, NJ, president, 1968-71; writer, 1970—. Teacher of writing workshops, lecturer. Delegate, White House Conference on Libraries and Information Services, 1979, New Jersey Governor's Conference on Libraries, 1979, and Council of State Libraries in the Northeast, 1985; member, Brooklyn Bridge Centennial Commission, 1981-83. *Member:* Author's Guild, Mystery Writers of America, Society of Children's Book Writers, Rutgers University Advisory Council on Children's Literature, New Jersey Literary Hall of Fame.

■ Awards, Honors

The Girl with Spunk, 1975, and *The Chinese Puzzle of Shag Island* and *By George, Bloomers!*, both 1976, were selected as Child Study Association of America's Children's Books of the Year; *By George, Bloomers!* was selected as one of *Saturday Review*'s Best Books for Spring, 1976; Edgar Allan Poe Award Runner-up for Best Young Adult Novel from the Mystery Writers of America, 1979, for *The Halloween Pumpkin Smasher; Haunted* was selected as the *New York Times* Best Mystery of the Year, 1980, and one of New York Public Library's Books for the Teen Age, 1981; American Book Award nomination, Golden Kite Award Nonfiction Honor Book from the Society of Children's Book Writers, Jefferson Cup Award Honor Book from the Virginia Library Association, one of *New York Times* Notable Books of the Year, an Outstanding Science Trade Book for Children from the National Council for Social Studies and the Children's Book Council, and a Notable Children's Trade Book in the Field of Social Studies from the National Council for Social Studies and the Children's Book Council, all 1982, and New York Academy of Sciences' Children's Science Book Award, 1983, all for *The Brooklyn Bridge: They Said It Couldn't Be Built.*

New Jersey Institute of Technology Authors Award, 1983, for *Do You See What I See?* and *In the Shadow of the Bear;* Golden Kite Award Nonfiction

Honor Book and Notable Children's Trade Book in the Field of Social Studies, both 1985, and Christopher Award, 1986, all for *The Mount Rushmore Story*; *What's Happening to My Junior Year?* was named a Recommended Book for Teenagers by the New York Public Library, 1987; *Panama Canal: Gateway to the World* earned a Golden Kite Award and was named a School Library Journal Best Book of the Year, both 1989; *The White House: Cornerstone of a Nation* was named a Recommended Book for Teenagers by the New York Public Library.

■ Writings

Turncoat Winter, Rebel Spring, Chilton, 1970.

The Girl with Spunk, illustrated by Charles Robinson, Putnam, 1975.

By George, Bloomers! (Junior Literary Guild selection), illustrated by Margot Tomes, Coward, 1976.

The Chinese Puzzle of Shag Island, Putnam, 1976.

The Shad Are Running, illustrated by Richard Cuffari, Putnam, 1977.

Shadow of the Shaman, Putnam, 1977.

The Secret of the Big House, Scholastic, 1977.

The Halloween Pumpkin Smasher, illustrated by M. Tomes, Putnam, 1978.

The Halo Wind, Putnam, 1978.

Mystery at St. Martin's, Putnam, 1979.

The Amazing Voyage of the "New Orleans" (Junior Literary Guild selection), illustrated by Glen Rounds, Putnam, 1980.

Haunted, Putnam, 1980.

Call Me Margo, Putnam, 1981.

The Mysterious Girl in the Garden, illustrated by M. Tomes, Putnam, 1981.

The Brooklyn Bridge: They Said It Couldn't Be Built (ALA Notable Book; Junior Literary Guild selection), Putnam, 1982.

Do You See What I See?, Putnam, 1982.

In the Shadow of the Bear (Junior Literary Guild selection), Putnam, 1983.

The Mount Rushmore Story (ALA Notable Book), Putnam, 1985.

What's Happening to My Junior Year? (Junior Literary Guild selection), Putnam, 1986.

Who's Scared? Not Me!, Putnam, 1987.

The Panama Canal: Gateway to the World (ALA Notable Book), Putnam, 1989.

The White House: Cornerstone of a Nation (Junior Literary Guild Selection), Putnam, 1990.

Mason and Dixon's Line of Fire (Junior Literary Guild Selection), Putnam, 1991.

■ Sidelights

Author of nonfiction as well as fiction and historical fiction for children and young adults, Judith St. George grew up in Westfield, New Jersey. She lived "an idyllic childhood with friends up and down block-long Maple Street," the author recalled during an interview for *AAYA*. "It was a street filled with young kids, my companions at Woodrow Wilson Grammar School—the same buddies I had from kindergarten all the way through the sixth grade."

"I was a typical 1930s and '40s tomboy.... In the winter I skated on a swamp pond and sledded. The rest of the year I played tennis and baseball," St. George commented in a 1976 *Junior Literary Guild* article. The author played second base on a team for boys, long before organized Little League was opened to girls. "Being the only girl on the team was a distinction which carried me a long way in those days," the author further told *AAYA*. "My brother was also athletic; I guess it was in the genes.

"One of my earliest attempts at writing came in the sixth grade, when I wrote a play and asked my teacher if my friends and I could produce it for the class. She agreed, and I have a vivid recollection of venturing out on the auditorium stage with my fellow classmates.

"Though not an academic star, I worked hard. Because I always did my homework like a good girl, I did fairly well in school. I can't remember a time when I didn't have my nose in a book, reading everything from mysteries and the Oz books (of which I owned thirty-six) to *The Secret Garden*. I also had the best comic book collection in the neighborhood as well as stacks of movie magazines. I can still tell you the life story of every movie star of the forties. In other words, I read some good books and some real trash." "To this day," St. George continued in the 1976 *Junior Literary Guild* article, "I never knock a kid reading 'garbage.' I know how my own tastes grew with time."

"Looking back," the author told *AAYA*, "I suppose historical novels like Carol R. Brink's *Caddie Woodlawn* and *Hitty: Her First Hundred Years* by Rachel Field must have made an impression upon me, because I devoured them when I was growing up. But since I didn't start writing seriously until much later, it would be hard for me to say that any one writer particularly influenced me."

Following a happy childhood, St. George's last two years in high school were spent at boarding school, where the teenager was far from happy. "Academically brilliant, my father excelled at both Yale undergraduate and law school," St. George told *AAYA*. "Consequently, there were always academic expectations, both spoken and unspoken, for my brother, sister, and me.

"My brother had gone away to school at a young age and adjusted well, so I suppose that there was no reason to assume I wouldn't do the same; but at fifteen, I was terribly shy. The two girls I roomed with had already been boarders for several years and were best friends, making it difficult for me to break in. Until then, I'd always had friends, but at boarding school I couldn't form any close relationships; it's surprising I wasn't even more homesick than I was. Since most of the other girls had already been boarders for three or four years, it was easy for a new kid to have a tough time, and being young for my class didn't help. Chaperones had to escort us everywhere, even to the movies, and there were other equally ridiculous regulations, but that wasn't the point. The point was, I just never fit in."

After graduation St. George entered Smith College, and life took a change for the better. "Though it was the 1950s when students still had house mothers, rules, and curfews," St. George told *AAYA*, "I was the ultimate happy college student. Ten of us who lived in the same house became immediate friends and have sustained that friendship ever since.

"I was editor in chief of the *Campus Cat*, our college humor magazine. Ours was a small, poverty-stricken publication, where everyone on the staff did everything from selling ads to writing articles.

"Although it was not a particularly political time, I'll never forget when Senator Joseph McCarthy came to Smith to speak to an assembly of two thousand young women. When he went into his usual spiel, 'I have here in my briefcase proof that Adlai Stevenson ... communism ... etc. ... etc.,' the entire auditorium burst into spontaneous laughter. It was really the most perfect reaction. I can still remember how utterly stunned McCarthy was when the wave of laughter washed over him.

"While in college, I had no idea that I'd someday become a professional writer, although as an English major, I did take a creative writing course at least four times with a professor who later taught at Columbia for many years. He allowed us to write about almost anything, but strangely enough, we were never required to do any rewriting. In the years since, I've come to learn that most of my writing is rewriting and rewriting and rewriting.

"With a number of excellent professors at Smith, the course that stands out in memory more than any other was Howard Patch's class on Geoffrey Chaucer. One of the leading authorities on Chaucer, Patch had been at Smith for many years, terrifying generations of students. The first day of the semester, he announced, 'At least once during the year, every student in my class will end up in tears.' Well, he never got me in tears, but I always took a deep breath before I entered his classroom. (Perhaps his methods worked—to this day I can still vividly recall my Chaucer.)

"After college, I worked for a year at Boston's Museum of Fine Arts as a secretary in the Painting Department. My brother was married, off to the Korean War as a Second Lieutenant, and I returned to Westfield to live at home.

While traveling to Oregon in 1845, thirteen-year-old Ella Jane meets an Indian girl who causes her to rethink some of her values.

"In those days we young women had jobs, not careers, and I decided, for convenience sake, to work in downtown New York. Starting at the tip of Manhattan, I walked into the first building on Broadway where I had an interview in the personnel office. 'We're interested in you, but we don't have any openings right now,' I was told. I crossed the street to the Cunard Steamship Building, intending to walk my way up Broadway until I found a job. But Cunard offered me a job and I worked happily at Cunard until my marriage a year later."

In 1954 the author married David St. George, a fledgling Episcopal minister. "When I met David," St. George related to *AAYA*, "he was dating one of my Smith friends, but they broke up and we didn't meet again for two years. Home from seminary during the summer of 1953, David asked me to go to the movies. That was it. Engaged at Christmas, we were married the following June and have been together now for thirty-seven years. Obviously the movie we saw, *From Here to Eternity*, was prophetic."

St. George's interest in making history come alive began during her first year of marriage when she and her husband lived in the Longfellow House in Cambridge, Massachusetts. "Built in 1759," St. George told *AAYA*, "the Longfellow House is one of America's great Georgian mansions, having been Washington's headquarters during the first year of the Revolution. Although the house was staffed by curators during the day, they liked to have it occupied at night, too. Typically, rooms were rented to a seminary couple for fifty dollars a month! We had many wonderful experiences in that house, some moving and some funny. We even had a midnight appearance of Mrs. Longfellow's ghost."

St. George didn't begin her first book, a historical novel, until the mid-1960s. "With four children in six years," St. George told *AAYA*, "I wasn't thinking or doing much else. But when the three oldest were in school, I began writing.

"Our house was near Jockey Hollow where the American troops were quartered during three winters of the American Revolution with George Washington living in nearby Morristown. Having researched quite a bit of the history, I decided to try my hand at writing a spy story set in Jockey Hollow. I had a portable typewriter from college which I'd take out during the day and put away before the kids came home from school. I was a bona fide closet writer, not telling anyone what I

was doing. I wanted to wait and see what came of it, because the moment you tell people you're writing a book, they want to know where they can buy it.

"Because I loved doing the research and did such an enormous amount of it, I simply included everything in the story that I'd learned. But the manuscript was rejected again and again. When it was returned the ninth time, I took a good look at the book, cut out the first three chapters as well as anything else that wasn't essential to the story. Once again I sent it out, and this time *Turncoat Winter, Rebel Spring* was sold, giving me a good lesson on how *not* to write historical fiction.

"With one book published, I figured I had my foot in the door, so I wrote another historical novel, this one about the Morris Canal and a runaway slave. It never crossed my mind that I might not get it published; but my original publisher didn't want the book. Around that same time, I met a fellow writer who belonged to the Westchester Writers' Workshop.

"Twice a month a group of published women writers got together to discuss their work. I was asked to join, and it was the workshop, not my first published book, that really got me going. Although the Morris Canal book never did get published, I began *The Girl with Spunk*, a story about a young farm-girl servant in Seneca Falls just before the first woman's rights convention. G. P. Putnam's picked up the book in 1974, and I've been with Putnam's ever since."

Although St. George's 1980 *Haunted* was without a controversial theme, the book introduced her to the unpleasant subject of censorship. The supernatural suspense story centers around a young man who spends his summer caretaking at a remote estate where an old man had killed both his wife and her cat before shooting himself. "The house in the story," St. George told *AAYA*, "is the one I grew up in—a very scary house that my father and his family had bought in 1914 and which we had moved into in 1940. It was my home until I was married in 1954.

"Planning to use *Haunted* in the fifth and sixth grade curriculum, the principal of our local school invited me to speak to the students. But before that day arrived, a sixth-grade girl's father, who had read the book, called every sixth-grade parent to protest using the book in the curriculum. Reading excerpts from the book out of context, he made his own editorial deletions, such as describing how the protagonist and his girlfriend take off their clothes by the pool without mentioning that they had bathing suits on underneath. He soon had the other parents up in arms, and the book was withdrawn from the curriculum.

"I didn't care whether *Haunted* was in the curriculum or not, but when I heard that it had been withdrawn, I hit the roof. I phoned all the members of the board of education to say that I would be attending their next meeting to discuss the decision. At the meeting, I discovered that they had all agreed to have the book withdrawn, but not one of them had read it! I didn't leave the meeting until I had made sure that the book was reinstated in the curriculum.

"Kids like the book because they love to be scared, and I have a hunch my own childhood fears permeate my mysteries." Growing up, "I was a timid child," St. George revealed in a publicity release, "the kind who always jumped from the doorway into bed so that whatever was under the bed couldn't grab my ankles. And I loved to scare myself by reading ghost stories by flashlight and listening to tales of terror on the radio with the lights out. Even today, whenever I'm working on a mystery, I'm nine years old again, alone in a dark house and frightening my adult-self half to death."

"When I've admitted my childhood fears to a school audience, any adults present always laugh, but not the kids," the author said to *AAYA*; she continued in a publicity release: "On the contrary, their hands shoot up, with [all of them] eager to tell me what's lying in wait to get them."

After her experience with censorship, St. George has fought to keep self-censorship from creeping into her work. "You begin to think, 'Am I going to get away with this? Maybe it would be safer to do something else, something less risky,'" St. George told *AAYA*. "It's terrible to think that way, to let that train of thought influence your writing. I've seen reviews from religious school libraries in which reviewers object to mild swearing. One of the father's complaints about *Haunted* was the line that was totally appropriate in context: 'You bastard!' He obviously has never ridden on a school bus filled with teenagers, or even pre-teenagers.

"A friend of mine wrote a book (probably her best) in which one of the characters touches a girl's breast. The novel was never picked up for paperback sales because of concern that school book clubs would reject it. 'The blander, the better.'"

In 1981 St. George's next book, *Call Me Margo*, was published. As a shy, fifteen-year-old girl away

This 1980 supernatural suspense story centers around a young man who spends the summer as caretaker at a creepy estate.

at boarding school, Margo experiences everything from a crippled English teacher who despises her, to teammates on the tennis team who cold-shoulder her, to a lesbian tennis coach who befriends her. "The ironic part is that our local school library has the book," St. George told *AAYA*. "Obviously, the father who tried to censor *Haunted* hasn't yet gotten his hands on *Call Me Margo*, or I'm sure I would have heard about it."

Though St. George does not usually incorporate her children's lives into her books, she acknowledges that Margo's story was a synthesis of her daughter's experiences, as well as her own. "When my daughter was playing on the high school field hockey team," St. George said to *AAYA*, "her female coach and the female assistant coach lived together, and had lived together for many years. Their relationship was accepted very matter-of-factly by the girls on the team. When I went to high school, that would never have happened, and I think the students' attitude was greatly to their credit.

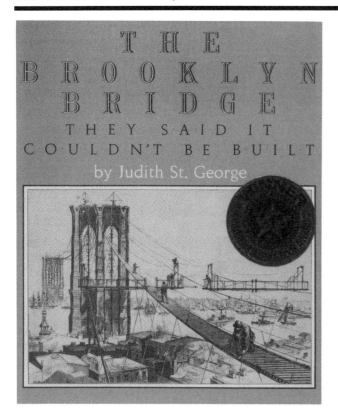

THE BROOKLYN BRIDGE
THEY SAID IT COULDN'T BE BUILT
by Judith St. George

St. George's 1982 multi-award-winning history tells how the Brooklyn Bridge was built despite numerous setbacks.

"Of course the boarding school part of *Call Me Margo* reflected my own boarding school years. By putting it all down on paper, I exorcised that experience forever."

Travelling extensively, the St. Georges have visited Europe, England, Russia, Canada, and Alaska. A trip to Panama was strictly for research. In 1989 the author's *Panama Canal: Gateway to the World* was published by Putnam. "When I finally finished *The Panama Canal: Gateway to the World*," St. George related to *AAYA*, "my editor remarked that it looked like an easy book. After a moment's astonishment, because the book had been the most difficult one I'd ever attempted, I reflected on the meaning of the word 'easy.' Easy.... But of course, that's what I'd intended; after all, I don't want somebody picking up my book saying, 'Whew! That must have been hard work.' No, I want somebody reading my book to be caught up in the flow of the story. And the flow of a book does not come easily to me. So, my editor's comment was, of course, a compliment."

"Our [four grown-up] children are all on their own now ... living in Alaska, California, Nevada," St. George said in a 1986-87 *Junior Literary Guild* article. "We miss them terribly and look forward for weeks to their visits. Their arrivals are the highlight of our year," the author told *AAYA*. "David and I are still enjoying tennis (me) and golf (him), and still using any and every excuse to travel," St. George continued in the *Junior Literary Guild* article. "As the years go by I find myself more and more involved in library causes and ever since attending the 1979 White House Conference on Libraries and Information Services as a delegate, I have served on various library boards at the state and regional level."

"I try to combat the isolation of work," St. George told *AAYA*, "by making an effort to connect in the afternoons with other people, usually in the form of a two-mile walk with a friend—she walks her dog, and I tag along. During the winter, I have a weekly indoor tennis game, and in warm weather I play outside whenever I can and swim daily in our local pool.

"David and I spend about forty-five minutes a day reading the *New York Times* while having a leisurely breakfast. From then on, it's go-go-go for the rest of the day. I stick to a strict schedule and work every morning from eight or nine until at least one. When I'm trying to finish a project, I sometimes get up at five thirty in the morning and work until after lunch. But normally, I only write four or five hours a day; my creative juices and energy don't hold up much beyond that.

"When working on a book, the idea has to strike me as being just right, or I won't write the story. Without passion and enthusiasm, I know the book would be flat, plus it takes too much time and effort to warrant the writing if I'm not in love with the subject. After all, the project is going to consume at least a year of my life.

"Sometimes, ideas just hit me. I saw a newspaper article about the White House's upcoming 1992 bicentennial, and it triggered my interest in writing about the White House. After growing up in a large house, living a year in the Longfellow House, and now owning a large, old and creaky home, large houses have always appealed to me.

"Faced with two hundred chronological years and forty presidents, I realized that it would be terribly boring to start with 1792 and proceed year by year up to the present. Instead, I decided to focus on how the social, political, and economic conditions in the country have influenced the White House during different periods throughout our country's history.

"I try not to limit myself by deciding I'm going to write about *this* and only *this* before I've begun my research," the author continued to relate to *AAYA*. "Occasionally I've started and stumbled because I was trying too hard to control the material. For me, it's important to let the material dictate my direction and theme, rather than trying to impose an artificial framework. Once I've dug into the research, into the subject, the theme naturally bubbles to the surface. Incidentally, I hate the negative term nonfiction and for my own books would prefer something like 'historical narrative'."

St. George seldom uses a computer for her early drafts. "The first time I wrote a book on computer," she told *AAYA*, "I put the entire manuscript on the machine without printing a page. When it was finished, my editor rejected it; I was shocked—that had never happened before. Later she called me back, saying we could work on it, but from then on I printed everything out as I worked, using the computer as a glorified typewriter. Lately, I've been using my typewriter more than my computer. For me, there's something solid and satisfying about the 'clunk-clunk' of the keys and immediately seeing the words in black print."

For the time being, St. George has no plans for future historical novels, having found that "although good historical fiction is being written, it is not a popular genre," she related to *AAYA*. "I'm in the schools a lot and talk to enough kids and librarians to know that if historical fiction is part of the curriculum, the kids will read it. But they won't seek it out on their own the way my generation did."

Both her historical fiction and nonfiction require a great deal of research. "Since writing my first book more than twenty years ago," St. George continued to tell *AAYA*, "I've done a lot of research for my novels, immersing myself in a period, discovering what was happening politically at the time, how people were living, what the economy was like. I hope that all that flavor comes through as an integral part of the story." St. George relies on children's nonfiction books for reference at the start of a project, because "the books are accurate, concise, better edited than adult books, and well-illustrated," she told *AAYA*. "From there, I go on to adult books, ending up my research at that national treasure, the New York Public Library."

In an exchange excerpted in *Journal of Youth Services in Libraries*, St. George tells of trying to help a friend, Liz, who called her and asked, "'I'm having a terrible time organizing material for a nonfiction book. Can I come over and pick your brain on how you do research?'

"Why not?," thought St. George. "Not only have I written ... nonfiction books, but I've also done extensive research for my historical fiction.... With all due modesty, I show Liz my system of beer cartons: a beer carton for my notes; another beer carton for correspondence; a third beer carton for brochures, pamphlets, and articles; and a fourth for Xeroxed copies of photographs. Research, library, and personal books are stacked [haphazardly around the room]. The A, B, C, D rewrites of my manuscript are [scattered] on the rug with red, blue, green, and purple reminders pinned to my workroom curtains—a different color for each rewrite.

"Liz is horror-struck. 'Judy, you've got to be kidding. *I'm* better organized than this.'

"One writer's organization apparently is another writer's disorganization," St. George continued in the article. "For me, writing a nonfiction book is akin to building a house, a project my family and I tackled some years ago. Because we were involved physically, it was a hands-on experience [beginning

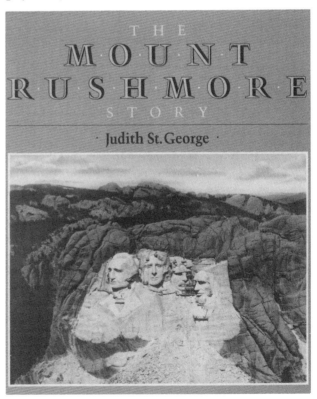

Winner of the 1986 Christopher Award, this history of the popular landmark was praised for its colorful detail.

Seventeen-year-old Matt tries to both adjust to life in a new town and solve a mystery in this 1983 thriller.

with a solid foundation], just as research is a hands-on experience."

"Occasionally it has occurred to me that I might have been born in a different time frame from this one," St. George declared in a publicity release. "Otherwise, why would I feel so much at home with long-ago people, their customs, language and everyday lives? The time frame doesn't seem to matter. I feel as comfortable with Andrew Jackson's White House years as I do with the Depression era of Mount Rushmore.

"People seem impressed by the amount of research needed to write a nonfiction book. But it's the research that's fun! I'm a library-freak, and for me, there's nothing like the high I get when I walk through the doors of a library, any library. As for visiting the setting of a nonfiction book, I always wait until the manuscript is finished before going to the physical site. There are always questions that can't be answered in libraries, and if I hadn't

already done most of the work, how could I know what I don't know?

"By the time ... David and I traveled to Panama for last-ditch (pun intended) research on the Panama Canal, I knew the working of the canal inside out and backwards. The day that we made a transit on the cargo ship from the Pacific to the Atlantic was one of the great experiences of my life as I mentally operated every valve, gate, and lock. (On the other hand, I hadn't counted on having to board the cargo ship, which was underway, by climbing up a thirty-foot rope ladder in the pitch dark from a launch that was also underway!)

"So, for me, the research is fun, both the library-kind and the physical-kind. It's the writing that's difficult. With every new book, I hear myself moaning, 'I can't believe that writing is this hard.' Is that because I'm making more demands on myself? I hope that's the reason but I'm not sure. All I know is that I want my readers to care as much about the outcome of historical events as if they were reading today's headlines. I want my

St. George's 1987 tale of mystery and mayhem.

readers to be aware that history is an 'ever-rolling stream' and that the past can't be separated from the present. Above all, I want the people in my books to come alive for my readers the way they come alive for me. . . .

"Kids mean a lot to me. . . . I really enjoy speaking to school groups and keeping in touch with what is going on in young people's lives. I especially enjoy the challenge of trying to entice the 'back-row kids' into exploring new worlds through books. But as for writing, I have to confess that I write for myself. After more than twenty years, it's how I define my *persona*. It's not only what I do, but also what I am."

■ Works Cited

"By George, Bloomers!," *Junior Literary Guild,* March, 1976, p. 24.
St. George, Judith, in an interview with Marc Caplan for *Authors and Artists for Young Adults.*
St. George, publicity.

St. George, "On Doing Research; or, How Did Mount Rushmore Get Its Name?," *Journal of Youth Services in Libraries,* fall, 1987, pp. 88-92.
"What's Happening to My Junior Year?," *Junior Literary Guild,* October, 1986-March, 1987, p. 61.

■ For More Information See

BOOKS

Contemporary Authors New Revisions Series, Volume 14, Gale, 1985.
Something about the Author, Volume 13, Gale, 1978.

PERIODICALS

Junior Literary Guild, March, 1980; March, 1982; September, 1983; April, 1990.
New York Times Book Review, July 13, 1980; January 25, 1981; April 25, 1982.

COLLECTIONS

Kerlan Collection at the University of Minnesota.

Edmund White

■ Awards, Honors

Hopwood Awards, 1961 and 1962, for fiction and drama; Ingram Merrill grants, 1973 and 1978; Guggenheim fellow, 1983; American Academy and Institute of Arts and Letters award for fiction, 1983; citation for appeal and value to youth from Enoch Pratt Free Library's Young Adult Advisory Board, 1988, for *The Beautiful Room Is Empty*.

■ Writings

NONFICTION

(With Peter Wood) *When Zeppelins Flew*, Time-Life, 1969.
(With Dale Browne) *The First Men*, Time-Life, 1973.
(With Charles Silverstein) *The Joy of Gay Sex: An Intimate Guide for Gay Men to the Pleasures of a Gay Lifestyle*, Crown, 1977.
States of Desire: Travels in Gay America, Dutton, 1980.

NOVELS

Forgetting Elena, Random House, 1973.
Nocturnes for the King of Naples, St. Martin's, 1978.
A Boy's Own Story, Dutton, 1982.
Caracole, Dutton, 1985.
The Beautiful Room Is Empty, Knopf, 1988.

OTHER

Blue Boy in Black (play), produced Off Broadway, 1963.

■ Personal

Born January 13, 1940, in Cincinnati, OH; son of Edmund Valentine II (an engineer) and Delilah (a psychologist; maiden name, Teddlie) White. *Education:* University of Michigan, B.A., 1962.

■ Addresses

Home—434 Lafayette St., New York, NY 10003; and 8 rue Poulletier, 75004 Paris, France. *Agent*—Maxine Groffsky, Maxine Groffsky Literary Agency, 2 Fifth Ave., New York, NY 10011.

■ Career

Time, Inc., Book Division, New York City, senior editor, 1972-73; Johns Hopkins University, Baltimore, MD, assistant professor of writing seminars, 1977-79; Columbia University School of the Arts, New York City, adjunct professor of creative writing, 1981-83; writer. Instructor in creative writing at Yale University, New York University, and George Mason University, Fairfax, VA. Executive director of New York Institute for the Humanities, 1981-82.

(With others) *Aphrodisiac* (short stories), Chatto, 1984.

(With Adam Mars-Jones) *The Darker Proof: Stories from a Crisis*, New American Library/Plume, 1988.

Also author of *Argument for Myth*. Author of six other plays. Contributor of articles and reviews to *Architectural Digest, Artforum, Home & Garden, Mother Jones, New York Times Book Review, Savvy Woman, Southwest Review*, and other periodicals. Editor, *Saturday Review*, and *Horizon*. Contributing editor, *Vogue* magazine, New York City.

■ **Work in Progress**

A novel.

■ **Sidelights**

Edmund White is a master stylist who has produced acclaimed novels, intrepid and insightful nonfiction on gay society, and semi-autobiographical novels that combine the best features of fiction and nonfiction. Known as a "gay writer," White also belongs among those writers whose literary reputations transcend simplistic labels. William Goldstein explains in *Publishers Weekly*, "To call Edmund White merely a gay writer is to oversimplify his work and his intentions. Although that two-word label … aptly sums up White's status, the first word no doubt helps obscure the fact that the second applies just as fittingly." White's fiction in particular has garnered critical acclaim; the author has received grants from the Ingram Merrill Foundation, the Guggenheim Foundation, and the American Academy and Institute of Arts and Letters. His semi-autobiographical novels have also won the appreciation of many young adult readers. *The Beautiful Room Is Empty* was chosen by the Enoch Pratt Free Library's Young Adult Advisory Board for its appeal and value to young adult readers. White's studies of the gay lifestyle and changing attitudes about homosexuality in America, including the impact of AIDS on the gay community, are important contributions to contemporary social history. Though male homosexuality is the subject of his writing, White offers insights into human behavior in general, according to reviewers. *Nation* contributor Carter Wilson comments, "Edmund White is to be envied not only for his productivity, … but because he is a gifted writer who has staked himself a distinguished claim in the rocky territory called desire."

White told *Publishers Weekly* that he is "happy to be considered a gay writer," even though that classification has resulted in some difficulties. "Since gay people have very little political representation, we have no gay spokespeople," he said. "What happens is that there is an enormous pressure placed on gay novelists because they are virtually the *only* spokespeople. The problem is that the novelist's first obligation is to be true to his own vision, not to be some sort of common denominator of public relations man to all gay people.… Everything is read as though it's a sort of allegory about the political dimensions of homosexuality as a general topic, rather than as a specific story about a specific person. That's understandable, because there are so few gay books, but it is regrettable because it is really an Early Stalinist view of art as propaganda." He intends his fiction to be "literary," by which he means that he hopes to attract the more serious and appreciative readers of fiction. "The market I'm going for, the kind of reader I'm looking for," he explained, "is one who is not simply looking for entertainment, but is looking for whatever we look for from art." He further explained, "I would hope that eventually my books would be good enough to be read simply as works of literature, as stories."

White has not always been comfortable identifying himself as a gay person. "I didn't want to be gay," the author told Leonard Schulman for a *Time* article. "I wanted to be normal, to have a wife and kids, not have a lonely old age." Yet, sometime after his parents' divorce, he believes he sympathized perhaps too strongly with his mother's desire for a husband. For years, he sought therapy as a means of eradicating homosexual behavior, but it was not until after his years at the University of Michigan that he met a gay psychoanalyst and accepted a gay lifestyle. He moved to Greenwich Village and discovered that the quality of his writing—and newly found self-esteem—would suffer unless it was frank about his sexuality and the emerging subculture in which it found expression.

White formed his lifelong commitment to reading and writing more easily. The author recalls in a *Town & Country* article that books afforded him his first flights of imagination. His social life as a child was limited because the family spent its summers in northern Michigan to relieve his sister's rose fever. White learned much of what he knew of social interaction from books because communication within his household was strictly limited. White's father, a civil engineer, enforced the rule of silence at the dinner table once by hitting him on the forehead with a soup spoon. "Music, the radio, books—those were the means by which emotion was conveyed in that stolid house where any more immediate outburst of feeling was forbidden or simply never displayed. Nor were we permitted to go to the movies, on the strange theory that they were corrupting to the young. Perhaps they were; they were certainly distressing." White recalls seeing Alan Ladd being flogged in the film *Two Years before the Mast* and feeling the wounds as if they were his own in nightmares for several weeks following. "That movie had been chosen because it was 'educational,' that is, based on a classic American book, but what such books and films taught me may not have been the lesson intended. From them I learned that 'real life' is savage, full of breathless incident and exotic locations—and at the same time imbued with an exacting moral refinement. Perhaps that's why the actual adult life I've come to lead has seemed so imperfect to me, so lackluster, for books taught me that a marriage can end over a subtle but fiercely held principle, that friendship can triumph over tyranny (even the tyranny of years), that a woman can rise in the world not solely on the basis of beauty or wealth but also through spiritual elegance, and that these ethical qualities sooner or later must become apparent to everyone."

Books became especially valuable to him, he explained in *Town & Country*, "because my father hated to see me reading, which he rightly considered an unhealthy substitute for sports or yard work and which he rightly feared would fill my head with funny ideas.... Whatever romances I've engineered or endured, whatever notions about the artist I've tried to live up to, whatever distant places I've traveled to or haunted in my imagination—they've all been footnotes to those pages I read as a child."

In the *Paris Review* interview with Jordan Elgrably, White talked about his first frustrating years as a writer. "I didn't get anything published until I was thirty-three and yet I'd written five novels and six or seven plays. The plays ... were dreadful," he said. When *Blue Boy in Black* was produced Off Broadway in 1963, critics commented that it began well, but they gave the play negative reviews. White decided that if he continued to write, he would stop "second-guessing" the New York market and would change his goals as a writer. He explained, "I decided to write something that would please me alone—that became my criterion—and that was when I wrote *Forgetting Elena*, the first novel I got published."

White had co-authored nonfiction books while a senior editor at Time, Inc. in New York City between 1969 and 1973. *When Zeppelins Flew*, written with Peter Wood, was published in 1969 and *The First Men*, written with Dale Browne, came out in 1973. After his debut as a novelist with *Forgetting Elena* in 1973 brought him acceptance in literary circles that included Susan Sontag and Richard Howard, White's concern about the commercial success of his books diminished. White told the *Paris Review*, "I have always made it a point of honor to write as though I had a million dollars; that is, I try to write in the most original way I know how, and that feels like a risk each time you do it. [French Nobel Prize winner] Andre Gide said that with each book you should lose the admirers you gained with the previous one."

White's first novel gained him many notable admirers, including master novelists Vladimir Nabokov and Gore Vidal. As White intended, *Forgetting Elena* transcended gay issues and was well-received as an intricately composed work of art. Critics applauded *Forgetting Elena* for its satiric and insightful look at social interaction as well as for its elegant prose. A first-person narrative of an amnesia victim struggling to determine his identity and the identities of those around him, *Forgetting Elena* exposes the subtle entrapments of social hierarchy and manners. White told the *Library Journal* that the novel's premise illustrates the "sinister" aspects of life in an artistically obsessed society. In such a culture, he explained, "Every word and gesture would ... convey a symbolic meaning. Ordinary morality would be obscured or forgotten. People would seek the beautiful and not the good—and, perhaps, cut free from the ethics, the beautiful would turn out to be merely pretty." Setting the novel's action at a fictitious resort reminiscent of New York's Fire Island, White creates, in the words of *Nation* contributor Simon Karlinsky, "a semiology of snobbery, its complete sign system." Karlinsky feels that "what might at first seem to be merely a witty parody of a particular subculture's foibles and vagaries actually turns out to be something far more serious and profound.... He has produced a parable about the nature of social interaction that transcends any given period and applies to the human predicament at large. To write of momentous and metaphysical matters in a light and graceful manner has almost become a lost art. It is refreshing and gratifying to encounter a new American novelist able to revive it."

EDMUND WHITE
Author of THE BEAUTIFUL ROOM IS EMPTY
FORGETTING ELENA

"An astonishing
first novel...
Uncannily beautiful."
The New York Times Book Review

(BB) Ballantine/Fiction/35862 (Canada $6.50) U.S. $4.95

White's 1973 novel is the first-person narrative of an amnesia victim trying to determine his identity.

Most critics consider *Forgetting Elena* a highly accomplished first novel. Karlinsky calls the work "an astounding piece of writing—profound, totally convincing and memorable." Alan Friedman likewise praises the book in the *New York Times Book Review*, though not without qualifications. Friedman writes, "There is something so unfailingly petty about the narrator's apprehensions ... and something so oppressive about his preoccupations ... that it is often difficult to be receptive to the book's genuine wonders." Friedman nevertheless concludes that this "tale of a sleuth who strives to detect the mystery of the self" is "an astonishing first novel, obsessively fussy, yet uncannily beautiful."

Larry McCaffery's introduction to an interview with White published in *Alive and Writing: Interviews* describes *Forgetting Elena* as "a hallucino-genic novel, part science fiction, part detective story, part comedy of manners. The work exudes mystery—the mystery of human desires and motives, the mystery of the signs and symbols we use to communicate those desires." In the interview, White credits Japanese literature with helping him to shape the peculiar consciousness he had while writing the novel: "One of the [Japanese] books that had a big impact on me was a tenth-century court diary called *The Pillow Book of Sei Shonagon* written by a woman who was a Heian courtier. She was the ultimate aesthete in a society dedicated to judging everything from an aesthetic point of view—in other words, morality had been replaced by aesthetics. That aesthetic overlay to everything became central to *Forgetting Elena*.... I was also very influenced by Susan Sontag's aesthetics when I was creating that book. In the introduction to *Against Interpretation* I seem to remember that she called a work of art a machine for creating sensation. That phrase haunted me."

White saw *Forgetting Elena* as a vehicle for "truth" as well as beauty, a mix that accounts for the book's more complicated features. He told McCaffery, "Beauty is all in favor of making a story that entertains, that's well-formed, that's lively, in which there are recognizable causes and effects, in which there are decisive experiences, turning points, crucial scenes—a sequence of events that cohere to the Aristotelian notions of drama." Truth, in contrast, said White, is less orderly. The memory is selective; causes, turning points, and personalities are not clearly defined. He said, "You are not a unitary character nor is your experience a unity (in fact, you are an extremely fragmented person who becomes different in almost every situation). Some of these are issues or questions that I tried to expose or dramatize in *Forgetting Elena*. I chose what I thought was an extreme metaphor for this condition: amnesia. But my narrator is an embarrassed amnesiac who doesn't want to admit to anyone that he can't remember who he is, much less who they are; he is constantly molding himself on other people's expectations. He's a skillful faker. An extreme version of any kind of social interaction."

White's second novel, *Nocturnes for the King of Naples*, published in 1978, has also won acclaim for its discerning treatment of human values and relationships. As John Yohalem explains in the *New York Times Book Review*, "*Nocturnes* is a series of apostrophes to a nameless, evidently famous dead lover, a man who awakened the much younger, also nameless narrator ... to the possibility of sexual friendship. It was an experience that the narrator feels he did not justly appreciate," Yohalem continues, "and that he has long and passionately—and fruitlessly—sought to replace on his own terms." David Shields of the *Chicago Tribune* offers this assessment of the novel's impact: "Because of the speaker's final realization of the impossibility of ever finding a ground for satisfaction, a home, this book is more a chronicle of sorrow and regret. It becomes, rather, a true elegy in which sorrow and self-knowledge combine and transform into a higher form of insight. This higher insight is the artistic intuition of the mortality of human things and ways."

According to J. D. McClatchy's *Shenandoah* review, White "is a superior stylist of both erotic theology and plangent contrition [i.e., loudly expressive remorse]. And his special gift is his ability to empty out our stale expectations from genres . . . and types . . . and to reimagine them in a wholly intriguing and convincing manner." While Doris Grumbach suggests in the *Washington Post Book World* that White "will seem to the careful reader to be the poet of the burgeoning homosexual literature," she also notes, "The music of White's prose is seductive. It is of course possible that a tone-deaf, a melody-indifferent reader might turn his back on White's homo-erotic narrative." However, she adds, White's prose in *Nocturnes* promises satisfaction to "the lover of good fictional writing who is open to this most subtle exploration of the many ways of love, desertion, loss, and regret."

Caracole, White's 1985 novel, goes back to an earlier century and retrieves a more elaborate fictional form. Lehmann-Haupt observes in his *New York Times* column that White has "certainly conceived a 19th century plot steeped in the conventions of romanticism" when he writes of two country lovers forcibly separated who turn to sexual escapades in a large city. The resulting story is a "puzzling melange of comic opera and sleek sensuality," says the reviewer. *New York Times Book Review* contributor David R. Slavitt describes *Caracole* as "a grand fantasy. . . . Shrewdness and self-awareness ooze from every intricate sentence, every linguistic arabesque and hothouse epigram." Though appreciative of the work, Slavitt suggests that one result of "the artificed quality of the book is the distance at which it puts its characters, who are . . . pastoral figures, vivid and cute, as if seen from the wrong end of a telescope. They can endure pleasure and pain that would be intolerable if they were more plausible and persuasive."

Slavitt concludes that *Caracole* "is, provokingly, a challenge to taste, which is likely to vary from one reader to another or even from moment to moment in the same reader. . . . But high and dry . . . Mr. White reigns and deigns, impishly looking down and loving the kind of delicious outrage he has worked so hard for in this book and has so richly earned."

Critics observe that each of White's books presents voices and literary strategies that differ from previous works. In the *Paris Review* interview, White commented that a writer who keeps changing his style "could be accused of dilettantism—or he could be defended as someone who resists the sort of packaging designed for quick product recognition and smooth consumption. Is a stylistically unpredictable writer a luxury product—or is he refusing to be a product? More subjectively, my mercurial literary personality reflects a general feeling of unreality. Like the narrator in *Forgetting Elena*, I'm an amnesiac—a guilty, not an innocent amnesiac. I keep feeling I've accomplished nothing, never written a 'real' novel. Today, when so many of my friends are dead or dying of AIDS, that feeling of unreality has been heightened. People say we should seize the day, but just *one* day turns out to be too cold (or slippery) to hold."

As this comment suggests, White's nonfiction on the gay life in America is as compelling as his fiction. *The Joy of Gay Sex: An Intimate Guide for Gay Men to the Pleasures of a Gay Lifestyle*, published in the late 1970s, attempted to make the topic less mysterious for curious heterosexuals and to provide useful information for gay men. In 1980, White published his second nonfiction work dealing with the male homosexual lifestyle, *States of Desire: Travels in Gay America*. A documentary on segments of homosexual life in fifteen major American cities, *States of Desire* contains interviews, autobiographical reminiscences, and accounts of cultural and entertainment centers for gays. According to Ned Rorem in the *Washington Post Book World*, *States of Desire* "poses as a documentary . . . on our national gay bourgeoisie. Actually it's an artist's selective vision . . . of human comportment which is and is not his own, mulled over, distilled, then spilled onto the page with a melancholy joy."

Some critics feel that White's scope and objectivity are limited in *States of Desire*. Richard Goldstein points out, "Nowhere in [the book] is there any sense of how different life is for a working-class homosexual, for a lesbian, or for a black." *New York Times Book Review* contributor Paul Cowan comments that White does not make "the promiscuous America he portrays ... even remotely attractive to an outsider." Cowan elaborates, "Though his book is partly autobiographical, [White] never tries to help readers who don't share his sexual preference to understand his assumptions or the assumptions of the people he describes." Despite these qualifications, critics express general praise for *States of Desire.* Rorem remarks that, flaws aside, "this book tenders its subject without apology and with the cultured clarity of an address to peers." Clemons feels that White's "novelistic gifts—curiosity about character (his own as well as others'), an alert ear and eye for revelatory detail—make this book absorbing." Richard Goldstein, too, commends White: "The author's persona, as open and appreciative as the ever-young men of San Francisco he describes, is a particularly attractive bonus to his intelligence.... His passion is evident throughout the trek, and so is his compassion for those who mediate less gracefully between affection and fantasy." In the *New York Times,* John Leonard concludes, "Mr. White comes out of the closet with a brass band and a Moog synthesizer. He acquaints us with terror and qualm. Simply as anthropology, *States of Desire* commands attention and respect."

Village Voice contributor Richard Goldstein feels that the best aspect of *States of Desire* "is White's attempt to explain the most tangible aspects of gay culture to homosexuals, who may be more confused by what they do than heterosexuals are by what they see.... In its demure way, this is as didactic a treatise on homosexual experience as has ever been written." Clemons notes that if White aims to provoke heterosexuals to rethink their views on gay men, he also intended to stir up the gay community. For example, he challenges gays to see that persecution of drag queens and transvestites by gays who live more conventional lives reveals a contradictory latent homophobia. White also diagnoses an important rift in the gay community: a conflict between gay "moderates," who seem to desire assimilation into the American mainstream, and the "radicals," who seek social change through militant confrontation. Clemons concludes, "[White] says he hopes his book 'will enable gays and straights to imagine other lives.' Often startlingly, it accomplishes that."

The Joy of Gay Sex and *States of Desire* qualified White as one of the most prominent spokespersons for gay men in America. He knew that publishing these works would engage him in politics, to some extent. He explained in a *Paris Review* interview,

"It was a political act for me to sign *The Joy of Sex* at the time. The publisher could not have cared less, but for me it was a big act of coming out. Charles Silverstein, my co-author, and I were both aware that we would be addressing a lot of people and so in that sense we were spokesmen. We always pictured our ideal reader as someone who thought he was the only homosexual in the world. *States of Desire* was an attempt to see the varieties of gay experience and also to suggest the enormous range of gay life to straight and gay people—to show that gays aren't just hairdressers, they're also petroleum engineers and ranchers and short-order cooks. Once I'd written *States of Desire* I felt it was important to show one gay life in particular depth, rather than all of these lives in a shorthand version. *A Boy's Own Story* and it's sequel, *The Beautiful Room Is Empty,* grew out of that."

In addition to his accomplished fiction and nonfiction, White has produced several semi-autobiographical novels that bring together the best features of both kinds of writing, beginning with *A Boy's Own Story,* a first-person narrative of a homosexual boy's adolescence during the 1950s. As a *Harper's* reviewer describes it, "*A Boy's Own Story* is a poignant combination of the two genres written with the flourish of a master stylist." The main conflict in this psychological novel is the narrator's battle against negative judgments from society and from within. *New York Times Book Review* contributor Catherine R. Stimpson believes, however, that the subject of the work is "less a particular boy than the bodies and souls of American men: the teachers and masters; the lovers, brothers, hustlers and friends; the flawed fathers who would be kings to sons who should be princes.... Like so many American novels about coming to maturity, 'A Boy's Own Story' asserts that growing up is a descent into painful knowledge, indecency and repression." Lehmann-Haupt of the *New York Times* likewise writes: "This is not exclusively a homosexual boy's story. It is any boy's story, to the marvelous degree that it evokes the incohate longing of late childhood and adolescence." Emotional turmoil related to homosexuality, though prominent in the novel, is only one difficulty among many related to coming of age, the *Harper's* reviewer observes: "[*A Boy's Own Story*] is an endearing portrait of a child's longing to be charming, popular, powerful, and loved, and of his struggles with adults, ... told with ... sensitivity and elegance."

More than one reviewer has called *A Boy's Own Story* a "classic" work. Comparing White to James

Baldwin, Herman Wouk, and Mary McCarthy, Thomas M. Disch writes in the *Washington Post Book World* that the novel "represents the strongest bid to date by a gay writer to do for his minority experience what the writers above did for theirs—offer it as a representative, all-American instance." Stimpson finds the book "as artful as [White's] earlier novels but more explicit and grounded in detail, far less fanciful and elusive.... Balancing the banal and the savage, the funny and the lovely, he achieves a wonderfully poised fiction." *Village Voice Literary Supplement* columnist Eliot Fremont-Smith concludes: "*A Boy's Own Story* seems intended to be liberating, as well as touching and clever and smart. It is something else as well: unsettling to the willing heart. This makes it a problem, with no happy solution guaranteed, which defines what's wrong with the book. But also what's right, what intrigues." Lehmann-Haupt calls the work "superior fiction," adding: "Somehow ... Mr. White does succeed in almost simultaneously elevating and demeaning his self-history. And these extremes of epiphany and emptiness are what is most universal about this haunting Bildungsroman."

In *The Beautiful Room Is Empty,* the sequel to *A Boy's Own Story,* the narrator alternately revels in his homosexuality and rejects himself for it. Psychoanalysis and increasing surrender to sensual activity escalate the young man's battle for self-acceptance. Though his sexuality troubles him, the excitement and audacity of his experiences with gay men in public restrooms seems a needed respite from the blandness of his suburban life. The gay characters easily upstage the others in the book with their outspoken opinions, witty banter, and daring sexual exploits, while "White takes us through [the narrator's] unsentimental education like an indulgent pal, making graceful introductions, filling in with pungent details, saving his harshest judgments for himself," Vince Aletti comments in the *Voice Literary Supplement.* Sometimes the adolescent makes bold moves, as when he shouts "Gay is good!" in a Greenwich Village demonstration. At other times, he acts out his self-loathing, as when he seduces his music teacher and betrays him to the authorities. By depicting both kinds of behavior, the narrator helps White to evoke "the cautious emergence of a gay consciousness" taking place in the surrounding culture, Aletti remarks. In the interview with McCaffery, White commented, "To have my boy turn out so creepy seemed to be a way of alienating some gay commissars. Nevertheless, I felt that the end-

ing made sense, even from a political point of view. You can't show somebody in a deforming period, like the 1950s in America, and then show him as happy, healthy, the perfect role model.... I felt that once I had written the end of the book, I had succeeded in presenting a truth about that deformation that would have been missing if I left it out."

Some readers did not see how one could come away from the book with a good feeling about homosexuality. In answer to these critics, White explained in a *Village Voice* interview that his role is not that of a propagandist, but that of a historian. He said, "I am more interested in being descriptive than prescriptive. That is, I like to describe the way people actually are. Some rather young people don't see the historical point of *The Beautiful Room Is Empty....* I was trying to point out that people were even more oppressed [in the 1960s] than they are today." Addressing the topic again in a *Publish-*

Written with sensitivity and insight, this 1982 novel tells of a homosexual boy's adolescence during the 1950s.

ers Weekly interview, the author said, "I feel it wouldn't be true to the experience of the characters if I showed them gliding blissfully through, when it was obviously a painful thing coming out in a period before gay liberation." A *Time* reviewer suggests, "In the era of AIDS, White's novel is a fiercely remembered plea not to push gays back into the closet."

Getting published was more difficult for gay writers in the 1960s. White recalled in the *Paris Review* interview, "I was writing gay books well before gay liberation and before there was a recognized gay reading public. One actually existed, although no publisher was aware of it. There was also a tremendous amount of self-repression among gay editors. A gay editor would turn down a gay book because if he admitted to liking it he would have to defend it at an editorial meeting, and that might lead other people to suspect *he* was gay." As attitudes about homosexuality changed, the publishing world became more receptive to books by gay writers. White told McCaffery, "In the mid-'70s, there was a kind of enthusiasm for publishing lots of gay titles, but a lot of junk was brought out that didn't do very well, so now the number of gay books has fallen off for commercial reasons. Interestingly enough, gays represent a large part of the reading market for serious fiction. In America most readers are middle-aged Jewish heterosexual women who are college educated. After that, I suspect that gay men in their thirties or forties, also college educated, are the second-biggest market for fiction and literature. Maybe college students are a distant third. But gay readers aren't obliged to read only gay books. Like everybody else, they want to read the best books they can."

At a time when books by gay writers are not as widely read as he hopes they will be, White, who once had a novel rejected by twenty-two different publishers, admits to being thrilled by the recognition his writing has received. "I know I'll always be doing this," he told *Publishers Weekly*, "and I know that I'll never make a living from my writing; but that's fine. It's enough to be published.... I don't have very exalted notions of what a writer's life should be like." Concurrent with his career as an author, White has taught creative writing at several East Coast universities, including Johns Hopkins, Columbia, and Yale. His reviews and profiles appear frequently in *Vogue* and other magazines. He also writes travel articles, and, from his home in Paris, reports on contemporary trends in art and politics, and French social history.

Paris is hospitable toward White and other journalists who take an interest in French culture, he reports. "Maybe we're liked because there are so few of us living here," White wrote in a 1985 *Vogue* column. "There are only about twenty-three thousand officially registered Americans in France—far below the forty thousand of the 1920s. But as one expatriate American who has lived here for most of his seventy years told me, the 1920s crowd was escaping Main Street and Prohibition and didn't give a damn about the French or their language, whereas today's expatriates usually study the language and the culture with seriousness, even reverence." White enjoys living in Paris because art is held in high esteem throughout France, and because Paris has become "*the* world clearinghouse for contemporary music, dance, theater, and video," as well as an important "channel for dispersing American art," he wrote in *Vogue.*

White is an astute observer of trends in French culture and politics. People from many nations now live in Paris where new attitudes about effective methods of political change are becoming apparent. Emphasis is being transferred from political philosophies, or ideologies, to confidence in improved interpersonal relations as the preferred means of social action. "The real change France is witnessing is the demise of ideology and the rise of a moderate, pragmatic politics," White related in *Vogue.* Nicholas Wahl, who explained these changes to White, credits this new attitude to the fact that Communism never appeared attractive to the French, "and to the belated recognition that we live in a world that requires patient adjustments, not fiery gestures, and compromise, not revolution."

Continuing his role as a social historian on the homosexual experience in America, White has written several intensely personal articles on the impact of AIDS on gay life and gay writers. He told Walter Kendrick of the *Village Voice,* "I think gay male life has been reduced both by the trade press, and, unfortunately, by many gays to the single issue of AIDS. At the same time, AIDS has been used to browbeat gays, and gays embrace AIDS as a way of feeling bad about themselves. There has been a terrible loss of confidence. [In *The Beautiful Room*] I was eager to write a fairly rousing testimonial to the importance of gay liberation."

White writes with authority about the gay liberation movement because he has been an active participant in the movement since the Stonewall riot in New York City in 1969. Police had raided the gay discotheque and gay men fought back in what is now seen as the official beginning of the campaign for gay rights. "The riot itself I considered a rather silly event at the time; it seemed more Dada than Bastille, a kind of romp," he said in the *Paris Review* interview. "But I participated in that and then was active from the very beginning in gay liberation. We had these gatherings which were patterned after women's and ultimately, I think, Maoist consciousness-raising sessions. Whether or not our sessions accomplished anything for society, they were certainly useful to all of us as a tool for changing ourselves." Before that time, he explained, gay men tended to think of themselves as primarily heterosexual except for certain "carelessly" acquired sexual habits—"but we weren't homosexuals as people. Even the notion of a homosexual culture would have seemed comical or ridiculous to us, certainly horrifying."

The spread of AIDS since the 1970s, he observes, has affected the way gay men see themselves. "Certainly the disease is encouraging homosexuals to question whether they want to go on defining themselves at all by their sexuality," White wrote in *Artforum.* "Maybe the French philosopher Michel Foucault was right in saying there are homosexual acts but not homosexual people. More concretely, when a society based on sex and expression is deeroticized, its very reason for being can vanish." Furthermore, he reports, the shadow of disease and death has become associated not only with gay sex but with many facets of gay life, significantly limiting the development of more positive attitudes toward homosexuality in America. In a 1985 *Rolling Stone* article, White observed, "The AIDS issue threatens to crowd out all other aspects of gay achievement and culture. A reading by gay poets, a performance by a gay dance company, a conference on the gay sensibility, all seem brave but marginal recollections of former hopes. For instance, when a respected young director . . . tried to get backing for a gay comedy film [in 1985], he was told in Hollywood that 'the industry' was interested in funding only AIDS movies. . . . Gay liberation, born in 1969, was an expression of the utopian Sixties belief in human perfectability through social experimentation; that belief has now collapsed before the crushing reality of disease."

In "Residence on Earth: Living with AIDS in the '80s," an article White wrote for *Life* magazine, he observes that the AIDS crisis has changed the general public's views of gay men: "Ten years ago gay men were perceived as playboys who put their selfish pleasures above family or community duties and responsibilities. Now they're seen as victims who have responded to a tragedy with dignity and courage. Above all, the lesbian and gay community is recognized as a *community,* one that is often angry and militant, generally well disciplined, always concerned," voluntarily raising funds and organizing support groups for AIDS sufferers, visiting the sick, and campaigning for responsible sex education.

White observes in the *Rolling Stone* that AIDS has caused the gay liberation movement some daunting setbacks. As White sees it, "Gay liberation opposed both the religious definition of homosexuality as sin and the medical model of homosexuality as a disease. But because of AIDS, preachers and doctors have gained back considerable ground. Many young gays are choosing to stay in the closet

White's 1988 sequel to *A Boy's Own Story* was praised for its appeal and value to young adults.

or to curtail almost all sexual behavior—understandable, but surely a source of frustration and bitterness." White warns that the "new moralism" has dangers of its own, including the tendency to see gays as scapegoats and to limit their civil liberties in the attempt to impede the spread of disease.

White feels that the gay liberation movement has succeeded, in part. In *Mother Jones,* White explained that nearly two decades after the Stonewall riot, "there is a great deal more self-acceptance among gays, even a welcome show of arrogance." In addition, he wrote, "Gay men no longer look longingly over their shoulders at straight life, and they take each other seriously as mentors, buddies, sidekicks, brothers, lovers." Women have also benefitted, no longer afraid that enjoying each other's company in public will lead others to suspect they are gay.

White observes that AIDS is not the only factor that accounts for the mixed success of the gay liberation movement. The movement has had some unanticipated side-effects. "Gay liberation grew out of the progressive spirit of the 1960s—a strange and exhilarating blend of socialism, feminism and the human potential movement. Accordingly, what gay leaders in the late 1960s were anticipating was the emergence of the androgyne [a person who is specifically neither masculine nor feminine], but what they got was the superbutch stud [a muscle-bound type whose homosexuality is a heightened form of masculine aggression]; what they expected was a communal hippie freedom from possessions, but what has developed is the acme of capitalist consumerism. Gays . . . consume expensive vacations, memberships in gyms and discos, cars, elegant furnishings, clothes, haircuts, theater tickets and records. . . . The success of gay liberation in the 1970s, of course, was largely political, but it was also, I'd contend, strongly related to the rise of the gay market. Unfortunately, today this rampant and ubiquitous consumerism not only characterizes gay spending habits but also infects attitudes toward sexuality: gays rate each other quantitatively according to age, physical dimensions and income; and all too many gays consume and dispose of each other, as though the act of possession brought about instant obsolescence." White points out that finding a solution to this problem, as it is for the AIDS epidemic, is important not just for gays, but for all Americans.

White believes that gay writers should recognize the historical significance of the AIDS epidemic in the context of the larger culture in which they live.

This 1988 collection reflects White's concern about the AIDS crisis.

For instance, the challenge to confront the AIDS crisis has brought to light a number of other serious American problems such as the prohibitive cost of health care. In a 1985 *Rolling Stone* article, he elaborated, "The AIDS epidemic has rolled back a big rotting log and revealed all the squirming life underneath it, since it involves, all at once, the main themes of our existence: sex, death, power, money, love, hate, disease and panic. No American phenomenon has been as compelling since the Vietnam War, which itself involved most of the same themes. Although obviously a greater tragedy, the war nevertheless took place on a different continent and invited a more familiar political analysis. We knew how to protest the war. In the rancorous debates over AIDS, all the issues are fuzzy and the moral imperatives all questions." Finding the answers to these questions has been made more difficult by the speed with which attitudes about homosexuality have changed. In *Artforum,* White observes, "To have been oppressed in the '50s, freed in the '60s, exalted in the

'70s, and wiped out [by AIDS] in the '80s is a quick itinerary for a whole culture to follow. For we are witnessing not just the death of individuals but a menace to an entire culture. All the more reason to bear witness to the cultural moment."

White states in the *Artforum* article that he believes gay writers have a further task ahead. "Art must compete with (rectify, purge) the media, which have thoroughly politicized AIDS in a process that is the subject of a book to be published shortly in England. It is *Policing Desire: Pornography, AIDS and the Media,* by Simon Watney.... To confront AIDS more honestly than the media have done, it must begin in tact, avoid humor, and end in anger." Tact is important, he says, "because we must not reduce individuals to their deaths," and "because we must not let the disease stand for other things." Humor is "grotesquely inappropriate to the occasion," since it "puts the public (indifferent when not uneasy) on cozy terms with what is an unspeakable scandal: death." He continues, "End in anger, I say, because it is only sane to rage against the dying of the light, because strategically anger is a political response, because psychologically anger replaces despondency, and because essentially anger lightens the solitude of frightened individuals."

White's concern about AIDS has also left its mark on his writing. White's stories in *The Darker Proof* focus on the experience of AIDS in order to make use of the way fiction can minister to deep emotional needs. He told Kendrick, "AIDS is a very isolating and frightening situation.... To show that someone else has the same thoughts, fears, hopes—the same daily anxiety—is one of the main things fiction does." White also told Stewart Kellerman in the *New York Times Book Review* that because of the AIDS epidemic, he sees "everything as a potential last work." Now that nearly forty of his friends and former students have died from AIDS, he feels "the urge to memorialize the dead, to honor their lives," he wrote in *Artforum.* He added, "There is an equally strong urge to record one's own past—one's own *life*—before it vanishes."

Apart from these imperatives, White believes that originality is the creative writer's foremost concern. He explained to McCaffery, "There are two ways of looking at literature. One is to feel that there is one great Platonic novel in the sky that we're all striving toward. I find that view to be very deadening, finally, and certainly it's a terrible view for a teacher or a critic to hold. The other view is that each person has a chance to write his or her own book in his or her own voice; maturing as an artist occurs when you find your own voice, when you write something that *only you* could have written. That's the view I have."

In keeping with his views on originality, White has resisted the pressure to meet popular expectations in his books. He remarked to McCaffery, "It's interesting how many gay readers are frustrated by how little explicit sexuality there is in my writing because most gay books published in the '50s and '60s were published specifically because there was a pornographic market for them.... Approaching the issue from a technical standpoint, I think that if you deal exclusively with sex in fiction, you inevitably end up only with an episodic structure."

In the *Paris Review* interview White described the two impulses—toward fiction and nonfiction—between which he balances his writing: "Writers can use literature as a mirror held up to the world, or they can use writing as a consolation for life (in the sense that literature is preferable to reality). I prefer the second approach, although clearly there has to be a blend of both. If the writing is pure fantasy it doesn't connect to any of our real feelings. But if it's grim realism, that doesn't seem like much of a gift. I think literature should be a gift to the reader, and that gift is in idealization. I don't mean it should be a whitewashing of problems, but something ideally energetic. Ordinary life is *blah,* whereas literature at its best is bristling with energy."

■ Works Cited

Aletti, Vince, review of *The Beautiful Room Is Empty, Voice Literary Supplement,* April, 1988, p. 3.

Allen, Bruce, review of *Forgetting Elena, Library Journal,* February 15, 1973.

Baylis, Jamie, review of *A Boy's Own Story, Harper's,* October, 1982, pp. 75-76.

Blaise, Clark, "Don't Give In to the Baggy Grown-Ups," *New York Times Book Review,* March 20, 1988, p. 7.

"Bookends," review of *The Beautiful Room Is Empty, Time,* April 11, 1988.

Clemons, Walter, "Gay Rites: A Tour Coast to Coast," *Newsweek,* February 11, 1980, pp. 92-93.

Cowan, Paul, "The Pursuit of Happiness," *New York Times Book Review,* February 4, 1980, p. 12.

Disch, Thomas M., "Memories of a Homosexual Boyhood," *Washington Post Book World*, October 17, 1982, p. 1.

Elgrably, Jordan, "The Art of Fiction CV: Edmund White," *Paris Review*, fall, 1988, pp. 46-80.

Friedman, Alan, review of *Forgetting Elena*, *New York Times Book Review*, March 25, 1973, p. 2.

Fremont-Smith, Eliot, "Making Book: Tease and Sympathy," *Village Voice Literary Supplement*, December, 1982, pp. 8-9.

Goldstein, Richard, "Modus Eroticus," *Village Voice*, January 28, 1980, pp. 41-42.

Goldstein, William, "Publishers Weekly Interviews: Edmund White," *Publishers Weekly*, September 24, 1982, pp. 6-8.

Grumbach, Doris, "Songs of Innocence and Experience," *Washington Post Book World*, November 12, 1978, p. 26.

Karlinsky, Simon, "America, Texas and Fire Island," *Nation*, January 5, 1974, pp. 23-24.

Kellerman, Stewart, "Everything Is Potentially Final," *New York Times Book Review*, March 20, 1988, p. 7.

Kendrick, Walter, "The Importance of Being: Armistad Maupin and Edmund White Interviewed by Walter Kendrick," *Village Voice*, June 28, 1988, pp. 22, 36.

Kuharski, Allan, "Elegies for the Eighties—New Gay Fiction," *San Francisco Review of Books*, winter, 1988-89, pp. 53-54.

Lehmann-Haupt, Christopher, *New York Times*, review of *A Boy's Own Story*, December 17, 1982, p. 26; review of *Caracole*, September 9, 1985, p. 19; "Edmund White's Tale of a Gay Youth," March 17, 1988, p. C29.

Leonard, John, review of *States of Desire*, *New York Times*, January 21, 1980, p. 3.

McCaffery, Larry, *Alive and Writing: Interviews*, University Press of Illinois, 1987, pp. 257-274.

McClatchy, J. D., "Baroque Inventions," *Shenandoah*, Volume 30, number 1, fall, 1978, pp. 97-98.

Rorem, Ned, "Cruising from Coast to Coast," *Washington Post Book World*, January 27, 1980, p. 3.

Schulman, Leonard, "Profile: Imagining Other Lives," *Time*, July 30, 1990, pp. 58-60.

Shields, David, "Elegy for the Phantom Past," *Chicago Tribune*, December 10, 1978, p. 7.

Slavitt, David R., review of *Caracole*, *New York Times Book Review*, September 15, 1985, p. 15.

Stimpson, Catherine R., "The Bodies and Souls of American Men," *The New York Times Book Review*, October 10, 1982, p. 15.

White, Edmund, "On Reading: An Exaltation of Dreams," *Town & Country*, May, 1983, pp. B22-B23.

White, Edmund, "Paradise Found: Gay Men Have Discovered There Is Friendship after Sex," *Mother Jones*, June, 1983, pp. 10-16.

White, Edmund, interview, *Library Journal*, February 15, 1973.

White, Edmund, "The Story of the Year: The AIDS Trauma Touched Everyone," *Rolling Stone*, December 19, 1985, pp. 121, 124.

White, Edmund, *Vogue*, "An Emperor of the Mind," November, 1984, p. 322; "Letter from Paris: Americans in Paris," May, 1985, pp. 152-155; "Letter from Paris: Tough Guys—The Late 'Saint Genet,' Depardieu, and a Pragmatic Chirac," July, 1986, pp. 120-122.

White, Edmund, *The Beautiful Room Is Empty*, Knopf, 1988.

White, Edmund, "Residence on Earth: Living with AIDS in the '80s," *Life*, fall, 1989, p. 135.

White, Edmund, *States of Desire*, Dutton, 1980.

White, Edmund, "Esthetics and Loss," *Artforum*, January, 1987, pp. 68-71.

White, Edmund, "Back to Mac," *House & Garden*, June, 1990, pp. 161-168.

Wilson, Carter, review of *A Boy's Own Story*, *Nation*, November 13, 1982, pp. 503.

Yohalem, John, "Apostrophes to a Dead Lover," *New York Times Book Review*, December 10, 1978, p. 12.

■ **For More Information See**

BOOKS

Contemporary Literary Criticism, Volume 27, Gale, 1984.

PERIODICALS

American Book Review, May, 1989.
Chicago Tribune, December 10, 1978; April 6, 1980.
Harper's, March, 1979; May, 1987.
Los Angeles Times Book Review, May 4, 1980; April 3, 1982.
London Review of Books, April 17, 1986; March 3, 1988.
Nation, March 1, 1980; November 16, 1985; April 9, 1988.
New Statesman, March 14, 1986; January 29, 1988.
Newsweek, April 30, 1973; January 17, 1983.
New York Times, September 8, 1985; March 17, 1988.

Observer, March 16, 1986; December 14, 1986;
  January 24, 1988; November 13, 1988.
Punch, March 19, 1986; January 8, 1988.
Spectator, March 5, 1988.
Times Literary Supplement, September 5, 1980;
  January 22, 1988.

Vogue, February, 1984; January, 1986; July, 1987.
Washington Post Book World, December 10, 1978;
  October 6, 1985; April 3, 1988.
West Coast Review of Books, Volume 14, number 1,
  1988.°

Elie Wiesel

■ Personal

Full name, Eliezer Wiesel; surname pronounced "we-*zell*"; born September 30, 1928, in Sighet, Romania; immigrated to United States, 1956, naturalized citizen, 1963; son of Shlomo and Sarah (Feig) Wiesel; married Marion Erster Rose, 1969; children: Shlomo Elisha; stepchildren: Jennifer. *Education:* Attended Sorbonne, University of Paris, 1948-51. *Religion:* Jewish.

■ Addresses

Office—The University Professors, Boston University, 745 Commonwealth Ave., Boston, MA 02215. *Agent*—Georges Borchardt, 136 East 57th St., New York, NY 10022.

■ Career

Worked variously as foreign correspondent for *Yedioth Ah'oronoth,* Tel Aviv, Israel, *L'Arche,* Paris, France, and *Jewish Daily Forward,* New York City, 1949-68; writer and lecturer, 1964—; City College of the City University of New York, New York City, Distinguished Professor of Judaic Studies, 1972-76; Boston University, Boston, MA, Universi-

ty Professor of Philosophy and Religious Studies and Andrew W. Mellon Professor in the Humanities, 1976—. Distinguished Visiting Professor of Literature and Philosophy, Florida International University, 1982; Henry Luce Visiting Scholar in the Humanities and Social Thought, Whitney Humanities Center, Yale University, 1982-83. Member of board of overseers, Bar-Ilan University, 1970—; member of board of directors, American Associates of Ben-Gurion University of the Negev, 1973—, National Committee on American Foreign Policy, 1983—, International Rescue Committee, 1985—, Hebrew Arts School, and Humanitas; member of board of governors, Tel-Aviv University, 1976—, Haifa University, 1977—, and Oxford Centre for Postgraduate Hebrew Studies, 1978—; member of board of trustees, Yeshiva University, 1977—, and American Jewish World Service, 1985—; chairman, U.S. President's Commission on the Holocaust, 1979-80, U.S. Holocaust Memorial Council, 1980-86; member of jury, 1984 Neustadt International Prize for Literature; chairman of advisory board, World Union of Jewish Students, 1985—; cofounder of National Jewish Center for Learning and Leadership; adviser, Boston University Institute for Philosophy and Religion, National Institute against Prejudice and Violence, and the International Center in New York, Inc. *Member:* Amnesty International; Foreign Press Association (honorary life member); U.N. Correspondents Association; American Gathering of Jewish Holocaust Survivors (honorary president, 1985); P.E.N.; Authors League; Writers Guild of America, East; Author's Guild; Writers and Artists for Peace in the Middle East; American Academy of Arts and Sciences (fellow); Royal Norwegian Society of Sciences and Letters; Jewish Academy of Arts and Sciences (fellow).

■ Awards, Honors

Prix Rivarol, 1963, for *The Town beyond the Wall;* Ingram Merrill Award, 1964; William and Janice Epstein Fiction Award from Jewish Book Council, 1965, for *The Town beyond the Wall;* National Jewish Book awards, 1965, for *The Town beyond the Wall,* and 1972, for *Souls on Fire;* International Remembrance Award from the World Federation of Bergen-Belsen Associations, 1965, for *The Town beyond the Wall* and all other writings; Jewish Heritage Award, 1966, for excellence in literature; Prix Medicis (France), 1968, for *Le Mendiant de Jerusalem;* Prix Bordin from French Academy, 1972, and Frank and Ethel S. Cohen Award from Jewish Book Council, 1973, both for *Souls on Fire;* Eleanor Roosevelt Memorial Award, 1972; American Liberties Medallion from American Jewish Committee, 1972; Literary Avodah Award from Jewish Teachers' Association, 1972; Martin Luther King, Jr., Medallion from City College of the City University of New York, 1973; Award for Distinguished Service to American Jewry from National Federation of Jewish Men's Clubs, 1973; Faculty Distinguished Scholar Award from Hofstra University, 1974; Scopus Award from Hebrew University of Jerusalem, 1974; Rambam Award from American Mizrachi Women, 1974; Holocaust Memorial Award from New York Society of Clinical Psychologists, 1975; Jewish Heritage Award from Haifa University, 1975; Spertus International Award, 1976; Myrtle Wreath Award from Hadassah, 1977; King Solomon Award, 1977; Humanitarian Award from B'rith Sholom, 1978; Joseph Prize for Human Rights from Anti-Defamation League of B'nai B'rith, 1978; Presidential Citation from New York University, 1979; Inaugural Award for Literature from Israeli Bonds Prime Minister's Committee, 1979; Zalman Shazar Award from the State of Israel, 1979.

Prix Livre-International and Bourse Goncourt, both 1980, and Prix des Bibliothecaires, 1981, all for *Le Testament d'un poete juif assassine;* Jabotinsky Medal from State of Israel, 1980; Rabbanit Sarah Herzog Award from Emunah Women of America, 1981; Jordan Davidson Humanitarian Award from Florida International University, 1983; Literary Lions Award from New York Public Library, 1983; fellow, Timothy Dwight College, Yale University, 1983; International Literary Prize for Peace from Royal Academy of Belgium, 1983;

Le Grand Prix de la Litterature de la Ville de Paris, 1983, for *La Cinquieme fils;* Le Grand Prix Litteraire de Festival International de Deauville, 1983; Anatoly Shcharansky Humanitarian Award, 1983; Commander de la Legion d'Honneur, France, 1984, elevated to Grand Officier, 1990; Congressional Gold Medal of Achievement, 1984; Distinguished Writers Award from Lincolnwood Library, 1984; Chancellor Joseph H. Lookstein Award from Bar-Ilan University, 1984; Sam Levenson Memorial Award from Jewish Community Relations Council, 1985; Comenius Award from Moravian College, 1985; Henrietta Szold Award from Hadassah, 1985; Anne Frank Award, 1985; International Holocaust Remembrance Award from State of Israel Bonds, 1985; Voice of Conscience Award from American Jewish Congress, 1985; Distinguished Community Service Award from Mutual of America, 1985; Covenant of Peace Award from Synagogue Council of America, 1985; Freedom of Worship Medal from Franklin D. Roosevelt Four Freedoms Foundation, 1985; Jacob Pat Award from World Congress of Jewish Culture, 1985; Humanitarian Award from International League of Human Rights, 1985.

Nobel Peace Prize, 1986; Distinguished Foreign-Born American Award from International Center, 1986; Freedom Cup Award from Women's League for Israel, 1986; Jacob Javits Humanitarian Award of U.J.A. Young Leadership, 1986; Medal of Liberty Award, 1986; Freedom Award from International Rescue Committee, 1987; Achievement Award from Artists and Writers for Peace in the Middle East, 1987; La Grande Medaille de Vermeil de la Ville de Paris, 1987; La Medaille l'Universite de Paris, 1987; La Medaille de la Chancellerie de l'Universite de Paris, 1987; Eitinger Prize from University of Oslo, 1987; Lifetime Achievement Award from *Present Tense* magazine, 1987; special Christopher Award, 1987; Profiles in Courage Award from B'nai B'rith, 1987; Achievement Award from State of Israel, 1987; Seminary Medal from Jewish Theological Seminary of America, 1987; Special Award from National Committee on American Foreign Policy, 1987; Metcalf Cup and Prize for Excellence in Teaching from Boston University, 1987; Gra-Cruz da Ordem Nacional do Cruzeiro do Sul, Brazil, 1987; Centennial Medal from University of Scranton, 1987; Golda Meir Senior Humanitarian Award, 1987; Hofstra University Presidential Medal, 1988; honorary fellow, Beth Hatefutsoth, 1988; Human Rights Law Award from International Human Rights Law Group, 1988; Herzl Literary Award; David Ben-Gurion

Award; International Kaplun Foundation Award from Hebrew University of Jerusalem; American-Israeli Friendship Award; S. Y. Agnon Gold Medal; approximately fifty honorary doctorates.

■ Writings

Un di velt hot geshvign (memoir; in Yiddish; title means "And the world has remained silent"), [Buenos Aires], 1956, abridged French translation published as *La Nuit*, foreword by Francois Mauriac, Minuit, 1958, translation by Stella Rodway published as *Night*, Hill & Wang, 1960, reprinted with preface by Robert McAfee Brown, Bantam, 1986.

L'Aube (novel), Seuil, 1960, translation by Frances Frenaye published as *Dawn*, Hill & Wang, 1961.

Le Jour (novel), Seuil, 1961, translation by Anne Borchardt published as *The Accident*, Hill & Wang, 1962.

La Ville de la chance (novel), Seuil, 1962, translation by Stephen Becker published as *The Town beyond the Wall*, Atheneum, 1964, new edition, Holt, 1967.

Les Portes de la foret (novel), Seuil, 1964, translation by Frenaye published as *The Gates of the Forest*, Holt, 1966.

Le Chant des morts (essays and stories), Seuil, 1966, translation by Steven Donadio published as *Legends of Our Time*, Holt, 1968.

Les Juifs du silence (originally published in Hebrew as a series of articles for newspaper *Yedioth Ah'oronoth*), Seuil, 1966, translation with afterword by Neal Kozodoy published as *The Jews of Silence: A Personal Report on Soviet Jewry*, Holt, 1966, revised edition, Schocken, 1987.

Zalmen; ou, La Folie de Dieu (play), Seuil, 1968, translation by Lily Edelman and Nathan Edelman published as *Zalmen; or, The Madness of God*, Holt, 1968.

Le Mendiant de Jerusalem (novel), Seuil, 1968, translation by the author and L. Edelman published as *A Beggar in Jerusalem*, Random House, 1970.

Entre deux soleils (essays and stories), Seuil, 1970, translation by the author and L. Edelman published as *One Generation After*, Random House, 1970.

Celebration hassidique: Portraits et legendes, Seuil, 1972, translation by wife, Marion Wiesel, published as *Souls on Fire: Portraits and Legends of Hasidic Masters*, Random House, 1972.

Le Serment de Kolvillag (novel), Seuil, 1973, translation by M. Wiesel published as *The Oath*, Random House, 1973.

(With music by Darius Milhaud) *Ani maamin: A Song Lost and Found Again* (cantata; first performed at Carnegie Hall, 1973), translation by M. Wiesel, Random House, 1974.

Celebration biblique: Portraits et legendes, Seuil, 1975, translation by M. Wiesel published as *Messengers of God: Biblical Portraits and Legends*, Random House, 1976.

Un Juif aujourd'hui: Recits, essais, dialogues, Seuil, 1977, translation by M. Wiesel published as *A Jew Today*, Random House, 1978.

Four Hasidic Masters and Their Struggle against Melancholy, University of Notre Dame Press, 1978.

(With others) *Dimensions of the Holocaust*, Indiana University Press, 1978.

Le proces de Shamgorod tel qu'il se deroula le 25 fevrier 1649: Piece en trois actes (first produced in Paris, 1981), Seuil, 1979, translation by M. Wiesel published as *The Trial of God (as It Was Held on February 25, 1649, in Shamgorod): A Play in Three Acts*, Random House, 1979.

Images from the Bible, illustrated with paintings by Shalom of Safed, Overlook Press, 1980.

Le Testament d'un poete juif assassine (novel), Seuil, 1980, translation by M. Wiesel published as *The Testament*, Simon & Schuster, 1981.

Five Biblical Portraits, University of Notre Dame Press, 1981.

The Haggadah (cantata), music by Elizabeth Swados, S. French, 1982.

Somewhere a Master: Further Hasidic Portraits and Legends, translation from the French by M. Wiesel, Simon & Schuster, 1982.

Paroles d'etranger (essays, stories, and dialogues), Seuil, 1982.

The Golem: The Story of a Legend as Told by Elie Wiesel (fiction), translation from the French by Borchardt, Summit, 1983.

Le Cinquieme Fils (novel), Grasset, 1983, translation by M. Wiesel published as *The Fifth Son*, Warner, 1985.

Signes d'Exode (essays, stories, and dialogues), Grasset, 1985.

Against Silence: The Voice and Vision of Elie Wiesel (collection), three volumes, edited by Irving Abrahamson, Holocaust Library, 1985.

(With Josy Eisenberg) *Job ou Dieu dans la Tempete* (dialogue and commentary) Grasset et Fasquelle, 1986.

Le Crepuscule, au loin (novel), Grasset et Fasquelle, 1987, translation by M. Wiesel published as *Twilight*, Summit, 1988.

(With Albert H. Friedlander) *The Six Days of Destruction: Meditations toward Hope,* Paulist Press, 1988.

L'oublie (novel), Seuil, 1989, translation by Stephen Becker published as *The Forgotten,* Summit, in press.

(With Philippe-Michael de Saint-Cheron) *Evil and Exile,* translation by Jon Rothschild, University of Notre Dame Press, 1990.

From the Kingdom of Memory (reminiscences), Summit, 1990.

(With John O'Connor) *A Journey of Faith: A Dialogue between Elie Wiesel and John Cardinal O'Connor,* Donald I. Fine, 1990.

Member of editorial boards, *Midstream, Religion and Literature* (University of Notre Dame), *Sh'ma: Journal of Jewish Responsibility,* and *Hadassah;* chairman of editorial board, *Holocaust and Genocide Studies: An International Journal.* Contributor to numerous periodicals.

■ Adaptations

Zalmen; or, The Madness of God was adapted for the stage by Marion Wiesel as *The Madness of God,* produced in Washington, DC, 1974.

Night was adapted as a sound recording, Caedmon, 1982.

■ Work in Progress

A book on Talmudic masters similar to his book of Hasidic portraits, *Souls on Fire.*

■ Sidelights

Elie Wiesel, who won the 1986 Nobel Peace Prize, has devoted much of his adult life to speaking out about and against oppression of many kinds. A Jew, he survived death camps, such as Auschwitz, where Nazis under Adolf Hitler murdered millions of European Jews—Hitler's "final solution" to the problem of what to do with people considered inferior to the "master race" he hoped to establish. Wiesel has revealed his experiences and those of others in memoirs, novels, plays, and lectures in the hope of preventing future horrors. He speaks to all ages but especially likes to talk to schoolchildren; as he said in a *Parade* magazine article by Jules Schwerin, "adults may not understand." Wiesel does not limit himself to Jewish concerns. As he wrote in an essay for *Contemporary Authors Autobiography Series (CAAS):* "We cannot delude ourselves that the massacre of any group will not affect the whole of civilization. We cannot wish for

the extermination of one people without placing all of humanity at risk. The final solution, aimed at the Jewish people, was an outline for the death of all peoples."

Wiesel was born in Sighet, Romania, near the border of what is now Hungary, on September 30, 1928, a Jewish holy day. He was the only boy in the family, with two older sisters and one younger. His father, Shlomo Wiesel, was a practical, hard-working shopkeeper—not particularly religious. In contrast, Elie Wiesel followed the leanings of his mother, a teacher and a devout Jew. According to Ted L. Estess in *Elie Wiesel,* she started him in heder, the basic Jewish schooling where he began learning to read scripture in Hebrew at the age of three. "It was she who brought me to *heder,* to make me a good Jew, loving only the wisdom and truth to be drawn from the Torah. And it was she who sent me as often as possible to the Rebbe of Wizsnitz to ask his blessing or simply to expose me to his radiance," Wiesel said.

He took to religious study early and avidly. Under a teacher of mysticism, Wiesel practiced his faith in ways that his parents didn't always know how to respond to, as when he and a schoolmate decided to honor the Sabbath day with complete silence. "How could I explain to them that one might, by a single profane word, violate the sanctity of the Sabbath? and that by silence one could enhance its beauty and prolong its reign?" he asked in his *CAAS* essay. "My interest in—my passion for—silence dates from those years. Sometimes I tell myself that my Master, thanks perhaps to unique powers, was trying to prepare me for the post-war years. . . . Did he suspect that language itself would fall mute before the Auschwitz that was to consume him?"

His maternal grandfather, another religious influence, also shaped Wiesel in a nonreligious way. Dodye Feig gave him a love for stories and storytelling. "A fabulous storyteller, he knew how to captivate an audience," Wiesel said in Estess's book. "He would say: 'Listen attentively, and above all, remember that true tales are meant to be transmitted—to keep them to oneself is to betray them.' He knew how intently I listened; he must have known that I would remember, but he had no way of knowing how closely I would follow his advice." Years later, Wiesel shared his grandfather's tales and many of his own in his numerous books. Legends he heard from Feig eventually saw print as *Souls on Fire.*

Wiesel (bottom right) in the Buchenwald concentration camp in 1945.

As a youth, however, Wiesel was focused only on his faith. "If someone had told me when I was a child that one day I would become a novelist, I would have turned away, convinced he was confusing me with someone else," he wrote in his book *One Generation After.* "The pattern of my future had then seemed clear. I would pursue my studies in the same surroundings with the same zeal, probing the sacred texts and opening the gates to the secret knowledge that permits fulfillment by transcending self. Novels I thought childish, reading them a waste of time. You had to be a fool to love the fictitious universe made of words when there was the other, immense and boundless, made of truth and presence. I preferred God to His creation, silence to revelation.... It took a war— and what a war—to make me change my road, if not my destiny."

Wiesel's quiet life in Sighet ended abruptly in 1944. The town shipped off its many Jews by train—packed into cattle cars—to the Nazi concentration camp at Birkenau, the receiving center for Auschwitz (known in Polish as Oswiecim). A local newspaper reported that "from now on, it would be possible to state one's place of residence without feeling shame," Wiesel recounted in *One Generation After.* Before the journey, the Jews of Sighet hastily buried their valuables to keep them from the Nazis. "In the early morning hours of that particular day, after a sleepless night, the ghetto was changed into a cemetery and its residents into gravediggers. We were digging feverishly in the courtyard, the garden, the cellar, consigning to the earth, temporarily we thought, whatever remained of the belongings accumulated by several generations, the sorrow and reward of long years of toil.

"My father took charge of the jewelry and valuable papers. His head bowed, he was silently digging near the barn. Not far away, my mother, crouched on the damp ground, was burying the silver candelabra she used only on Shabbat eve; she was moaning softly, and I avoided her eyes. My sisters burrowed near the cellar. The youngest, Tziporah, had chosen the garden, like me. Solemnly shoveling, she declined my help. What did she have to hide? Her toys? Her school notebooks? As for me, my only possession was my watch." Wiesel had received the watch from his parents at his bar mitzvah, the ritual passing into adulthood of Jewish boys. "It meant a lot to me. And so I decided to bury it in a dark, deep hole, three paces away from the fence, under a poplar tree whose thick, strong foliage seemed to provide a reasonably secure shelter.

"All of us expected to recover our treasures. On our return, the earth would give them back to us. Until then, until the end of the storm, they would be safe. Yes, we were naive. We could not foresee that the very same evening, before the last train had time to leave the station, an excited mob of well-informed friendly neighbors would be rushing through the ghetto's wide-open houses and court-yards, leaving not a stone or beam unturned, throwing themselves upon the loot."

In fact, however, Wiesel's watch remained. Twenty years later he returned to his birthplace, to his house, now a stranger's home. With his hands he dug in the place he remembered and discovered the watch in its box, just as he had buried it, though covered with dirt and rust. It was a link with his past. First he felt disgust at its poor condition, then "a strange kind of gratitude" overtook him. "This thing, this nameless, lifeless thing had survived for the sole purpose of welcoming me on my return and providing an epilogue to my childhood." He almost took it with him, but instead, in a gesture he found hard to explain, he returned it to its grave. "I tell myself that probably I simply wanted to leave behind me, underneath the silent soil, a reflection of my presence. Or that somehow I wanted to transform my watch into an instrument of delayed vengeance: one day, a child would play in the garden, dig near the tree and stumble upon a metal box. He would thus learn that his parents were usurpers, and that among the inhabitants of his town, once upon a time, there had been Jews and Jewish children, children robbed of their future."

Not quite fifteen years old, Wiesel went with his family and neighbors to Auschwitz-Birkenau, where more than two million Jews died during the war. There he and his father were separated from his mother and sisters. A "noncommissioned officer came to meet us, a truncheon in his hand," wrote Wiesel in *Night*. "He gave the order: 'Men to the left! Women to the right!' Eight words spoken quietly, indifferently, without emotion. Eight short, simple words. Yet that was the moment when I parted from my mother. I had not had time to think, but already I felt the pressure of my father's hand: we were alone. For a part of a second I glimpsed my mother and my sisters moving away to the right. Tzipora held Mother's hand. I saw them disappear into the distance; my mother was stroking my sister's fair hair, as though to protect her, while I walked on with my father and the other men. And I did not know that in that place, at that moment, I was parting from my mother and Tzipora forever. I went on walking. My father held onto my hand.... Not far from us, flames were leaping up from a ditch, gigantic flames. They were burning something. A lorry drew up at the pit and delivered its load—little children. Babies! Yes, I saw it—saw it with my own eyes ... those children in the flames. (Is it surprising that I could not sleep after that? Sleep had fled from my eyes.)

"So this was where we were going. A little farther on was another and larger ditch for adults. I pinched my face. Was I still alive? Was I awake? I could not believe it. How could it be possible for them to burn people, children, and for the world to keep silent? No, none of this could be true. It was a nightmare.... Soon I should wake with a start, my heart pounding, and find myself back in the bedroom of my childhood, among my books...." As they walked, Wiesel's father seemed resigned to his fate, but young Elie thought instead of throwing himself into the electric fence nearby. Then someone began reciting the Jewish prayer for the dead, the Kaddish. "I do not know if it has ever happened before, in the long history of the Jews, that people have ever recited the prayer for the dead for themselves....

"We continued our march. We were gradually drawing close to the ditch, from which an infernal heat was rising. Still twenty steps to go. If I wanted to bring about my own death, this was the moment. Our line had now only fifteen paces to cover. I bit my lips so that my father would not hear my teeth chattering. Ten steps still. Eight. Seven. We marched slowly on, as though following a hearse at our own funeral. Four steps more. Three steps. There it was now, right in front of us, the pit and its flames. I gathered all that was left of my strength, so that I could break from the ranks and throw myself upon the barbed wire. In the depths of my heart, I bade farewell to my father, to the whole universe; and, in spite of myself, the words [of the Kaddish] formed themselves and issued in a whisper from my lips: *Yitgadal veyitkadach shme raba....* May His name be blessed and magnified.... My heart was bursting. The moment had come. I was face to face with the Angel of Death.... No. Two steps from the pit we were ordered to turn to the left and made to go into a barracks.

"Never shall I forget that night, the first night in camp, which has turned my life into one long night, seven times cursed and seven times sealed. Never shall I forget that smoke. Never shall I forget the little faces of the children, whose bodies I saw turned into wreaths of smoke beneath a silent blue sky. Never shall I forget those flames which consumed my faith forever. Never shall I forget that nocturnal silence which deprived me, for all eternity, of the desire to live. Never shall I forget those moments which murdered my God and my soul and turned my dreams to dust. Never shall I forget these things, even if I am condemned to live as long as God himself. Never."

After such an introduction to the place of death, Wiesel faced the harsh life of a prisoner. He and the other men survived on a little bread and soup, and those who could had to work hard and long. They slept on what amounted to bare shelves, the most people crammed into the smallest space possible. In *One Generation After* Wiesel recalled a man there who helped him keep a shred of his faith alive. Before coming to Birkenau, Wiesel was sure, the man had been "respected and admired for his erudition and wisdom. Here, like all of us, he was ravaged by hunger, lost in anonymity. But to him, this was unimportant. What mattered was to be able, thanks to a single disciple, to become Rosh-Yeshiva [a spiritual teacher] again, even here, in the camp. Since I was ready to receive, he knew he could give. And as long as he went on giving, he was as strong as life, even stronger perhaps. To me, he became the personification of the Jew's characteristic need to transmit his legacy; and he knew that he was timeless and indestructible...

"We studied together many hours, sometimes without interruption, losing our awareness of what surrounded us." The man, whose name Wiesel does not remember, knew the whole Talmud—all of Jewish scriptural tradition—by heart. While laboring side by side for their captors, the two were able to continue Wiesel's religious study where it had ended in Sighet. The man emphasized to Wiesel that they must not let their souls fall into evil, even—especially—in the camp. "The soul is important and the enemy knows it; that's why he tries to corrupt it before destroying us. Do not let him. The soul counts for more than the body."

Near the end of the war, Wiesel and his father were moved more than two hundred miles west to Buchenwald, a concentration camp in eastern Germany. Wiesel's father died there. Ill, he was beaten by other prisoners, who stole his food. Wiesel would give his father food from his own small ration, and he stayed with him as much as he could. The head of the barrack block said Wiesel should stop trying to help his father and think only of himself. Secretly Wiesel agreed, but he immediately felt guilty about it. He went on sharing his food and staying with his father. In *Night* Wiesel chronicled the end of this difficult time. One night his father begged Wiesel for a drink of water and was struck in the head by a guard. When the guard left, Wiesel got down from his bunk and sat by his father for more than an hour. "Then I had to go to bed. I climbed into my bunk, above my father, who

This autobiographical account covers Wiesel's deportation to Auschwitz in 1944 and his liberation from Buchenwald in 1945.

Wiesel's study of Jewish history and religious practices culminated in this 1972 volume.

was still alive. It was January 28, 1945. I awoke on January 29 at dawn. In my father's place lay another invalid. They must have taken him away before dawn and carried him to the crematory. He may still have been breathing.

"There were no prayers at his grave. No candles were lit in his memory. . . . I did not weep, and it pained me that I could not weep. But I had no more tears. And, in the depths of my being, in the recesses of my weakened conscience, could I have searched it, I might perhaps have found something like—free at last!

"I had to stay at Buchenwald until April eleventh. I have nothing to say of my life during this period. It no longer mattered. After my father's death, nothing could touch me any more. . . . I spent my days in a state of total idleness. And I had but one desire—to eat. I no longer thought of my father or of my mother. From time to time I would dream of a drop of soup, of an extra ration of soup. . . ."

As Wiesel commented in his *CAAS* essay, "We were all dead, but did not know it. But we knew that we would never be alive again, that no return was possible from where we were now. . . . Others were perhaps stronger and more confident; but not I. I never succeeded in imagining myself free, happy, whole; I never managed to think myself, to project myself, beyond the barbed wire. The night around us and the night within us merged in an opaque black curtain."

In April of 1945 American soldiers reached Buchenwald and freed the remaining prisoners. Sixteen years old and with no family or home to return to, Wiesel went to France along with several hundred other orphaned survivors. There he learned that his two older sisters, Batya and Hilda, had also survived.

After the war, Wiesel was often troubled by "an absurd and yet painful conviction: for me to survive, another had to die. Who was it?" he asked in his autobiographical essay. "Often as I write, my thoughts dwell upon him. Have I the right to speak in his name? Better: have I the right to speak at all knowing that I will never succeed in stating the essential?" Instead of telling about his experiences, Wiesel made a ten-year vow of silence on the subject. The vow stood firm in spite of inner conflict. Wiesel had "absorbed not only the suffering, which was not mine alone—suffering everywhere in the camps—but I absorbed, unwittingly, perhaps unconsciously, the obsession to tell the tale, to bear witness." According to Estess, he said, "I knew that anyone who remained alive had to become a storyteller, a messenger, had to speak up." But he could not speak up immediately. Instead he returned to his religious studies, immersing himself in them. Later he looked back on this time amazed. "How could I shift with no transition from Buchenwald to the faith and prayers of my childhood?

"This is the only possible explanation: we were too rudely awakened. We needed several months to believe that we were truly out of danger; and alive. In the meantime we let ourselves be carried along by old habits revived, habits of body as well as of mind. . . . In a way it was a kind of protest: to show the enemy that he had not won the battle. . . . He had not succeeded in permanently interrupting our prayers."

The time in the camps had severely shaken Wiesel's faith, if not quite destroyed it. He still believed in God, but he was tormented by the question of how God could have allowed such atrocities against his people. "How can God and his silence be justified?" Wiesel wrote in his *CAAS* essay. "One cannot conceive of Auschwitz with God or without God." When he renewed his religious studies it was no longer an attempt "to master doctrines that he believed implicitly," Estess revealed. "Now he was passionately questioning for himself, attempting almost desperately to understand how the Holocaust had been possible. He argued with God and he challenged man, inquiring as if his life and world meaning depended on the outcome of his inquiry."

From 1948 to 1951 Wiesel became fluent in French and studied literature, psychology, and philosophy at the Sorbonne, earning money working as a tutor, choir director, and translator. "All I wanted was to study in a very autodidactic manner," he said in Estess's article. Learning French was part of beginning a new life, making new friends, entering a new world. Since then he has worked almost exclusively in French, with his wife translating his books into English. "Why do I write in French? I write in French because it was the language I learned at sixteen, and it is valuable to me. Except for non-fiction, I don't try to write in English. A language is like a person, it doesn't like infidelity," he wrote in *Against Silence: The Voice and Vision of Elie Wiesel.*

Wiesel also became a journalist for a French newspaper in the late 1940s, and in 1949 he visited Israel to report on the new country's independence. After several months there, he returned to Paris, where he was hired as a foreign correspondent for the Israeli paper *Yedioth Ah'oronoth.* In 1954 one of his newspaper interviews, with Christian novelist Francois Mauriac, changed his life again. The subject of the Holocaust arose, and although Wiesel did not specifically speak of his experience in the concentration camps, Mauriac encouraged him to write about it. "My meeting with Mauriac coincided with the tenth anniversary of my deportation," Wiesel recalled in *CAAS.* "I sensed clearly that the time had come to begin translating ten years of patient silence into words. In Yiddish it was *And the World Kept Silent,* which was to become *Night.* Why had I chosen Yiddish? Sentimentality? Fidelity? Both. I felt an obligation to make my first book an offering to a culture, an atmosphere, a climate which were those of my childhood."

Night, an autobiographical account covering Wiesel's life from deportation to liberation, deals with his fears, guilt, and questions concerning the Holocaust. This memoir, adapted and translated

Wiesel continues his study of Hasidic teachers and spiritual leaders in this 1982 sequel.

into eighteen languages, became his best-known work. It is the first of his books witnessing to the horrors of the Holocaust, the only one specifically about Wiesel's own experiences. In the *Dictionary of Literary Biography Yearbook: 1987* article on Wiesel by John K. Roth, Wiesel asserted that "all my subsequent books are built around it." He commented, "I have never spoken about the Holocaust except in one book, *Night*—the very first—where I tried to tell a tale directly, as though face to face with the experience."

He felt driven to avoid a literary approach. "No literature; above all do not produce literature," he asserted in his *CAAS* essay. "Nor try to please by flattering the reader or critic. Say only the essential—say only what no other could say.... Speak as a witness on the stand speaks. With no indulgence to others or oneself." In his preface to the twenty-fifth anniversary edition of *Night,* Robert McAfee Brown remarked that the world was not particularly eager to hear Wiesel's testimony. "Such depressing subject matter," he observed. "But we cannot indefinitely avoid depressing subject matter, particularly if it is true.... *Night* has been the most influential book in forcing that confrontation. Lean, taut, and sparse in style, employing no tricks, but providing no avenues of escape for its readers, it remains today a book we must read and reread if we are to accept responsibility for our past and to learn from that past for the sake of our future."

Night was first published, under the Yiddish title *Un di velt hot geshvign,* in 1956. That same year Wiesel visited the United States on a newspaper assignment to report on the United Nations and was struck by a taxicab in Times Square. While recovering from the accident, Wiesel could not renew the documents permitting him to live in France as a non-citizen, and he decided he would stay in the United States. In 1963 he was granted U.S. citizenship.

In the United States Wiesel worked for the *Jewish Daily Forward* and kept a busy schedule. "I slept less and less, and never took a vacation," he said in the *CAAS* essay, "because in addition to my professional duties, and along with my novelist's tasks, I continued my studies of the Jewish tradition's sacred texts." For seventeen years he studied privately with Harav Saul Lieberman, "the greatest Talmudist in many generations." Twice a week the two met for hours to explore the Talmud and commentaries on it, and Wiesel came to rely on him as a close personal friend as well as spiritual master. Lieberman officiated at Wiesel's 1969 wedding to Marion Erster Rose, another Holocaust survivor.

Since marrying, Wiesel has made his home in New York City and occasionally visits Paris and Israel. "I can't say today that I could be attached to anyplace, or anything," he confessed in a *Washington Star-News* interview. "I can't own anything in gold. It's like I'm allergic to it. One night the German officers in camp ordered all valuables to be thrown in a pile. I saw a mountain of wedding rings and watches and jewelry. And it hit me. For this, my mother and father struggled all their lives."

Although known primarily as a Holocaust writer, Wiesel feels passionately for all victims of prejudice, black or white, capitalist or communist, Jewish or Christian or Moslem. "By struggling on behalf of Russian, Arab or Polish Jews, I fight for human rights everywhere," he wrote in *One Generation After.* "By calling for peace in the Middle East, I take a stand against every aggression, every war. By protesting the fanatical exhortations to 'holy wars' against my people, I protest against the stifling of freedom in Prague [Czechoslovakia]. By

This 1981 novel won awards internationally.

striving to keep alive the memory of the holocaust, I denounce the massacres in Biafra [Nigeria] and the nuclear menace. Only by drawing on his unique Jewish experience can the Jew help others. A Jew fulfills his role as man only from inside his Jewishness. That is why, in my writings, the Jewish theme predominates. It helps me approach and probe the theme of man.

"Of course, had there been no war, I would have sought self-realization in other ways. I would not, for example, have become a writer, or at least, I would have written something other than novels. And in the small yeshiva where I would have stayed, indefinitely poring over the same page of the same book, I would never have imagined one could justify one's existence except by strictly observing the 613 commandments of the Torah. Today I know this is not enough. The war turned everything upside down, changing the order and substance of priorities. For me, to be a Jew today means telling the story of this change. For whoever lives through a trial, or takes part in an event that weighs on man's destiny or frees him, is duty-bound to transmit what he has seen, felt and feared. The Jew has always been obsessed by this obligation. He has always known that to live an experience or create a vision, and not transform it into link and promise, is to turn it into a gift to death.

"To be a Jew today, therefore, means: to testify. To bear witness to what is, and to what is no longer. One can testify with joy—a true and fervent joy, though tainted with sadness—by aiding Israel. Or with anger—restrained, harnessed anger, free of sterile bitterness—by raking over the ashes of the holocaust. For the contemporary Jewish writer, there can be no theme more human, no project more universal."

During President Jimmy Carter's administration Wiesel was named chairman of the President's Commission on the Holocaust, then chairman of the U.S. Holocaust Memorial Council, a post he held until 1986. As chairman of the council, Wiesel instituted National Days of Remembrance in the United States, and his leadership inspired the introduction of Holocaust curricula in numerous schools throughout the country.

Wiesel, who also studies and occasionally teaches mystical Jewish texts and stories, was named Andrew W. Mellon Professor in the Humanities at Boston University in 1976. He enjoys writing for children and speaking to students. His message to one group of junior high school students in New York City, observed Schwerin, was that "every people, every human being is different. You have the same right, pride and authority as anyone else. The worst enemy to humankind is indifference.... We are always the children of the same family."

Wiesel is dedicated to bringing justice to all people and ensuring human rights everywhere. He serves as writer, witness, teacher, and moral activist. "After the event, we tried to teach, we felt we had to do something with our knowledge," he wrote in *Against Silence*. "We had to communicate, to share, but it was not easy. Behind every word we said, a hundred remained unsaid. For every tear, a thousand remained unshed. For every Jewish child we saw, a hundred remained unseen.... What can I tell you as a teacher who teaches young people? It is more than a matter of communicating knowledge. Whoever emerges in the field of teaching the Holocaust becomes a missionary, a messenger."

In 1986 Wiesel won the Nobel Peace Prize for witnessing to the Holocaust and speaking out on behalf of the persecuted everywhere. In his accep-tance speech, quoted by Steve Fagin in the *Day*, he said: "No one may speak for the dead, no one may interpret their mutilated dreams and visions. And yet, I sense their presence. I always do—and at this moment more than ever. The presence of my parents, that of my little sister...." In his Nobel lecture, printed in the *Dictionary of Literary Biography Yearbook: 1986*, he reminded his listeners: "Remembering is a noble and necessary act.... The rejection of memory becomes a divine curse, one that would doom us to repeat past disasters, past wars." He urged people to work for universal peace. "None of us is in a position to eliminate war, but it is our obligation to denounce it and expose it in all its hideousness. War leaves no victors, only victims.... Mankind needs to remember more than ever. Mankind needs peace more than ever, for our entire planet, threatened by nuclear war, is in danger of total destruction. A destruction only man can provoke, only man can prevent. Mankind must remember that peace is not God's gift to his creatures, it is our gift to each other."

"When I was in the camps," Wiesel said in *Parade*, "evil had attained such dimensions that they made it invincible. The fallout of that hate is still here, all around us. If we don't learn from what happened, if we remain indifferent, we are lost. I must—*we* must—bear witness." As he wrote in *CAAS*, "Auschwitz was perhaps a warning." He is somewhat encouraged by the response of survivors to their experiences. "Logically, they should have given up on mankind. Kept their distance, and spat on society and its idols.... But they chose faith and compassion. In that, they show us the path to follow."

In his essay Wiesel spoke of taking stock of his life. He is proud that some of his books are taught in schools, that he has reached some people. "I am satisfied with what has been offered me. With the years comes a skeptical serenity that helps us carry on," he noted. "Praises do not turn my head and blame does not disturb my rest. With the years comes a desire to concentrate on the essential.... A writer's purpose should not be to please, but to unsettle, and I might even say, to unsettle himself. Personally I am rarely satisfied. Is that why I am always venturing into new territory? When no one was paying attention to the Holocaust, I was talking about it; now that everybody is talking about it, I say little." He turned to the plight of Russian Jews, oppressed by an atheist government for decades, and later took on the threat of nuclear war. He is still writing. "When all is said and done, I know no other way," he confessed. "I set down words and do my best to make them speak the truth, or at least to let them tell no lies."

■ Works Cited

Contemporary Authors Autobiography Series, Volume 4, Gale, 1986, pp. 353-62.

Elenko, Stuart S., "The 1986 Nobel Peace Prize: Elie Wiesel," Dictionary of Literary Biography Yearbook: 1986, Gale, 1987, pp. 19-28.

Estess, Ted, Elie Wiesel, Ungar, 1980.

Fagin, Steve, "For Wiesel, Strochlitz, a Bond of Friendship, Love Steeped in Tragedy," Day (New London, CT), December 14, 1986, p. A16.

Richards, David, interview in Washington Star-News, May 7, 1974.

Roth, John K., "Elie Wiesel," Dictionary of Literary Biography Yearbook: 1987,, Gale, 1988, pp. 388-401.

Schwerin, Jules, "Can Prejudice Be Overcome?," Parade, February 23, 1986, pp. 12-15.

Wiesel, Elie, One Generation After, Random House, 1970.

Wiesel, Against Silence: The Voice and Vision of Elie Wiesel, Holocaust Library, 1985.

Wiesel, Night, preface by Robert McAfee Brown, Bantam, 1986.

■ For More Information See

BOOKS

Abramowitz, Molly, Elie Wiesel: A Bibliography, Scarecrow, 1974.

Berenbaum, Michael G., The Vision of the Void: Theological Reflections on the Works of Elie Wiesel, Wesleyan University Press, 1979.

Brown, Robert McAfee, and H. J. Cargas, Face to Face, Anti-Defamation League, 1978.

Brown, Elie Wiesel: Messenger to All Humanity, University of Notre Dame Press, 1983.

Cargas, Harry James, Conversations with Elie Wiesel, Paulist Press, 1976.

Cargas, Responses to Elie Wiesel, Persea, 1979.

Contemporary Issues Criticism, Volume 1, Gale, 1982.

Contemporary Literary Criticism, Gale, Volume 3, 1975, Volume 5, 1976, Volume 11, 1979, Volume 37, 1986.

Dictionary of Literary Biography, Volume 83: French Novelists since 1960, Gale, 1989.

Fine, Ellen S., Legacy of Night: The Literary Universe of Elie Wiesel, State University of New York Press, 1982.

Frost, Christopher J., Religious Melancholy or Psychological Depression? Some Issues Involved in Relating Psychology and Religion as Illustrated in a Study of Elie Wiesel, University Press of America, 1985.

Greene, Carol, Elie Wiesel: Messenger from the Holocaust, Childrens Press, 1987.

Halperin, Irving, Messengers from the Dead, Westminster Press (Philadelphia), 1970.

Koppel, Gene, and Henry Kaufmann, Elie Wiesel: A Small Measure of Victory, University of Arizona, 1974.

Langer, Lawrence L., The Holocaust and the Literary Imagination, Yale University Press, 1975.

Rosenfeld, Alvin, and Irving Greenberg, editors, Confronting the Holocaust: The Impact of Elie Wiesel, Indiana University Press, 1979.

Roth, John K., A Consuming Fire: Encounters with Elie Wiesel and the Holocaust, John Knox Press, 1979.

PERIODICALS

Atlantic Monthly, November, 1968.

Best Sellers, March 15, 1970; May, 1981.

Book Week, May 29, 1966.

Central Conference of American Rabbis Journal, Number 19, 1972.

Chicago Tribune Book World, October 29, 1978; March 29, 1981.

Christian Century, January 18, 1961; June 17, 1970; June 3, 1981.

Christian Science Monitor, November 21, 1968; February 19, 1970; November 22, 1978.

Commonweal, December 9, 1960; January 6, 1961; March 13, 1964; October 14, 1966.

Contemporary Literature, April, 1974.

Globe and Mail (Toronto), April 20, 1985; August 6, 1988.

Los Angeles Times Book Review, June 19, 1988.

Nation, October 17, 1966; February 24, 1969; March 16, 1970; January 5, 1974.

National Jewish Monthly, November, 1973.

National Observer, February 2, 1970.

National Review, June 12, 1981.

New Leader, December 30, 1968; June 15, 1981.

New Republic, July 5, 1964; December 14, 1968.

Newsweek, May 25, 1964; February 9, 1970.

New Yorker, March 18, 1961; January 9, 1965; August 20, 1966; July 6, 1970; July 12, 1976.

New York Herald Tribune Lively Arts, January 1, 1961; April 30, 1961.

New York Review of Books, July 28, 1966; January 2, 1969; May 7, 1970.

New York Times, December 15, 1970; March 10, 1972; April 3, 1981; April 16, 1984; March 21, 1985; October 15, 1986; June 10, 1988.

New York Times Book Review, July 16, 1961; April 15, 1962; July 5, 1964; June 12, 1966; January 12, 1969; January 25, 1970; January 20, 1976; January 21, 1979; April 12, 1981; August 15, 1982; April 30, 1989.

People, October 22, 1979.

Saturday Review, December 17, 1960; July 8, 1961; July 25, 1964; May 28, 1966; October 19, 1968; January 31, 1970; November 21, 1970.

Soundings, summer, 1972.

Time, March 16, 1970; May 8, 1972; July 12, 1976; December 25, 1978; April 20, 1981; March 18, 1985.

Times (London), September 3, 1981.

Times Literary Supplement, August 19, 1960; November 20, 1981; June 6, 1986.

TV Guide, February 15, 1969.

Washington Post, October 26, 1968; February 6, 1970; November 15, 1986; November 4, 1989.

Washington Post Book World, October 20, 1968; January 18, 1970; August 8, 1976; October 29, 1978; April 12, 1981; May 29, 1988.

—*Sketch verified by Martha Hauptman, assistant to Elie Wiesel*

—*Sketch by Polly A. Vedder*

Roger Zelazny

■ Personal

Full name, Roger Joseph Zelazny; occasional pseudonym, Harrison Denmark; born May 13, 1937, in Cleveland, OH; son of Joseph Frank and Josephine (Sweet) Zelazny; married Judith Alene Callahan (an attorney), August 20, 1966; children: Devin, Trent (sons), Shannon (daughter). *Education:* Western Reserve University (now Case Western Reserve University), B.A., 1959; Columbia University, M.A., 1962.

■ Addresses

Home—Santa Fe, NM. *Agent*—Kirby McCauley, 432 Park Ave. S., Suite 1509, New York, NY 10016.

■ Career

Writer, 1969—. U.S. Social Security Administration, claims representative in Cleveland, OH, 1962-65, claims policy specialist in Baltimore, MD, 1965-69. Lecturer at colleges, universities, and at writing workshops and conferences. *Military service:* Served three years each in National Guard and U.S. Army Reserve, c. early 1960s. *Member:*

Authors Guild, Authors League of America, School of American Research, Science Fiction Oral History Association, Science Fiction Research Association, Science Fiction Writers of America (secretary-treasurer, 1967-68), Ohioana Library Association, Santa Fe Chamber of Commerce.

■ Awards, Honors

Nebula Award, Science Fiction Writers of America, 1965, for best novella, "He Who Shapes," 1965, for best novelette, "The Doors of His Face, the Lamps of His Mouth," and 1975, for best novella, "Home Is the Hangman"; Hugo Award, World Science Fiction Convention, 1966, for best novel, *This Immortal,* 1968, for best novel, *Lord of Light,* 1975, for best novella, "Home Is the Hangman," 1983, for best novelette, "Unicorn Variations," 1986, for best novella, "Twenty-Four Views of Mount Fuji by Hokusai," and 1987, for best novelette, "Permafrost"; Prix Apollo, 1972, for French edition of *Isle of the Dead;* Guest of Honor, World Science Fiction Convention, 1974, Australian National Science Fiction Convention, 1978, European Science Fiction Convention, 1984, and at numerous regional and local science fiction conventions; *Doorways in the Sand* named one of the best young adult books of the year, 1976, American Library Association; Balrog Award, 1980, for best story, "The Last Defender of Camelot," and 1984, for best collection, *Unicorn Variations; Locus* Award, 1984, for collection *Unicorn Variations,* and 1986, for novel *Trumps of Doom.*

■ Writings

SCIENCE FICTION AND FANTASY NOVELS

This Immortal, Ace Books, 1966.
The Dream Master, Ace Books, 1966.
Lord of Light, Doubleday, 1967.
Isle of the Dead, Ace Books, 1969.
Creatures of Light and Darkness, Doubleday, 1969.
Damnation Alley, Putnam, 1969.
Jack of Shadows, Walker & Co., 1971.
Today We Choose Faces, Signet, 1973.
To Die in Italbar, Doubleday, 1973.
Doorways in the Sand, Harper, 1976.
Bridge of Ashes, New American Library, 1976.
(With Philip K. Dick) *Deus Irae*, Doubleday, 1976.
Roadmarks, Ballantine, 1979.
Changeling, Ace Books, 1980.
The Changing Land, Ballantine, 1981.
Madwand, Ace Books, 1981.
(With Fred Saberhagen) *Coils*, Simon & Schuster, 1982.
Eye of Cat, Ultramarine, 1982.
Dilvish, the Damned, Ballantine, 1983.
(With others) *Berserker Base*, Tor Books, 1985.
A Dark Traveling, Walker & Co., 1987.
(With Saberhagen) *The Black Throne*, Baen, 1990.
(With Thomas T. Thomas) *The Mask of Loki*, Baen, 1990.

"AMBER" SERIES; NOVELS, EXCEPT AS INDICATED

Nine Princes in Amber (also see below), Doubleday, 1970.
The Guns of Avalon (also see below), Doubleday, 1972.
Sign of the Unicorn (also see below), Doubleday, 1975.
The Hand of Oberon (also see below), Doubleday, 1976.
The Courts of Chaos (also see below), Doubleday, 1978.
The Chronicles of Amber (contains *Nine Princes in Amber*, *The Guns of Avalon*, *Sign of the Unicorn*, *The Hand of Oberon*, and *The Courts of Chaos*), Doubleday, 1979.
Trumps of Doom, Arbor House, 1985.
Blood of Amber, Arbor House, 1986.
Sign of Chaos, Arbor House, 1987.
(With Neil Randall) *Roger Zelazny's Visual Guide to Castle Amber*, Avon, 1988.
Knight of Shadows, Morrow, 1989.
Prince of Chaos, Morrow, 1991.

STORY COLLECTIONS

Four for Tomorrow, Ace Books, 1967 (published in England as *A Rose for Ecclesiastes*, Hart Davis, 1969).
The Doors of His Face, the Lamps of His Mouth, and Other Stories, Doubleday, 1971.
My Name Is Legion, Ballantine, 1976.
The Last Defender of Camelot, Pocket Books, 1980.
Unicorn Variations, Pocket Books, 1983.
Frost and Fire: Fantasy and Science Fiction Stories, Morrow, 1989.

OTHER

(Author of introduction) Harlan Ellison, *From the Land of Fear*, Belmont/Tower, 1967.
(Author of introduction) Philip Jose Farmer, *A Private Cosmos*, Ace Books, 1968.
(Editor) *Nebula Award Stories 3*, Doubleday, 1968.
Poems, Discon, 1974.
(Author of introduction) Bruce Gillespie, editor, *Philip K. Dick: Electric Shepherd*, Norstrilia Press, 1975.
(With Gray Morrow) *The Illustrated Roger Zelazny*, Baronet, 1978.
The Bells of Shoredan (booklet), Underwood/Miller, 1979.
When Pussywillows Last in the Catyard Bloomed (poems), Norstrilia Press, 1980.
For a Breath I Tarry, Underwood/Miller, 1980.
To Spin Is Miracle Cat (poems), Underwood/Miller, 1982.
He Who Shapes: The Infinity Box (novella), Tor Books, 1989.
Wizard World, Baen Books, 1989.
(With Robert Sheckley) *Bring Me the Head of Prince Charming*, Bantam, 1991.

CONTRIBUTOR

Avram Davidson, editor, *The Best from Fantasy and Science Fiction*, Doubleday, 1965.
Ellison, editor, *Dangerous Visions: 33 Original Stories*, Doubleday, 1967.
Terry Carr, editor, *New Worlds of Fantasy #2*, Ace Books, 1970.
Robert Silverberg, editor, *The Science Fiction Hall of Fame*, Doubleday, 1970.
Silverberg, editor, *Great Short Novels of SF*, Ballantine, 1970.
Ted White, editor, *The Best from Amazing*, Manor Books, 1973.
White, editor, *The Best from Fantastic*, Manor Books, 1973.
Isaac Asimov, Martin Henry Greenberg, and Joseph T. Olander, editors, *100 Great Science Fiction Short Short Stories*, Doubleday, 1978.

Ben Bova, editor, *The Best of Analog,* Baronet, 1978.

Also contributor to other books. Contributor of more than one hundred stories, sometimes under pseudonym Harrison Denmark, to *New Worlds, Omni, Magazine of Fantasy and Science Fiction, Fantastic Stories, Amazing Stories,* and *Galaxy.*

■ Adaptations

Damnation Alley was adapted for a film of the same title, Twentieth Century-Fox, 1977; the short story "The Last Defender of Camelot" was adapted for television as a *Twilight Zone* episode of the same title, 1986.

■ Sidelights

Roger Zelazny is one of America's best-loved authors of science fiction and fantasy. He has been praised for his vivid writing and his ability to create intricate narratives with characters that call to mind the larger-than-life figures of ancient myth. As a fledgling novelist in the 1960s, Zelazny gained renown by recasting legends from such diverse sources as ancient India and Egypt. He then went on to create a lengthy series of novels about a complex world of his own imagining—Amber—that exists in all times and all places at once. "It occurs to me ... that there is a relationship between the entire body of science fiction and that high literary form, the epic," he wrote in "Some Science Fiction Parameters," included in his anthology *Unicorn Variations.* "Traditionally, the epic was regarded as representing the spirit of an entire people—The *Iliad,* the *Mahabharata,* the *Aeneid* showing us the values, the concerns, the hoped-for destinies of the Greeks, the ancient Indians, the Romans. Science fiction is less provincial, for it really deals with humanity as such. I am not so temerarious as to suggest that any single work of science fiction has ever come near the epic level ... but wish rather to observe that the impulse behind it is akin to that of the epic chronicler, and is reflected in the desire to deal with the future of humanity, describing in every way possible the spirit and destiny of not a single nation but of Man."

In his biography of Zelazny, Carl Yoke saw two special qualities that have made the author a "great science fiction writer": "First, he is insatiably curious," Yoke declared. "His appetite for knowledge drives his reading. Though he finds the odd, or the unusual, particularly interesting, he is attracted to any new idea, person, or circumstance.

His ability to absorb material is unmatched. It is this quality which makes him difficult to research, for nearly everything he reads turns up eventually in his fiction. Second, he is a keen student of people. He is extremely sensitive to them, and he meets everyone initially with compassion and sympathy. For him, each individual is a source of new knowledge about man and a possible adventure."

"[Zelazny is] not easily categorized," wrote Michael Vance and Bill Eads in *Fantasy Newsletter.* "He seems at home swimming with or against the main currents of science fiction." The author, Vance suggested, "wins awards and sells books because he weaves wordspells that transport readers into the farthest reaches of space or the darkest mysteries of magic with equal ease."

Though he went on to write interstellar epics, Zelazny spent a seemingly typical American youth in metropolitan Cleveland, Ohio. He was already beginning to show the wild imagination that would make him famous, however. He was writing funny monster stories even in elementary school, and before he had graduated from high school he had composed a string of tales about two gruesome but oafish secret agents who lived in tunnels beneath Paris. "These stories are marked by humor, impossible situations, and sophisticated word play," wrote Yoke, who grew up with the author. "More importantly, they gave Zelazny an opportunity to exercise his imagination, and the structuring of their mythologies taught him to discipline his mind and his evolving skills." In his early teens Zelazny made many efforts to have his stories published, but none were successful.

"[Science fiction] was a childhood addiction," Zelazny told W. B. Thompson in *Future Life.* "I started reading in the field when I was about 11 years old. In those days you could go to the Salvation Army store and get a box of old pulp magazines for next to nothing. That was where it was born. I wanted to write ever since I was a kid. It was something I always felt I would do one day. So I sort of directed myself toward setting up a situation where I could write full-time."

Zelazny entered Cleveland's Western Reserve University in 1955 as a psychology major, learning the teachings of such classic personality theorists as Sigmund Freud and Carl Jung. He grew disenchanted with the psychology department, wrote biographer Theodore Krulik, when it became dominated by a group of behaviorist professors "more interested in running rats through mazes than studying established theorists." So Zelazny switched his major to English, reading such deep literary thinkers as philosophical novelist Thomas Mann, poet Rainer Maria Rilke, and the symbolist poets of France. He won Western Reserve's Holden Essay Award for a discussion of medieval storyteller Geoffrey Chaucer and twice won the school's Finley Foster Poetry Prize. Then he went to graduate school at New York's Columbia University. Zelazny later noted that his studies there—in Elizabethan and Jacobean drama—had a substantial effect on the themes and style of his work. During this time the author also served six months active duty in the National Guard. In 1962 Zelazny graduated from Columbia and began a seven-year stint handling claims for the U.S. Social Security Administration. He also began a rapid rise in the world of science fiction.

As a university student, Zelazny had wanted to write but often couldn't find the time. Now, as a federal office worker, he made time during the evenings and on weekends. For a week he examined all the contemporary science-fiction magazines and a few paperbacks, and then he wrote furiously. "Zelazny's procedure," declared Joseph Sanders in *Roger Zelazny: A Primary and Secondary Bibliography*, "was to write one story an evening and to polish it the following night." Working his way down an alphabetical list, Zelazny began sending the stories to major science-fiction magazines, and he received particular encouragement from the editor of *Amazing Stories*. Within a few months his first story, "Passion Play," was published in *Amazing*; within a year, he had sold nearly twenty more.

This early success, confided Zelazny in *The Last Defender of Camelot*, only came after he had confronted his previous failures: before writing "Passion Play" he forced himself to read and ponder the many stories that magazines had already rejected. "I was overexplaining," he realized. "I was describing settings, events and character motivations in too much detail. I decided, in viewing these stories now that they had grown cold, that I would find it insulting to have anyone explain anything to me at that length. I resolved thereafter to treat the reader as I would be treated myself." Thus inspired, he looked for a new story idea. Leafing through a doctor's-office copy of *Life* magazine, he saw a feature on the death of a racing-car driver, and he invented the plot of "Passion Play" within a few minutes. The story follows the magazine article—with a few twists. The tale is told from the driver's point of view. And the driver is a fully conscious robot.

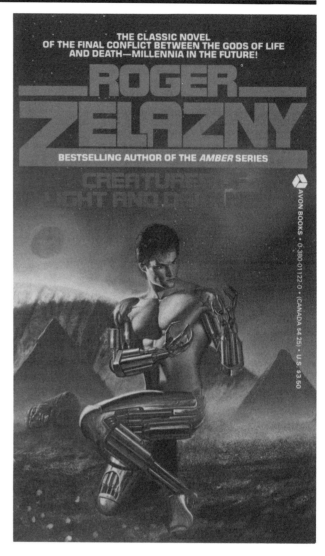

Zelazny describes this 1969 novel as one of his most experimental works.

"After I sold this story ... I suddenly felt like a writer," Zelazny recalled in *Camelot*. "This feeling seems to feed something back into the act of composition itself, providing more than simple assurance. Actual changes in approach, structure, style, tone, began to occur for me almost of their own accord. Noting this, I began to do it intentionally. I made a list of all the things I wanted to know how to handle and began writing them into my stories."

So Zelazny strove to improve his work by *deliberately* writing about things that were, to some extent, difficult for him. The gambles paid off—he was nominated for the Hugo and Nebula awards sixteen times by 1969—and experiments became a normal part of his work. "I operate under a continuing need to experiment," he told Jeffrey Smith in *Alien Critic* in 1973, "and the nature of the experimenting requires that at least part of the time I write from weakness. It would be easy to write a (I think) very good book by not purposely introducing the [experimental] element, by consciously avoiding it, by writing around and slicking over my deficiencies. If I were to do this though, and do it repeatedly, I would have strong books for a while—and then someone would notice that they were sounding more and more alike. I might as well be stamping them out with a cookie-cutter. I would start to shrivel up as a writer."

Two stories from the 1960s, "A Rose for Ecclesiastes" and "The Doors of His Face, the Lamps of His Mouth," are examples of the experiments that made Zelazny successful. Both works are really novellas, far longer than the "short short" stories that he originally fired off to magazines. Both are also a deliberate effort to capture elements of a science-fiction tradition that Zelazny realized was about to disappear. With the coming of interplanetary satellites and more sophisticated telescopes in the 1960s, the old vision of Venus and Mars as habitable worlds brimming with exotic people and animals was rapidly disappearing. Zelazny seized the opportunity to pay one last tribute to the classic era of early science fiction—and, while doing so, forged a poetic, perceptive writing style that became part of his own tradition.

"A Rose for Ecclesiastes" focuses on Gallinger, an Earthman who goes to Mars to study the remnants of its dying civilization. The men of Mars have become sterile, and the Martians have accepted racial extinction as an act of God. Gallinger has an affair with a Martian woman named Braxa, who becomes pregnant as a result. Deeply in love with Braxa, Gallinger knows that the child of this illicit union would ordinarily be condemned to death lest it contradict the Martians' belief that they are fated to disappear. To save the child, he engages in an elaborate ruse designed to prove that he is the "Bringer of Life" who, according to Martian religious texts, will come from the heavens to revive the Martian race. Since the Bringer of Life is said to mock Martian beliefs, Gallinger flouts the elders' sense of resignation by presenting them with a live rose and belittles their scriptures by reading to them from the biblical Book of Ecclesiastes, with its famous assertion that "all is vanity." He thus secures the child's life, only to discover that Braxa has merely pretended to love him for the sake of her people's future. The dismayed Gallinger attempts suicide, but survives to become a new man with a profound sense of humility. "['A Rose for Ecclesiastes'] revitalized

science fiction," wrote Thomas D. Clareson in *Voices for the Future: Essays on Major Science Fiction Writers.* "Zelazny introduced color, poetry, metaphor, and a deeper psychological dimension into science fiction." As Yoke explained in the *Dictionary of Literary Biography,* the story "brilliantly explores man's capability to grow from his experience."

To help give his characters psychological depth, Zelazny provides them with vivid past lives. In "A Rose for Ecclesiastes," for example, readers learn that Gallinger became a religious scholar in order to evade his father's demands that he become a minister. And as Gallinger ponders the actions of Braxa, he talks to another man who shares details of his own disquieting love affair. "In general, I do not like pastless characters," wrote Zelazny in "The Parts That Are Only Glimpsed," an essay reprinted in *Unicorn Variations.* "Over the years I have read too many novels where the main characters seemed to come into existence on the first page and plunge immediately into whatever conflict was brewing." More complex characterization, he explained, is valuable even when it does not motivate actions or further the plot. "Somewhere, sometime early I came to believe in tossing in a bit of gratuitous characterization as I went along," he noted. "It works to expand the setting of the entire piece and to provide evidence of the larger reality surrounding the action by giving the reader a momentary, possibly even subliminal, feeling that there is something more there."

Like "A Rose for Ecclesiastes," "The Doors of His Face, the Lamps of His Mouth" shows a man who undergoes radical psychological change. The story's broad theme—the conflict between one man's ego and enormous forces beyond his control—has reminded readers of everything from the biblical Book of Job (source of the title) to Herman Melville's epic novel *Moby-Dick.* Like Job, Zelazny's protagonist Carlton Davits is originally affluent and self-assured. Davits goes to Venus on a foolhardy quest to be the first man to capture one of the planet's fearsome sea monsters. Like Melville's Captain Ahab, he leads his crew to utter destruction before the monster's fury. Davits withdraws to alcoholism and bankruptcy, but like Job, he has a chance for redemption by honestly facing his fallibility. He reconciles with his equally proud and competitive wife, and together the two find the inner strength needed to successfully confront the beast. As biographer Theodore Krulik observed, "A Rose for Ecclesiastes" and "The Doors of His Face, the Lamps of His Mouth" have

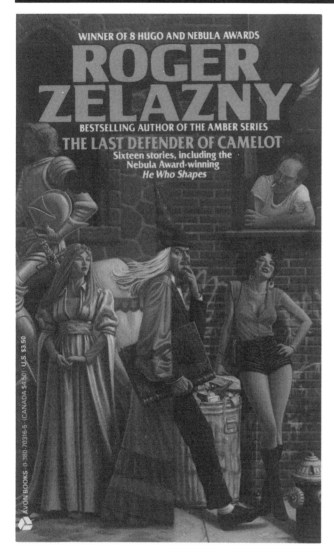

WINNER OF 8 HUGO AND NEBULA AWARDS

ROGER ZELAZNY

BESTSELLING AUTHOR OF THE AMBER SERIES

THE LAST DEFENDER OF CAMELOT

Sixteen stories, including the
Nebula Award-winning
He Who Shapes

This collection of Zelazny's award-winning stories, published in 1980, includes a survey of his early works.

important similarities that anticipate much of Zelazny's later work. "More than most writers," Krulik declared, "Zelazny persists in reworking a persona composed of a single literary vision. This vision is the unraveling of a complex personality with special abilities, intelligent, cultured, experienced in many areas, but who is fallible, needing emotional maturity, and who candidly reflects upon the losses in his life. This complex literary persona cuts across all of Zelazny's writings." "The Doors of His Face, the Lamps of His Mouth" brought Zelazny one of his first two Nebula awards in 1965.

With his well-wrought prose and daring mix of mythology, learned allusions, and high technology, Zelazny quickly became known as a major science-fiction talent. "In an important sense Zelazny really was without fear and without blame," wrote Sidney Coleman in the *Magazine of Fantasy and Science Fiction*. "He would try the most daring tricks, and bring them off. Zelazny's famous skill as a culture-magpie is an outstanding instance: He would cast a computer as both Faust and Adam, mix grail legend with electric psychotherapy, work a line from the *Cantos* into a story whose basic plot was the old pulp chestnut about the white hunter and Miss Richbitch ... [and] he made it work."

Four for Tomorrow, Zelazny's first anthology of short fiction, appeared in 1967, and Theodore Sturgeon, who had been writing science fiction since Zelazny was a small child, wrote an introduction that warmly welcomed him to the field. "Genuine prose-poets we have seen, but quite often they fail when the measures of pace and structure are applied," Sturgeon observed. "And we have certainly had great storytellers, whose narrative architecture is solidly based [and] soundly built ... but more often than not this is done completely with a homogenized, nuts-and-bolts kind of prose. And there has been a regrettably small handful of what I call 'people experts'— those especially gifted to create memorable characters, something more than real ones well-photographed—*living* ones who change.... But there again, 'people experts' have a tendency to turn their rare gift into a preoccupation." However, he declared, "Zelazny delivers all these treasures and avoids all these oversights.... He has full measures of substance and structure, means and ends, texture, cadence and pace." "The curve [Zelazny] has drawn with his early work can be extended into true greatness," Sturgeon predicted. "He has given no evidence to date that he has stopped growing or that he ever will. Do you know how rare this is?"

Having conquered the short story and the novella, Zelazny soon moved onto longer works. "The nature of my work and my working habits shifted radically in the late 60's," he noted in his introduction to *The Last Defender of Camelot*. "I went in more heavily for the writing of novels. I had started out as a short story writer, and I still enjoy writing short stories though I no longer do nearly as many as I used to in a year's time. The reason is mainly economic." In 1969, flush with success, Zelazny left behind his government job and became a full-time writer. "It is a fact of writing life that, word for word, novels work harder for their creators when it comes to providing the necessities and joys of existence. Which would sound cold and cynical, except that I enjoy writing novels, too." With the novel, Zelazny's flair for characterization became central to his work. "With shorter fiction I generally get the idea first, and then develop a character to fit whatever it is I want to do," he wrote in *Science Fiction Chronicle*. "With my novels, I tend to think of the characters first. The story begins to develop as I try these characters in different situations."

Such an approach helped Zelazny to overcome the hurdle of writing his first novel—*This Immortal*, which was published in 1966. "At the time of its inception, anything over 25,000 words in length seemed next to infinite," he recalled in *Alien Critic*. So the author had a mental dialogue with himself. "*Question:* What could I do to be assured an ample supply of material? *Answer:* Have lots of characters representing different attitudes, so that the narrator would always have someone to talk to or talk about. *Question:* Who does this very well? *Answer:* Aldous Huxley. *Decision:* Bear him in mind when constructing the cast of characters, ... but take nothing else. Do not lean too heavily on anyone."

The germ of *This Immortal* came during Zelazny's three years of service in the U.S. Army Reserve, when he spent some time in an Arts, Monuments, and Archives Unit dedicated to preserving historical and cultural landmarks in occupied foreign countries. In the novel the guardian of monuments is Conrad, an immortal human who watches over an Earth that war has turned into a nuclear wasteland. Vegans have taken control of the planet, and most Earthlings have accepted the aliens' offer of homes on other worlds in exchange for menial labor. Conrad, who had once been an active political opponent of the Vegan takeover, is filled with loathing when he is assigned to give a tour of Earth to the wealthy Vegan Myshtigo. Myshtigo, by contrast, is silently evaluating Conrad for the challenging job of leading the rebuilding of the Earth.

For the benefit of his planet, Conrad must rise above his years of Earthly chauvinism and accept the fact that he shares common concerns with the aliens. The novel depicts Conrad's transformation. Having seen the passing of many human generations, Conrad has learned to face the diverse, ever-changing nature of human existence. In an essay in *Death and the Serpent: Immortality in Science Fiction and Fantasy*, Joseph Sanders summarizes Conrad's wisdom as "things, places, people are real; judgments that might have applied to reality in the past, though, cannot be trusted." When Conrad relinquishes his instinctive hatred of aliens,

he is granted charge of the restoration of Earth. "Conrad passes from being a destroyer, disrupter, and fighter to being a creator, restorer, and peacemaker," said Joseph Francavilla in *Extrapolation*. As Sanders observed: "the successful immortal, such as Conrad, who not only stays alive but does something satisfying with his life, does so by avoiding confinement within a set of rules or preconceptions." *This Immortal* brought Zelazny his first Hugo Award.

Lord of Light, like *This Immortal*, features an immortal human whose personal redemption brings about the redemption of an entire planet. In *Lord of Light*, a small upper class uses highly advanced technology to dominate a world full of their less fortunate peers. Members of the upper class achieve godlike powers through such scientific means as neurosurgery and drugs. In their pride they model themselves on Hindu gods, and Zelazny makes liberal use of Indian mythology to dramatize their existence. One of the rulers eventually reaches a state of enlightenment more in accord with true Hindu religious values, and he sees that his fellows are nothing but tyrants. He rebels in order to free the enslaved masses. *Lord of Light* brought Zelazny his second Hugo in 1968, just two years after the first. Writing in the *Washington Post Book World* more than a dozen years later, *Science Fiction Encyclopedia* editor Peter Nicholls hailed the work as a "vastly entertaining novel" and placed it on his list of sixteen books from the whole history of the genre that could show readers "what makes good science fiction interesting."

Science and ancient myth blend once again in *Creatures of Light and Darkness*, one of Zelazny's most experimental works. In a highly intricate plot, the book depicts a struggle for knowledge and power among the ancient Egyptian gods. Zelazny freely reshapes the mythological material, and, as Pauline F. Micciche wrote in *Library Journal*, the result is "a warp of Christian, Greek, Egyptian and Norse myths spun into one thread." "*Creatures of Light and Darkness* was written for my own amusement," Zelazny told Theodore Krulik. "I doubted that any publisher would really be interested in it since I did so many different things: all the small chapters, and the shifting back and forth, and doing a chapter in free verse, and one as a closet drama." Fellow science fiction author Samuel Delany got a Doubleday editor interested in the book. The book is so experimental, Zelazny suggested in *Alien Critic*, that it is "down near the break-even point" in being a viable work. None-

HUGO AND NEBULA AWARD WINNER

ROGER Zelazny

Author of TRUMPS OF DOOM

THE COURTS OF CHAOS

Corwin journeys beyond Shadow... to confront the ultimate destructive force

The final volume in the first series of "Amber" novels holds the climactic confrontation between Amber and its evil enemies.

theless, he asserted, "I probably learned more from writing this book than I have from any other."

In novels such as *This Immortal, Lord of Light,* and *Creatures of Light and Darkness,* Zelazny added a new characteristic to the flawed geniuses who starred in his earlier novellas: the heroes now possess godlike powers—immortality, at the least. But as Yoke suggested in an essay in *The Mechanical God: Machines in Science Fiction,* Zelazny's godlike protagonists must still confront personal challenges that make them surprisingly similar to the mortal men of "A Rose for Ecclesiastes" or "The Doors of His Face, the Lamps of His Mouth." In the novels, though, the problems are larger, and superhuman powers are required to overcome them. "To live forever simply means to have time enough to experience, learn, develop, and to

increase one's self-awareness—to define oneself," observed Francavilla in *Extrapolation.* "In his quest for self-definition and for the reconciliation of disharmonious parts of his personality, the immortal hero in Zelazny's works defines what it means to be human by expanding man's potential and by boldly extending the boundaries of the human into the region of the divine."

Interestingly, at the same time that Zelazny was beginning to explore the epic and the divine, he remained versatile enough to depict a technological hell. *Damnation Alley* (1969) is one of the rare Zelazny novels in which the main character is generally despicable. The book was inspired partly by *Hell's Angels,* Hunter Thompson's first-person account of California's most notorious motorcycle gang, and partly by a biker who served with Zelazny in the National Guard. *Damnation Alley* opens in the sovereign republic of California, one of the few areas of the United States where civilization continues to exist in the wake of atomic war. A messenger arrives from the sister republic of Boston, begging for medical help against an outbreak of plague. California decides to send a vaccine, but the only way back to Boston is through Damnation Alley, a transcontinental route that abounds in atomic waste and vicious mutants. The mission will likely be fatal—the messenger from Boston dies of radiation poisoning—and authorities offer the job to a convict, Hell Tanner. If he survives, he can go free. Tanner battles mutant humans, motorcycle gangs, and even the Boston police to deliver his cargo. His freedom secured, he defaces a monument built to commemorate his own heroism and then steals a few cars as he leaves the city. "With extreme pessimism," wrote Krulik, "Zelazny shows us characters who have given up on a normalization of civilized values. They are part of a sick society that is straining for existence after civilization as a whole has committed suicide." Is *Damnation Alley* a prediction of where high technology will lead America? "No," the author assured Vance and Eads in *Fantasy Newsletter.* "Most full time writers turn out a lot of material," he explained. "Their real aim is basically to tell a good story. It may not necessarily be something they particularly endorse. If it's a good story they're gonna go ahead and write it."

Zelazny's search for a good story has lead him easily back and forth across the invisible line that traditionally separates science fiction, with its interest in technology, and fantasy, with its interest in magic and legend. When Zelazny defined science fiction for *Fantasy Newsletter,* he avoided such a distinction. "[Science fiction] is, for me, a special way of looking at anything, really—by pulling it out of context and into a different situation," he said. "Sometimes you just ask yourself, 'What if?' And you make up something that's considered unlikely to happen, just to take a look at it. Much has been said about science fiction being purely based on scientific ideas, just pushing them into the future. But that was a product of the '20s, '30s and '40s when it was just getting started. The same questions came to be asked later on about non-scientific things, social questions and religious and political issues."

Beginning with the 1970s, observers suggested, Zelazny has increasingly turned away from technology in his work and become more interested in the trappings of fantasy—including, notably, magic. Biographer Krulik pointed out that Zelazny has sometimes viewed magic and science almost as if they were two complementary philosophies of life: while science strives to control everyday reality, magic evokes "a world beyond simple human control." The disparity, Krulik continued, is clearly conveyed in a 1980 Zelazny novel, *Changeling*. The novel posits two parallel realities, one dominated by magic and the other by science. Though each world fears the powers of the other, their mutual existence is somehow necessary to maintain "the Balance" that keeps the universe stable. Conflict ensues when a wizard switches Pol, a child of the magical world, with Mark, a child of the scientific one. When Mark grows to adulthood he begins creating scientific inventions in the world of magic, and Pol must return to the magical world and confront Mark to ensure that the Balance of the universe is preserved. In *Changeling* "I wanted to show that [magic and science] weren't necessarily two things that were completely opposed," Zelazny told Krulik. "Possibly they were both aspects of the same thing. . . . special cases of some more general law."

Probably Zelazny's finest evocation of magic and fantasy is his series of "Amber" novels, named for the imaginary world of Amber. The books have appeared in two series. The first—*Nine Princes in Amber, The Guns of Avalon, Sign of the Unicorn, The Hand of Oberon,* and *The Courts of Chaos*—was published in single volumes between 1970 and 1978. The second began in 1985 with *Trumps of Doom* and has continued with *Blood of Amber, Sign of Chaos,* and *Knight of Shadows.* Amber is not bounded by the familiar limits of time and space: in a sense, it includes within itself all times and places. The immortal natives of Amber use magic

to travel among an infinite variety of alternate worlds, all of which—including Earth—are pale reflections of Amber's higher reality. "Amber is a place, a city, a state, a 'world'," wrote Edwin Morgan of the *Times Literary Supplement.* "[It] is the perfect place, the Substance to which everything else is Shadow. It is not in our space and time, and its inhabitants, although they talk and act for the most part in human ways, are not human. Since they have enormous powers, they appear at times like gods." To visualize the world of Amber, some observers recall an analogy by the ancient Greek philosopher Socrates, as quoted in Plato's book *The Republic.* The difference between our everyday world and the greater reality of ideas, Socrates suggests, is like the difference between a shadow and the person who casts it.

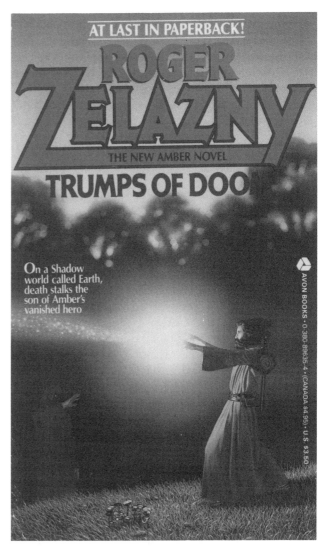

Winner of a Locus Award, the debut novel in the second "Amber" series introduces the adventures of Corwin's son Merlin.

The first series of Amber novels focuses on Corwin, a prince of the strife-torn ruling house of Amber. He is a classic Zelazny hero—a larger-than-life figure who in the course of long and exotic adventures grows in virtue and wisdom. To help readers understand Corwin's saga, biographer Krulik suggested that each book in the series be viewed as a distinct *type* of novel. *Nine Princes in Amber* can be seen as a mystery story or, Krulik notes, as a "typical space opera: the protagonist starts his adventures in our reality and moves into more and more fantastic worlds." The novel begins as Corwin awakes in a hospital bed on Earth, suffering from amnesia. Discovering he has relatives nearby, he quickly seeks them out; with help from his brother Random, he returns to Amber and regains the full memory of his princely status. Corwin recovers his health by being exposed to "the Pattern," a sort of magic work of art that contains within it the pattern of Amber and the entire universe. He learns that his father, king Oberon, has mysteriously disappeared, and that his evil brother Eric has usurped the throne. Blind with rage, Corwin wages an ill-fated attack on Eric and, symbolically enough, is punished by being imprisoned and having his eyes put out. His sight restored by his own superhuman regenerative power, Corwin uses magic to escape his prison and, on the way out, levels a vicious curse on Eric.

In *The Guns of Avalon* Corwin redeems himself by successfully undergoing a series of ordeals and battles reminiscent of medieval romances about the legendary King Arthur and the Knights of the Round Table. As the novel opens Corwin meets a knight named Lancelot—one of the most famous members of the Round Table. Corwin helps the injured knight to recover from his wounds by carrying him to the castle of the noble Ganelon. Together with his new companions, Corwin helps to save the alternate world of Avalon from attack by evil creatures who have invaded from an ominous Black Road. The Black Road, Corwin and Ganelon discover, allows the forces of evil to access many alternate worlds; at the end of the novel the two men return to Amber to save Eric from a similar attack. Eric, fatally wounded, passes the throne of Amber to Corwin by giving him the magic Jewel of Judgment.

Sign of the Unicorn, Krulik suggests, is a variation on the detective mystery. The book begins when Corwin calls together his quarreling relatives for a family reconciliation; instead, Corwin and his brother Brand are quickly stabbed by an invisible attacker. Corwin begins a long effort to compre-

Mysterious villains and alternate worlds abound in this action-packed fantasy.

hend the family intrigues. Eventually he reaches a bleak plain where, to his surprise, a unicorn shows him a manifestation of the Pattern. This is the one true Pattern, Corwin learns—it is a source of immense power, for it is the higher reality of which Amber itself is only a pale reflection.

The Hand of Oberon clears up many of the mysteries that the first three contain. Corwin, his brother Random, and Ganelon investigate the one true Pattern, discovering a dark stain that is apparently linked to the Black Road and the evil beings that travel it. Brand, they learn, has been scheming for power, secretly walking over the Pattern to draw on its magic; the stain is the spot where he conjured up Random's son and stabbed him. Worse yet, Corwin learns that Brand has absconded with the Jewel of Judgment and seems poised to combine its power with the power of the Pattern and create his own universe. Convinced that his father Oberon is still alive somewhere, Corwin attempts to conjure him up, and Ganelon answers. Thus disguised, Oberon has been taking part in the battle against evil.

The Courts of Chaos shows the climactic confrontation between Amber and its evil enemies. The title refers to the source of all evil—Chaos, a world of disorder out of which, paradoxically, all other worlds have been created. Amber and Chaos, perfect form and utter formlessness, thus remain in eternal conflict. "In the Amber series, as Corwin finally comes to understand," Sanders wrote in his Zelazny bibliography, "life exists between two poles, Pattern and Chaos. Neither 'wins'. The difficult, creative tension between them continues, just as life continues." At Oberon's command, the forces of Amber attack the courts of Chaos to create a diversion while Oberon tries to repair the one true Pattern. He dies in the attempt, but the Pattern is restored, and Corwin regains the Jewel of Judgement just long enough to create an entirely new Pattern in addition to the old. Finally the evil Brand is killed and, in a magical apparition, a unicorn bestows the Jewel of Judgment on Corwin's brother Random, making him the new king of Amber. Corwin joins the others in pledging his loyalty. No longer rash and alienated, Corwin has matured to become a noble servant of his people.

The first series of Amber novels boosted Zelazny to new heights of popularity. When *The Courts of Chaos* appeared in 1978, it sold more copies in hardcover than any previous Zelazny book, and the works as a group brought their author more fan mail than all his other writings combined. Reviewers also endorsed the series, with occasional reservations. "Zelazny kept his inventiveness and the rich feeling of the story fresh and vigorous from the first volume in 1970 to the fourth in 1976— and that's a long stretch for a writer to continue without flagging," observed Lester del Rey in *Analog.* "Unfortunately, *The Courts of Chaos* seems to have lost.... some of the inventiveness, potential, and freshness of the other books." Del Rey regretted that Zelazny's publisher did not afford him the chance to write the whole chronicle as a single effort, perhaps for one long volume. He concluded: "Had that been done, this could well have been a genuinely superb piece of fantasy. As it is, it's a good story—no more. Two years is too long to wait between installments of a serial, both for the reader and the writer."

By contrast, Marshall Tymn, Kenneth Zoharski, and Robert Boyer suggested in their volume *Fanta-sy Literature* that the Amber books had improved over time. "The series starts out like many standard sword and sinew works," they explained, "but after the comparatively weak *Nine Princes in Amber* it "develops rapidly in literary quality. Characterization improves; style becomes more polished; and philosophical complexities emerge." Overall, the authors found the first five Amber books "excellent, both for their unusually original fantasy elements and for their literary qualities," and they called Amber "one of the more ingeniously conceived secondary worlds in fantasy literature."

In the 1980s Zelazny began his second Amber series, in which Corwin's son Merlin is pursued by mysterious villains as he travels the network of alternate worlds. *Trumps of Doom,* the debut novel, won a Locus Award in 1986. The next year, after *Blood of Amber* had appeared, the Toronto *Globe and Mail's* H. J. Kirchhoff declared: "As usual in the Amber books, Zelazny parlays hip dialogue, quirky characters and an anything-is-possible multiple universe into a winning swords-and-sorcery adventure."

Zelazny has become one of the most enduring figures in imaginative fiction, and, not surprisingly, many observers have come forward to assess his overall achievement. Even Carl Yoke, one of his most prominent admirers, acknowledged in *Dictionary of Literary Biography* that the verdict is mixed. "Some critics," he noted, "feel that Zelazny has not achieved the stature which was projected for him when he first broke on the science fiction scene." An example might be Sidney Coleman, who suggested in a 1974 article in *Magazine of Fantasy and Science Fiction* that Zelazny had lost the flair for subtle shifts in literary tone that had made his writing so effective during the 1960s. "We once had something unique and wonderful, and it is gone," Coleman wrote, "and what we have in its place is only a superior writer of preposterous adventures." Yoke was much more enthusiastic. "There is no question of [Zelazny's] stature," the critic declared. "He has contributed major works to the field, and perhaps more than any other writer has brought the techniques, style, and language of serious literature to science fiction. His greatest contribution, however, may be that he has brought to a literature famous for its cardboard figures, characters who are psychologically credible, who are sympathetic, who have scope and dimension."

As the creator of so many alternative worlds, Zelazny is sometimes asked about the future of his own. "There have always been troubles through-

Zelazny's 1989 continuation of his enormously popular series.

out history," he said in *Fantasy Newsletter*. "It's just that they change character from time to time. If you stop and think about how 200 generations ago we were living in caves and had all the problems associated with that sort of life, the fact that we made it through all the wars and things that characterize our history makes me optimistic. I think problems and troubles are part of the human condition, and I also think that humanity is a fairly tough institution and should be able to adapt." Such faith, perhaps, enabled Zelazny to create the epic vision of his novels. As Yoke wrote in *The Mechanical God*, "Those who know [Zelazny's] writing well . . . know that in many ways his work is primarily a celebration of the nature of man."

■ Works Cited

Clareson, Thomas D., editor and contributor, *Voices for the Future: Essays on Major Science Fiction Writers*, Bowling Green State University, 1979.

Coleman, Sidney, review of *To Die in Italbar*, in *Magazine of Fantasy and Science Fiction*, August, 1974, pp. 51-55.

Del Rey, Lester, "Ex Uno Plurimum," in *Analog*, February, 1979, pp. 168-70.

Francavilla, Joseph V., "These Immortals: An Alternative View of Immortality in Roger Zelazny's Science Fiction," in *Extrapolation*, spring, 1984, pp. 20-33.

Kirchhoff, H. J., review of *Blood of Amber*, in *Globe and Mail* (Toronto), February 14, 1987.

Krulik, Theodore, *Roger Zelazny*, Ungar, 1986.

Micciche, Pauline F., review of *Creatures of Light and Darkness*, in *Library Journal*, September 15, 1969, p. 3086.

Morgan, Edwin, "Forever Amber," in *Times Literary Supplement*, February 13, 1981, p. 158.

Nicholls, Peter, "The Stars, Their Designation: An Introduction to SF," in *Washington Post Book World*, July 26, 1981, pp. 6-7.

Sanders, Joseph, "Introduction," in his *Roger Zelazny: A Primary and Secondary Bibliography*, G. K. Hall, 1980, pp. ix-xxvii.

Sanders, "Dancing on the Tightrope: Immortality in Roger Zelazny," in *Death and the Serpent: Immortality in Science Fiction and Fantasy*, edited by Carl B. Yoke and Donald M. Hassler, Greenwood Press, 1985, pp. 135-143.

Smith, Jeffrey B., "Up against the Wall, Roger Zelazny," in *Alien Critic*, November, 1973, pp. 35-40.

Sturgeon, Theodore, "Introduction," in Roger Zelazny's *Four for Tomorrow*, Ace Books, 1967, pp. 7-13.

Thompson, W. B., "Roger Zelazny: The Popular Author of *Lord of Light* Talks about His Craft," in *Future Life*, March, 1981, pp. 40-42.

Tymn, Marshall B., Kenneth J. Zoharski, and Robert H. Boyer, "Core Collection: Novels and Short Story Collections," in their *Fantasy Literature: A Core Collection and Reference Guide*, Bowker, 1979, pp. 181-84.

Vance, Michael, and Bill Eads, "An Interview with Roger Zelazny," *Fantasy Newsletter*, January, 1983, pp. 8-10.

Yoke, Carl B., *Roger Zelazny*, Starmont House, 1979.

Yoke, "Roger Zelazny," in *Dictionary of Literary Biography*, Volume 8: *Twentieth-Century American Science Fiction Writers*, Gale, 1981, pp. 213-220.

Yoke, "What a Piece of Work Is a Man: Mechanical Gods in the Fiction of Roger Zelazny," in *The Mechanical God: Machines in Science Fiction*, edited by Thomas P. Dunn and Richard D. Erlich, Greenwood Press, 1982, pp. 63-74.

Zelazny, Roger, "Introduction" and "Introduction [to] 'Passion Play,'" in his *The Last Defender of Camelot*, Pocket Books, 1980, pp. 1-3 and pp. 4-6.

Zelazny, "The Parts That Are Only Glimpsed: Three Reflexes" and "Some Science Fiction Parameters: A Biased View," in his *Unicorn Variations*, Timescape Books, 1983, pp. 67-70 and 245-252.

Zelazny, "The Process of Composing," in *Science Fiction Chronicle*, January, 1985, p. 22.

■ For More Information See

BOOKS

Collins, R. A., editor, *Scope of the Fantastic: Culture, Biography, Themes in Children's Literature*, Greenwood Press, 1985.

Contemporary Literary Criticism, Volume 21, Gale, 1982.

Levack, Daniel J. H., *Amber Dreams: A Roger Zelazny Bibliography*, Underwood/Miller, 1983.

Reilly, Robert, editor, *The Transcendent Adventure*, Greenwood Press, 1984.

Science Fiction and Fantasy Authors: A Bibliography of First Printings of Their Science Fiction and Selected Nonfiction, G. K. Hall, 1979.

Staicar, Tom, editor, *Critical Encounters II*, Ungar, 1982.

Walker, Paul, *Speaking of Science Fiction*, Luna Publications, 1978.

Yoke, *Roger Zelazny and Andre Norton: Proponents of Individualism*, State Library of Ohio, 1979.

PERIODICALS

Algol, summer, 1976.

Amazing Stories, July, 1984.

Analog, March 2, 1981; March, 1983.

Baltimore Sun, January 29, 1967.

Best Sellers, September, 1976; June, 1978.

Extrapolation, December, 1973; summer, 1980.

Fantasy Newsletter, October, 1980; September, 1983.

Foundation, March, 1977.

Journal of American Culture, summer, 1979.

Locus, October, 1983.

Los Angeles Times Book Review, January 11, 1981.

Magazine of Fantasy and Science Fiction, May, 1971; February, 1982.

Media Sight, summer, 1984.

Mosaic, winter, 1981.

New Scientist, February 23, 1978.

New York Review of Books, October 2, 1975.

New York Times Book Review, May 23, 1976; December 19, 1982.

Observer, June 24, 1979.

Riverside Quarterly, June, 1970; August, 1973.

Science Fiction: A Review of Speculative Literature, June, 1978; December, 1979.

Science Fiction Review, May, 1980; August, 1980.

SF Commentary, November, 1978.

Times Literary Supplement, February 29, 1968; March 28, 1968.

Washington Post Book World, December 23, 1979; January 25, 1981; December 25, 1983.

Acknowledgments

Acknowledgments

Grateful acknowledgment is made to the following publishers,
authors, and artists for their kind permission to reproduce copyrighted material.

MAYA ANGELOU. Jacket of *I Know Why the Caged Bird Sings*, by Maya Angelou. Random House, Inc., 1969. Copyright © 1969 by Random House, Inc. Jacket design by Janet Halverson. Reprinted by permission of Random House, Inc./ Jacket of *I Shall Not Be Moved*, by Maya Angelou. Random House, Inc., 1969. Copyright © 1990 by Random House, Inc. Jacket design by Susan Shapiro. Jacket photograph by Johan Elber, courtesy of Alvin Ailey American Dance Theatre. Reprinted by permission of Random House, Inc./ Cover of *Gather Together in My Name*, by Maya Angelou. Random House, Inc., 1974. Copyright © 1974 by Maya Angelou. Reprinted by permission of Random House, Inc./ Jacket of *Oh Pray My Wings Are Gonna Fit Me Well*, by Maya Angelou. Random House, Inc., 1975. Copyright © 1975 by Random House, Inc. Jacket design by Janet Halverson. Reprinted by permission of Random House, Inc./ Photograph by Tim Richmond/Katz Pictures./ Photograph of Angelou during an interview, © Mary Ellen Mark, Archive Pictures, Inc./ Scene from *I Know Why the Caged Bird Sings*, courtesy of CBS Television.

JEAN M. AUEL. Jacket of *The Clan of the Cave Bear*, by Jean M. Auel. Crown Publishers, Inc., 1980. Jacket typography © 1980 by Paul Bacon. Jacket painting © 1980 by Hiroko. Reprinted by permission of Crown Publishers, a division of Random House, Inc./ Cover of *The Mammoth Hunters*, by Jean M. Auel. Crown Publishers, Inc., 1985. Cover design by Jean M. Auel. Reprinted by permission of Crown Publishers, a division of Random House, Inc./ Jacket of *The Plains of Passage*, by Jean M. Auel. Crown Publishers, Inc., 1990. Copyright © 1990 by Crown Publishers, Inc. Jacket painting by Hiroko. Jacket typography by Paul Bacon. Reprinted by permission of Crown Publishers, a division of Random House, Inc./ Photographs © 1985 by John Emmerling./ Scene from *The Clan of the Cave Bear*, Copyright © 1986 by Warner Bros., Inc. and Jonesfilms.

CLAUDE BROWN. Cover of *Manchild in the Promised Land*, by Claude Brown. New American Library, 1965. Copyright © 1965 by Claude Brown. Cover © 1965 by New American Library. Used by permission of New American Library, a division of Penguin Books USA Inc./ Jacket of *The Children of Ham*, by Claude Brown. Stein and Day/Publishers, 1976. Copyright © 1973, 1976 by Claude Brown. Jacket design by Tim Gaydos. Reprinted with permission of Scarborough House/Publishers./ Photograph by James Hamilton./ Photograph of Brown with a child, courtesy of Claude Brown.

DANIEL COHEN. Jacket of *Ancient Egypt*, by Daniel Cohen. Doubleday, 1990. Jacket illustration by Gary A. Lippincott, copyright © 1990 by Daniel Cohen. Jacket design by Cathy Saska. Illustrations copyright © 1990 by Gary A. Lippincott. Used by permission of Doubleday, a division of Bantam Doubleday Dell Publishing Group, Inc./ Illustration from *Ancient Egypt*, by Daniel Cohen. Doubleday, 1990. Text copyright © 1990 by Daniel Cohen. Illustrations copyright © 1990 by Gary A. Lippincott. Used by permission of Doubleday, a division of Bantam Doubleday Dell Publishing Group, Inc./ Jacket of *Ancient Greece*, by Daniel Cohen. Doubleday, 1990. Jacket painting by James Seward. Jacket design by Cathy Saska. Copyright © 1990 by Daniel Cohen. Used by permission of Doubleday, a division of Bantam Doubleday Dell Publishing Group, Inc./ Jacket of *The Ghosts of War*, by Daniel Cohen. G.P. Putnam's Sons, 1990. Jacket art © 1990 by Stephen Marchesi. Reprinted by permission of The Putnam Publishing Group./ Jacket of *Phone Call from a Ghost*, by Daniel Cohen. A Minstrel Book, 1991. Copyright © 1988 by Daniel Cohen. Cover art by Lisa Falkenstern. Illustrations by David Linn. Reprinted by permission of Minstrel Books, a division of Simon & Schuster, Inc./ Photograph © Jerry Bauer.

EVAN S. CONNELL. Cover of *Mrs. Bridge*, by Evan S. Connell. Copyright © 1959 by Evan S. Connell. Cover photograph by Mikki Ansin, © by Merchant Ivory Productions. Cover design by David Bullen. Reprinted by permission of Merchant Ivory Productions./ Cover of *Mr. Bridge*, by Evan S. Connell. Copyright © 1969 by Evan S. Connell. Cover photograph by Mikki Ansin, © by Merchant Ivory Productions. Cover design by David Bullen. Reprinted by permission of Merchant Ivory Productions./ Jacket of *Son of the Morning Star*, by Evan S. Connell. Harper & Row, Publishers, 1984. Copyright © 1984 by Evan S. Connell. Cover painting © by Wendell Minor. Reprinted by permission of HarperCollins Publishers, Inc./ Photograph © Jerry Bauer./ Advertisement for *Son of the Morning Star*, courtesy of ABC Television.

THOMAS J. DYGARD. Cover of *Soccer Duel*, by Thomas J. Dygard. Puffin Books, 1981. Copyright © 1981 by Thomas J. Dygard. Cover illustration copyright © 1990 by Todd Doney. Reproduced by permission of Penguin USA Inc./ Cover of *Rebound Caper*, by Thomas J. Dygard. William Morrow and Company, Inc., 1983. Copyright © 1983 by Thomas J. Dygard. Jacket illustration © 1983 by Michael Garland. Reprinted by permission of William Morrow and Company, Inc./

Jacket of *Tournament Upstart,* by Thomas J. Dygard. William Morrow and Company, Inc., 1984. Copyright © 1984 by Thomas J. Dygard. Jacket illustration by Frederick Porter. Reprinted by permission of William Morrow and Company, Inc./ Jacket of *Wilderness Peril,* by Thomas J. Dygard. William Morrow and Company, Inc., 1985. Copyright © 1985 by Thomas J. Dygard. Jacket illustration © 1985 by Sandy Appleoff. Reprinted by permission of William Morrow and Company, Inc./ Cover of *Halfback Tough,* by Thomas J. Dygard. Puffin Books, 1986. Copyright © 1986 by Thomas J. Dygard. Cover illustration copyright © 1989 by Todd Doney. Reproduced by permission of Penguin USA Inc./ Jacket of *The Rookie Arrives,* by Thomas J. Dygard. Morrow Junior Books, 1988. Copyright © 1988 by Thomas J. Dygard. Jacket illustration © 1988 by Mike Wimmer. Reprinted by permission of William Morrow and Company, Inc./ Cover of *Winning Kicker,* by Thomas J. Dygard. Puffin Books, 1990. Copyright © 1978 by Thomas J. Dygard. Cover illustration copyright © 1990 by Todd Doney. Reproduced by permission of Penguin USA Inc./ Photograph courtesy of Thomas J. Dygard.

WILLIAM FAULKNER. Cover of *The Sound and the Fury,* by William Faulkner. Vintage Books, 1954. Copyright 1929 by William Faulkner. Copyright renewed 1956, by William Faulkner. Copyright 1946 by Random House, Inc. Reprinted by permission of Random House, Inc./ Cover of *The Hamlet: A Novel of the Snopes Family,* by William Faulkner. Vintage Books, 1956. Reprinted by permission of Random House, Inc./ Cover of *Absalom Absalom!,* by William Faulkner. Vintage Books Edition, 1972. Copyright 1936 by William Faulkner. Renewed copyright © 1964 by Estelle Faulkner and Jill Faulkner Summer. Cover photograph by Robert Wenkam. Reprinted by permission of Random House, Inc./ Cover of *As I Lay Dying,* by William Faulkner. Vintage Books, 1985. Copyright 1930 by William Faulkner. Copyright renewed 1957 by William Faulkner. Cover illustration by David Tamura. Reprinted by permission of Random House, Inc./ Scene from *The Long Hot Summer,* courtesy of Twentieth-Century Fox./ William Faulkner, "Introduction," to *Sanctuary,* Random House, 1931. Copyright 1931 and renewed 1959 by William Faulkner. Reprinted by permission of Random House, Inc./ William Faulkner, *Essays, Speeches & Public Letters,* edited by James B. Meriwether, Random House, 1965. Copyright © 1965 by Random House, Inc. Reprinted by permission of Random House, Inc./ William Faulkner, *Lion in the Garden: Interviews with William Faulkner, 1926-1962,* edited by James B. Meriwether and Michael Millgate, Random House, 1968. University of Nebraska Press, 1980. Copyright © 1968 by James B. Meriwether and Michael Millgate. Reprinted by permission of the University of Nebraska Press./ Joseph Blotner, *Faulkner: A Biography,* Random House, 1974. Copyright. © 1974 by Joseph Blotner. Reprinted by permission of Random House, Inc./ William Faulkner, *Selected Letters of William Faulkner,* edited by Joseph Blotner, Random House, 1977. Copyright © 1977 by Jill Faulkner Summers. Reprinted by permission of Random House, Inc.

CHESTER GOULD. Photograph courtesy of New York Daily News./ Cover of Daily News Magazine, reproduced by permission of Tribune Media Services./ Illustration by Peter Sorel/© Touchstone Pictures. All Rights Reserved.

BETTE GREENE. Cover of *Philip Hall Likes Me. I Reckon Maybe.,* by Bette Greene. Dell Publishing, 1974. Text copyright © 1974 by Bette Greene. Pictures copyright © 1974 by Dial Press. Reprinted by permission of Dell Publishing Co., a division of Bantam Doubleday Dell Publishing Group, Inc./ Cover of *Summer of My German Soldier,* by Bette Greene. A Bantam Starfire Book, 1974. Reprinted by permission of Bantam Books, Inc., a division of Bantam Doubleday Dell Publishing Group, Inc./ Jacket of *Get on Out of Here, Philip Hall,* by Bette Greene. Dial Books For Young Readers, 1981. Jacket painting © 1980 by Charles Lilly. Reprinted by permission of Dial Books For Young Readers, a division of Penguin Books USA Inc./ Photograph by Ken Rome./ Scenes from *Summer of My German Soldier,* courtesy of Highgate Pictures, a division of Learning Corporation of America.

CONSTANCE C. GREENE. Cover of *A Girl Called Al,* by Constance C. Greene. Dell Publishing, 1969. Copyright © 1969 by Constance C. Greene. Cover illustration by Paul Tankersley. Reprinted by permission of Dell Publishing Co., Inc., a division of Bantam Doubleday Dell Publishing Group. Inc./ Cover of *I Know You, Al,* by Constance C. Greene. Dell Publishing, 1975. Text copyright © 1975 by Constance C. Greene. Cover illustration by Paul Tankersley. Reprinted by permission of Dell Publishing Co., Inc., a division of Bantam Doulbeday Dell Publishing Group, Inc./ Cover of *Al(exandra) the Great,* by Constance C. Greene. Dell, 1982. Copyright © 1982 by Constance C. Greene. Cover illustration by Paul Tankersley. Reprinted by permission of Dell Publishing Co., Inc., a division of Bantam Doubleday Dell Publishing Group. Inc./ Jacket of *The Love Letters of J. Timothy Owen,* by Constance C. Greene. Harper & Row, Publishers, 1986. Copyright © 1986 by Constance C. Greene. Jacket art © 1986 by Marla Frazee. Jacket © 1986 by Harper & Row, Publishers, Inc. Reprinted by permission of HarperCollins Publishers, Inc./ Jacket of *Monday I Love You,* by Constance C. Greene. Harper & Row, Publishers, 1988. Jacket art © 1988 by Daniel LaVigne. Jacket © 1988 by Harper & Row, Publishers, Inc. Reprinted by permission of HarperCollins Publishers, Inc./ Photograph courtesy of Constance C. Greene./ Scene from *Very Good Friends,* courtesy of Learning Corporation of America.

JUDITH GUEST. Cover of *Ordinary People,* by Judith Guest. Ballantine Books, 1976. Copyright © 1976 by Judith Guest. Reprinted by permission of Ballantine Books, a division of Random House, Inc./ Cover of *Second Heaven,* by Judith Guest. New American Library, 1982. Copyright © 1982 by Judith Guest. Cover © 1982 by New American Library. Used by permission of New American Library, a division of Penguin Books USA Inc./ Cover of *Killing Time in St. Cloud,* by Judith Guest. Dell, 1988. Copyright © 1988 by Judith Guest and Rebecca Hill. Reprinted by permission of Dell Publishing Co., Inc., a division of Bantam Doubleday Dell Publishing Group, Inc./ Photograph by Timothy Francisco./ Scene from *Ordinary People,* courtesy of Movie Star News.

JAMAKE HIGHWATER. Jacket of *Anpao: An American Indian Odyssey,* by Jamake Highwater. Lippincott, 1977. Jacket painting by Fritz Scholder. Reprinted by permission of HarperCollins Publishers, Inc./ Jacket of *The Ceremony of Innocence,* by Jamake Highwater. Harper & Row, Publishers, 1985. Jacket art by Blackbear Bosin, © 1985 by Nola Bosin

Kimble. Jacket © 1985 by Harper & Row, Publishers, Inc. Reprinted by permission of HarperCollins Publishers, Inc./ Jacket of *Eyes of Darkness*, by Jamake Highwater. Lothrop, Lee & Shepard Books, 1985. Jacket painting copyright © 1985 by David Montiel. Reprinted by permission of Lothrop, Lee & Shepard Books, a division of William Morrow and Company, Inc./ Jacket of *I Wear the Morning Star*, by Jamake Highwater. Harper & Row, Publishers, 1986. Jacket art © 1986 by David P. Bradley. Jacket © 1986 by Harper & Row, Publishers, Inc. Reprinted by permission of HarperCollins Publishers, Inc./ Photograph by Henry Kurth./ Photograph of Highwater in 1988, © 1988 by Johan Elber.

JOHN HUGHES. Photograph by Paul Natkin./ Scene from *Ferris Bueller's Day Off*, courtesy of Paramount Pictures./ Scene from *She's Having a Baby*, courtesy of Paramount Pictures./ Scene from *Some Kind of Wonderful*, courtesy of Paramount Pictures./ Scene from *Home Alone*, by Don Smetzer./ Scene from *The Breakfast Club*, courtesy of Universal Pictures.

W.P. KINSELLA. Jacket of *Dance Me Outside: More Tales from the Ermineskin Reserve*, by W.P. Kinsella. David R. Godine Publishers, Inc. 1977. Copyright © 1977 by W.P. Kinsella. Jacket illustration by Gaylord Schanilec. Reprinted by permission of David R.Godine Publishers, Inc./ Jacket of *Shoeless Joe*, by W.P. Kinsella. Ballantine Books, 1982. Reprinted by permission of Ballantine Books, a division of Random House, Inc./ Jacket of *The Iowa Baseball Confederacy*, by W.P. Kinsella. Houghton Mifflin Company, 1986. Copyright © 1986 by William P. Kinsella. Jacket design © 1986 by Wendell Minor. Reprinted by permission of Wendell Minor./ Photograph by Robert Morfey.

ROBERT LIPSYTE. Cover of *One Fat Summer*, by Robert Lipsyte. Bantam Books, 1977. Copyright © 1977 by Robert M. Lipsyte. Reprinted by permission of Bantam Books, Inc., a division of Bantam Doubleday Dell Publishing Group, Inc./ Jacket of *Free to be Muhammad Ali*, by Robert Lipsyte. Harper & Row, Publishers, 1978. Copyright © 1978 by Robert M. Lipsyte. Jacket photograph by Gaffney/Liaison. Jacket design by Jay J. Smith. Reprinted by permission of HarperCollins Publishers, Inc./ Jacket of *Summer Rules*, by Robert Lipsyte. Harper & Row, Publishers, 1981. Copyright © 1981 by Robert M. Lipsyte. Reprinted by permission of HarperCollins Publishers, Inc./ Jacket of *Jock and Jill*, by Robert Lipsyte. Harper & Row, Publishers, Inc. 1982. Copyright © 1982 by Robert M. Lipsyte. Jacket designed by Al Cetta. Reprinted by permission of HarperCollins Publishers, Inc./ Cover of *The Contender*, by Robert Lipsyte. Harper & Row, Publishers, 1987. Copyright © 1967 by Robert M. Lipsyte. Cover art © 1987 by Ed Acuna. Cover © 1987 by Harper & Row, Publishers, Inc. Reprinted by permission of HarperCollins Publishers, Inc./ Photograph by Anon Rupo.

MONTY PYTHON. Illustration from *Monty Python and the Holy Grail (Book)*, by Graham Chapman, Terry Jones, Terry Gilliam, Michael Palin, Eric Idle, and John Cleese. Eyre Methuen Ltd., 1981. Copyright © 1977 by the National Film Trustee Company Ltd. Reprinted by permission of Python Productions, Ltd./ Cover of *The Meaning of Life*, by Graham Chapman, John Cleese, Terry Gilliam, Eric Idle, Terry Jones, and Michael Palin. Methuen London Ltd., 1983. Copyright © 1983 by The Monty Python Partnership. Book designed by James Campus. Stills photography by David Appleby. Reprinted by permission of Python Productions, Ltd./ Cover illustration by James Victore from *The Adventures of Baron Munchausen*, by Terry Gilliam and Charles McKeown. Applause Theatre Book Publishers, 1989. Copyright © 1988 by Columbia Pictures, a division of Columbia Pictures Industries, Inc. Illustrations by James Victore and Joyce L. Houlihan. Reprinted by permission of Applause Theatre Books, 211 West 71st Street, New York, NY 10023./ The Pythons in a publicity photo, courtesy of the Python Organization./ John Cleese and gang in *Time Bandits*, © 1981 The HandMade Film Partnership./ Scene from *Monty Python's Life of Brian*, Copyright © 1979 Python (Monty) Pictures Ltd./ Scene from *Brazil*, copyright © 1985 by Twentieth-Century Fox Film Corporation./ Scene from *Monty Python's Meaning of Life*, courtesy of The Movie Channel./ The Pythons in a sketch from *Monty Python's Flying Circus*, Hulton Picture Company/Bettmann Newphotos./ Group photograph, copyright © Python Productions, Ltd.

FLANNERY O'CONNOR. Cover of *The Habit of Being*, by Flannery O'Connor. Copyright © 1979 by Regina O'Connor. Cover design by Janet Halverson. Reprinted by permission of Farrar, Straus and Giroux, Inc./ Cover of *Everything That Rises Must Converge*, by Flannery O'Connor. Farrar, Straus and Giroux, Inc., 1989. Copyright © 1965 by the Estate of Mary Flannery O'Connor. Reprinted by permission of Farrar, Straus and Giroux, Inc./ Cover of *Wise Blood*, by Flannery O'Connor. Farrar, Straus and Giroux, Inc, 1989. Copyright © 1949, 1952, 1962 by Flannery O'Connor. Cover design by Milton Glaser. Reprinted by permission of Farrar, Straus and Giroux, Inc./ Cover of *A Good Man Is Hard To Find*, by Flannery O'Connor. A Harvest/HBJ Book, 1983. Reprinted by permission of Harcourt Brace Jovanovich, Inc.

JUDITH ST. GEORGE. Jacket of *The Halo Wind*, by Judith St. George. G.P. Putnam's Sons, 1978. Copyright © 1978 by Judith St. George. Jacket illustration by Diane de Groat. Reprinted by permission of The Putnam Publishing Group./ Jacket of *Haunted*, by Judith St. George. G.P. Putnam's Sons, 1980. Copyright © 1980 by Judith St. George. Jacket illustration by Judy Clifford. Reprinted by permission of The Putnam Publishing Group./ Jacket of *The Brooklyn Bridge: They Said It Couldn't Be Built*, by Judith St. George. G.P. Putnam's Sons, 1982. Copyright © 1982 by Judith St. George. Jacket design by Kathleen Westray. Reprinted by permission of The Putnam Publishing Group./ Jacket of *Do You See What I See?*, by Judith St. George. G.P. Putnam's Sons, 1982. Copyright © 1982 by Judith St. George. Jacket illustration by Karen Kolada. Reprinted by permission of The Putnam Publishing Group./ Jacket of *The Mount Rushmore Story*, by Judith St. George. G.P. Putnam's Sons, 1985. Jacket design by Kathleen Westray. Cover photograph courtesy of the National Park Service, Department of Interior. Reprinted by permission of The Putnam Publishing Group./ Jacket of *Who's Scared? Not Me!*, by Judith St.George. G.P. Putnam's Sons, 1987. Copyright © 1987 by Judith St. George. Jacket illustration copyright © 1987 by Eric Velasquez. Reprinted by permission of The Putnam Publishing Group./ Photograph courtesy of Judith St. George.

EDMUND WHITE. Cover of *A Boy's Own Story,* by Edmund White. New American Library, 1982. Copyright © 1982 by Edmund White. Cover photograph by Dan Weaks. Cover copyright © 1983 by New American Library. Cover design by Earl Tidwell. Used by permission of New American Library, a division of Penguin Books USA, Inc./ Cover of *The Darker Proof: Stories From a Crisis,* by Edmund White and Adam Mars-Jones. New American Library, 1988. Cover copyright © 1988 by New American Library. Used by permission of New American Library, a division of Penguin USA Inc./ Cover of *The Beautiful Room is Empty,* by Edmund White. Ballantine Books, 1989. Copyright © 1988 by Edmund White. Reprinted by permission of Ballantine Books, a division of Random House, Inc./ Cover of *Forgetting Elena,* by Edmund White. Ballantine Books, 1990. Copyright © 1973 by Edmund White. Reprinted by permission of Ballantine Books, a division of Random House, Inc./ Photograph © Thomas Victor.

ELIE WIESEL. Jacket of *Souls on Fire: Portraits and Legends of Hasidic Masters,* by Elie Wiesel. Summit Books, 1972. Copyright © 1972 by Elie Wiesel. Jacket design by Fred Marcellino. Reprinted by permission of Summit Books, a division of Simon & Schuster, Inc./ Jacket of *The Testament,* by Elie Wiesel. Summit Books, 1981. Copyright © 1981 by Elirion Associates, Inc. Jacket illustration by Paul Bacon. Reprinted by permission of Summit Books, a division of Simon & Schuster, Inc./ Cover of *Night,* by Elie Wiesel. Bantam Books, 1982. Copyright © 1960 by Mac Gibbon & Kee. Reprinted by permission of Bantam Books, Inc., a division of Bantam Doubleday Dell Publishing Group, Inc./ Jacket of *Somewhere a Master: Further Hasidic Portraits and Legends,* by Elie Wiesel. Summit Books, 1982. Copyright © 1982 by Elirion Associates, Inc. Jacket design by Fred Marcellino. Reprinted by permission of Summit Books, a division of Simon & Schuster, Inc./ Photograph by Roman Vishniac./ Group photograph of Wiesel in a concentration camp, AP/Wide World Photos.

ROGER ZELAZNY. Cover of *Creatures of Light and Darkness,* by Roger Zelazny. Avon Books, 1969. Copyright © 1969 by Roger Zelazny. Reprinted by permission of Avon Books, New York./ Cover of *The Courts of Chaos,* by Roger Zelazny. Avon Books, 1978. Copyright © 1978 by Roger Zelazny. Cover illustration by Tim White. Reprinted by permission of Avon Books, New York./ Cover of *Trumps of Doom,* by Roger Zelazny. Avon Books, 1985. Copyright © 1985 by The Amber Corporation. Cover illustration by Tim White. Reprinted by permission of Avon Books./ Cover of *Blood Amber,* by Roger Zelazny. Avon Books, 1986. Copyright © 1986 by The Amber Corporation. Cover illustration by Tim White. Reprinted by permission of Avon Books, New York./ Cover of *The Last Defender of Camelot,* by Roger Zelazny. Avon Books, 1988. Copyright © 1980 by The Amber Corporation. Front cover illustration by James Warhola. Reprinted by permission of Avon Books, New York./ Jacket of *Knight of Shadows,* by Roger Zelazny. William Morrow and Company, 1989. Copyright © 1989 by The Amber Corporation. Jacket design by Teresa Bonner. Reprinted by permission of William Morrow and Company, Inc./ Photograph courtesy of Kirby McCauley Ltd.

Cumulative Index

Author/Artist Index

The following index gives the number of the volume
in which an author/artist's biographical sketch appears.

245